Greenwich Council
Library & Information Service

IN HOUSE
QUALITY
SYSTEMS

Woolwich Library
Calderwood Street, SE18 6QZ
020 8921 5750

RE

Please return by the last date shown

1 6 MAR 2010		
RE 14/4		
EL 26.9.12		
1 9 OCT 2012		
	Thank You!	

To renew, please contact any Greenwich library

D1345061

A GOOD WALK SPOILED

Also by John Feinstein

Hard Courts

Forever's Team

A Season Inside

A Season on the Brink

Play Ball

Running Mates
(A MYSTERY)

A Good Walk Spoiled

Days and Nights on the PGA Tour

JOHN FEINSTEIN

LITTLE, BROWN AND COMPANY

A *Little, Brown* Book

First published in Great Britain in 1995
by Little, Brown and Company

Copyright © 1995 John Feinstein

The moral right of the author has been asserted.

All photographs taken by Fred Vuich, copyright *Golf* magazine,
except those of Jeff Cook and Paul Goydos.

Photograph of Jeff Cook by Sam Greenwood; photograph of Paul
Goydos by Pete Fontaine. The PGA Tour holds copyright for both.

A CIP catalogue record for this book
is available from the British Library.

ISBN 0 316 87707 7

Printed in England by Clays Ltd, St Ives plc

Little, Brown and Company (UK)
Brettenham House
Lancaster Place
London WC2E 7EN

FOR MOM . . .

FOR DANNY

With the hope that I can pass on to him the love that she gave me

CONTENTS

	Acknowledgments	ix
	Introduction	xiii
1	"The Only Time Your Legs Ever Shake"	3
2	In the Arena	23
3	"It's Not Good News, Paul . . ."	54
4	The Fall Classic	67
5	The Sounds of Silence	89
6	Tales of Tommy, Johnny, Billy, and Deane	104
7	Struggling	119
8	Hope Springs Eternal?	143
9	Who's the Boss?	162
10	Arnie . . . and Friends	191
11	Shark Attack	209
12	The Men of the Masters	239
13	Springtime in the South	282
14	Goliath Beats David . . . Barely	301
15	Who's the Boss?	318
16	Open Heat	331
17	Nike Daze	361
18	Two Hands on the Jug	371
19	Welcome Back, Zinger	407
20	The New King	420
	Epilogue	446

ACKNOWLEDGMENTS

ANYONE WHO HAS EVER PLAYED GOLF would doubtless agree that there are days when Mark Twain's famous assessment of the game, "Golf is a good walk spoiled," is 100 percent accurate. My wife, who does not play, always asks me, "If you love golf so much, then why are you always in such a bad mood coming off the golf course?"

It is a question I can't answer. A golfer understands; a nongolfer can't. Golf is addictive and aggravating. It is also energizing and enervating. But I think I can honestly say I have finally found a way to come off the golf course in a good mood: go out and *watch* great players. That's what I've done for the last fifteen months and, at the same time, I've had the chance to get to know and (I hope) understand what makes them tick.

My game plan starting this book was to work with a smaller group of athletes than I have in some of my other books; to try and really get inside the heads of the players and to take the readers there with me. If I have succeeded, it is because of the remarkable patience of my core group. As someone who has covered just about every sport there is, I can honestly say that I found golfers the most open and cooperative group I have ever dealt with. In fact, the list of people I need to thank is — as you are about to find out — a very long one.

There is no way I can possibly give enough thanks to the men who became jokingly known around the press rooms on tour as Team Feinstein: Davis Love III, Curtis Strange, Tom Watson, Paul Azinger, Jeff Sluman, Billy Andrade, Nick Price, Mike Donald, John Cook,

Lee Janzen, Greg Norman, Nick Faldo, Tom Kite, Bruce Fleisher, Paul Goydos, Brian Henninger, and Jeff Cook. Their willingness to share their time and their thoughts with me made it possible for me to write this book the way I wanted to: not only from inside the ropes and the locker room, but from inside their minds.

I also owe special thanks to a number of others who gave me large chunks of time: Frank Chirkinian, the executive producer of CBS's golf coverage; Arnold Palmer and Jack Nicklaus; and the tour's two commissioners during my research: Deane Beman and Tim Finchem. Several other players were also generous with their time and thoughts. They include Jay Haas, Peter Jacobsen, Fred Couples, Brian Claar, Ben Crenshaw, Brad Faxon, Jim Gallagher Jr., Glen Day, Mike Hulbert, Robert Wrenn, Brad Lardon, and Patrick Burke.

A number of caddies also helped make my life easier and more enjoyable on tour, most notably Frank Williams and Jimmy Walker, but also Mike Hicks, Craig Cimarolli, Jim Mackay, Jeff (Squeeky) Medlen, Bruce Edwards, Joe LaCava, Pete Bender, Ken McCluskey, Tony Navarro, Mike Carrick, and Chris Mazziotti.

Several agents went out of their way to help me, notably Ken Kennerly of Golden Bear; Chuck Rubin of Assured Management; Vinny Giles of Pros Inc.; Frank Williams of Great White Shark (wonder who he works for); Doc Giffin of Arnold Palmer Enterprises; and Bev Norwood of IMG, whose assistance was absolutely invaluable.

Terry Hanson was a guide, an adviser, a friend, and an ear always willing to take time to listen throughout the process.

The people at the PGA Tour had no particular reason to go out of their way to make my life more enjoyable, but they did anyway. John Morris and his communications staff were as patient as the players, answering questions, clearing the way for me to get into tournaments without any hassles (not to mention dealing with the security goons who didn't know anything about the rules of the tour or of common courtesy at the L.A. Open), and bending over backward virtually all the time. My sincere thanks go to all of them: Marty (CS) Caffey, (Hi) Chuck Adams, Mark Mitchell, Dave Lancer, James Cramer, Bob Hyde, Denise Taylor, Vicki Page, Dianne Reed, Jodi Herb, Leslie Sinadinos, and, last but certainly not least, America's number one stats guy, Wes Seeley, who had the answer for every conceivable question and some that were inconceivable.

Thanks also to Sid Wilson, regardless of his lack of taste when it comes to Mexican food, and to Cathy Hurlburt and Patty Cianfrocca. Sam Greenwood, whether he is one arm's length from the ropes or not, and Pete Fontaine took lots of pictures and walked lots of holes and helped make it all fun.

The rules and promotions people also acted above and beyond the call of duty on more than one occasion, most notably rules gurus Ben Nelson, George Boutell, Wade Cagle, Slugger White, Arvin Ginn, and the two guys who no one is better than, Mark Russell and Jon Brendle. In promotions, Don Wallace, Lee Kaplan, Malcolm Turner, Rich Pierson, Gerald Goodman, and Larry Strong always had answers for my various and sundry questions.

That's a lot of people. Wait, there's more. At the PGA of America: Joe Steranka and the always groovy Julius Mason. At the U.S. Golf Association: Mark Carlson and Craig Smith. At the Royal & Ancient: David Begg. At the European PGA Tour: Mitchell Platts.

I received a good deal of advice from a number of writers who have been around the sport a lot longer than I have: Dave Kindred, who has been my mentor for more years than either one of us wants to think about, made more important suggestions than I can possibly count; Len Shapiro has also given me coaching and counsel forever; and Bob Woodward may not break 90 very often, but his suggestions on how to focus the book were — as always — invaluable.

There were many other writers, too numerous to list, who went out of their way to be kind, but I would be remiss if I didn't mention Larry Dorman, Tim Rosaforte, Jaime Diaz, Dan Jenkins, Gary Van Sickle, Geoff Russell, Robinson Holloway, Bob Verdi, Jo-Ann Barnus, and Michael Bamberger.

I am also extremely grateful to the people at *Golf* magazine for taking a rookie golf writer onboard at the very beginning. Mike Purkey came up with the idea for an On Tour column and convinced George Peper and Jim Frank to let me write it. I hope they enjoyed it half as much as I did. Thanks also to Fred Vuich for stepping in on short notice to provide the pictures for this book.

None of my books would ever get published without my agent, Esther Newberg, who is, of course, far more than an agent and has been ever since I got into this business. That has been especially true during the past eighteen months. Since Esther and I each have exactly no patience, we desperately need someone with great patience as our liaison. That person is her assistant, Amanda Beesley.

I have also been extremely fortunate to have a friend and publisher and editor like Peter Gethers during the last seven years, and equally fortunate that, when Peter chose to pursue his own writing career, Charlie Hayward and Michael Pietsch at Little, Brown were willing to step into the considerable void caused by his career change. This book is the product of a great deal of hard work done by Esther, Amanda, Peter, Charlie, and Michael.

At the request of my wife, I am not going to list all my friends because I always go on far too long and invariably leave someone out. They all know who they are and how much they mean to me. I do have to mention (sorry, Mary) Norbert Doyle, the world's most underrated golfer, and Tim Maloney, whose heroics eighteen months ago will not soon be forgotten.

Finally (please stop cheering) there is my family: Mary, Danny, Dad, Margaret, Bobby, and last, but certainly not least, David, whose yeoman efforts in tracking down printer ribbons for me rescued this project. Dealing with the loss of my mother during these last eighteen months has been the most difficult thing any of us has ever gone through. I would like to think the support we have given one another is a tribute to her constant insistence that nothing in life is more important than your family.

It was my mother who first took me onto a golf course. She taught me early on that you didn't have to be a great player to love the game. Every Sunday afternoon, she would turn on the television and watch the pros. She always told her friends, "I'm the world's leading golf voyeur."

During the last fifteen months, I've had the chance to play that role. I loved every minute of it. As in so many other things, my mother taught me extremely well.

INTRODUCTION

IT was one of those spectacular days in the California desert, a December afternoon in Palm Springs when you walk around in shirtsleeves staring at the scenery and all the gorgeous houses thinking that winter could go by very quickly in a place like this. I had just finished walking 18 holes on the Dunes Course at LaQuinta Country Club with Brian Henninger during round two of the 1993 PGA Tour Qualifying School, and I was in the car racing back to the Jack Nicklaus Resort Course at PGA West to find out how several other players had fared that day.

As I waited impatiently at a light, it suddenly struck me how wrapped up I was in this whole thing. Among the seventeen players I was following over the course of a year on the PGA Tour, four — Henninger, Mike Donald, Paul Goydos, and Jeff Cook — were competing at the school for their spot on the 1994 Tour. The reason I was so impatient was that I didn't know yet how Donald, Goydos, and Cook had done. There are no scoreboards or computers at Q-School, so the only way to find out how players have done is to check the main scoreboard next to the 18th green at the host course. There, the scores were recorded by hand, a long, tedious process, very different than the instantaneous computerized updates one grew accustomed to on tour.

But even as I focused on their efforts, I couldn't help but wonder about some of the other players I was encountering daily. Henninger had a friend named John Kennaday who had come back from cancer and was now trying to find work playing the game he loved. Walking with Goydos, I had encountered Brad Lardon, a player who had been on the tour once, then off it for three years. His caddy was his brother Mike, a psychiatrist. How appropriate for this event. On another afternoon I walked with Glen Day, a friendly Oklahoman who had played the European tour for several years and was dying to come home. John Maginnes, who played with Mike Donald one day, had pooled his financial resources with his brother just to get to Palm Springs. Bobby Cole had won the Q-School as a phenom at age nineteen and was back, twenty-six years later, trying again, not so much a has-been as a never-was.

Everywhere I turned, there was another story.

Reporters aren't supposed to care who wins or loses, whether they're covering an election, a basketball game, or a golf tournament. But it would have been silly for me to pretend that I didn't care how "my" four players were doing. You can't spend hours and hours with people, know their life stories, know their families, know the kind of effort that goes into making a living playing golf, and not want to see them do well.

Especially at Q-School, where failure means wondering if you can continue playing a game you have played your whole life. Almost always, they go on, win or lose, because the alternatives — working as a club pro, selling golf equipment, or getting out of golf completely — aren't nearly as attractive. They all want the chance to get to or return to the big tour, as everyone calls it. Sure, there are fallbacks — the Nike Tour, mini-tours, playing overseas — but no one turns pro dreaming about playing anyplace *but* the big tour. That is the major leagues. Everything else is Triple-A. Or worse.

It occurred to me as I pulled into the parking lot at the Nicklaus Course that most golf fans didn't care very much about the fate of Henninger, Goydos, Donald, Cook, or any of the other 186 players at the Q-School. There were stories in the local paper each day about the fact that the tournament was being played in Palm Springs and still the galleries numbered only in the dozens. Friends and family and that was just about it.

"This tournament should be on television every year," Goydos said, "because this is real pressure. All those tournaments on TV, someone misses a putt to finish second, he still makes more than $100,000. You have a putt where your livelihood is at stake, *that's* pressure."

I knew perfectly well that if I was going to write a golf book, I had better be able to tell readers about John Daly and Greg Norman; Jack Nicklaus and Arnold Palmer; Tom Watson and Tom Kite; Nick Faldo and Nick Price. And yet, there was a part of me that believed that Goydos and Henninger and Donald and Cook were more interesting.

I've always been that way, though, someone who thinks that the unknown fighting for his life is a better story than the millionaire fighting for his next million. I've always been fascinated by the struggle of sports and that was exactly what Q-School epitomized.

As I researched this book, though, what I found is that *everyone* in golf struggles. John and Greg; Jack and Arnie; Tom and Tom; Nick and Nick; even Mr. Laid-back, Fred Couples. All of them. Sure, the struggles are at different levels with different stakes, but what you find when you spend time with golfers is that what they do is make something that is very hard look very easy.

Of course all athletes do that to some degree. But the notion that has caught on in recent years about golfers being a bunch of faceless clones who have identical, effortless swings is untrue at best, viciously inaccurate at worst.

Golf is the least precise game in the world. More often than not, golfers are at a loss to explain exactly why they start playing well or playing poorly. And, almost without fail, it is a lot easier to lose your rhythm and your confidence than it is to find them. When you are in the so-called zone, you know it isn't going to last; when you fall out of the zone and can't find a fairway, you worry that it may last forever.

When Nick Faldo looked at tapes of his golf swing in 1994, he thought it was technically better than it had been in 1990 and 1992. But in those years, he was the game's dominant player. In 1994, he failed to make a serious run in any major tournament. Nick Price tied for thirty-fifth at the Masters in 1994, then missed the cut at the U.S. Open. He wondered if he was destined to be one of those guys who won at Memphis and Hartford but had only one major title to show for an entire career. Then, in five weeks, he won the British Open *and* the PGA. Lee Janzen won the U.S. Open in June 1993, making three birdies in the last five holes to hold off Payne Stewart. It was an extraordinary performance. During the next eleven months he didn't finish in the top twenty in a single tournament.

It happens to everyone who has ever picked up a golf club. One day it is there, the next day it isn't. One week you've discovered the secret to the game; the next week you never want to play it again. How can Greg Norman play four rounds in 24 under par at the Players Championship and then go 26 straight holes without a single birdie two weeks later at the Masters? How can Curtis Strange win back-to-back U.S. Opens and then all but disappear for four full years? How can Davis Love shoot 60 on Friday and then not be able to break 70 on Saturday or Sunday on the same golf course under virtually the same conditions?

On the other hand, how is it that Goydos can go from being a substitute schoolteacher to a successful touring pro five years later? How can Loren Roberts and Tom Lehman struggle to make a living their entire lives and then almost win the U.S. Open and the Masters at a time when most people would have thought they would be giving lessons for a living? How can Mike Donald win a total of $70,000 in just under two years and then win $100,000 in a little more than a month?

No one has the answers. That's why the golf magazines are full of instruction sections: because everyone is looking for a secret that doesn't exist. Hard work can make you better but it won't *always* make you better. Sometimes, it will make you worse.

Golf has no guarantees. And what makes it even more difficult, there are no excuses. Sure, you can moan occasionally about a wind gust or a spike mark, but when a player goes home at night and looks in the mirror, he knows that only one person was responsible for the 75 he shot that day and he's looking at him.

No one ever gets a bad call in golf. No one strikes you out or tackles you or blocks your shot or hits a forehand so hard you can't get to it. The ball doesn't move and neither does the hole. You either get the ball into the hole quickly or not quickly enough. Period. Your teammates don't let you down, and the coach or manager doesn't keep you on the bench or play you out of position.

Golfers fire teachers and caddies and change balls and putters and clubs, but it is all just a rationalization. In the end, they all know that they control their own fate entirely. That is a terrifying thought, one that drives a lot of golfers slightly (or more than slightly) crazy. There is no sport as solitary as golf. No sport humanizes you like golf. The greatest players in history have days when they can't break 80. There may be no lonelier feeling in sports than shooting 78 on Sunday or three-putting the 18th on Friday to miss the cut. No one did it to you, you did it to yourself.

The sport that golf is most often compared to is tennis, since both are individual sports. But life on the tennis tour is much easier than life on the golf tour. Not only do the stars receive appearance fees almost every week, the stars and nonstars are guaranteed a free hotel room at every tournament on the men's tour for the entire week and a paycheck just for playing in the tournament — in singles and doubles.

There are no appearance fees on the PGA Tour, although top players do sometimes get paid big money to play in an outing the Monday before or after a tournament. But they *work* for that money, spending the day glad-handing and playing with a bunch of amateurs who expect a lot of attention for the cash they've shelled out to be in the presence of the greats — and nongreats. There are no free hotel rooms and you don't get paid a nickel until you've beaten half the field by making the cut on Friday. Golf is the only sport left where you pay to compete: it costs $100 to enter a PGA Tour event. No exceptions.

To win a Grand Slam tennis tournament, you have to beat only seven players. Sure, 128 players are in the field, but you have to play only seven of them. If Pete Sampras loses early because his foot hurts, you don't have to beat him. To win any golf tournament, you have to beat the entire field. In 1994, Fuzzy Zoeller was a remarkable 20 under par at the Players Championship, shattering the tournament record. He didn't win, though, because Greg Norman was four shots better and there wasn't a damn thing Zoeller could do about it.

There are no second chances in golf. You can't fall two sets behind, then rally to win and get to start all over again the next day. Every shot counts. Every mistake is recorded, in ink. Billy Andrade, who is friendly with a number of major league baseball players, likes to tell them, "You can strike out your first three times up and still be a hero by hitting a homer your fourth time up. In golf, you make three errors and you're dead."

Or, as Sam Snead once pointed out to Ted Williams, "In golf, you have to play your foul balls."

Successful golfers live a wonderful life. They make a lot of money and they are pampered everywhere they go. Purses on the PGA Tour have skyrocketed in the last twenty years. Once, the only players on tour who owned their own airplanes were Palmer and Nicklaus. Now it seems as if half the players on tour have their own jets.

"I was the first golfer to buy a plane," Palmer said. "But when I bought one, I'd already won the Masters twice. These days it seems like if you win somewhere, *anywhere* — you go out and buy a plane."

But success can be fleeting. For every plane owner on tour, there are a dozen guys trying to find bargain-basement nonrefundable coach fares with a Saturday night stay-over. And there are a dozen more who are back on the Nike Tour, driving from event to event. And a dozen more after that who wish they were on the Nike Tour. Everyone has a story about a player who had it made one year and couldn't, as the players say, "play dead" the next year.

Golfers love the life they lead and want to stay out for as long as possible. Nowadays, almost all of them want to stay out until they're fifty so they can jump right over to the senior tour and not miss a beat. That is one area where golfers have a huge advantage over other athletes: the best and luckiest of them can still make an excellent living playing the game into their sixties. Most athletes are looking for a life by the time they are thirty-five; some golfers haven't even peaked by then.

But they all struggle. Not just the ones at Q-School, every single one of them. They all spend hours and hours on the range searching for the feeling they had when they knew every shot was going exactly where they wanted it to go. Then they head for the putting green because they know the stroke that was knocking every putt in just a couple of weeks ago is there somewhere.

Think about this: golfers are the only athletes in the world who routinely practice, often for hours, *after* they are finished playing for the day. Occasionally, a tennis player will go out to practice after an easy match; the real gym rats might find a basketball hoop to shoot at after a poor game; but that's about it. Ninety-nine point nine percent of the golfers on the PGA Tour can't sleep at night if they don't hit balls after a round.

"That's when you do your work," Nick Price said. "When you hit balls before a round, you're just warming up. After your round is when you can fix things, change things, find out what's gone wrong."

So I followed these seventeen golfers, famous and not so famous, for a little over a year, on tour, from Q-School to the Masters to the Ryder Cup with plenty of Pebble Beach, Greensboro, and Williamsburg mixed in. What did I find out in those fifteen months? That golf is *hard,* not just for all of us who hack away and can't *really* play the game, but for the very best players in the world, from the ones who fight through Q-School to the millionaires who show up on television every week. They put in long hours with less certainty they will be successful than any athletes in the world. Being a star one year means absolutely nothing the next year. Everyone starts at zero and there are very few long-term guaranteed contracts. They all worry that they'll wake up one morning and the magic swing or putting stroke will be gone.

"Until I won the PGA [and a ten-year exemption] I started every year worrying I might end up back in Q-School," Paul Azinger said. "That sounds crazy, but you do think about it. That's just the way the game is."

In the end, that's what this book is about: the way the game is and how difficult it is to live with, day in and day out, even for those who love it, eat, drink and sleep it, and play it better than anyone else in the world.

Most people think that professional athletes are motivated by money, by the huge sums they can make nowadays if they are successful. I can honestly say that I have never met a great athlete in any sport who started out to become a millionaire. If money was all that drove them, they would lose their drive the moment they cashed their first check with six or seven numbers in it.

I found this to be especially true of golfers. They love working at the game, they cherish the pressure even if they know that they will fail at least as often — probably far more often — as they will succeed. "The failure is what makes succeeding so sweet," Greg Norman said. "In golf, failure is a great thing — an absolutely necessary thing."

When Norman went through his twenty-seven-month victory drought between 1990 and 1992, he didn't miss the money or the trophies or the glory the most. "I missed the feeling on Sunday afternoon," he said. "I missed the pressure of being there."

They all want to *be there* because they know the work that goes into getting there. Shortly after Curtis Strange had come up one stroke short of making the playoff at last year's U.S. Open, I ran into him in the empty locker room at Oakmont.

I asked him if he would sleep that night.

"Probably not," he said. "I'll probably go through every shot and every thought."

He smiled. "But you know what? That's okay. It's disappointing, but goddamn it, I was *there*. I hadn't had that feeling in a long time. This is what you play the game for — to get yourself in position on Sunday at the U.S. Open so you can throw up all over yourself."

He was glowing. "My God," he said, "it felt great."

He hadn't won. But he had had a chance right to the very end. All the work was worth it, just to have that feeling. That's what they all search for: the chance to be *there* on Sunday afternoon. They live to have the chance to choke. At the Q-School; at Hartford or Memphis; at Augusta or Oakmont.

A GOOD WALK SPOILED

1

"THE ONLY TIME YOUR LEGS EVER SHAKE"

DON'T THROW UP.

That thought had occurred to Davis Love III on more than one occasion during his golf career. Only this time it was different. To Love, "throw up" was not a literal term, it was part of the golf vernacular as in "I was one shot off the lead with four holes left and then I threw up all over myself."

Nerves take over. The pressure caves in on you. In other sports you choke. In golf, you throw up. Leave yourself a four-foot putt on 18 and you are in the dreaded throw-up zone. Every golfer has thrown up on himself.

Only at this instant, a cool, cloudy, English autumn Sunday afternoon in September of 1993, Love wasn't thinking about throwing up in a golf sense. That would come later. Right now, standing in the middle of the 18th fairway at the Belfry, a golf course that looked and felt like a Florida resort but happened to be located in the English Midlands, Love was thinking about *literally* throwing up in front of several million people.

He wanted to bend over, put his hands on his knees, and take several deep breaths to calm himself, but he knew he couldn't do that. He couldn't let his teammates, standing a few yards behind him on the left side of the fairway, see that. He certainly couldn't let anyone on the European team see even a trace of nerves. Not now. Not with his opponent, Costantino Rocca, facing an almost impossible shot out of the right rough.

No way could he let anyone know the thoughts churning through his brain. He looked at his golf ball, sitting safely in the fairway, exactly 148 yards from the pin, and then he looked back at Rocca, who was trying to figure out some way to carry his second shot over the water that protected the green both in front and to the left.

I can't lose, he thought. Then he mentally slapped himself across the face for letting that notion slip into his head for even a split second. If there was any one lesson he had learned during the last three days it was how quickly things could change during a Ryder Cup match.

The last thirty minutes had been proof — again — of that. Walking down the 16th fairway, trying not to feel frustrated, Love had looked up and seen a welcoming committee of sorts waiting for him at the green. Tom Watson, the American captain, was there. So were a number of his teammates, their matches already over. Most of the American caddies and just about all the wives were there too.

Love had been checking the scoreboards around the golf course all day, trying to figure how his team was doing. It was confusing, though, and changed so quickly from hole to hole that he couldn't calculate exactly what was going on. He knew a red number was good — that meant the American player was leading — and blue was bad — that meant the European player was in front. And he also knew that any roar that sounded like a tidal wave was *very* bad. It meant that a European had done something spectacular. Early in the afternoon, there had been a comforting calmness and quiet. Listen for the quiet, Watson had told his team, that means we're getting the job done.

But as the afternoon stretched on, the quiet had disappeared. In the last hour there had been too many roars. Playing the seventh of eleven matches, Love knew there weren't many points left to be decided. He had led through most of the front nine, but never by more than one hole. Then Rocca, a chunky Italian with a solid record in Europe but a complete unknown in the U.S., had won back-to-back holes at 13 and 14 and, suddenly, Love was one down.

And so, as he walked onto the 16th green and saw the American contingent, Love knew exactly where the competition stood. This match decides the whole thing, he thought. His stomach, which had seemed to be in a permanent knot since Friday morning, did the impossible. It twisted a little tighter.

He and Rocca both two-putted for par at 16, so Love was still one down with two holes to play. Watson was waiting for him on the 17th tee, hands jammed into the pockets of his windbreaker. "We really need this match," he said, his voice as quiet as Love had ever heard it. Love didn't answer right away because the first thought that came into his head wouldn't have sounded very good: "No shit, Tom."

Instead, he took a deep breath and said, "All I know is, I'm due to make a putt and he's due to miss one."

The 17th at the Belfry is a long par-five, the kind of hole that should give a big hitter like Love an advantage over most players. Sure enough, he was within wedge distance of the green after two shots and Rocca was way back in the fairway, hitting a five-iron. But Rocca hit the shot brilliantly, leaving himself a 25-foot birdie putt. When Love's wedge spun to a stop 18 disappointing feet below the hole, it looked like another halve was likely. And that wasn't good enough.

Rocca lined up his putt carefully, then trickled it down the hill toward the cup. For one terrifying second, Love thought it was going in the hole. But it slid by, inches above the cup, and rolled farther than Rocca had thought it would, leaving him a little more than three feet coming back. Love noticed that Rocca had started walking as the ball got close to the hole, thinking he had a tap-in for par. Then, when it kept on going, he stopped dead in his tracks. "He was surprised it went so far," Love said. "He thought he was going to have an easy tap-in. For the first time all day, he looked just a tiny bit scared."

Love couldn't think about that though. He had to try to make his putt so Rocca's wouldn't matter. He hit a solid-looking putt, but inches short of the hole it died right. Rocca conceded the par and Love picked the ball up, angry for a moment, but then hopeful again. Rocca took forever looking over his putt.

Standing next to his caddy, Frank Williams, Love broke the first rule of Ryder Cup that his teammates had drilled into him all week: he made a prediction. "He may miss this," he whispered.

With the huge crowd so quiet you could have heard a ball marker drop, Rocca finally stroked the putt that would clinch at least a tie — a one-hole lead with one to play. Only he pushed it. The putt spun right as Rocca stared in disbelief and the crowd gasped in horror. They were even.

So were their teams. At that moment, the Americans had 12½

points and were leading in one match. The Europeans had 12½ and were leading in one. This match would almost certainly decide the outcome.

Love's first instinct was to run to the 18th tee, take out his driver, and hit the ball nine miles. But he could hear his friend, mentor, and partner Tom Kite's voice in his head. "Take your time. Don't rush. Let *them* think about what you're doing behind them."

And so, as the marshals cleared the way for Rocca to walk the 50 yards up the hill to the 18th, Love remained behind. The next match was a full hole behind, so there was no need to clear the green immediately. He dropped a ball on the green and said to Williams, "I just want to hit a few putts uphill."

He hit several putts, then walked slowly through the crowd to the tee where Rocca was waiting. Everyone was shouting at the two players, but for some reason, Love heard only Bruce Edwards, Watson's regular caddy, who had been working for Lanny Wadkins during the week, since Watson wasn't playing. "You're going to win, Davis," Edwards kept saying. "You're going to win."

Watson was waiting on the tee again. Bernard Gallacher, the European captain, stood with Rocca. Love wondered for a split second if Gallacher was telling Rocca that his team really needed this match.

The 18th at the Belfry is a great finishing hole on what is a rather ordinary golf course. It is a slight dogleg left, with water all the way down the left side that widens out in front of the green. The fairway is narrow for about 250 yards, then widens. There are bunkers on the right side from which the green is virtually unreachable.

If you play boldly down the left side and try to carry too much water, you will end up wet, as several Americans had on the final day of the biennial matches in 1989. If you play too timidly, aiming away from the water, you will probably catch the bunkers or the rough, bringing the water into play on your second shot. Into the wind, a driver aimed right is the correct play. Downwind, a driver can be too much club unless you are willing to play way left, because the ball will run through the fairway into trouble.

The Americans had spent hours practicing this shot during the week. They had calculated yardage to different spots and had noted exactly how far the ball would carry based on the wind. Watson had stood in the middle of the fairway marking landing areas and targets while his players hit shot after shot in his direction.

Love and Watson walked to the front of the tee. The hole was playing downwind. "What have guys been hitting here?" Love asked Watson.

"I'm not certain," Watson said. "I've been all over the course all day. But it isn't a driver for you today."

Love knew that. The question in his mind was whether to hit a three-wood or a one-iron.

Watson read his mind. "It could be a one-iron," he said.

Love could get a one-iron safely to the fairway, he knew that. But he wanted to put as much pressure on Rocca as he possibly could. A well-struck three-wood down the left side would roll way down the fairway, leaving Love in perfect position. That would make Rocca's tee shot that much more difficult.

Love knew that if he put his shot in the water he would be remembered as the goat of the 1993 Ryder Cup. But he couldn't think that way. He had to think he could pull off a tough shot when it mattered most. Otherwise, why play?

He took out the three-wood and glanced at Watson. Arms folded, Watson nodded, almost imperceptibly. He wasn't about to tell Love what to do in this situation but clearly he approved of the choice. A man who loves challenges, he appreciated Love's not backing away from this one.

Love took his practice swing, set up to the ball, and took the club back in the long, sweeping arc that was the envy of most players on tour. As soon as he followed through, he knew he had hit a perfect shot. The ball flew down the left side, climbed over the corner of the water where Love had aimed, and bounced safely onto the wide part of the fairway, well past the bunkers.

The Americans were screaming, and Love could hear an appreciative roar coming from where the ball had landed. There were a few groans mixed in and then it was very quiet. The European fans, who had rooted ardently for their team all weekend without any of the ugliness displayed by the American fans in 1991, knew Love had hit a superb shot. They were disappointed but impressed.

Rocca's turn. All day he had struck the ball well. The silence now was even more deafening than it had been on the 17th green. Rocca stepped up to the ball and took a deep breath. Suddenly, a huge roar, the loudest of the weekend, erupted from several holes back. It had to be Paul Azinger and Nick Faldo, the last match of the day. The last time Love had looked, the two anchors had been even. This roar made it clear that Faldo had done something remarkable. Rocca settled back over the ball, but the roar erupted again. What the hell had Faldo done? Only later would the players learn that Faldo had aced the 14th hole.

"It may have been the only time in Ryder Cup history that a hole in one actually hurt the team that made it," Love said later, remembering how Rocca had to step back twice.

Finally, there was quiet again. Rocca went through his preshot routine a third time and swung. Love knew two things right away: the shot was safely right of the water, but it was not where Rocca wanted to be. It was right, a pop-up type of drive that landed between the bunkers, more than 200 yards from the green.

The Americans were almost delirious. Walking across the footbridge that led from the tee to the fairway, Love wondered if anyone could hear his heart pounding. "Hit one good shot and the Ryder Cup's coming home," he told himself. "Just one more good shot."

As he walked to his ball, Love could see the packed grandstands behind the green and to the right. Flags were waving all over the place. The players and caddies all walked to the left side of the fairway for a better view. The wives were on the right side, over by the ropes. Love didn't look there. He was afraid if he saw his mother, who was walking with his wife, he might start thinking about his dad and this was absolutely not the time for that.

Even so, as he stood in the fairway with Williams, waiting for Rocca to play his shot, his stomach felt as if it was upside down on a roller coaster.

Please hang on, he thought, hoping his stomach would hear him. Don't throw up. Not now. Hang on for ten more minutes.

He took a deep breath and folded his arms, hoping to look calm. It seemed to him that it had been about ten years since he had last felt calm. It had actually been sixty hours.

The first person to warn Love about Ryder Cup nerves was Tom Kite. Before their first match as partners on Friday, Kite had pulled him aside. "Remember one thing," he had said. "If they've got a sixty-foot putt, expect them to make it. If they're in an unplayable spot, figure they'll find a play. If you're sure we've won a hole, flush the thought. Things are going to happen you've never seen happen before in your entire life."

Love had tremendous respect for Kite. He knew he had been through five Ryder Cups and spoke from experience. But all week long, as the American and European teams prepared for what had become golf's most emotional event, Love had thought everyone was making just a little bit too big a deal of the whole thing.

"I know you boys have played a lot of golf in a lot of places around the world," Watson had said to Love and the three other first-time Ryder Cuppers on the team. "You've played majors, been in position to win majors, but you've never experienced anything like this. This is the only event in the world that will make your legs shake."

By Thursday night, the eve of the matches, Love thought he had heard enough. He had read all about the European juggernaut that was bound and determined to take the cup back after barely losing it on American soil in 1991. He had heard all about what Ryder Cup did to Seve Ballesteros, the spiritual and emotional leader of the Europeans, who never seemed to lose a cup match. He had read reams of copy about the indomitable Nick Faldo and unshakable Bernhard Langer. He had walked the 18th hole with his teammates and heard all the stories about the disasters that had befallen the American team there in 1989.

Ryder Cup pressure. European supermen. Impossible shots becoming possible. Love enjoyed hearing it all. He didn't doubt this was a monumental happening, the most important thing he had ever been a part of in golf.

But he still didn't quite buy all the hype. When Watson gathered his twelve players and their wives for dinner on Thursday night, Love listened some more to the veterans as they talked about what had to be done and what had to be avoided, in order to win. The theme seemed to be this: keep the match close during the first two days of team play, when 16 points were at stake, then take advantage of the superior depth on the American side during the twelve singles matches on Sunday. The goal was 14½ points; somehow, someway. The secondary goal was 14 — a tie — because as the holders the Americans would retain the cup if the twenty-eight matches did not produce a winner.

That was what had happened the last time the matches had been staged at the Belfry, four years earlier: a 14–14 tie. Only then, Europe had held the cup and the American team flew home feeling like losers. After all, the cup was still in Europe.

As he listened and looked around the dining room, Love was a bit awed by the talent he saw. Fred Couples, the 1992 Masters champion, perhaps the most naturally talented player in the game; Paul Azinger, the toughest competitor Love had ever met, who was coming off his first victory in a major — the PGA — a month earlier; Corey Pavin, who could hit every shot in the bag; Lanny Wadkins and Raymond Floyd, the old men who had seen and done it all in Ryder Cup and in golf; Chip Beck, the man who never seemed to have a negative thought on the golf course or in life; Payne Stewart, who had won a U.S. Open and a PGA and, of course, his buddy Kite, who was only the leading money winner of all time in the sport.

Then there were the four so-called rookies: Lee Janzen — all he had done this year was win the U.S. Open; Jim Gallagher Jr., one of the best-kept secrets in the game, a guy who could hit the ball as long as just about anyone not named John Daly; and John Cook, who had almost won two majors the year before and had won more than $1 million. Love was no slouch either. He had won seven tournaments before the age of thirty and had finished second to Couples on the U.S. money list in 1992.

How could this team possibly lose? Hell, they were so deep that Watson wasn't even playing Janzen, the reigning U.S. Open champion, in the first four matches the next morning.

"You know what I think," Love finally said during a lull in the conversation. "I think all this talk of staying close and getting to fourteen and a half is kind of silly. Why don't we just go out there with the idea that we're going to win *every single match?* Why don't we make it our goal for Saturday, not to be close, but to have the cup *clinched* before we go to bed? There's sixteen matches the first two days. Why can't we think about winning all of them?"

They had all stared at him in disbelief for a split second as if someone had spiked his drink. Then they started to laugh. Love didn't get it. "Just wait till tomorrow," they all said. "Then you'll understand." Then they laughed some more.

Love shrugged. He wasn't trying to put down the Europeans or downplay the magnitude of the event. But for goodness sake, he'd been playing golf since he was old enough to walk and he'd been in every major tournament there was, both as an amateur and a professional. He thought about what Watson had said about Ryder Cup making your legs shake.

I'll be nervous, I know that, he thought. But *shaking?* Come on, Tom, be serious. I've played golf my whole life. He was used to the knot in his stomach in big moments, had come to expect it. But never *ever* had he felt wobbly-legged on a golf course.

And then came Friday morning. The weather was awful, foggy and drizzly and cold. There was no way to play golf at the scheduled 8 A.M. starting time. Since the players on both teams were staying on-site at the Belfry Hotel, they were all downstairs, trying to kill time, first on the putting green, then on the driving range, then back inside to get out of the cold and wet. Love and Kite were playing the third match against Seve Ballesteros and José María Olazabal, the so-called Spanish Armada. Of the four American rookies, Love was the only one playing in the four morning matches. There would be four more matches that afternoon.

When he walked outside to look around, Love was amazed. Even in the awful weather, the grounds were packed by 8 o'clock. Everywhere he looked, he saw people, bundled against the cold, hands wrapped around coffee and tea containers. No one knew how long the wait would be, but they were all there, ready, excited, hoping to will the European victory they wanted so much.

Love hung around with his teammates, chipping and putting and hitting a few balls. Finally, shortly before 10, the fog began to lift. Word came down from the two captains: if the weather didn't worsen again, play would begin at 10:30.

And that's when Davis Love first felt his legs shake. "All of a sudden it hit me just how big a deal this really was," he said. "It wasn't as if I hadn't known it before. But watching on television, just rooting for the U.S., is an entirely different thing. I mean, there were thousands of people there and, unlike at a tournament, they were going to be watching just four matches — and I was playing in one of them."

No money — not a nickel — was at stake. The Ryder Cup is about national pride and coming through for your teammates. Love now knew that kind of pressure was a lot more intense than playing to collect a check.

The morning format was alternate shot — two-man teams playing with one ball, alternating shots until the ball was in the cup. Kite, having studied the golf course, had suggested that Love hit the tee shot on the odd-numbered holes since the two par-fives on the back nine were the 15th and the 17th, holes where Love's length would come into play off the tee.

Love hadn't given it much thought, but it seemed to make sense, so he had told Kite that was fine with him. Now, Love was having second thoughts. As Corey Pavin and Lanny Wadkins left the putting green and headed for the first tee for the opening match, it occurred to Love that one was an odd number. That meant he would hit the first shot of the match.

"Hey, Tom," he said, trying to sound nonchalant, "are you sure you want me to take the odd holes?"

Kite, understanding, smiled. "I'm sure, Davis," he said. "You'll be just fine."

Fifteen minutes later, match number 3 was called to the first tee. Love was shivering. Must be the cold, he told himself. Probably isn't, he thought a few seconds later. They were walking now, escorted by several security guards, through a phalanx of people to the tee. Ballesteros and Olazabal were a few yards in front of them in matching red sweaters. The crowd grew louder with each step they took.

"Look, Tom, I really think you should take the odd holes," Love said. His tone was almost pleading. "I just think . . ."

"I know exactly what you're thinking," Kite said, a hand on his shoulder. "Trust me, you're going to be just fine."

Love looked at his caddy, who always seemed to know the right thing to say when the pressure on his player was greatest. Williams was white as a sheet. "He looked worse than I felt," Love said. "And I didn't feel very good at all."

Watson and Gallacher waited on the tee to greet the four players. Pictures were taken. The players were introduced. And then Love heard the dreaded words, "On the tee, representing the United States of America, Davis Love the Third!"

Love didn't hear the polite applause. Somehow, he managed to get his ball on the tee. He took a deep breath and went through his preshot routine. Down the fairway he could see people standing eight and ten deep, straining to see where his shot would land. The first hole at the Belfry is short and rather narrow. Love had his three-metal out rather than his driver.

Everyone grew quiet. Love forced his mind to go blank. He checked his target and let twenty-five years of instinct take over. The ball flew in a high arc down the right side of the fairway. Perfect. Shakily, Love picked up his tee and smiled in response to the applause. He didn't even hear the huge cheer that greeted the introduction of Olazabal.

Six months later, paired with Watson during the first round of the Players Championship, Love would hit a similar tee shot on the opening hole. "Just like the Ryder Cup," Watson said as the ball landed.

Love shook his head. "Wrong, Tom," he said. "My legs aren't shaking."

When the European PGA finds a Ryder Cup captain it is comfortable with, the job is his for as long as he wants. Tony Jacklin, the onetime U.S. and British Open champion who captained the Europeans three times, probably could have been captain for life if he had so desired, especially after winning the cup in 1985 and 1987 and retaining it with a tie in 1989. Bernard Gallacher, Jacklin's successor, kept the job in spite of losing in 1991 and was asked back again after 1993 — even though he had said before the matches that he intended to step down.

The PGA of America, which governs the Ryder Cup in the United States, takes the opposite approach. Although repeat Ryder Cup captains were once the norm — Walter Hagen was the American captain the first six times the matches were played — nowadays the captaincy is considered a one-shot deal. If you are asked a second time, it will undoubtedly be several years down the road from the first time. So, even though he would have liked to have kept the job, Dave Stockton knew his work was over in 1991 as soon as Bernhard Langer's six-foot par putt on the final hole of the final match had slid past the cup, giving the U.S. a 14½ to 13½ victory and returning the cup to the U.S. for the first time since 1985.

And there was very little doubt about who would defend the title Stockton had helped win: Thomas Sturges Watson.

Until Nick Price's recent emergence, Watson was golf's last truly dominant player. Between 1975 and 1983 he won eight major titles — five British Opens, two Masters, and one U.S. Open. He was player of the year six times and led the PGA Tour money list five times. Three times he went head-to-head with Jack Nicklaus down the stretch in majors and beat him. When he chipped in on the 71st hole of the 1982 U.S. Open at Pebble Beach to steal that title from Nicklaus, the greatest player in the game's history looked him in the eye and said, "You did it to me again, you little SOB."

Nicklaus was joking, but there was a large chunk of truth in what he said. Every great athlete has a mean streak in him somewhere. You can't consistently destroy the dreams of your competitors without it. If you pause to think what a victory will mean to the other guy, you may not be quite as willing to step on him when you need to. Especially in golf, where the margin for error is usually so razor thin, that tiny kernel of doubt often turns winners into losers.

Tom Watson never doubts. And he never backs away from a fight. He once thought he saw Nicklaus gesture at him with his putter — as if to say, "Take *that*" — after Nicklaus made a bomb to regain the lead during the final round of the Masters in 1977. Watson angrily took the gesture personally, birdied two of the last four holes, and won. When he learned later that Nicklaus hadn't been gesturing at him, Watson apologized for his thoughts but certainly not for his victory.

Watson never *thinks* something, he *knows* it, whether the subject is golf or politics or wine. It is no coincidence that his nickname on tour is Carnac Junior. Nicklaus was the original Carnac, Watson his successor, because both men, like the old Johnny Carson character Carnac the Magnificent, always seem to know the answers before you ask the questions.

Nicklaus, ten years younger than Arnold Palmer, had unseated The

King as the game's best player. In 1977, Watson, ten years younger than Nicklaus, succeeded him at the top of the sport. But unlike Nicklaus, who kept winning major titles until he was forty-six, Watson lost the hunger somewhere along the way. When he won his fifth British Open in 1983 he was thirty-four, the same age Palmer had been when he won his fourth Masters and seventh major. Like Palmer, who never won another major, Watson stopped winning. He should have won another British Open in 1984, but he let it slip away to Seve Ballesteros on the back nine at St. Andrews and was never quite the same again. He was still good — very good at times — but never dominant.

"I accomplished a lot of my goals in a relatively short period of time and I made a lot of money," Watson said ten years later. "When I was younger, before I had children and money, all I wanted to do was play golf, work at my golf, get better at my golf. But when the children came [Meg in 1979 and Michael in 1982] my time with them was very important to me.

"For a long time, I thought that was the major reason I didn't play as well. But it wasn't that simple. I definitely lost some edge. I didn't work as hard at my game. It just wasn't quite as important to me."

No one wins year in and year out, especially in the tournaments that matter most, without being an SOB. Somewhere, some of the SOB seeped out of Watson and the winning that had occurred so regularly — thirty-nine times in twelve years — came to a sudden halt. By the time he was named Ryder Cup captain late in 1991, Watson was eight years past his last major title and four years distant from his last win on tour.

Even so, he was still one of the game's most revered figures. He had always been popular with the fans, even as the young upstart challenger to Nicklaus. He was shy and almost obsessively private, but he had the kind of swashbuckling look and game that appealed to many. At 5-foot-9 he wasn't eye-catching, but he had Popeye-sized arms, reddish-brown hair, and a friendly gap-toothed grin that caused writers obsessively to compare him to Huck Finn.

And, like Palmer, he made golf into an adventure. He had a long, looping swing that sent the ball great distances, not always in the right direction. A round of golf with Watson was often a whirlwind tour of trees, meadows, water, and sand. Somehow, when he emerged eighteen holes later, Watson had scrambled and chipped and putted his way into the lead or close to it.

No one could get out of trouble the way Watson could. He was a genius around the greens and the boldest putter anyone ever saw. His putts never dropped over the front lip, they banged the back of the cup, bounced in the air, and then dropped in. Watson was so good at making miraculous recoveries that the ultimate compliment you could pay another player who had found a way out of trouble to make par was to tell him, "That was a Watson par."

Away from the golf course, Watson wasn't much different from the kids he had grown up with outside Kansas City or the ones he had gone to Stanford with. But golf made him special. He became so good at it that he became a part of the game's history and lore. A hundred years from now they will still talk about Nicklaus and Watson dueling down the stretch at Turnberry in 1977, and everyone who ever plays Pebble Beach will walk over to the spot on 17 where Watson hit The Chip and look at the thick grass and shake their heads and say, "How in the world did he do that?"

Great golfers are remembered forever. Watson reveled in that. He became a student of the game's history and of its great players. Byron Nelson became his teacher, mentor, and inspiration after he blew up in the last round of the 1974 U.S. Open, shooting 79 at Winged Foot after leading for fifty-four holes.

Watson absorbed Nelson's teachings and he read every book he could find on Vardon and Hagen and Hogan and Jones. After he won his first Masters in 1977, he sat and listened intently each year at the Champions Dinner to all the great players who had won the title before him. "It was like going to an annual seminar on the history of the game," he said.

By dint of his hard work, he became a part of that history. His five British Open victories put him behind only Vardon's six. That made the near miss at St. Andrews in 1984 that much more disappointing. Even so, he became an adopted son in all of Great Britain, but most of all in Scotland. Growing up in Kansas City, he had been Tommy Watson, but to the rest of the world he was Tom — except in Scotland, where he again became Tommy — or "Toom." They cheered him as if he were one of their own. He returned the feeling. This was, after all, the ancestral home of golf and if these people felt an attachment to him, then it meant he was part of something special.

All those feelings led Watson to seek the Ryder Cup captaincy for 1993. As a young player he had dreamed of playing Ryder Cup. He knew all about the traditions that dated back to 1927 and loved the idea of being part of a team, something one almost never got to do in golf. Even in college, although you were on a team, you always played stroke play, meaning that it wasn't really much different from playing in a tournament.

In Ryder Cup, though, everything was match play: head-to-head. You spent two days playing with a partner, then played one singles match on Sunday. There were twelve players on each team, and for one week every other year, golfers actually meshed into a unit, rooting for one another, living together, sometimes dying together.

Watson's first Ryder Cup as a player had been in 1977, the last year that Great Britain took on the United States without the rest of Europe. The U.S. won easily — as it always did in those days — but Watson's memories of the week were vivid. It was at the opening ceremony that he decided he wanted to be a Ryder Cup captain someday.

"It was a classic gray English day and the ceremony was behind the clubhouse at Royal Lytham and St. Anne's," he said. "Just as the flags were being raised, a gust of wind blew through and the flags unfurled perfectly, just stood straight up and out. Dow Finsterwald was our captain and he talked about what it meant to be part of a Ryder Cup, about all the great players who had taken part and how honored he was to follow in the footsteps of all the captains who had come before him. I just stood there with these shivers going down my back thinking, I want to do that someday."

The Europeans were added to the British team in 1979, a change that pumped new life into the matches. The European victories in 1985 and 1987, followed by the draw in 1989, had turned the Ryder Cup from a virtually unnoticed biennial competition into an event as big as — perhaps even bigger than — any of the majors.

Watson wasn't on the American teams that lost in 1985 or 1987 but did play in 1989, the last time the matches had been played in

Europe. He knew then that he wanted to captain an American team that would go to Europe and take the cup home.

"I definitely wanted to be the captain over there," he said. "Winning at home just wasn't quite the same challenge. I love golf in Britain, I love the fans, and I love their knowledge of the game. They just have a feel for the game that no one else in the world has. Even people who don't play over there understand the sport. There's nothing like it."

Watson had watched the 1991 matches played on Kiawah Island, in South Carolina, on television and, like a lot of people, was dismayed by what he saw. The matches had been dubbed The War by the Shore before they even began and nothing that happened during the three days dispelled that notion. The American fans were surly and ugly; the feeling between the teams bordered on bitter and sometimes spilled over beyond that border.

Watching the final day of the match at Kiawah, seeing all that tension and bitterness, had made Watson uncomfortable. He knew that the next American captain would have a lot of work to do not only trying to retain the cup on foreign soil, but also trying to put the proper feeling back into the matches.

Still, he wanted the job. A meeting was set up with Jim Awtrey, the executive director of the PGA, and when it was over, Awtrey stood up, reached his hand across the table, and said, "Well, Tom, you're our choice." Watson was amazed. He had walked into the meeting hoping to be a candidate and walked out of it as the captain.

As part of his preparation, Watson talked at length with Nick Faldo about the hard feelings between the two teams at Kiawah. Faldo told him he thought a lot of the problems dated back to 1989, when Raymond Floyd, that year's American captain, had stood up at the gala dinner held before the start of the matches and had introduced his team as "The twelve best golfers in the world." Floyd had stolen the line from Ben Hogan, who as captain in 1967 had introduced his team that way. Back then, it had been close to the truth. In 1989, it wasn't. "We all told Tony [Jacklin] that he should get up and introduce Seve as the thirteenth best player in the world," Faldo said. "We knew what Raymond was trying to do, but considering the fact that we had beaten them pretty soundly the previous two matches, it just wasn't appropriate."

The Europeans felt slighted again at the 1991 dinner when a film on the history of the Ryder Cup that the PGA had put together barely made mention of anyone who wasn't an American. There had been angry words on the golf course between Ballesteros and Paul Azinger. Some of the Americans had even shown up wearing camouflage shirts to emphasize that this really was war.

Watson agreed with Faldo that it had all gone too far. He made a point whenever he was asked about his role as captain to talk about the need to bring good feeling back to the competition. The tradition of competing was as important to him as winning.

"This isn't war," he said. "This is golf. We're going to go over there and try like hell to kick their butts. And they're going to try like hell to kick ours. That's as it should be. But when it's over, we should be able to all go off together, lift a glass, and toast one another. That's what the Ryder Cup is about."

Anyone who took that statement to mean that Watson would be satisfied to see his team give it the old college try and go home gallant losers didn't understand the man. For this Ryder Cup to become part of the glorious résumé he had pieced together, the U.S. had to win. Even a tie, although it would retain the cup, would not be good enough. Watson wanted to take a team into Europe and win. No American team had done that since 1981.

Watson's preparation was exhaustive. Ten of his players would be selected for him through a points system. The other two he would choose. The most logical picks were Raymond Floyd and Lanny Wadkins, two men who had about as much Ryder Cup experience as anyone alive. Both — especially Wadkins — were friends. Both would be natural leaders on what was shaping up as a relatively inexperienced American team.

But Watson didn't want to rule anyone out. He talked to other players about who they thought would perform well in the crucible of Ryder Cup competition. He encouraged potential team members to play money matches during their Tuesday practice rounds to get used to head-to-head match play. He studied statistics to see who drove the ball consistently, who made the most birdies, who was most adept at getting the ball up and down from tough spots.

But statistics weren't going to choose Watson's players for him. His gut would. There was a good deal of public clamoring for John

Daly, golf's Paul Bunyan. The thinking was that Daly, with his huge drives, would intimidate the Europeans and, in a match-play situation, his bad holes wouldn't matter as much as they did in stroke play.

Watson liked Daly and thought the huge crowds he brought out were good for golf. But he never considered him for the team. "You can't take someone over there who has a give-up attitude, and that's what John has," he said. "If things go wrong, he picks up or gives up. You can't have that in Ryder Cup, because if he does that he doesn't just hurt himself, he hurts the whole team. I couldn't count on John to go out there for thirty-six holes a day and not give up."

Other names cropped up. Larry Mize and Fuzzy Zoeller were both experienced and both were playing well as the August 16 deadline for Watson to make his picks approached. And, almost from out of nowhere, Curtis Strange, dormant for more than three years, had suddenly played himself into contention with four straight top-ten finishes. Like Floyd and Wadkins, Strange had Ryder Cup experience and, like Floyd and Wadkins, there was no questioning his heart or his toughness.

Watson knew he wanted Floyd on the team regardless of how he was playing, especially since he had been the captain at the Belfry in 1989. But if Strange had played well at the PGA — the last tournament before the deadline — he would have almost been compelled to pick him ahead of Wadkins, who had struggled for most of the summer.

That would have been an extremely difficult choice for Watson, especially since Wadkins had a better Ryder Cup record than anyone else who would be on the American team. But Strange and Wadkins both rescued Watson from his dilemma: Strange missed the cut at the PGA, and Wadkins stayed on the leader board until the back nine on Sunday. The next morning Watson surprised no one when he named Floyd and Wadkins.

By then, with the help of the PGA, Watson had put together a detailed itinerary and schedule that outlined for the players and their wives virtually everything they would be doing throughout every moment of Ryder Cup week. The thirty-page booklet included travel schedules, daily schedules for players and wives, *and* instructions on what to wear each day. Also included was a detailed Ryder Cup rule-book, a daily dining schedule, the match schedule, and instructions on how to prepare luggage for the Concorde.

Watson thought of everything. There were notes that said things like "Remember to send dress shirt to laundry today." And, "Be sure to bring plug adaptors and converters. The electrical outlets are 220V."

Watson's biggest concern was not his ability to organize a team or to make certain that the players all wore red on the days he wanted them to wear red. He knew he could handle all that. What he worried about was the unknown: his ability to coach.

That is, after all, exactly what a Ryder Cup captain is: a coach. Watson had never coached and didn't know much about coaching. Always a reader, he began studying successful coaches and what they said about motivation, about dealing with players who have failed, about making sure a team is getting along. He also met with Roy Williams, the basketball coach at Kansas University.

Williams is an avid golfer, a seven-handicapper, and he was more than happy to talk to Watson. A few weeks before the team was scheduled to leave for England, he and Watson met at a golf course halfway between Lawrence and Kansas City. It was late in the afternoon so, instead of playing, Watson and Williams drove a cart to the far end of the range and sat and talked while the sun set and the range emptied.

Watson had been concerned throughout the summer about the pressure of playing on the road and the advantage the Europeans would have with the backing of their crowd. He remembered how the American team had failed to respond down the stretch on the final day in 1989 and it worried him.

"You know it can work both ways," Williams told him. "There's always pressure on the home team because they're *supposed* to win. We always tell our players that there's nothing better than quieting the other team's crowd. I tell them to listen for the silence, because you'll never hear anything sweeter, and to be sure to look up at the end and watch the stands empty out when we're ahead."

Watson liked that. He had another question: Do you try to match players who get along or do you throw opposites in together?

"Depends," Williams said. "But if you've got one guy who is always up and confident and another guy who tends to get down, they might be perfect together."

Watson made a note of that too. He had a hundred different playing combinations in his head and he was looking for anything that might help his decision. It was almost dark when they finally returned to the clubhouse. Watson felt good as he drove away hearing Williams's words in his head. "Listen for the silence."

2

IN THE ARENA

WHEN THE CONCORDE carrying the American Ryder Cup team
set down on the tarmac at Birmingham Airport at a few minutes before 9 o'clock on a rainy Monday evening, everyone breathed a deep
sigh of relief.

Not that the flight had been bumpy. In fact, it had been very fast
and quite enjoyable. It was just that when the plane departed from
Dulles Airport in Washington that morning, it had left behind several
weeks of controversy and embarrassment.

It all started because the president of the United States, an enthusiastic golfer, wanted to meet the Ryder Cup team before it went off to
do battle with Europe. There was just one small problem: most of the
team had no desire to meet him.

There wasn't a single member of the team who had voted for Bill
Clinton in 1992. None of them liked the Clinton plan to tax the
wealthy one bit. The politics of the team were probably best summed
up by U.S. Open champion Lee Janzen, who said, "Where I grew up
you were better off telling people you were a garbage man than a
Democrat."

That's true for most of the PGA Tour, not so much because all the
players grew up with Republican silver spoons in their mouths, but
because most of them grew up around country clubs and business
people who tended to fall on the conservative side of most political
issues. If an open election for president were held on the PGA Tour,
the winner would probably be Rush Limbaugh.

When the word first got out that Clinton had invited the team to come to the White House on the Monday they were scheduled to fly to England, several players were asked how they felt about such a visit.

Paul Azinger, who not only had voted for Bush but had canceled his subscription to his hometown newspaper after it endorsed Clinton, was diplomatic when he was asked about the trip. He said he would certainly go as part of the team and that a trip to the White House was an honor no matter who was president. But Azinger also told his close friend Payne Stewart, "I don't want to shake hands with a draft dodger."

The reference was to Clinton's failure to serve during the Vietnam War. Azinger's father had fought in Vietnam, and he still had memories of talking to him on the phone from there as a little boy. "I remember you always had to say 'over' when you were finished talking," he said. "Once I forgot to say 'over,' and Dad didn't say anything. I guess you weren't allowed to. It scared the hell out of me. Finally, I remembered and said 'over,' and he started talking. The whole thing blew my mind."

Azinger's mind was also blown when he found that his buddy Stewart had repeated his crack about Clinton to a reporter and it had shown up in print. Later, when he was able to joke about the incident, Azinger shook his head and said, "I guess I should have told Payne that we were talking off the record."

Others had spoken on the record. John Cook had said that Clinton's tax plan penalized people who worked hard in order to help those who did not. Janzen, jokingly, had said he wanted to make the trip but wouldn't be able to afford it after he paid his taxes. Others had simply said they didn't want to go.

A public firestorm ensued. Here was a team going off to represent the United States saying it didn't want to meet the president. Here also was a group of wealthy men complaining about having to pay taxes.

It was Watson who finally put an end to all the talk. "It doesn't matter who the president is, if you're invited to the White House, you go," he said. "The president is the country's First Golfer. We'll be there."

Watson's political background was a little different from that of his players. He had grown up in a Republican household but had gone through a radical period at Stanford, taking part in antiwar marches while letting his hair grow long. He graduated in 1971 and a year later voted for George McGovern for president. When he informed his father of his intent to vote for McGovern, his father looked at him and said, "You're an idiot."

Twenty-two years later, after having voted twice for Ronald Reagan and twice for George Bush, Watson laughed at his father's words. "He was right," he said. "I was an idiot."

Watson's conservatism isn't lockstep vote-your-pocketbook stuff. For one thing, he believes drugs should be legalized so that the U.S. can at least reap the tax benefits from their sale. "We can't seem to curb their use," he said, "so why not legalize them, collect the taxes, and say that if you break a law while on drugs you are subject to a stiffer penalty? That's what we do with alcohol, isn't it?"

Watson's players knew nothing about his politics. Except for Floyd and Wadkins, none of them knew him very well. He was someone they all respected but couldn't quite get a handle on. Watson was always friendly, but never very warm or open. He was not an easy person to talk to once the conversation went beyond small talk or locker room humor.

One of Davis Love's first memories of Watson dated back to the 1988 British Open. He had been working on the putting green the day before the tournament began when Watson arrived and began putting. After a few minutes, Watson asked Love if he would mind taking a look at his stroke.

Only in golf do players who are, after all, playing against one another, routinely help one another out during practice sessions. Love was nervous though. He was twenty-four years old, in his second year on tour, and here was the great Tom Watson asking him for a putting lesson. "I didn't want to tell him something that was going to mess him up the day before the British Open started," he said. "I wanted to help if I could, but I also thought I better be careful."

Love stood behind Watson and watched him stroke a few putts. Suddenly, something his father had told him many times as a boy flashed into his head. "You know, Tom, almost all the great putters keep their eyes directly over the ball or inside the ball," he said.

"Yours look to me like they might be outside the ball."

Love was pleased with himself. "I knew what I was saying was right and it was simple. It couldn't possibly mess him up."

Watson didn't even look up when Love had finished with his tip. "Nah," he said. "I don't buy that. You're wrong."

Love walked away baffled. "If he knew the answer," he said later, "why did he ask me the question?"

It was a more open Watson who greeted the players when they began turning up on Sunday evening at the Sheraton-Carlton Hotel in Washington. At dinner that night, he spoke emotionally about the adventure they were about to embark on together and how difficult it would be. But he also told them he had no doubt they were up to the task.

The players were a bit nervous about the next morning's White House visit. Clinton was bound to be aware of their comments about him. "So what?" Watson said. "Believe me, he's used to people disagreeing with him. It's his job to deal with people like that every day."

The group arrived the next morning just as Chelsea Clinton was leaving for school and the president was returning from his run with his Secret Service/media entourage trailing in his wake. Socks the Cat was playing on the lawn. "Well," said Azinger, who'd arrived at dinner the night before with Bill and Hillary masks, "I think I've seen enough."

Watson had thought long and hard about what he should say to Clinton. A week earlier, he had bolted awake one morning with the answer. After all the players had been introduced to Clinton, he gripped a golf club and said, "You know, Mr. President, the golf grip is a lot like politics. If you hold the club too far to the right, you're going to get in trouble on the left. If you hold it too far to the left, you're going to have trouble from the right. But if you hold it in the middle . . ."

"You'll get it just right," Clinton said, finishing the thought for him on cue. Everyone laughed. The tension broke. Watson had said the right thing.

All the politics and pressure were forgotten when the Concorde landed in England and the players saw that every nook and cranny of the airport was filled with golf fans. Two barricades had been set up so the players could walk unimpeded through the lobby to the curb where a car and driver awaited each of them. As each player made his way through the crowd, a cheer went up — the loudest, of course, for Watson. This was the opposition, but it was respected and — in the case of Watson — revered.

"It made you realize once and for all," John Cook said later, "that this was a really big deal."

At the Belfry, a light dinner awaited them after check-in and then the players started playing their favorite board game, Pass the Pigs. Since the flight had only been about three hours and their bodies were still on East Coast time, they weren't the least bit tired. Shortly before midnight, Watson walked in, tapped his watch and said, "It's eleven forty-five, boys. Let's get a good night's sleep and an early start tomorrow."

He turned to walk out, then stopped. "In case you were wondering, that was a subtle hint," he said.

The game stopped. Tired or not, the players headed for bed. Their captain had spoken.

The next two days were routine. Watson assigned practice groups each day and spent some extra time on the range with John Cook and Chip Beck, both of whom were struggling with their swings. The players weren't certain who would play with whom on Friday, but they had ideas. Love and Kite were campaigning to play together. Everyone assumed that Fred Couples and Raymond Floyd, who had been unbeatable at Kiawah, would stay together, and it seemed likely that Corey Pavin and Wadkins, both scrappers, would be paired. That would leave Azinger and his press spokesman Stewart as the likely fourth team, with the rookies Cook, Jim Gallagher Jr., and Janzen sitting out the first morning along with Beck.

The European lineup also seemed set. Ballesteros and Olazabal, as always, would be paired, and Nick Faldo and Colin Montgomerie were also a lock. Gallacher also had four rookies and he seemed to be leaning toward leaving all of them out of the morning matches. That would probably mean that two British veterans, Sam Torrance and Mark James, would play together with Bernhard Langer and Ian Woosnam — three Masters titles among them — as the fourth team.

The Americans spent a lot of time learning and relearning the Belfry's Brabazon Course. The reason the Ryder Cup was being staged here for a third time was simple: money. The Belfry had offered the European PGA huge dollars to establish its headquarters at the resort and to play the Ryder Cup on the Brabazon Course every four years.

Everything at the Belfry was built around the Ryder Cup connection. Each wing of the hotel was named after a different Ryder Cup captain. The Americans were in the Lee Trevino wing, the Euros in the Tony Jacklin wing.

The Brabazon Course is a fairly ordinary golf course with two fabulous match-play holes: the short par-four 10th, where players had to decide whether to risk hitting a tee shot over water to a narrow green, and the long, difficult 18th. How much did the Ryder Cup connection mean to the resort? Well, if you wanted to play the other Belfry course, the Derby, the cost was £18. But if you wanted to tread the Brabazon, the same ground where Ryder Cups had been decided, you had to come up with £50.

The players who had played at the Brabazon before noticed two things: a wet summer and early fall had left the course soft and playing longer than they remembered. And there was almost no rough.

"Seve rough," Azinger said one day walking through it. "They've got it set up so he can play."

Seve Ballesteros loomed as the biggest question mark on the European team. He had been the unquestioned spiritual leader for the Europeans throughout the 1980s but he was having a miserable year. Always wild off the tee, he was now so wild that even with his unparalleled ability to manufacture shots, he couldn't recover well enough to score. The lighter the rough the better it would be for Seve.

Everything was set up according to a very precise schedule and every desire of the players was met almost immediately. Watson did request one change in the dining room that had been set up for the team to eat in. Three tables that could sit about ten people each were in place when the team arrived. Watson wanted one long table. The team would eat together.

They ate together on Wednesday but not at the new table. Instead, they all put on their best dress clothes (PGA-supplied of course) and traveled ten miles down the road to the Metropole Hotel for the gala dinner. Eight hundred people would pay £150 apiece for the privilege of eating in the same ballroom as the two teams.

Watson dreaded the gala dinner. Tradition called for the teams to sit through not only the dinner and speeches but also the musical acts that came afterward. It would be after midnight before they returned to the Belfry, and he knew that was bound to make everyone a little cranky with barely more than twenty-four hours left before the matches began.

He also knew from experience that the gala dinner tended to turn into an autograph fest for the paying public. Inevitably, they would line up at the two team tables to have their menus signed. Watson made a decision: his players would not spend their evening signing autographs. He told them that if anyone asked, they should politely ask that menus or anything else people wanted signed be sent to the American team room with the promise that everything would be signed and returned before week's end.

The players felt awkward about this. On the one hand, they liked the idea that Watson was willing to play bad guy for them and give them an excuse not to spend the whole night signing menus. On the other hand, they knew that saying no to a crowd that had paid big bucks (or heavy pounds) to rub shoulders with them would probably be uncomfortable.

Sure enough, shortly after the meal was served, the fans began lining up at the two tables. The Europeans dutifully signed. The Americans politely said no. The evening might have passed with only a few feelings mildly hurt if Sam Torrance had not asked Watson to sign his menu.

Torrance was the most outgoing member of the European team, a forty-two-year-old chain-smoking Scotsman with a keen, dry wit. When he leaned over Watson's shoulder and asked him to sign a menu, Watson shook his head.

"You know what will happen if I sign, Sam," he said. "We'll spend the whole night signing."

"But, Tom, it's part of the tradition of the night to sign menus for one another."

Watson shook his head again. "No, Sam, it's not," he said. "At the victory dinner on Sunday we do that. Not here."

Insulted and hurt, Torrance stalked back to his team's table, indicating that Watson had snubbed him. Sensing a problem, Watson followed him back to the table. "Look, Sam, I don't want you to feel insulted," he said. "If you send the menus to our team room, I promise we'll sign every one of them."

Torrance waved him off. "Forget it, Tom," he said. "Just forget it."

Boom! The very thing Watson wanted so desperately to avoid, controversy and tension between the teams, had just arrived full force because of a decision he had made. There was no way this would stay secret, not with eight hundred people in the room, many of them smarting from being snubbed for signatures. Watson knew the British tabloids would run wild with the story. He returned to the table shaken and upset.

"I was trying to make things easier for my team," he said later. "I probably made a mistake, but it didn't have to become as big a deal as it did."

By the next morning it had become a huge deal. The tabloids were — of course — running amok. "Fork Off!" read one headline. Another said, "Tom Watson You Are A Disgrace!"

Watson walked into breakfast looking ashen. He hadn't slept well at all, waking up from different dreams throughout the night. The players had never seen the Tom Watson they saw that morning. "I got myself into this and I'll handle it," he said. "You guys just go out and play and don't worry about it."

The words were Watson, but the tone wasn't. His voice was soft, filled with sadness and uncertainty. Some of the players thought he sounded choked up. "It did shake me up," he said. "I know how the tabloids are over there, but some of the things that were said by people hurt. It was exactly what I didn't want to have happen. I just couldn't understand why people would get upset with me for not wanting my team to have to sign eight hundred autographs during a formal dinner. I know from experience that I can sign three hundred and twenty-two autographs in an hour. That means you're signing for two and a half hours. Asking people to do that is rude."

Watson knew the only way to put the incident behind him was to deal with it. So when he met with the media that day for the traditional captains' press conference, he brought the subject up. He apologized to Torrance (even though he was angry with him for not letting the issue die) and to anyone else who had been insulted by his decision.

Later, Gallacher made light of the whole thing, saying he had taken care of Torrance by forging Watson's autograph on his menu since he was quite familiar with it. Someone asked if signing autographs had ruined his team's evening. Gallacher grinned wickedly. "Well, Seve did struggle a bit with his fromage . . ."

The American players did as they were told. They went out and played and let Watson handle the situation. By now, the crowds had grown huge and the players signed autographs all day long. "Remember, we're bad guys, we don't sign," Azinger said as he waded through a crowd signing everything in sight.

By the time the opening ceremony was held late Thursday afternoon, the hue and cry had quieted. Torrance, after telling reporters in the morning that he intended to show Watson and the Americans how he felt about being insulted when the matches began, had backed off — no doubt under orders from Gallacher.

Sixteen years after getting chills as the flags went up at Lytham and St. Anne's, Watson led an American team into another flag-raising ceremony. When he had finished introducing his team, Watson turned to the players and said, "Gentlemen, I cannot tell you how proud I am to be your captain."

The flags went up, the anthems were played. Finally, it was time to play golf.

Even so, the autographing incident had already had a tangible effect. At nightfall Wednesday, the British bookies had made the Americans 11–10 favorites. Twenty-four hours later, the Europeans were favored by the same odds. Menugate had replaced Clintongate as everyone's favorite topic.

If the players had any doubts about how intense Watson was about this competition, they were erased when they saw, at the bottom of their schedules for Friday, September 26 — the opening day of play — his "thought for the day."

It was simple and direct: "Remember," it said, "everything they invented, we perfected."

That, they thought, is the way he really feels about this whole thing. The sportsmanship and good feeling are all well and good, but once the first ball is hit, winning was what they had come for.

"What we all liked about it," Davis Love said, "was the message that the niceties are over; let's go kick their butts."

That was exactly the message Watson wanted to deliver.

By the time the matches finally began, everyone was having trouble with his nerves, even the most experienced players. The two-hour fog delay heightened the tension. As Watson stood on the first tee waiting for Pavin and Wadkins, who would lead off for his team against Torrance and James, he tried to force a smile. "Usually I don't worry about what I can't control," he said. "But in this case, I have to worry."

The Ryder Cup format is simple: On Friday and Saturday there are eight matches. The four morning matches are alternate shot, the four afternoon matches are best ball. Ironically, the Americans had done well in recent years in the alternate-shot matches even though it was a format they never played. It was in the best-ball matches — the format most Americans play week in and week out at country clubs and the pros play in their practice-round betting matches — that the Europeans had dominated.

Even so, the Americans didn't feel too bad when the first morning ended in a 2–2 tie, for one reason: the supposedly unbeatable Spaniards, Olazabal and Ballesteros, had been beaten by Tom Kite and Davis Love.

Ballesteros had become a legendary Ryder Cup figure over the years, not only for his brilliant play, but for his gamesmanship. He was famous for coughing at the wrong (or right) moment, for creating a confrontation (like the one with Azinger in 1991) to throw off an opponent's concentration, for somehow finding a way to get to the psyche of the opposition.

He also made Olazabal a better player. The younger Spaniard had also had a difficult year, but Ballesteros had spent the whole week building him up, saying he was the best player in the world. When the two of them played together, they paced the fairway shoulder-to-shoulder as if connected by an invisible cord.

Kite and Love knew all this. Just before the match began, several of the American wives had handed Love a package of cough lozenges.

"First time he coughs," they said, "take this out and give it to him."

It never came to that. On the first hole, Kite had a putt of less than two feet to halve the hole. Ballesteros waited until he had marked the ball and started lining the putt up before he said, "That's good."

Kite picked the ball up without a word and walked to the tee. "Tom, you didn't hear me say the putt was good before you put it down?" Ballesteros said.

"No, Seve, I didn't," Kite said, smiling. "I guess the crowd was just so loud I couldn't hear."

That set the tone. The Americans weren't going to be drawn into any arguments. On a couple of occasions when Love started to charge down the fairway at the same accelerated pace as the Spaniards, Kite slowed him down. "No need to rush," he said. "They aren't going anywhere without us."

Love, quaking legs and all, played extremely well in his Ryder Cup debut. The Americans took the lead on the second hole with a birdie and the Spaniards never caught them. What's more, they won the match with the kind of bravura that Ballesteros and Olazabal were famous for.

Having reached the turn one up, the two Americans watched in amazement as Ballesteros, after what seemed like an endless discussion with Olazabal, pulled out an iron and laid up short of the water on the 10th. Seve laying up? Unthinkable. Apparently, he still lacked confidence off the tee.

Kite didn't pause a beat before he grabbed his three-wood and took dead aim at the green. The ball rose in a high arc and several thousand people held their breath as the ball hung over the water for a split second, then landed softly on the green and rolled to a stop six feet from the pin.

"Yeah!" Kite screamed, jumping straight up into the air. Maybe he had been this excited when he won the U.S. Open. Maybe. Racing down the fairway, his wife, Christy, shook a fist herself and said, "Who says he's conservative?"

Kite's shot wouldn't mean much if the Americans didn't win the hole. Olazabal wedged the ball to within nine feet, and Ballesteros sank the birdie putt, looking at Love as if to say, "The pressure's all on you now."

Love calmly stroked the putt in for an eagle two. The Americans had the hole and a two-up lead. They had also given the Spaniards a large dose of their own medicine. Ballesteros and Olazabal never got any closer, and Love finished the match off with a three-foot par putt at 17.

Pavin and Wadkins had won their match to open the day, but the two American teams that should have been strongest, Azinger-Stewart and Couples-Floyd, had both been beaten soundly. Watson decided to shake things up in the afternoon. He sat Stewart and Floyd, paired Couples with Azinger, and brought two of the rookies, Janzen and Gallagher, off the bench together.

Pavin and Wadkins came through again, but Kite and Love, matched a second time with the Spaniards, didn't have the same luck in best ball as they had in alternate shot, losing on the 15th hole. Janzen and Gallagher lost a tough match on 18 when one of the European rookies, Peter Baker, rolled in a 25-foot birdie putt. That put the Europeans up 4–3 with one match still on the course: Azinger-Couples against Faldo-Montgomerie.

Golf rarely gets any more melodramatic than this. There was no love lost in this foursome. Faldo was so obsessed and intense that he almost never spoke to anyone on the golf course, even his partner. Montgomerie wasn't much of a talker either unless he was snapping at someone. Azinger talked all the time but was wound just as tight as Faldo. Couples, for all of his laid-back appearance, wanted badly to make up for his Sunday failure on this golf course four years before.

Birdies flew everywhere. When Azinger stuffed an eight-iron one foot from the flag at 16, the Americans went one up. It was now virtually dark and everyone on the grounds was following this match. Azinger walked off the 16th green, his face a mask of tension, and said to Watson, "I want to beat these guys *so* bad . . ."

Easier said than done. With everyone literally feeling his way, Faldo somehow knocked a five-iron to five feet at 17 and made the birdie putt. The match was even and it was pitch black. The captains agreed to finish at 8 o'clock the next morning.

"It's gonna be a long night waiting to play one hole," Azinger said walking up 18 in the dark. "I'm already exhausted and we've got two days to go."

*   *   *

Dinner in the Belfry's Stafford Room — the U.S. team room — was very quiet that night. The uncertainty surrounding the postponed match had left everyone a little bit nervous. A 4–4 tie was possible, but so was a 5–3 deficit. Everyone remembered what a Waterloo the 18th had been in 1989. The hole had come into play only once on Friday and the Europeans had won it on Baker's birdie.

Normally a voracious eater, Davis Love had been having trouble eating all day. He knew it was just nerves, but when he noticed his wife not eating at dinner he wondered what was going on. Unlike some wives, Robin didn't get nervous about golf.

"You okay?" he asked.

"I don't feel great," she said. "I think I could use some Tylenol."

Almost seven months pregnant, Robin Love had walked the entire 18 holes that morning. During the lunch break, Davis had suggested that she take the afternoon off or just walk a few holes. Robin walked for a little while, started to feel weary, and went back to the hotel to rest. That was fine with her husband. The doctor at home had told her she could walk but should quit if she started to tire.

Love wanted to go over to the fitness trailer to get stretched before he went to bed, so he suggested Robin walk there with him to get some Tylenol. When they arrived, the trainers said they didn't have any Tylenol but suggested that if they checked with the front desk some could surely be found.

Robin went back to find Tylenol while Davis got stretched. A little while later he walked back to the team room. Robin wasn't there. Neither was Linda Watson.

"Where did Robin and Linda go?" he asked.

"They went to find Tylenol" was the answer.

Love wasn't sure why Robin needed Linda's help to find Tylenol and the tone of the answer told him that it wasn't that simple. Something's going on here, he said to himself and went upstairs to find out. There were security guards patrolling the floors to make sure no unwanted fans or media could get up there. Love asked one of them if he had seen his wife.

"They're in your room," the guard said.

They?

Love opened the door and found three people crowded into the small room. Linda Watson was sitting next to the bed. A doctor was standing over the bed, and his wife was lying flat on her back with her legs in the air.

Instinctively, Love told himself to stay calm. He knew if he started panicking that Robin would panic too. "What's going on?" he asked quietly.

"It looks like the baby has dropped," the doctor said. "Your wife has overdone it. I've checked the baby's heartbeat and it's fine. But she may be leaking amniotic fluid. Right now, I think she just needs to stay in bed for the next twenty-four hours. If she starts to feel any worse, there's an OBGYN right nearby we can call."

Love thanked the doctor and, as soon as he had left, called Robin's doctor at home in Georgia. He explained what had happened and the local doctor's theory. "If it was amniotic fluid, it would just keep coming," the doctor said. "My guess is that the baby's dropped and is pushing on her bladder. She's probably leaking urine. If she keeps leaking, you're going to have to take her to the hospital and she's going to have the baby. Otherwise, she should be okay if you can convince her to stay in bed."

That wouldn't be easy. Within a few minutes of the doctor's departure Robin was claiming she felt fine and wanted to get up. "I thought I might have to get straps for her," Love said.

The other wives were put on call to keep Robin company the next morning while the matches were going on and to make certain she stayed in bed. Love slept fitfully during the night. He kept rolling over in bed thinking it must be morning only to learn that it was fifteen minutes later than the last time he had thought it was morning.

Azinger had predicted a long night. Interminable was more like it.

It was 7:55 the next morning when the carts carrying Azinger, Couples, Faldo, and Montgomerie pulled up to the 18th tee. It was overcast, but at least there was no fog. It was also freezing. The official temperature reading at 8 o'clock was 49 degrees with gusty winds. Everyone knew what was at stake, including the fans who had already turned out in force and had started jostling for position at sunrise.

Montgomerie hit first, pushing a weak but safe shot into the right rough. With his partner dry, Faldo was able to aim down the left and bite off a large chunk of the water. For a split second, it looked as if he had bitten off too much. But the ball landed safely in the left fairway and a huge cheer went up as the ball bounced into the view of the gallery.

Couples led off for the Americans. The minute his ball left the club it was dead. It started left and hooked. It splashed into the water as another cheer went up. One American down, one to go.

Azinger had not been this nervous during his PGA playoff a month earlier against Greg Norman. He *had* to get the ball into the fairway in position to reach the green. He couldn't let Faldo win the hole with a par and put the Europeans two points up.

He was shaking with nerves and the cold. "My Florida bones can't take that kind of cold," he said. "When I saw Freddy's ball get wet, I thought, Oh boy, it's all on me now."

Under the circumstances, the shot may have been as good as any Azinger has ever hit. It flew on almost the same line as Faldo's ball, landed in the fairway, and rolled 15 yards beyond Faldo. The crowd applauded appreciatively, knowing a great shot under pressure when it saw one.

"Great tee shot," Watson said, his hands stuffed in his pockets to ward off the cold.

They made their way up the fairway. Montgomerie was first to play. From a bad lie, he hit his ball weakly into the water. Groans. Faldo, standing behind his ball in the fairway, showed no emotion at all. Mentally though, he flinched.

God, now it's one against one, he thought. I bloody well better hit this one well and put some pressure on Azinger.

He didn't. His seven-iron shot reached the green well short of the pin, leaving him with a 50-foot uphill putt. Azinger was 163 yards from the pin. Watson walked up next to him. "Great tee shot," he said again.

Azinger stood behind his ball for what seemed like forever, tossing grass into the air to check the wind over and over. He and his caddy, Mark Jiminez, finally decided on an eight-iron. The shot was almost perfect. It landed pin high, but just a tad right — about 18 feet from the flag.

Advantage, U.S.

The other twenty players, having finished their warm-ups for the matches that would begin at 8:30, were now sitting greenside. Couples and Montgomerie, both now spectators too, joined them. The green, the stage and pendulum of the match, belonged to Azinger and Faldo.

Their rivalry stretched back to 1987, when Azinger had bogeyed the last two holes of the British Open to give Faldo a one-shot victory and his first major title. Azinger had carried that wound with him for years. It had been exacerbated when Faldo was quoted as making fun of Azinger's unorthodox grip. During the last round of the PGA when Azinger had seen Faldo's name at the top of the leader board along with his and Norman's, his resolve had seemed to double.

"It was nothing personal," he claimed. "But I didn't want to lose another major to *him*."

He didn't. Now the two men were face-to-face in a totally different situation. Each was a millionaire and there wasn't a penny at stake. But both could feel the almost unbearable tension as they walked onto the 18th green. Their teammates were yelling encouragement, but neither man heard a word.

Faldo putted first. The 18th was probably the slowest green on the golf course, especially early in the morning. Faldo knew it was slow, but not how slow, and his putt stopped 10 feet short. No one on the American team thought for one second that he would miss the second putt, no matter how difficult it might be.

They were all hoping that Azinger would make Faldo's putt irrelevant. He walked around the ball, lining it up from all angles. Kneeling nearby, Watson heard a TV technician's walkie-talkie crackle.

His head snapped around. "Turn that thing down!" he demanded.

Azinger's putt looked like it was in until it got to within a yard of the hole, when it started to slide just right. Azinger threw his head back, his eyes closed, and let out a deep sigh of frustration. He walked up and tapped the ball in for par.

The Americans could do no worse than tie. If Faldo somehow missed, the first day's play would end 4–4 *and* the U.S. would start day two with a full head of steam. But Faldo's putt was never going anywhere but dead center. The crowd screamed for joy and the Europeans surrounded him on the green. Europe was ahead, 4½–3½.

Faldo grabbed Torrance's hand as if he was going to fall over.

"What's for breakfast?" he said. Then his knees buckled and he bent over and let out a huge sigh of relief.

The rest of the morning was a disaster for the Americans. Seemingly spurred by Faldo, the Europeans won three of four matches. The only U.S. victory came from the newly created team of Raymond Floyd and Payne Stewart. By lunchtime, Europe led 7½ to 4½ and it looked like a rout was in the offing.

Watson had to come up with something for the afternoon. He still hadn't played Cook and Beck, and he knew they were losing their minds waiting. But who should he pair them with? He remembered what Roy Williams had said about putting a confident player with a player who tended to get down on himself. No one was more up or confident than Beck. Cook was much more mercurial. He decided to gamble and put them together.

The two men were on the driving range when a PGA official came up to them carrying a walkie-talkie. He handed the walkie to Cook and said, "Tom wants to talk to you."

Cook heard Watson's voice crackle at the other end. "Cookie, you ready to go?" he asked.

"Dying to," Cook answered.

"Good. Let me talk to Chip." He repeated his question to Beck, who repeated Cook's answer. "Fine then," Watson said. "You guys are going out in the first match against Faldo and Montgomerie. We could really use a boost."

Cook looked at Beck. "Nothing like skipping the frying pan and going straight into the fire, huh?" he said.

"Don't worry about a thing," Beck said. "No reason why we can't whip them."

It may well be that there has never been a golfer with a more positive attitude than Beck. Other players say that he is the only man on tour who can knock a ball in the water and say, in all seriousness, "Boy, this is great. Now I get a chance to get up and down from there for a par!"

Beck had been subjected to severe criticism from the media and other players when he had laid up from the 15th fairway at Augusta during the last round of the Masters earlier in the year. He had trailed

Langer by three shots at the time, and a lot of people felt that by not going for the green and a possible eagle, he had been protecting second place rather than going all out for first. Beck had said a million times that he just didn't think he could get the ball over the water from where he was and thought laying up was the best way to make birdie. A lot of people didn't buy it, and Beck had literally had his manhood questioned for months.

Here was a chance to make everyone forget all that. The Americans' situation could not have been much worse. A split of the afternoon matches simply wasn't going to be good enough because a three-point deficit going into the twelve singles matches would probably be too much to overcome.

When Faldo knocked in a birdie putt at the first hole it looked as if the afternoon would be a continuation of the morning. Cook didn't blink. He rolled his birdie putt in right on top of Faldo.

That set the tone for the match. Every time it seemed the Europeans might grab an advantage, Cook or Beck came up with a shot. On the fourth hole, Cook was lining up another birdie putt. He asked Beck if he wanted to take a look at it for him.

"Heck no," Beck answered. "I don't need to look at that putt, you know what it will do. You're going to knock it dead center." He pointed across the green where Faldo and Montgomerie and their caddies were lining up a putt from a hundred different angles, circling the ball and the hole over and over again. "Look at those guys. They got everyone in the world trying to figure out what to do over there. John, we got 'em confused! They're shaking over there! We got 'em!"

Cook cracked up. He also made his putt after both Europeans had missed. The Americans were one-up. The rest of the afternoon was fraught with peril, but Cook and Beck never gave up their slender lead. When Cook went cold on the back nine, Beck kept the team in the match. He got up and down at 12, 13, and 14 for pars, then blasted out of a bunker to five feet for a birdie at 15 that matched Faldo. The Americans were still one-up when they arrived at the 18th. It had been ten hours since Faldo and Azinger had confronted one another on this hole.

The scoreboards tracking the other three matches showed that Pavin and Gallagher were easily beating Mark James and Costantino

Rocca, but Ian Woosnam and Peter Baker were doing the same to Couples and Azinger. Stewart and Floyd had a slim lead on Olazabal and Joakim Haeggman. Ballesteros had asked Gallacher for the afternoon off to work on his swing for the Sunday singles. With a three-point lead, Gallacher had felt comfortable granting the request.

If Cook and Beck could hang on at 18, the Americans would have a shot at a 3–1 afternoon margin, which would bring them within one. If both remaining matches were halved, the Europeans would have a two-point lead going into Sunday.

Beck had carried the team for most of the back nine. Now, though, Cook stepped up again. He hit a perfect drive and crushed his second shot to almost the same spot where Azinger had hit his second shot in the morning. Montgomerie was out of the hole again, but Faldo being Faldo stuck his shot 10 feet below the hole. If he made the putt, Cook would have to make his to win the match.

This time, though, Faldo turned human. The putt slid right at the last second. Cook now only needed to two-putt. Faldo didn't even ask him to go through the exercise. He walked over and shook hands, conceding the match. Cook and Beck had turned the entire match around. When Stewart rolled in a birdie putt at 17 a few minutes later to give the U.S. its third victory of the afternoon, you never would have known that the Europeans were still leading 8½ to 7½. The Americans were jubilant — and relieved.

"If I were a betting man," Azinger said, "I'd have bet all I had on us right then. John and Chip just turned the whole thing around."

One other thing that had picked up the Americans' spirits immeasurably was the near-miraculous recovery of Robin Love. After staying in bed all morning, she had announced at lunchtime that she felt 100 percent better and wanted to get up and walk around a little. Okay, everyone said, but just a little.

When Davis Love found out that Watson was going to sit him out in the afternoon, he suggested to Robin that they rest together and then walk out to the ninth green to watch the afternoon matches come through. Robin said that was fine. She was going to walk out to the first tee with Tracy Stewart and then she would come right back to the room. Exhausted and drained, Love went upstairs and promptly fell asleep. When he awoke almost two hours later, Robin was no-where in sight.

He walked to the ninth green. Robin wasn't there either. The first two matches had already gone through, and Couples and Azinger were standing on the green trailing Woosnam and Baker by three holes. Watson was there watching. He told Love that Robin was fine and, he thought, with Linda.

At that moment, Watson was more concerned with Couples than anything else. Except for the epic Friday night/Saturday morning match, Couples had played poorly. After the morning matches, he had asked Watson to let him sit out the afternoon so he could practice and try to get his game in shape for Sunday. Unlike Gallacher, Watson didn't have the luxury of a three-point lead. Couples had to play.

But Couples hadn't come around. He and Azinger were getting waxed by the red-hot Baker and Woosnam. As the players came off the ninth green, Watson tried to give Couples a pep talk. "You're only three down, Fred. There's plenty of time to come back," he said. "Don't get down on yourself."

Couples had been hearing pep talks and encouragement for two days now. Everyone meant well. But there's nothing a golfer hates more than being told everything is just fine when he knows it isn't. As languid as he may look on the golf course with his long, easy swing and ambling gait, Couples gets down on himself as quickly as anyone. The difference has always been his ability to bounce back.

"Freddie can go out and have a good dinner or watch a good ball game and get in a good mood just from that after a bad round," Love said. "The rest of us have to go figure out what's wrong. Freddie can just show up the next day and turn wrong into right."

It wasn't happening this weekend, though, and Couples was aggra-vated. When Watson added his voice to the chorus of "everything's all right, don't worry about a thing," Couples snapped. "Just leave me alone, Tom," he said angrily. "I don't need any pep talks right now."

He stalked to the 10th tee. Love turned to Watson. "You think I should try to talk to him?" Watson wasn't sure. Love found Couples's caddy, Joe LaCava, and pulled him aside. "Do you think I should talk to Freddie?" he asked. LaCava shook his head emphatically.

"He told me a couple holes ago that he was sick and tired of pep talks and the next person who said something to him he would probably kill."

That person had been Watson. Love decided to follow the match. Couples and Azinger didn't get any better, and Baker and Woosnam closed them out on the 13th hole, winning 7 and 5. Cook and Beck had just won, and Pavin and Gallagher had won too. The only match left on the course was Floyd and Stewart against Olazabal and Haeggman. One of the caddies suggested that everyone should race over to 16 to watch that match. Couples shook his head. "I've had enough golf," he said. "I'm going in."

He began walking over to a cart that would take him back to the clubhouse. Love took a deep breath and followed him. "Look, Freddie, I know you're pissed off, but I really think you should come out and watch Payne and Raymond. You're very important to this team, especially to the young guys like me, and if you go around with a bad attitude, especially tonight, it's going to affect everybody. You're one of the leaders of this team."

"I got you," Couples said, and he nodded to the driver that he was ready to go.

Love put a hand on his arm. "No, Fred, I'm not sure you do get me. You *are* important to this team. Your attitude the rest of today and tomorrow *will* affect how the other guys feel."

Couples didn't say anything. The driver started the cart. Love followed the others to the 16th green. As the players approached the green, he noticed a familiar figure walking with the wives: Robin.

"What in the world?" he demanded.

She put a hand up. "I know, I know. I started out to walk one hole, but it was just too exciting. I had to keep going. I still feel great, so don't worry."

Love didn't know whether to worry, to feel angry, or to feel happy. His wife had never in her life found golf exciting. "I've never wanted her life to go up or down based on me making or missing four-footers," he said. "But it was kind of nice that she was so into this. Payne told me later that seeing her out there really gave him a lift."

Love got a lift of his own a few minutes later. As he and Robin walked up 17, he noticed Couples and his girlfriend, Tawnya Dodd. "Thanks for coming out," he said to Couples.

"I *did* get your message," Couples said.

Love didn't say another word. He had been disappointed when Watson had told him he wasn't playing in the afternoon. Now he felt like it had been worth it.

The mood in the American team room that night was 180 degrees different than the night before. One point down with twelve matches left, having taken back the momentum in the afternoon, confidence was soaring. Cook and Beck, the forgotten men of Friday and Saturday morning, were now heroes.

"You know, positive thinking can overcome a mechanical break down," Beck kept saying. "And I was having a mechanical breakdown out there."

With his North Carolina accent, Beck is easy to imitate. That became the rallying cry for the evening: "Positive thinking can overcome a mechanical breakdown!"

The only down note of the evening came when Watson returned from the captains' meeting. Gallacher had informed him that Sam Torrance had an infection of his big toe that had flared up on him. There was a good chance he might not play on Sunday.

Under Ryder Cup rules, if one player cannot play in the singles, the other team removes one player from its lineup and each team is credited with half a point for the match not played. The U.S. had benefitted from this rule in 1991 when Steve Pate, who had been injured in an automobile accident en route to the gala dinner, sat out the singles. Since Pate had played on Saturday, the Europeans had wondered if the Americans weren't trying to steal half a point. Now, since Torrance had played Friday — and played poorly — the same thought occurred to some of the Americans. What, they wondered, would have happend if Faldo had an infected toe? Would he sit out? Not likely. More likely he would play on a broken leg if necessary.

This wasn't Faldo, though, it was Torrance, and given his toe injury, the possibility that he would sit out was quite real. When Watson walked into the team room with the news, the first two people he told were John Cook and Lee Janzen. They looked at one another. Each man had the same thought: I'm going to be the one who sits out.

Under the rules, Watson had to place the name of one player in an envelope. The next morning, if Gallacher announced that Torrance couldn't play, Watson would hand over the envelope. Before Watson had a chance to give much thought to who should go into the envelope, Wadkins came into the room. He had just heard about Torrance. He grabbed Watson, took him aside, and said, "Put me into the envelope."

That was unthinkable. Wadkins was as accomplished a Ryder Cup singles player as the team had and he was scheduled to play Sunday against Ballesteros. The Americans were convinced that if anyone on the team was certain to beat Ballesteros, it was Wadkins.

But as Wadkins talked, Watson realized his argument made sense. The player in the envelope, Wadkins said, should be either him or Floyd because the other ten players had earned their spots on the team while he and Floyd had been selected by Watson. Floyd had played superbly on Saturday, Wadkins not so well. Watson thought about it briefly and decided Wadkins was right.

"Lanny made a very difficult situation a lot easier for me," Watson said later. "The more he talked, the more I realized it was absolutely the right thing to do. I think the other guys understood the sacrifice he was making, because no one wanted to play more than Lanny. It was one of the great gestures I've ever seen anyone make."

Wadkins knew he was making the right gesture, but at the time, he was thinking that was all it was — a gesture. "I went to bed that night convinced Sam would play and I would be playing Seve," he said. "It wasn't until Tom came back the next morning and said Sam was out that it really hit me that I wasn't going to play."

The Europeans had a potentially far more serious problem than Torrance's toe to deal with that night. Peter Baker's eleven-month-old daughter had been rushed to a hospital with what appeared to be spinal meningitis. Under the rules, if two players from one team could not play, the opposition was entitled to claim a forfeit of the second match. When they heard about Baker's daughter, the Americans discussed that possibility.

"It wouldn't be right to do that," Floyd said. "That's not in the spirit of the Ryder Cup. If Peter can't play because his child is sick, I'll sit out too."

While that was being bounced around, Love asked Watson if it would be appropriate to send a note to Gallacher asking him to let Baker and his wife know that they were in the thoughts of the American players. Having dealt with a crisis involving an unborn child the night before, Love had an idea of the anguish and fear Baker had to be feeling.

Watson liked the idea. Love wrote the note, walked it across the hall, and asked a security guard to deliver it to Gallacher. The next morning he received a thank-you note from Gallacher with the news that all was well. Baker's daughter had an ear infection, nothing more, and was doing just fine.

With that settled and with Torrance definitely out, there were eleven singles matches to play and the day would begin with the Europeans now leading 9–8, each team having picked up half a point for the unplayed match. The U.S. needed 6 points to create a 14–14 tie, 6½ to win the cup again outright.

The day was cool, overcast, and windy. Watson's final thoughts were brief: If you start to feel down do two things: think about Lanny and how much he wanted to play and don't stop smiling whether you're four up or four down.

If the Americans were smiling early in the day it was only because they were remembering Watson's words. At one point, early in the afternoon, the Europeans were leading in the first five matches. But the last day of a Ryder Cup is a roller coaster. At 1 o'clock, Europe looked like a winner; at 2 o'clock the Americans were in control. By three, Europe was in command again. An hour later, it was anybody's ball game. The day was exhausting and exhilarating with eleven matches on the golf course at once and roars and shouts coming from everywhere. This was golf at its simplest: mano-a-mano, low score wins the hole, add up the holes at the finish.

Couples, playing in the leadoff match, started the American turn-around (the first one) by coming from two down with six holes left to halve his match with Woosnam. Right behind him came Beck, fighting another mechanical breakdown.

Through thirteen holes, Beck was three down to Barry Lane. Watson, bouncing from match to match, showed up on the 14th tee, hoping to give Beck a boost. As Watson approached, he heard Beck yelling at him: "Hey, Tom, where's your smile?" As instructed, Beck was grinning as if he were three up, rather than three down. Watson hadn't followed his own orders. "Keep smiling, Tom. I'm gonna get him for you, don't you worry about a thing."

Clearly, Beck didn't need any cheering up. Watson got back in his cart and went to look for someone who did. Beck was as good as his word. He won the 14th hole, eagled the 15th, won the 16th to get even, and then won the 18th to win the match.

That victory was huge for the Americans. Instead of trailing by two points, they were now even at 9½. Around the golf course, checking the scoreboards constantly, the other players shook their heads in wonder thinking about Beck and his unshakable attitude.

"And people questioned the man's toughness," Azinger said later. "They ought to look in the mirror."

The joy over Beck's comeback was short-lived however. The Europeans won the next three matches, Montgomerie beating Janzen; Baker, completing a remarkable week, beating Pavin; and Haeggman beating Cook. The last result was particularly tough to take. Haeggman and Cook had been even on the 18th tee, and Haeggman's tee shot looked to be dead in the water the second it left the club. Somehow, he just cleared the corner and reached the fairway. Cook put his drive in the right bunker and, with Haeggman way down the fairway, had to try to reach the green from there. His ball hit the bank on the edge of the water, popped in the air, and then rolled back into the water. Cook stood staring at the spot in disbelief.

At that moment, Europe led 12½ to 9½. But the Americans had comfortable leads in three matches: Payne Stewart was on the verge of closing out Mark James; Tom Kite, playing the best golf of the day, was hammering Bernhard Langer; and Jim Gallagher, playing in Wadkins's slot, was easily beating Ballesteros.

Without Olazabal around to dig him out of trouble, Ballesteros was almost helpless. He couldn't have found a fairway with a compass on the front nine, and he shot an embarrassing 42 — six over par. Gallagher took the lead on the first hole and never looked back.

With those three matches in hand, the U.S. also had 12½ points. In the remaining matches, Floyd was leading Olazabal and Faldo was leading Azinger. If those two leads held up, each team would have 13½ points. Which explains why all eyes were on Love and Rocca as they walked up 18 with their match even: Love in the fairway, Rocca in the rough.

Standing in back of his ball, arms folded, trying to look as nonchalant as possible, Love couldn't help but drink in the scene: the packed stands, his friends and teammates standing a few yards away trying to will him to victory. He remembered what his mother had said on the first practice day: "I can't believe that my little boy is actually playing in the Ryder Cup."

Now her little boy was probably going to *decide* the Ryder Cup. Love took a deep breath. He knew now what this was all about. I've waited my whole life for this, he thought, and took one more deep breath.

Rocca had finally decided on a club. It was getting close to 5 o'clock and the temperature, which had climbed at midday, was dropping quickly. He had a long shot from a sidehill lie in the rough and, like John Cook an hour earlier, he had no choice but to try and clear the water.

The ball came out of the rough low and stayed low. It looked for a second like it would drop into the water, but it held its height just long enough to clear the bank and bounce on the hill in front of the green. It stopped there, short of the putting surface, but visible. The crowd screamed with relief. Rocca still had a chance.

Not a very good one, Love was thinking. From where Rocca was, he would have to make a great chip to get close and have a chance at par. Of course the way to take all the suspense out of the matter was to stick this shot close and make a birdie.

He had a nine-iron in his hands but wasn't entirely sure that was the right club. All week long, he had been hitting long irons into this green. But having crushed the ball downwind, he had only 148 yards to the pin and wondered if perhaps he should hit a pitching wedge.

He decided on the nine. "What I should have done was aimed it left and let it drift back into the flag," he said. "I didn't think enough about the slope in front of the pin and the fact that with a short iron, the ball wasn't going to bounce very much at all."

Love liked the shot when it came off the club, but when it landed he could see that it was well short of the pin. It began rolling backward off the slope as the cheers got louder and louder. By the time it stopped rolling, the ball was barely on the green, 50 feet short of the pin.

Love stared as the ball rolled in the wrong direction, thinking, whoa, that's way down there. Then he remembered something. "On Thursday afternoon, we had spent a lot of time practicing long putts from all over the green," he said. "I knew the putt would be slow, but that if I remembered to hit it I should be able to get it close. And I still thought he was going to have trouble making par."

Even so, what had been a huge advantage for Love off the tee was now a decidedly smaller one. The noise was deafening as the players walked to the green. Love walked up to the top tier so he would have a good view of Rocca's chip from below. Cries of "Come on, Rocky, you can do it!" were coming from everywhere.

Love had another thought: In the movie, Rocky came close, but he lost.

Rocca's chip skittered up the hill and, for a moment, the crowd thought he had knocked it stiff. "Yes!" came the shouts. Standing behind the hole, Love could see that the ball wasn't going to stop. It rolled 18 feet past the cup.

Love's turn. He looked the putt over carefully and reminded himself how slow the green was. But he didn't want to go crazy, knock the putt six feet past, and have to putt downhill coming back. So, at the last second, he eased up just a little. He heard the groans from his teammates as the putt rolled dead, six feet short of the pin.

"Dammit," he said under his breath. "You knew it was slow and you didn't hit it."

Rocca had life again. In fact, if he could somehow curl his putt in, the pressure on Love to make his just to get a halve would be brutal. Rocca's putt trickled toward the hole but veered left and went 18 inches past. Love thought briefly about making him mark the ball; after all, under this kind of pressure, no putt was an absolute gimme. Then he changed his mind.

I'm going to give him this and knock mine in and this thing's going to be over, he told himself.

He reached down, picked Rocca's ball up, and flipped it to him. Then he re-marked his ball and he and Williams took a long look at it. Williams thought the putt would break only slightly, that it should be aimed at the right edge of the hole. Love saw more break in it than that. "It's just outside right," he told Williams.

He stepped up to the ball and went through the routine he had developed through the years working with sports psychologist Bob Rotella: Pick a spot, take aim, take a practice putt, line up, and putt. Don't overthink.

But just as he was about to draw the putter back, Love felt himself starting to shake. Something in his brain said, "Don't putt it!"

He stood up and stepped back. By now, no one was breathing. The Americans, seeing Love step back, fidgeted. A player backing off a putt is usually a sign of doubt. Love looked at it differently. Rotella had told him that if you weren't ready to make a putt, you should always back off. He had backed off a putt in 1990 that he needed to make to win a tournament and, watching on television, his younger brother Mark had panicked. Love made the putt. Later, he told Mark, "If you ever see me back off a big putt, it means I'm thinking clearly about what I'm doing and I'm going to make the putt."

As he started his routine again, Love thought about Mark. "I knew he was thinking, now Davis is going to make this."

He picked his spot and took his practice stroke. Now he felt ready. He stroked the ball, and it rolled dead center. "Sometimes, when you make a putt like that, you think later, boy that was easy," Love said. "Rotella says it's like driving a car when you let instinct take over and you start thinking about something else. The next thing you know, you've driven fifty miles and you didn't even notice. I let instinct take over on that putt."

He did the same thing after the putt hit the hole. His arms went straight up into the air and he stood frozen on the spot as his teammates mobbed him. In the midst of the pandemonium he heard Lanny Wadkins's voice above all the others: "The cup is on the Concorde!" Wadkins kept saying. "The cup's coming home!"

It was. Floyd had just gone three up on Olazabal with three holes to play. Love's victory gave the U.S. 13½ points, and since Floyd could now do no worse than halve his match, the Americans had clinched the 14 points that would tie the match and retain the cup.

Love was still listening to Wadkins when it occurred to him that he had never had a chance to shake hands with Rocca. "Where's Costantino?" he asked. Rocca had waited to shake hands, but when

Love was mobbed he had given up and started walking toward the clubhouse.

Love broke away from the revelers and ran after Rocca. He was walking with his arm around his wife and had just reached the gate next to the stands leading back to the locker room when Love caught him. Love grabbed his shoulder. When Rocca turned around, Love could see tears in his eyes.

For a split second, Love felt his despair. After all, he easily could have been in Rocca's shoes. "I hope you're proud of the way you played," he said. "And I hope your country's proud of you. It should be."

The two men shook hands and then Rocca hugged Love. He walked away slowly. Love watched him briefly, then was engulfed again.

The cup was on the Concorde, but Floyd still needed to halve one more hole to clinch the victory. Faldo was still one up on Azinger thanks to his hole in one at 14.

The Americans headed out to 17. Floyd was now two up with two holes left. Olazabal birdied 17. Floyd was one up. Could the Europeans still pull out a tie?

No. Olazabal hooked his tee shot on the 18th into the water. A moment later, when Floyd put his second shot safely on the green, he conceded the hole and the match.

As the Americans celebrated, Love walked up to Tom Watson. "Can you hear it?" he asked.

"Hear what?" Watson asked.

Love pointed at the rapidly emptying stands. "The silence," he said.

Watson grinned. He could hear it. "That," he said, "is as sweet a sound as I think I've ever heard."

Watson had known for weeks exactly what he was going to say during the closing ceremony — win, lose, or draw. He had read an excerpt from Theodore Roosevelt's famous "Man in the Arena" speech several years earlier in, of all things, a letter for parents sent home from one of his children's school. He had been so impressed by the words that he had taped them to the mirror in his bathroom.

Watson often tapes things to his mirror: newspaper columns that he likes, sayings he wants to remember, letters from friends. His wife does the same thing on the kitchen refrigerator. When he started thinking about what he would say at the closing ceremony, Watson thought almost immediately about the speech taped to his mirror.

"It hit exactly the right note for both teams," he said. "It said exactly what I wanted to say about the competition. The world had seen a great show, but most people were going to forget about it, except for who won and who lost. But for the players, it was different. They *were* in the arena and they would always remember what they had felt, right to their dying day.

"Golf is such a solitary sport and the Ryder Cup is so much about being a part of a team. The feelings you have for one another because of what you go through together will never go away."

And so, after he had been presented with the Ryder Cup as the winning captain, Watson read Roosevelt's words.

> It is not the critic who counts, not the one who points out how the strong man stumbled or how the doer of deeds might have done them better. The credit belongs to the man who is actually in the arena; whose face is marred with sweat and dust and blood; who strives valiantly; who errs and comes short again and again; who knows the great enthusiasms, the great devotions and spends himself in a worthy cause and who, if he fails, at least fails while bearing greatly so that his place shall never be with those cold and timid souls who know neither victory nor defeat.

When he was finished, Watson turned to his team and repeated what he had said at the opening ceremony on Thursday: "Gentlemen, I cannot tell you how proud I am to be your captain."

In the end, it had turned out almost exactly the way Watson had wanted it to turn out. The menu flap had hurt, but it had been buried by the dramatics of the golf and by the fellowship that had grown between the competitors as the weekend wore on.

There had been only one incident of any seriousness and it had been brief. On Saturday, Maria Floyd had heard Ballesteros speaking to Olazabal in Spanish during the afternoon match that Ballesteros didn't play in. Coaching by anyone but the captain is against the rules.

"I know what you're doing," Maria Floyd said to Ballesteros. "I speak Spanish and you're coaching him."

Ballesteros hotly denied the accusation and walked away. Nothing more came of it. On Sunday, watching the Azinger-Faldo match — which was by then meaningless — come up 18, Ballesteros had said to Love, "I enjoyed competing against you and Tom [Kite]. It was the way competition should be."

Love agreed. So did everyone else. The Europeans could not have been more gracious in defeat. They were disappointed to lose, but thrilled with the way all the players had conducted themselves.

"The whole thing was brilliant," Faldo said later. "I give a lot of credit to Tom Watson. He listened to what we all told him about what was wrong at Kiawah. Everyone on both sides tried like hell and in the end they were a little bit better. Even so, it was a great week of golf."

Greatest of all, perhaps, for Watson. He called it his biggest thrill in golf, bigger even than the eight major titles. "I couldn't control a lot of what happened and that's what made it so tough," he said. "To be honest, the week stopped being fun for me after the menu flap and didn't start being fun again until Davis made his putt on Sunday. Everything in between was pressure and nerves and hoping to make the right decisions. I really didn't have a chance to enjoy myself again until Sunday night. Then I didn't want to go to sleep."

He was the only one. Everyone else was exhausted. The victory dinner — during which all menus on both sides were signed — was raucous and even got a little bit rowdy near the end. But by 1 A.M. everyone on the American side was ready for a good night's sleep. Payne Stewart was the last to leave and Linda Watson told her husband she was going to bed.

A couple of hours later, Lee Janzen woke up from a sound sleep to hear a television set blasting away in the hospitality room that was across the hall from the Watsons' suite. He walked down the hall to see what was going on and found one person in the room: Tom Watson. A cigar in one hand, a glass of wine in the other, his feet up on a chair in front of him, Watson was watching the BBC replay of the last few minutes of the match with the sound turned all the way up.

"I couldn't enjoy it the first time," Watson said when Janzen walked in. "Now I don't want it to end."

3

"IT'S NOT GOOD NEWS, PAUL . . ."

THE TOUR CHAMPIONSHIP, played in the last week of October, is the last official event on the golf calendar. The year's top thirty money winners qualify for the event and play for a $3 million purse that includes a first prize of $540,000. Most of the major awards are decided at the Tour Championship: leading money winner, player of the year, and the Vardon Trophy, which goes to the player with the lowest stroke-per-round average for the year.

November and December, which are supposed to be golf's off-season, are now dominated by a series of made-for-TV events in which the money is quite real but unofficial. No one adds it up or gives away any awards based on who plays well in these events.

That doesn't prevent most of the top players from participating. Not only is the prize money too good to pass up, but since these are unofficial events, most of them offer appearance money to top players just for showing up. Players fly all over the globe in November and December lining their pockets with the gold that promoters willingly throw their way.

As a result, a lot of players are so exhausted by the time the official tour starts up again in January that they will skip all or most of the West Coast events during the first two months of the season. In 1994, for example, Nick Price, the 1993 player of the year, didn't play in a PGA Tour event until the first week in March. Greg Norman played once, Fred Couples twice. A year earlier, coming off his player-of-the-year title, Couples admitted he was exhausted by all of his November-December play and needed a vacation.

This trend doesn't please the men who run the tour, but there isn't much they can do about it. After all, if the promoters of the Sun City Challenge in South Africa are going to put up $1 million as first prize and invite twelve players to take a shot at it with the last-place finisher getting $100,000, how is the Tour going to say no, you can't go, especially now that South Africa's political sanctions have been lifted? Every week there is a tournament somewhere with big money, a good chunk of it guaranteed, to be played for.

During his twenty years as commissioner, Deane Beman had always walked a tightrope, trying to ensure that his top players would play often enough at home to keep his sponsors happy, while allowing them enough opportunity to play overseas for appearance fees, which, for players like Norman and Couples and John Daly, can easily reach $250,000 a pop. Other top players receive six-figure offers almost routinely.

Beman had finally decided that the best he could do was try to limit the stars' overseas appearances during the "official" season, then let them do whatever they wanted for two months at the end of the year. He was also quite aware of the benefits of made-for-TV golf.

In the 1960s, two taped made-for-TV events had played a major role in increasing the game's popularity. The CBS Golf Classic paired players into two-man teams and had them play one another in the same best-ball format that most amateurs play on weekends. Producer Frank Chirkinian came up with the idea of miking the players so the audience could listen in on their conversations and reactions, and the Classic, shown on tape in one-hour segments throughout the cold winter months, was immensely popular.

So was Shell's Wonderful World of Golf. While the CBS Classic was taped at one course during one week and then replayed all winter, World traveled everywhere, taping head-to-head, medal-play matches. The format was simple: two players meeting on a great golf course somewhere in the world every week. Again, the show was taped and shown in one hour.

There was no downtime, no long walks between shots, no tedious waits for slow players. The action was almost continuous and, since there was no real pressure, the audience got to see the players relaxed and enjoying themselves. When live TV golf became a weekly staple on the networks in the 1970s, both made-for-TV events gave way, although World has now been brought back in limited form by Jack Nicklaus's production company. It was not until 1984, when Don Ohlmeyer came up with the idea for the Skins Game, that taped, TV-created events began to make a comeback.

Ohlmeyer, the one-time executive producer at NBC who had started his own production company, had a simple idea: get four top players and have them play for two days, nine holes a day, for skins. Next to four-ball best ball, skins is probably the game played most often by weekend hackers. Each hole is worth one skin, every man for himself. If a skin is worth one dollar, then the player with the lowest score on a hole wins the skin and a dollar. However, if there is a tie, whether it is among two, three, or four players, everyone ties and the skin carries over to the next hole.

Of course it wasn't likely that four top players were going to show up someplace and put up their own money to play a skins match. Ohlmeyer found several corporations willing to do so, though, and created the Skins Game. He added some spice to it by increasing the value of the skins every six holes. The first six holes would be worth $10,000 apiece, the next six $15,000, the last six $20,000. That meant, with carryovers, you could have players lining up putts worth six figures.

Skins was a success from the start. The fact that Ohlmeyer was able to get golf's Big Three of the 1960s — Arnold Palmer, Jack Nicklaus, and Gary Player — along with the man who had succeeded them as the dominant name in the game, Tom Watson, to play in the first Skins Game helped.

So did the fact that Watson accused Player of cheating at a crucial moment late in the second day. The controversy made headlines and Skins had a permanent place in the Thanksgiving Weekend TV lineup.

One star who rarely played much TV golf in November and December was Paul Azinger. There were several reasons for this, not the least of which was Azinger's aversion to flying. But there was more to it than that. Azinger, who liked being at home in Sarasota, Florida, with his wife and two daughters, didn't like going overseas unless he had to and thought that the extra money he might make by working the last two months of the year wasn't worth it if it affected his ability to start well the next year.

Azinger was like a lot of players in that he worried that next year might be the year in which the magic that had made him great disappeared.

His approach in 1993 was different than in the past. For one thing, having won the PGA in August, he now had a ten-year exemption, meaning the earliest he might have to face Q-School again was in December 2003. For another, as the PGA champion, he was invited, for the first time, to play in the Skins Game.

Skins was appealing to Azinger for several reasons. His buddy, Payne Stewart, was the defending champion and was automatically reinvited. The Azingers could fly to Palm Springs with the Stewarts, spend Thanksgiving together out there, and then Paul could play on Saturday and Sunday.

There was also the little matter of seeing Dr. Frank Jobe about his shoulder.

Shoulder problems were nothing new to Azinger. In fact, he couldn't remember a time in his career when he hadn't had some sort of shoulder pain. He had been operated on once, in 1991, but the pain had flared again early in the 1993 season and Azinger had gone through a bone scan in late June.

By July, the pain was bad enough that Azinger was popping up to twenty Tylenols a day to control it. "It doesn't affect my golf though," he said one day at the New England Classic, where he was leading the tournament in spite of the pain and the pills. "I can't raise my arm above my shoulder, but I can take the club back without feeling a thing."

When the pain persisted, Azinger had an MRI done just before leaving for Toledo for the PGA. It was there, shortly after he finished his second round, that Jobe called him. "There's an abnormality in the shoulder I don't like," Jobe said. "I'd like you to come out here next week for a biopsy."

When Azinger heard the word biopsy, it brought him up a little short. "When you hear biopsy, you think cancer," he said. It didn't panic him though. When Jobe had cleaned out the shoulder in 1991, he had done a biopsy as a precaution. It showed nothing. Azinger assumed this was another precaution and it would again show nothing.

"Look, Doc, I'm playing pretty good," he said. "I don't have time right now."

Jobe didn't push him. And when Azinger won the tournament two days later, Jobe called to congratulate him and tell him he could hold off on the biopsy but to call him right away if the pain got any worse.

The pain never went away, but the anti-inflammatories controlled it throughout the Ryder Cup and most of the fall. Then in November, after Azinger had played in the Grand Slam of Golf, a four-man event that includes the four Grand Slam Tournament winners of that year, the pain got worse. He went in for another bone scan and an MRI the week before the Skins game.

When Jobe saw the results, he called Azinger again. This time there was no negotiating. "No ifs, ands, or buts," Jobe said. "We've got to do a biopsy." They made a date for the Tuesday after the Skins Game. Jobe sent him a copy of the bone scan. When Azinger looked at it he was shocked. The shoulder was completely black.

The Skins Game turned out to be no fun at all. By now, the shoulder was affecting his swing and Azinger didn't win a single skin all weekend. He would say months later that he hadn't seriously thought about cancer at that stage, but it did seem to be on his mind.

A month earlier, at the Las Vegas Invitational, he had brought up Heather Farr's name repeatedly during a lengthy interview. Farr had played on the women's tour until contracting cancer. She had gone through a long, painful two-year fight with the disease before dying that month.

"Sometimes, I feel like the worst hypocrite in the world," Azinger said that day. "I just get *so* mad on the golf course and I know that's wrong. Today, I made a double bogey on number sixteen and I walked off the green cursing myself. I was so bitter about it, I was just brutal. Then I started thinking, Heather Farr would love to be here right now making double bogey, you idiot. Just shut your yap and play."

A few minutes later, Farr came up again: "We all think we're in control of our lives, but really we're not. Heather Farr thought she had control of her life until one day when a doctor told her she had cancer. That can happen to any one of us. We can walk into a doctor and he can tell us something's wrong with the arteries leading to our heart or we have cancer or who knows what. Then what kind of control do you have?"

Azinger, his wife, Toni, and their two daughters flew to Los Angeles after the Skins Game and, as planned, Jobe performed the biopsy on Tuesday. He told Azinger it might be as much as a week before any results came back. Two nights later, he called. "Can you be here at one o'clock tomorrow?" he asked.

Azinger hung up the phone and looked at Toni. "Something's up," he said. "If it was good news, he'd just tell me, you're fine, no problem, go home."

His instinct was right. Jobe got right to the point. "It's not good news, Paul. You have cancer."

Azinger suppressed the first question that came into his mind because his daughters, Sarah Jean and Josie Lynn, were in the room: "Am I going to die?" Instead, he asked the question euphemistically. "What do we do next?"

"We find out," Jobe said, "if it's spread."

The lymphoma Jobe had discovered is one of the most curable forms of the disease. That was the good news. The question now was whether it was confined to the shoulder. The answer didn't come for three days. "I did a lot of thinking about a lot of things those three days," Azinger said. "It was the first time in my life that I really understood that I wasn't bulletproof. When you're thirty-three and you feel like you're at the peak of your career and you've got a great family and more money than you ever dreamed of making, you don't think about dying.

"I still think of myself as a kid, just a big kid. Now someone was telling me I might die. There's no clever answer when someone tells you that."

There had been very few times in Paul Azinger's life when he found himself without a clever answer. He was his mother's third son, his father's first. Jean Gaudino had two sons — Jeff and Joe — with her first husband, John Gaudino, before he was killed in a military plane crash. A couple of years later, she re-met Ralph Azinger, someone she had known growing up, and they were married. Paul was born in 1960, Jed two years later.

Ralph and Jean and all four boys played golf. Jean was the family's best player, a five-handicapper before back problems slowed her down. She was also a fierce competitor, a quality she passed on to her third child.

Ralph Azinger was a lieutenant colonel in the Air Force. He was a navigator on a C-141 during the Vietnam War before retiring from the Air Force in 1972 to go into the boat and marina business. If he has any horror stories about Vietnam, Paul has never heard them. But he has heard his father's philosophy of life hundreds of times: the military approach is the best approach.

"Every round of golf should be approached like a mission," Ralph would tell his son. "You have to map out a course of action and follow it to the letter. Without a good navigator, you're lost."

Paul's trip to golf stardom was not very direct however. In fact, he lost his way more than once. Although his father always told him he had a "whoosh" in his swing that the other boys didn't, he was never a prodigy. He played Little League baseball for four years, losing just one game as a pitcher — "I had a gun, I could really throw that sucker," he remembered with a wide smile — but gave it up when his family moved back to Florida after a brief sojourn in New Jersey.

After that, it was all golf. By seventh grade, he could break 40 for nine holes. Three years later, he quit his high school team because he couldn't stand the coach. "The guy was brutal," Azinger remembered. "He was a football coach, a little-bitty guy with big fat fingers who would walk up and poke you in the chest and tell you how bad you were. I couldn't stand him. He drove me away from the game."

He probably wouldn't have played golf in college if not for a kid named Rick Stallings, who won the state championship in 10th grade. Believing that Stallings and Azinger were good friends, the coach at Brevard Junior College recruited Azinger, thinking that might help him land Stallings. Azinger and Stallings weren't friends but they did both decide to go to Brevard.

As a freshman, Azinger was the number three man on Brevard's C team. But it was during that year that he met John Redman, who was giving lessons on a driving range in Titusville. Even though Azinger had a grip and a swing that Nick Faldo would later describe as "a baseball grip and a hatchet swing," Redman saw something special in him right away. He worked with him for hours and, since

Azinger had no money, he didn't charge him. "We'd work all day, then I'd buy a six-pack of beer," Azinger said. "That was the only pay John ever got back then."

Azinger went from occasionally breaking 80 as a freshman to being the number one player on the team as a sophomore. In fact, he improved so much that he beat Rick Stallings out for the number one spot. Stallings was so shocked and angry he transferred. A year later, Azinger landed at Florida State. It was there that he met Toni. They were married in January 1982, one month after Paul had survived his first Q-School. After the honeymoon, Paul set out to try and make it on tour while Toni finished school.

They spent the next three years living in a motor home as Paul went from the big tour back to the mini-tours after losing his card in 1982 and flunking Q-School (there was no Hogan or Nike Tour back then) and then back to the big tour in 1984. Azinger thinks now that the year he spent on the mini-tour after his first failure on the big tour turned his career around.

"I really didn't believe I was good enough my first year on tour, and I played that way," he said. "But when I went back to the mini-tour my attitude was Hey, I've played against the best, I'll whip up on these guys — and I did. I thought I could beat them, so I did. That's so important out here. You have to think you can play in order to play."

Azinger was still trying to convince himself when he got back on tour in 1984. He spent a lot of time in Monday qualifiers and trying to make cuts. "I always seemed to come up just short for a while," he said. "I would make a double bogey on the eighteenth or bogey the last three or lose in a playoff. I was choking all over the place. I wondered if I had what it took to produce under pressure."

It was a question that would continue to haunt Azinger at different levels as he went up the golf ladder. He finished 144th on the money list in 1984 and went back to school again. He got his card back for a third time and finally broke through in 1985, making $81,179. That was good enough for ninety-third on the money list and, although he didn't know it, he was through with school forever.

He and Toni sold the motor home and bought a house. Two years later, Azinger really broke through, winning three times on tour and almost winning the British Open. He led that tournament for seventy holes before finishing bogey–bogey to hand the title to Faldo. A year later he led the PGA for three rounds before Jeff Sluman shot 65 on the last day to pass him and win.

Azinger kept winning and making big money. He became a key member of the U.S. Ryder Cup team. He was considered as tough a Sunday player as there was in the game. He was proud of what he had accomplished, proud that he had taken the "baseball grip and hatchet swing" and, through hours and hours of work, produced a swing that could repeat under pressure. He developed one of the best short games in the sport.

He also made a few enemies along the way. Azinger is, if nothing else, outspoken. He wears his heart and his politics on his sleeve and if people don't like what they see or hear, that's fine with him. He had a couple of notorious run-ins with Ballesteros at the Ryder Cup, and when he brought up the Gulf War in the context of the Ryder Cup in 1991, a lot of people thought he had gone way over the line.

And, as he continued winning, he heard the whispers, the ones about winning a major. They got louder after Tom Kite won the U.S. Open in 1992 because the mantle of "best player never to have won a major" fell squarely on his shoulders. He insisted that it didn't worry him or bother him, but deep down it did. It was only after he had finally removed the yoke with his win in the PGA that he understood just how important it had been to him.

"That last day at the PGA, I was all over myself," he said. "I didn't get mad the way I sometimes do, but I kept saying, Do you have the balls to do this? Can you hit the big shots now when everything is at stake? Are you man enough to stand up to the pressure or are you going to fold again?"

He was firing at flags down the stretch and he caught Greg Norman and Faldo from behind. On the second playoff hole, he hit the shot of his life, a perfect sand wedge that stopped eight feet from the pin. Norman hit his shot 25 feet past the cup, then left his first putt five feet short.

Azinger didn't even want to think about Norman's chances of making that putt. He wanted to ram his birdie putt in and end all the doubts. Only he couldn't do it. The putt slid right at the last second and all the doubts came back again. If Norman made his putt, they would go to a third playoff hole and his best chance to win might have slipped away.

Azinger tapped in for his par, then backed up to watch Norman putt. Standing there, he looked across the green and saw several reporters he knew crouched on the hill by the side of the green watching. His face never changed expression but his heart sank.

I'm never going to live this down, he thought. They'll never let me forget that I had an eight-foot putt to win my first major and I couldn't get it in the hole. I'm going to get blasted.

Azinger took a deep breath and tried not to think about losing. He looked over at the 11th tee and tried to think about the next hole. "Greg's going to make this and you're going to have to go up that hill to the tee and hit another good shot. Come on, regroup, get your brain working again."

He was still trying to regroup when Norman missed his par putt. Suddenly, all the questions had been answered. He was the PGA champion and CBS's Jim Nantz was asking him how he felt. For a split second Azinger — for perhaps the first time in his life — couldn't think of anything to say. Finally, his mind clicked back on and he talked about how thankful he was and how comforting the presence of God had been to him throughout the day. It was one of the very few times he had ever mentioned his Christianity in public.

"I'm not a preacher" is something Azinger says a lot. "I believe what the Bible says and I believe in salvation. But I'm not here to tell anyone else what to believe."

Azinger has gone to the Wednesday night Bible studies conducted on tour for years, but says his Christianity wasn't really a consistent factor in his life until 1990. Even after that, he frequently questioned himself because of his temper and the anger he often felt on the golf course.

But winning the PGA brought him a different kind of peace. "I realized after I won that even though I had told people and told myself that I didn't have anything to prove, that I did. We're all so fragile out here, it's unbelievable. If Greg had made that putt and I'd lost the playoff on the next hole, I would have left there destroyed. Instead, I left feeling as good about myself as a player as I've ever felt. Of course two weeks later I was killing myself out there again and calling myself names, but deep down I knew that I had the courage to hold up when the pressure was the greatest and that meant a lot to me.

"I've always been someone with a great fear of failure. I hate losing and I really hate answering questions about why I lost. I can't stand going home and having people ask me what went wrong or why haven't I been playing better.

"I know guys out here who fear success, who don't want the pressure that comes with success or the attention. Heck, I've seen guys back off on Sunday afternoon because they know if they win they'll have to give a speech and they're afraid of giving a speech.

"That was never my problem. I always feared having to go home a failure. After the PGA I knew, for the first time, that I wasn't going to go home a failure. If I never played again or if I died tomorrow, people would say I was a damn good player."

And then, on the afternoon of December 2, Frank Jobe told him that never playing again might be the least of his worries. Three long days later, he was back in Jobe's office. The cancer hadn't spread. It was curable. The next six months would be painful and difficult. But the prognosis looked good. For three days, Azinger couldn't stop thinking about his daughters. Sara Jean was going to be eight later in the month and Josie Lynn was five.

"I'm not afraid of dying because I believe in eternal life," he said. "But I didn't want my daughters to have to watch me die when I was only thirty-four. That scared me. When the doctor said it was curable but I needed six chemotherapy treatments, I said, 'Let's get at it.' My attitude was simple. I was going to kick cancer's butt."

Anyone who has ever spent more than five minutes with Paul Azinger would never have assumed for one second that he would think any other way.

The news of Azinger's cancer was as shocking as any that had hit the golf world since Tony Lema's plane had crashed in 1965, killing the 1963 British Open champion.

Like Lema, Azinger was at his peak. He had just finished his best year ever, and now no one knew when, or if, he would play again. Beyond that, as Azinger said himself, he had always been the tour's biggest kid. He was the guy who showed up for the Ryder Cup with

Bill and Hillary Clinton masks. He was the guy always trading practical jokes with his best pal, Payne Stewart. He was the guy always running his mouth in the locker room, cutting up, making fun of everyone and anyone, including himself.

Disbelief was followed by sadness. Then came the questions. Just how sick was he? Stewart, Azinger's closest friend on tour, was bombarded with questions. At that stage, though, he didn't have a lot of answers.

Azinger went through his first chemotherapy session shortly after Jobe's diagnosis. It was just as bad as he had heard it would be, and worse. Now he knew the *real* definition of throwing up. All the side effects followed. His hair began to fall out. He couldn't stand the smell of *anything*. He had no appetite and he began to dread the thought of going through this five more times.

Once he was home in Florida, the phone didn't stop ringing. Eventually, he had to change his number because he just didn't feel right ducking the calls. The mail poured in from around the world. Ballesteros wrote. So did Olazabal. And Faldo. "Guys I really hadn't always gotten along with," he said. "They all said the same thing: we want you back out here."

Some calls were inspirational. Gene Littler, who had beaten cancer twenty years earlier and returned to the tour. Johnny Miller, who gave him the line he kept repeating over and over again: "It's not important what we accomplish in life, but what we overcome."

Azinger was both touched and moved by the outpouring of affection and concern. There were times during the first month that he got down, way down, especially when the side effects of the chemo were at their worst. Curtis Strange called one day in late December and came away from the conversation shaken.

Azinger told him the side effects were eating him up. They frightened him. He had looked up some stories on Heather Farr because he had admired her courage throughout her battle with the disease. "The stories on Heather when she first got sick are almost exactly like the stories on me now," Azinger said. "You could swap the names and the stories would be the same. *Exactly the same.*"

Strange couldn't get those three words out of his head for weeks: *exactly the same.*

It wasn't until after the side effects of the second chemo session in January began to wear off that friends started to hear some of the old Zinger on the phone. He began telling people they could stop by and rub his bald head for luck, and he started putting out warnings to watch out for him come July because he was coming back with a vengeance. When Stewart began to struggle with his game, Azinger told him, "It's really gonna be embarrassing if I only play four months this year and still kick your butt on the money list."

That line was passed around the locker room with glee. It sounded so much like Zinger. If he was back to giving Stewart grief, then he must be feeling better.

4

THE FALL CLASSIC

TO THE STARS, the last two months of every year is a gravy train, a time to pick and choose among the made-for-TV goodies that are available to them week after week.

That is the side of golf the public sees as the holidays approach: the Kapalua Invitational on Maui leading to the Shark Shootout in California, which comes before the Skins Game in Palm Springs and just before the zillion-dollar Johnnie Walker Invitational in Jamaica. One corporate sponsor after another lines up to play Santa Claus to the game's millionaires.

The side the public doesn't see is entirely different. For most players trying to make a living playing golf, November and December are the months that determine where they will be playing during the next twelve months. Will they be on the Big Tour, playing for million-dollar purses every week, trying to decide whether they prefer the blue courtesy car or the red? Or will they be slogging along on the Nike Tour, playing for 20 percent of what they play for on the big tour, hoping their car can crisscross the country without needing a new engine. Many won't even make the Nike Tour; they will be forced to play in Asia or Africa or South America or, if they don't want to go overseas, on the various mini-tours around North America, where you have to finish in the top ten most weeks just to recoup your entry fee.

All of them dream about walking the fairways with the TV cameras shining and the crowds screaming. But to have any chance at all to be one of the elite, they all have to go through the same labyrinth, one that often seems to have no exit.

On tour, they call it school. It is school — in the same sense that swimming the Atlantic might be called a workout.

On a picture-postcard December afternoon in Palm Springs, the Dunes Course of the La Quinta Golf Club looked no different than it looks almost every day of the year. The temperature was in the 70s; the afternoon shadows, which begin closing in by 3 o'clock during the winter, were beginning to darken the surrounding mountains; and as far as the eye could see, there were golfers.

But these golfers weren't playing for a dollar or for five dollars or even for that night's dinner. They were playing for their lives.

If the Ryder Cup is the event all golfers dream about, the PGA Tour's annual Qualifying School is the event they all have nightmares about. Many of those nightmares are quite real. Almost everyone who has ever collected a check on tour has a story about Q-School. The first time Curtis Strange went through the school he bogeyed the last three holes to miss qualifying for the tour by one shot. "Choked my guts out," he said years later. "I doubt if I've ever choked that bad any other time in my life."

His wife, Sarah, remembers that night vividly. "We just sat in the hotel room staring at one another, thinking *now* what do we do?"

Back then what you did was wait six months for another chance, because there were two schools each year. Now the wait is twelve months. Some have likened the brutal pressure one goes through at Q-School to taking a bar exam. Brian Henninger, a tour rookie in 1993 who had just missed keeping his playing privileges, was at Q-School for the fourth time. To him Q-School is tougher than law school. "At least if you pass the bar, you're done," he said. "Here, you can pass the test one year and be right back taking it again the next year. And the year after and the year after."

More than any other professional sport, golf forces players to perform each year in order to continue to play. There are no long-term, guaranteed contracts like the ones in team sports. In tennis, players are paid just for getting into a tournament, and if their singles play falters, they can fall back on doubles as a career. In golf, you have to beat half the field every week to make any money and there's no such thing as doubles.

Everyone starts each year at zero. There are two ways to avoid the hell of qualifying: winning and earning. Winning a tournament earns you an exemption for two years. Seven tournaments carry a ten-year exemption: the four majors (the Masters, the U.S. Open, the British Open, and the PGA), the World Series of Golf, the Tour Championship, and the Players Championship. That means there are usually about a dozen players with a long-term playing guarantee and perhaps thirty to forty others who have two-year guarantees. Everyone else is playing for a spot among the year's top 125 money earners. If you don't make that list you go back to school, where the top forty scorers (and anyone tied for fortieth) earn a spot on the next year's PGA Tour.

On this day — the third day of the 1993 school — Wendy Goydos stood on the 13th tee at the Dunes with a look of complete terror on her face. Unlike on tour, where everyone must walk — carts look bad on TV — players are allowed to use carts during Q-School. Wendy Goydos was caddying for her husband, Paul. That meant she was driving the cart, keeping his clubs clean, and trying to keep him from — his words — "turning into a Tasmanian Devil."

Like Henninger, Goydos had been a tour rookie in 1993. He had struggled, finishing in the top twenty in one tournament. But he had improved as the year went on. He had played steady golf for two days, shooting 71–71. That put him in a tie for fifty-seventh place, not brilliant, but comfortable with four more days to play. Now though, after knocking his ball in the water at the 10th hole and making double bogey, Goydos was one over par on his third round. If he went any higher, he would be digging a hole for himself.

"There's just no margin for error right now," Wendy Goydos said quietly. "Right now, I'm dying." She took a deep breath. "I don't think I'll be able to breathe until I see that ball safely on dry land."

The ball in question was, at that moment, resting near her husband's feet. He had a nine-iron in his hands and was taking aim at a long, narrow green 147 yards away. The 13th hole at the Dunes is a simple-looking par-three, but it has water in front and a couple of deep bunkers behind it. On this day, the pin was cut up front, near the water. If you tried to get the ball close, you risked the water. If you played safe, you could find the bunkers or have a very long putt.

"Friend of mine made eight here yesterday," Goydos said casually, waiting for the group in front to clear the green. Wendy looked slightly ill.

Goydos pulled the nine-iron back, made a smooth pass at the ball, and it flew toward the green. "Is it enough?" Wendy Goydos asked.

It was. The ball hit and stopped 10 feet behind the pin. "I smothered it," Goydos said, handing the nine-iron to Wendy, not willing to concede that he had hit a superb shot.

Wendy Goydos was breathing again. Barely. "And just think," she said, "after today, we're still only halfway there. Paul will make it. I'm not sure I will."

There are three stages of Q-School each year. In 1993 there were eight hundred entries. The entry fee is $3,000 for most players. Based on their earnings that year, about a hundred players are exempt from the first stage. Their entry fee is $2,750. About thirty more are exempt into the finals based on finishing 126th to 150th on the money list or because of career earnings. Their fee is a mere $2,500.

How often do players go back to school? Consider the field of 191 players who reached the Q-School finals in 1993: seventeen of them had won at least one tournament on tour. Of the forty-three players who had made it through the school in 1992, only twelve had retained their playing privileges at the end of 1993. Two — Brett Ogle and Grant Waite — had won tournaments. Ten others finished in the top 125. The other thirty-one headed back to school. Four of those thirty-one were exempt into the finals because they had finished between 126th and 150th on the money list. The rest were exempt from only the first stage.

The players who gathered in Palm Springs to begin play on December 1 ranged in age from twenty-two to forty-five. The oldest player in the field was Bobby Cole, who, twenty-six years earlier as a nineteen-year-old phenom out of South Africa, had won the Qualifying School. Stardom had been predicted for him then. Instead, his major claim to fame had become his marriage to Laura Baugh, a phenom herself on the women's tour as much for her blond good looks as her golf swing. Now, with five children at home, Cole was hoping for one more shot at the tour.

George Burns was also forty-five, and he was trying to get back on tour too. Twelve years earlier, with nine holes left in the U.S. Open at Merion Country Club outside Philadelphia, Burns had led the tournament. David Graham caught him on the back nine, and Burns never came close in a major again.

And then there was Mike Donald. Among the 191 players, Donald was probably the most famous. Anyone who followed golf at all remembered Donald's 1990 U.S. Open. He was the career journeyman, the lifelong tour grinder who, in his eleventh year on tour, almost won the Open. It could have been Jack Fleck in 1955, Orville Moody in 1969, Mike Donald in 1990; men whose names appeared out of place on a list that included Hogan, Palmer, Nicklaus, and Watson, but were there nonetheless.

Donald led for most of the last two rounds, and he still led with three holes to play. If Hale Irwin had not holed the greatest putt of his career over hill and dale from 60 feet away on the 18th hole, Donald would have had a two-stroke lead.

Instead, it was a one-stroke lead. And so, when he bogeyed the 16th, he ended up tied with Irwin, creating an 18-hole playoff the next day. Donald led all afternoon. This time he did have a two-shot lead with three holes to play. But Irwin birdied the 16th and Donald bogeyed the 18th and they were tied again. Halfway to the hole, Donald's par putt at the 18th, a 15-footer, looked like it was going to go in. Donald certainly thought so. He started to walk sideways, preparing to celebrate. But as it got closer, Donald stopped. He could see it was dying to the right. "I was hoping it might just nip the side door and spin in."

An inch more left, maybe two, and it would have done just that. By that margin, Donald missed a ten-year exemption and all that comes with spending the rest of your life being introduced as a U.S. Open champion. Instead, Irwin birdied the first hole of sudden death and, after ninety-one holes of golf, Donald had come up an inch and a half short.

But he was one of those runners-up people don't soon forget. The son of an auto mechanic, Donald was the antithesis of what most people perceive PGA Tour pros to be. He had grown up playing public courses in south Florida and had scrambled his way through college and onto the tour. He went into the last tournament of his rookie year knowing he needed to make the cut to make enough money that week to retain his playing privileges for the next year.

He played well the first two days, made the cut, and walked into the scorer's tent to sign his scorecard. A round of golf isn't official on tour until a player has checked his score and signed his card. Suddenly, Donald felt woozy and dizzy. He actually thought he might faint. The numbers on his card were blurry. Hoping they were right, he managed to sign his name and stumble out of the tent.

"It just hit me when I walked in there that if I signed my card right, I was still on tour," he said. "Next thing I knew, I couldn't see straight."

He saw straight enough to improve steadily year after year. His only win was at Williamsburg in 1989, but he made a solid, comfortable living doing what he loved to do most — play golf.

He looked like — and was — the kind of guy who would be just as comfortable having a beer in a truck stop or playing cards at the local muni-course as sitting in the clubhouse at a fancy country club. He had a beer belly and a friendly, round, ruddy face. Since he was single, the most photographed member of his gallery during that 1990 Open was Pearl Donald, his mom. The announcers kept mentioning that he was a bachelor, which didn't make his girlfriend, who was watching on television, terribly happy. He was a gracious loser, someone who never whined about his fate or complained about bad luck. About the closest he ever came to expressing regret was an occasional shake of the head and a whispered "I had him by the short hairs" when he talked about the playoff.

He ended up having his best year on tour in 1990 — finishing twenty-second on the money list — but in December of that year, his mother got sick. She was in and out of the hospital for the next month, growing weaker and weaker. She died in January at the age of sixty-four and, suddenly, the person Donald called first after a good round wasn't there anymore.

He stayed home at the beginning of 1991 to make sure his dad was okay. When his father finally insisted he get back to playing, he flew to California for the Bob Hope Desert Classic. The pros play the first four days of the Hope with amateur partners, so Donald found himself walking down the first fairway on the opening day of the tournament with a 15-handicapper he had just met.

"How you been playing this year?" the 15-handicapper asked.

"To tell you the truth, I haven't played the last few weeks," Donald said. "My mom passed away last month and I wanted to spend some time at home with my dad."

The 15-handicapper shrugged. "Buy him a dog and he'll be fine."

Welcome back to the tour, Mike.

Most people weren't nearly that insensitive (how could they be?) and many of the other players went out of their way to tell Donald how sorry they were. But Donald simply couldn't shake the angry, hurt feelings he had been left with after his mother's death. It was as if the fool from the Bob Hope kept following him around repeating his boorish mantra.

For most of his career, Donald had been outgoing and friendly with his fellow pros. He was popular enough to be elected as one of the four player members of the tour's board in 1987 (beating Tom Watson) and had fond memories of his early days on tour when everyone drove from one tournament to the next and the tour was as much a fraternity as it was a business.

It was all different by 1991. Now everyone flew and most players traveled with their families. A lot of Donald's buddies were married or off the tour. He spent a lot of nights alone in his hotel room asking himself, what the hell am I doing here?

His attitude affected his play, and by the end of the year, Donald had finished out of the top 125 for the first time in his career. He went back to school and again came up short. Even so, he was able to get in most of the places he wanted to play in 1992 because when he wrote and asked for sponsor's exemptions almost everyone said yes, partly because they remembered 1990 and partly because Donald had always been one of the tour's good guys.

He managed to get his card back at the end of 1992 — finishing 120th on the money list — but 1993 had been a disaster. He had missed the cut in his last eleven tournaments and finished the year 184th on the money list. He had made only $51,113.

Donald turned thirty-eight in July and talked often about quitting. His father kept telling him that he could probably live a very happy life back home in Hollywood, Florida, especially if he was as miserable as he said he was on tour. Donald certainly wasn't happy.

"There's a saying out here that when someone asks you how you played and you tell them you shot eighty, half of them are thrilled and the other half wish it had been eighty-one," he said one afternoon shortly after another missed cut. "It's an exaggeration, but there's a lot to it. Sure, we're all friendly to one another and we get along. In fact, most of the guys out here are good guys. But when you get right down to it, do any of them really give a damn about Mike Donald?

"Of course not. Why should they? They've got lives of their own and problems of their own. The only ones who really care about you are your family and I don't have any family out here. I'm not complaining. I enjoy spending time alone, I really do. But it can be a very lonely life."

It had gotten extremely lonely for Donald in 1991. For years, Fred Couples had been one of his best friends on tour. They had come up through the ranks together, and even after Couples had become a star, they had stayed friends. Couples was one of the few players who had called Donald during his mother's illness to see how she was doing. Given Couples's famous aversion to the telephone, Donald was touched by the fact that Couples had picked up the phone to call him.

But Couples had gone through a divorce in 1992 and was now traveling most of the time with his girlfriend, Tawnya Dodd. There wasn't as much time for friends as there once had been, and although Donald would never admit it, he missed that friendship. What's more, when a player is going badly and gets down on himself and on tour life the way Donald had, other players can sense it and feel it. They don't want to pick up those vibes themselves, so they tend to steer clear. Donald knew he was giving off negative vibes at the end of 1993, but he couldn't stop himself.

"Every week I show up and say, okay, new start, let's have a good attitude and get something going," he said as the end of the year closed in. "Then something goes wrong on Thursday and the next thing I know I've put up another goddamm seventy-four and here we go again.

"There's part of me that wants to quit, go home, and not pick up a golf club for a long time. But there's another part of me that says this is what I do best and this is what I want to keep doing."

On the first night back at school, Donald and one of his old friends, Lance Ten Broeck, walked into a bar to have a quick beer before turning in. When the owner of the bar saw Donald, he stopped dead in his tracks.

"Hey, Mike Donald!" he shouted. "Mike Donald! God, I'll never forget that Open back in '90. I watched every second of it, every single second. It almost killed me when you lost that playoff!"

Donald had heard this speech in various forms before. Most of the time, he smiled, thanked the person for remembering, signed an autograph, and promised to do better the next time. Now, though, back in school for the second time in three years, he looked at the man, smiled wanly, and said, "Almost killed *you?*"

Players call the Q-School finals the Fall Classic, a term more readily associated with baseball's World Series. The World Series is watched by millions, the Q-School by a couple hundred. And yet the pressure that is palpable, even to a spectator, is extraordinary.

The golf course is almost eerily silent, a silence that is only occasionally broken by a cry of anguish, a scream of pain, or the *plunk* that a thrown club makes when it lands in a water hazard.

There are no scoreboards, no microphones in the cups to make the ball rattle for TV, no white paint inside them to help the camera pick them up. There are no gallery ropes, because there is virtually no gallery; no concession stands, souvenir tents, or ticket takers. And there isn't a single corporate tent or logo anywhere in sight.

There is also no computerized scoring system, which means that at the end of each day, players, families, and friends gather around a large scoreboard set up near the 18th green at the host course and watch as the scores trickle in and are posted by hand. Once all the scores have gone up, everyone stands around analyzing and interpreting what it all means and what needs to be done the next day. Then they go home to worry about it and hope they can sleep.

The Q-School finals last six days. During the first four days, the players are spread out over two golf courses. After seventy-two holes, the field is cut to the low 90 scores and ties, and the last two rounds are played on one course. The host course in 1993 was the Jack

Nicklaus Resort Course that is part of the sprawling PGA West complex. La Quinta, about five miles away, was the second course.

The Q-School is grueling not only because it is six days long, but because of the mental strain on all the players. They all know they are one step from the promised land of The Tour, but they also know that most of them won't get there. Even though most players use carts, the pace of play is brutally slow. On tour, the average round for a threesome is about four and a half hours. At Q-School, it is closer to five and a half.

"Just wait till the last day," said Paul Goydos, who was in the finals for the third time. "You'll see guys absolutely freeze over one-foot putts. They won't be able to draw their putters back."

To Goydos, surviving the school was important. He was twenty-nine and had a wife, a three-year-old daughter, and a one-year-old daughter. But his route to this point had been so different from most players' that he was able to joke occasionally about the nerves and the tension he was feeling.

"I never expected to get to this level in golf," he said. "I didn't think about it seriously as a career until a couple of years ago. Other guys will tell you they've worked their whole lives to get on tour. I can honestly say I haven't."

Goydos grew up in Long Beach, the youngest of three boys. His father was a former navy chief who became an administrator at Long Beach State University. Goydos took up golf after being beaned in the head three times in one Little League baseball game. His father had some old clubs in the hall closet, left over from his navy days, that had gone unused for years. Goydos pulled them out and began knocking whiffle balls around the backyard. Eventually his parents bought him a series of six lessons at a nearby municipal course and he got hooked on the game.

"My parents bought me a $20 monthly ticket at this muni-course that was called the boneyard because almost everyone who played there was so old," he said. "I was the only kid there. I'd just stand around the first tee waiting for the starter to hook me up with some old guys so I could play."

He was always good, but never a star. His high school golf coach was married to the golf coach at Long Beach State. She talked him into giving Goydos a scholarship and he lived at home while he was in college because his parents lived a block from campus.

During his senior year, he began to have trouble with his hands. They would swell up on him to the point where he couldn't make a tight enough fist to grip a golf club. The pain and swelling stopped when he didn't play, so after reaching the third round of the U.S. Public Links Championship at the end of his senior year, he quit the game, got his degree in finance, and began looking for a job.

He had met George Madak, a local mortgage broker, at the club where Long Beach State played its home matches and he went to work for him. Madak had a daughter named Wendy, a pretty blonde who taught kindergarten. She liked Goydos's dry sense of humor and he liked everything about her. They were married on New Year's Eve in 1989.

By then, Goydos was playing golf again. When the mortgage business began to die in 1988, Goydos began working part-time as a starter at a nine-hole golf course to supplement his dwindling income. On a slow afternoon he found himself leafing through a golf magazine and saw an ad for oversized grips, designed for people with arthritis. He wasn't certain if his problem was arthritis, but he decided the grips were worth a try and ordered a set.

He hadn't touched a club for close to a year, but when the grips allowed him to play pain free, he started to play again. He entered several mini-tour events in California as an amateur and played well enough that Doug Ives, a local newspaperman who ran the mini-tour, urged him to turn pro.

Since Goydos had never declared himself a pro, he hadn't collected any prize money that summer. But Ives had kept track of what his winnings would have been and allowed him to apply that money to his entry fees for the following summer. He turned pro, played well again, collected his money, and decided to give Q-School a try in the fall of 1989.

The first stage in his region was at Fort Ord. Goydos shot 70 the first day, signed his scorecard, walked outside, and felt the ground start to shake. It was the San Francisco earthquake. "San Francisco was eighty miles from Santa Cruz, where the quake actually hit; we were thirty," he said. "I figured, that's it, they'll have to call this thing off. There was no electricity anyplace, the aftershocks kept hitting constantly, and the only food, electricity, and water was through the backup generator they had on the army base. It was ridiculous."

They played, though, and Goydos ended up winning in spite of the fact that he was up running for doorways several times a night when the aftershocks hit. He went to the second stage and missed making the finals by a stroke — losing in a nine-man playoff for the last seven spots. "The last guy to get in was Ed Dougherty," he remembered. "He made a forty-footer and I missed from fifteen, then he got his card and made five hundred grand the next three years."

Goydos had no card and nothing approaching five hundred grand. After he and Wendy got married, she suggested he do some substitute teaching in the Long Beach city schools. The money was decent — $110 a day — and the work was from eight to three, leaving afternoons free for practice.

A lot of substitute work in public school systems is in the inner city, and Goydos spent a lot of time teaching kids from the tougher neighborhoods. It opened his eyes to a lot of things. "The life we lead on tour isn't real," he said. "We're in our own little world out here, and most people don't understand how horrible things are outside that world. Golf, for some reason, is recession proof. I would hate to have to go back and look for a job in Long Beach right now."

Goydos had his adventures as a teacher. One morning one of his eighth-grade students came to him and said he had a problem. "What's the problem?" Goydos asked.

"I think my friends and I just killed someone."

It had been a street fight that got out of hand. Goydos stayed with the youngster through the hearing process and was glad when he was cleared of wrongdoing. "Most of the time, these aren't bad kids," he said. "They're just in a very bad situation."

On another afternoon, during a recess, Goydos was in the schoolyard watching a group of kids play basketball. A fight broke out in the housing project across the street and a man ran out of one house, heading straight for the schoolyard, followed by another man who was shooting at him. The gunshots began spraying the schoolyard and everyone hit the deck for several terrifying minutes. The man was finally disarmed with no one injured.

"It wasn't that big a deal," Goydos said. "It's not like the guy was shooting at us. He was just shooting." Just not the kind of shooting most professional golfers are exposed to.

Goydos returned to the California mini-tour in the summer of 1990 and struggled. He was down to his last $800 — with his first child on the way — and used it to pay the $400 entry fees for the last two big events of the summer, the Long Beach Open and the Queen Mary Open. "If something didn't happen at one of them, I was through," he said. "We'd have hung by a thread until fall when I could start subbing again."

Something happened. He won the Long Beach Open and $20,000. "It felt like all the money in the world," he said, laughing.

The victory kept him playing until Q-School rolled around again. This time he made it through the first two stages but shot "a million" in the finals.

"I played the last two days with Dudley Hart and Mike Standly," he said. "They were both twenty-two and right out of college and they both made it. I was twenty-six, married, and had a kid. I started thinking, you're too old to be bumming around as a part-time golfer. Maybe it's time to look for a real job."

But by making it to the finals he had qualified to play part-time on the fledgling Ben Hogan Tour. The PGA Tour, believing that a proving ground was needed for young players, started the Hogan Tour in 1990. The prize money was a tenth of that on the regular tour — or, as the Hogan players called it, "the big tour" — but it gave players who didn't make the big tour a place to play and sharpen their games without having to go overseas.

The first seventy players who miss the cut at Q-School are exempt for the Hogan Tour. Goydos hadn't even made that group, so he had only a partial exemption, meaning he figured to get into only a handful of Hogan Tour events. He wasn't even going to bother, but the first two events were in California and Arizona, so he figured he might as well play if he got in. He made $800 the first week, then got in the next week as the last alternate. He birdied the last three holes on the last day and made $8,000.

That windfall put him high enough on the money list to make him exempt for most events on the Hogan Tour. The Goydoses decided it was now or never. Wendy quit her job, Paul bought a Cherokee, and the whole family — Paul, Wendy, and their infant daughter, Chelsea — set out to see the country. Goydos ended up playing twenty-five events in 1991 and made $30,000 to finish thirty-ninth on the money list.

The only real setback came when Goydos woke up one morning, looked out the window, and saw nothing in the parking space where he had parked the Cherokee. "Did you move the car?" he asked Wendy.

"No."

"Well, someone did." The police found the car — abandoned — a week later.

The $30,000 just about covered travel expenses and also made him exempt from the first stage of qualifying at the 1991 Q-School. The second stage was at his favorite golf course, Fort Ord. "I figured I was a lock to make the finals," he said. Not quite. He ended up as first alternate and flew to Greenlefe in central Florida because he had been told that first alternates *always* got in. Not always. "They said it was the first time in history everyone showed up."

His place on the Hogan money list left him partially exempt again starting 1992. Again, he thought seriously about getting a job. But his golf was improving steadily, he hadn't had any pain in his hands, and he wanted to give it one more try. But time was really running short. Wendy was pregnant again, and it was a sure bet that they weren't going to be able to live out of the Cherokee with two little children. Since Wendy had given up her job, money was even tighter than it had been before. Goydos went back to subbing in January and February and waited to find out if he would again get in at Yuma as an alternate the way he had the year before.

Wednesday night, word came. He was in. The family hopped in the Cherokee, made the drive overnight to Yuma, and arrived in the middle of a hailstorm. There was no chance to practice Thursday and no chance to find a caddy so Wendy carried the bag.

Goydos won. The Cherokee went back into full-time service. By the end of 1992, Goydos was seventeenth on the Hogan money list. That put him straight into the 1992 Q-School finals. He was also a vastly more experienced golfer than he had been during his first trip to the finals two years earlier. He had played in fifty tournaments in two years and had learned how to deal with pressure and with mistakes. He kept his cool for six days, didn't let the frigid weather at the Woodlands (outside Houston) bother him, and cruised home in eighteenth place. At twenty-eight, about to become a father for the second time, he had made it to the big tour.

But for how long?

Goydos showed up for his first tournament in Hawaii wondering how he would fit in on tour. He went to the range late one afternoon and began hitting balls. A few yards away, he noticed someone else hitting balls. The guy was tall and blond and had a swing that looked like it had been chiseled to perfection for years. Goydos was transfixed, watching one rocket after another.

Who *is* that guy? he wondered. I've never seen him in my life and I can't come *close* to hitting a ball like that. If everyone out here is this good, I've got no chance. Absolutely no chance.

Discouraged, Goydos picked up his clubs and started back to the clubhouse. As he walked by the golden-ball striker he happened to glance at his bag. The name on it was Payne Stewart. Wearing a baseball cap and regular clothes on a practice day instead of his trademark knickers, Stewart had looked like everyone else on tour looks and not like Payne Stewart. Goydos breathed a huge sigh of relief. "I already knew I couldn't beat Payne Stewart," he said. "I could live with that."

He missed the cut in Hawaii — "by a million" — but made the cut the next week in Tucson, curling in a six-foot putt on the 18th hole that just caught the edge to get in on the number. He played well on the weekend, made $8,000, and began to think that maybe he could play with the big boys.

It wasn't easy. He made a reasonable number of cuts, but had trouble when the pressure began to build on the weekends. Getting the putter back on a four-footer was a lot tougher on Sunday afternoon than on Thursday morning, especially when every shot was worth a couple grand.

His goal at the start of the year had been to make the top 125 and keep his card. But as the year drew to a close, it became apparent that the top 150 was more realistic. If he did that, he would at least be straight back into the finals at school. The pressure kept building.

At the Southern in early October, he needed one birdie on the last three holes to make the cut and didn't get it. A week later, at Disney, he shot 66 the first day but gagged the last nine holes on Saturday (the tournament cuts after fifty-four holes), shot 38, and missed by one again. Another miss at Texas and there was only one tournament left — the Las Vegas Invitational.

Las Vegas is one of two ninety-hole tournaments on tour. The cut comes after fifty-four holes. With nine holes left, Goydos knew he was in trouble, needing at least three birdies, maybe four, to get to the number. He got two, but came to the last hole knowing he needed one more birdie to have a chance. He hit his third shot to 10 feet and drained the putt for birdie.

Still, he wasn't sure if he was in because the tournament is played at three sites the first three days and scores are tabulated at only one. He called the press room at the host course and reached Chuck Adams, one of the tour's media officials.

"Chuck, I want to find out if I made the cut," he said.

Adams looked through the computer and found Goydos at four under par. The cut, he knew, was five. He also knew how desperately Goydos needed to make the cut.

"Paul, I'm really sorry," he said. "It looks like you missed by one."

Even though he knew that had been a possibility, Goydos was stunned by the finality of it. "So the number went to six," he said. "I had really hoped it would be five."

Now it was Adams who was stunned — or at least confused. "Paul, the number is five," he said. "You're at four."

Goydos's heart leaped. The computer was wrong! For some reason, his final birdie wasn't in there yet. "Chuck, you're *sure* the cut is five?"

"Positive."

Goydos explained to Adams that his score in the computer was wrong. A few minutes later, when his scorecard — which was his official score — reached the scorekeeper, it confirmed the computer's error. Goydos lived to play the weekend.

Deep down he harbored a long-shot hope to shoot lights-out the last two days and blow by enough people to make enough money to make the top 125. Tenth place, worth $35,000, would have done it, but Goydos would have had to shoot 133 the last two rounds to get there. That didn't happen, but he did shoot 68–72, good enough to give him a tie for forty-third and earn him $4,760 for the week. That put his winnings at $87,804 for the year, which put him into 152nd place on the money list. Since two of the players ahead of him, Bernhard Langer and Nick Faldo, were members of the European tour, he was exactly 150th on the list among PGA Tour members, meaning he was the last player exempt from the first two stages of the school.

In all, Goydos had finished sixteenth in earnings among the 1992 Q-School graduates. "It was a strange year," he said. "There were times when I was absolutely convinced I was the worst player in the history of the game. Then I found out that *everyone* feels that way at one time or another. I know so much more about golf and about the tour now than I did a year ago, it isn't even funny.

"That's the weird thing. I don't know if I can get through the school again, but I'm convinced if I do I'll be a much better player next year because of what I've learned this year. The question is, can I survive the school? I think I can, but you never know. There's no logic to that thing. You just have to hope you can get through six days without a disaster."

The disaster that Wendy Goydos had worried about on the 13th hole on the third day of Q-School had been averted. In fact, after getting his tee shot to within 10 feet, Paul made his putt for birdie to get back to even par. He bogeyed the next hole when his drive landed in the middle of a divot but birdied 18 for an even par 72. That left him at two under par 214. He was tied for sixty-eighth place. Not brilliant, but a long way from needing to panic.

"I haven't done anything great, but I haven't done anything horrible yet either," he said. "I'm hitting the ball well. If I get my putter going just a little, I'll be okay."

For Goydos that qualified as a comment of unparalleled optimism. In a sport where everyone gets down on himself, Goydos stands near the top when it comes to getting down. One of his good friends on tour, Patrick Burke, is always telling him to "have some cheese with all that whine."

Goydos knows Burke is right. "I do whine all the time," he said.

"But I'm getting better. I've actually admitted to playing well a couple times this year."

Goydos was standing behind the 18th green waiting for his friend Jeff Cook to putt out. It was shortly after 4 o'clock by now and the temperature in the desert was plummeting as sunset closed in. Still, Goydos waited to find out how Cook — playing three groups behind him — had done.

Cook, Goydos, and Brian Henninger had all been rookies on the big tour during 1993. They had known each other from the Hogan Tour and, since they were all going through a similar experience, they kept track of one another as the year wore on.

On the surface, they had little in common. Goydos was the kid from the city with the dry wit and the somewhat skeptical view of the world at large. Henninger was just the opposite, born and raised in Oregon with a love for the outdoors and a wide-eyed, upbeat approach to life. Goydos played poker when he had free time; Henninger went hunting with his brother. In a moment of complete rapture Goydos was apt to say something like "I played okay"; Henninger had tears of joy in his eyes when his wife dropped him off *before* his first round on tour. Henninger was a year older than Goydos but looked as if he should be getting ready to go back to college in the fall.

Cook, at thirty-one, was the oldest of the three but the only one who was still single. That was a statistic not likely to change in the near future for the simple reason that being single was too much fun for Cook to give up. Cook had traveled the world to play golf and had many stories — some of them even true — about his adventures. He came across as the ultimate carefree bachelor, the rare exception to the tour rule that says there's no time to have a good time.

But there was also a serious side to Cook. He had overcome dyslexia as a kid to earn a scholarship to Indiana and a degree in business. On Christmas Eve of 1991, he had discovered what turned out to be testicular cancer, a finding made even scarier by the fact that his father had died of cancer at the age of forty-seven. He had surgery and returned to the Hogan Tour six weeks later.

What the three of them shared was a desire to continue playing a sport that had never been thrust upon them. All were essentially self-taught. They had been shown a grip and a stance as kids and then gone off to play. Because he focused on tennis as a teenager, Henninger was only a five-handicapper when he decided to try to walk onto the team at Southern California. Cook's scholarship to Indiana was for academics, not golf.

Of the three, it was Henninger who had seemed most likely to avoid a return trip to the school. In July, he had finished tied for fourth at the Western Open, shooting 68 on the final day even though he had to deal with the pressure of being paired with Fred Couples. That check — $52,000 — had put him over $90,000 for the year and seemed to seal his spot in the top 125. But after another top-twenty finish at New England two weeks later, Henninger's game went south. He began playing to make the cut rather than just playing, a sure way to ensure missed cuts.

Like Goydos, he had gone to Vegas needing badly to make the cut. He had earned $110,000 for the year, and it looked like $118,000 would make the top 125. That meant he needed a top-thirty finish to avoid the school. Like Goydos, he birdied the 18th hole on Friday to finish five under. There were no computer glitches with his score, but since he had played early in the day, he spent the afternoon pacing his hotel room, wondering if five under would be good enough to make the cut.

He and his wife Cathy had planned the trip as a fun week together. Their four-month-old daughter, Carlin, was home with her grandparents and this was the Henningers' first chance since her birth to spend some time together and relax without worrying about middle-of-the-night feedings and diaper changes.

"Poor Cathy," Henninger said later. "We were supposed to be having a good time and I'm pacing up and down losing my mind."

Every so often, he would call the course to check. For a while, five looked safe, then, no, it might be six. Finally, just before nightfall, he found out he was in. Still, that was a long way from the top thirty. A couple of late bogeys the next day meant a 72, and Henninger figured he needed to shoot 66 on Sunday to have a chance. He was wrong, 67 would have made it. Since he shot 77, it was a moot point.

He finished with a double bogey and a headache. Cathy, who had walked every step of the way with him, wondered if the double bogey might have killed his chances. "Don't think so," Henninger said. "My chances died a lot earlier than that."

Henninger was in a foul mood when he left the golf course. He felt he had failed as a golfer, that he had let Cathy and Carlin down, and now he was going back to school. As he pulled around a corner, he saw a man sitting by the curb holding a sign: "I'm homeless, I'm hungry and I need help," it said.

It wasn't the first time Henninger had seen a beggar, but the timing shook him up. Here he was, driving a comfortable car, leaving a fancy country club to go check out of his four-star hotel, and he was feeling sorry for himself. He had suffered a setback and he was angry at himself for not dealing with the pressure of the last few months better. But he was convinced he would learn from the experience and, beyond that, his family wasn't going to go hungry because of his failure. He and Cathy were still going ahead with plans to buy a house. Henninger wasn't homeless, hungry, or helpless.

He was a very lucky guy. "Sometimes, you just need to be reminded," he said. "Sometimes, I guess, we all need to be reminded."

Jeff Cook wasn't feeling very lucky when he holed out that afternoon on 18. Even after finishing 164th on the money list he had felt confident that he would get through the school again and back on tour. Like Henninger and Goydos, he was convinced that a year on tour had made him a better and smarter player.

Forced to go back to the second stage because he hadn't made the top 150, he had cruised through, finishing sixth at a regional in which the top twenty-four players qualified for the finals. But he had arrived in Palm Springs fighting the flu. He had felt so lousy the first few nights that he had gone straight back to the condo he was sharing with Rick Dalpos — who was playing in his twelfth school — and gone directly to bed.

Even so, he managed a 72 the first day and a 70 the second. He felt better starting the third day and played his best golf, getting to three under through sixteen holes. Two pars would give him a 69 and, he knew, jump him over a whole lot of people.

On the 17th tee at the Dunes is a sign that says, "Rated one of the toughest holes in America." Given what the players go through at Q-

School it seems almost cruel to leave the sign up during the week.

The hole is a par-four that bends around a lake that runs along the left side all the way up to the green. It is a little bit like the 18th at the Belfry in that the player who plays safely to the right is going to have a long, tough second shot over still more water, while the player who tries to shorten the hole by cutting across the water runs the risk of getting wet off the tee.

Cook played safe on his drive, then pulled not one but two shots into the lake. By the time he had putted out he had a triple-bogey seven, and the three shots under par he had worked so diligently all day for were gone. He managed to par the 18th but came off the green feeling frustrated at a wasted opportunity.

"How'd it go?" Goydos asked.

"Even," Cook answered. "I was three under until I made triple at seventeen."

Henninger, who had played the back nine first and had just arrived from playing his last hole — the ninth — joined the group.

"Play any good?" Cook asked.

"Three under," Henninger said, unable to suppress a smile. "You guys?"

"Even," they both answered. Then Cook briefly retold his story about the disaster at 17. At no point had anyone uttered the words, "What did you shoot?"

Pros never ask that question. It is too dangerous because the answer can be embarrassing. Sometimes, when a player has done poorly and he is asked, "Did you play any good?" his answer will simply be no. Or, if it is a Friday — cut day — he may just say, "Trunk-slammer," which means "I missed the cut, so I'm loading up my clubs, slamming the trunk, and getting out of here."

If you have played well enough to answer the question, you never say, "I shot sixty-nine." You say, as Henninger had, "Three under." And, once you have established that you are solidly under par for a tournament, you drop the "under." Henninger was now at seven; Goydos and Cook were at two. The "number" the next day — the score it would take to make the cut — would probably be either one or two.

At school, no one even wanted to think about a trunk-slammer.

They had all worked too hard too long to get to this point. And the next year of their lives was hanging on how they played the next three days.

The three friends stood in the setting sun assessing where they were. They wouldn't know exactly how they stood until they drove back to the Nicklaus Course and checked the scoreboard.

Henninger, at seven, was clearly in good shape. Cook and Goydos, both at two, were probably in solid shape for the cut that would come the next day, but would need to do some moving the next two days to get into good position for the final day.

When they all made the drive back to the scoreboard, their suspicions were confirmed: Henninger was now tied for eleventh, only five shots behind the leader, a Frenchman named Thomas Levet. Goydos and Cook were in a large group that was tied for 68th — two shots away from the top forty. The good news was that there was lots of golf to play. It was also, as Wendy Goydos might have pointed out, the bad news.

5

THE SOUNDS OF SILENCE

MIKE DONALD spent a lot of time in front of the scoreboard that afternoon. He had played his third round at the Nicklaus Course because he had been in the bottom half of the field after two rounds. The top ninety-five players played their third round at the Dunes and their fourth at the Nicklaus while the bottom ninety-five — there had been one withdrawal after the first day — did just the opposite.

Donald had started the tournament extremely well on Wednesday, getting to four under par after 14 holes. But the 15th, a short par-five with an island green, had destroyed him. He had put two balls in the water there and made a 10. That turned a good round into a horrible one; he finished at 76. The next day had been only a little better — a 73 — and then he had again started strong in the third round. This time he was six under through 13 before he knocked his tee shot under a bush and triple-bogeyed the 14th. He still finished two under for the day, but he knew he had blown a chance to make up a lot of ground.

Now, at three over par 219, he found himself tied for 145th place, meaning he had one day to jump over fifty-five players if he didn't want to slam his trunk the next evening. He knew he was capable of going low; his starts on the first and third days were evidence of that. But he also knew that his recent history said that something — a 10, a 7, or just a bunch of missed putts — would prevent that from happening.

Arms folded, he stood at the back of the pack watching the scores go up and wondered again if this was where he wanted to be. "I'm not the oldest guy here by any means," he said. "But sometimes I feel like I am." He waved a hand at those assembled in front of him. "I doubt if there are fifty guys in this field who can play on tour, I mean really play, make money at it. There might be only thirty. But they're all going to have to learn the hard way how tough it is. I mean, look at how many of these guys are repeaters. A year from now, wherever they hold the school, you'll see a lot of the same faces."

There was weariness in Donald's voice as he spoke, as if he knew that he had reached a fork in the road but wasn't quite sure which direction to go in next. It was as if the Scarecrow from *The Wizard of Oz* was whispering in his ear, "Well, you could go that way, but on the other hand, *that* way is quite nice too."

Donald's problem was that *no* way seemed very appealing at the moment. For now, he knew he had one round of golf to play the next day and he was going to need to go low if he was going to get anywhere close to the number and have another round to play on Sunday.

For the first time all week there was a hint of humidity in the air the next morning when Donald's group teed off at the Dunes. If there was ever a threesome that defined the disparate routes players took to get to the school, this was it.

Donald had almost won a U.S. Open and had been on tour for fourteen years. John Maginnes was twenty-five, a golfing nomad who had grown up in North Carolina and had come to the school hoping to at least make the four-day cut and earn a full exemption onto what was now the Nike Tour, Nike having taken over the corporate sponsorship from the Hogan Company at the start of 1993.

Maginnes and his brother Philip, who was caddying for him, had pooled their resources to pay expenses for the week. After arriving, Maginnes filled out a bio-form for the tour. Each player is asked to fill one out at the start of the week to be used if he makes the next year's media guide. Under special interests, John Maginnes had written "Beer, tobacco and TV."

His interest in tobacco was apparent on the golf course. He chain-smoked throughout the round, proving that at least in one area of the game he could keep up with John Daly. Maginnes started the day at 217 — two shots ahead of Donald — knowing he needed to shoot no worse than 70 to get close to the number.

The third member of the group, Tom Dolby, had absolutely no chance at coming close to the number and really didn't care. He was a club pro from Minneapolis who had entered the school after playing well enough the previous summer to qualify for the 1994 PGA Tournament. "I figured it was a chance to play with some good players," he said.

He had surprised himself by getting to the finals and was delighted to have a few midwinter days in the desert sun. But he was eager to get back to his pro shop because there was work to be done before Christmas and to start getting ready for next spring.

At thirty-one, he had long ago abandoned the dream of playing on tour and was one of a small handful of players in the field who saw the school as a lark, a vacation, something to enjoy. He could hit the ball a long way — he made 18 birdies in four days — but he also tossed in enough bogeys and double bogeys that he ended up finishing ahead of only four players in the field.

That hardly bothered Dolby. He spent most of the last day rooting for his two struggling playing partners. Both men had their chances. Playing the back nine first, Donald started fast again — two under through seven holes — but he three-putted "One of the Toughest Holes in America" for bogey and then made another bogey at 18. That put him back to three over par for the tournament, meaning he needed to play his last nine holes in no worse than four under.

Maginnes started out at one over par and was still one over with two holes to play. The strain he was feeling was apparent all day. After making a 10-foot par putt on his 14th hole of the day, Maginnes bent over, put his hands on his knees, and took several long, deep breaths. "This isn't golf," he said. "This is combat."

"I need two birdies to make the cut," he told his brother as they walked to the par-three eighth hole. Donald had made seven straight pars on his second nine and was still at three over. He knew now he had no chance to play the last two days.

As had been the case throughout the day, the threesome had a long wait on the eighth tee. Almost all the players on the Dunes were trying to come from behind to make the cut and the pace of play had been ludicrous from the start. The round was now more than five hours old and there were still two holes to play.

"Right now, all I want to do is go home, put my clubs somewhere I can't find them, and not pick them up for a long, long time," Donald said as the wait continued. "I just want to get out of here and not even think about golf. I'm beat. This whole year has just beaten me up."

Maginnes was on the tee. Donald and Dolby watched as he slashed a five-iron straight into the water. Maginnes stared at the spot where the ball had disappeared as if he thought some force of nature might push it out of the water and onto the green. Donald reached for a club and shook his head. He knew what it meant to Maginnes to make the cut. "That's really too bad," he said softly.

Maginnes dropped, wedged onto the green, and missed his bogey putt. When he made the four-footer coming back for his five, Donald said, "You know, that's a really good putt there."

Maginnes didn't answer. He walked to the ninth tee, lit another cigarette, and stood staring into the distance while the group waited yet again to hit. "Oh God," he said. "Oh God, oh God, oh God."

All three players birdied the par-five ninth. Both Donald and Maginnes had eagle putts. Maginnes came up six inches short. Donald went three feet past. He had hit 289 shots and he knew he was a goner. He carefully marked his ball, checked the line, took a practice putt, then knocked it in.

"I was thinking that I might need that putt to be totally exempt on the Nike Tour next year," he said.

No matter how much the game had beaten him up, Donald clearly wasn't going to put the clubs away for very long. He was a golfer. Golfers play golf.

As the three players shook hands and wished each other luck, Maginnes said to Donald, "What's next for you?"

Donald shook his head. "You know, to tell you the truth, I have no idea."

While Donald was slamming his trunk, Goydos, Henninger, and Cook were at the Nicklaus Course jockeying for position with the top half of the field. Henninger and Cook both struggled, Henninger shooting 73, Cook 72. Cook's 72 put him perilously close to the number, which turned out to be two, not one, as most players had predicted. Cook was right at two — tied for seventy-eighth place. Henninger was comfortably in at five, but was passed by thirty-one players, dropping from eleventh to forty-second.

One of the players who passed him was Goydos. That didn't make Henninger unusual, though, since Goydos passed fifty-nine players by shooting 65. Four other players would shoot 65 during the six days, but no one would shoot lower than that.

"I've never done that in my life," Goydos said. "I mean, I walked off the eighteenth green and said to myself, Where did that come from?" It came from continuing to hit the ball well and from making every putt he looked at. Goydos was three under par for four holes and just kept on going.

"If nothing else that round was an example of what I mean about the experience I picked up on tour this year," he said. "Once, I would have been satisfied at three under, I would have started thinking that if I just didn't make any mistakes I would shoot sixty-nine and wouldn't that be a good score. Now I know that to be successful you have to make lots and lots of birdies every week. If you need to be twenty under to win or ten under to make a good check, there's nothing wrong with getting seven or eight of that on the same day."

The 65 vaulted Goydos into a tie for ninth place. It also meant that Wendy Goydos, who had been sleeping very little, might get some sleep. "Of course now I have to make sure I don't come out tomorrow and throw up all over myself," Goydos said, always able to find the cloud in any silver lining. He was almost smiling though. He knew he had taken a giant step toward surviving.

A total of ninety-eight players had survived to play the last two days. Among those who missed the number were Bobby Cole, the onetime boy wonder, who had missed by two shots, and Bobby Clampett, another former phenom trying to get back on tour. He was also two shots out. David DuVal, who had finished four straight years as an All American at Georgia Tech in the spring and had then won twice on the Nike Tour, finished eagle-birdie to get to one under and thought he had made the cut only to learn he had missed by one. He would return to the Nike Tour for another year, proving exactly how much being a four-time All American is worth in the world of professional golf. Donald and Maginnes both finished four shots off the cut, in the group tied for 137th. Maginnes was two shots away from his goal of a full exemption on the Nike Tour. Donald's pal Lance Ten Broeck finished one shot behind him. Goydos's buddy Patrick Burke was one shot further back after sailing his putter into the lake in front of the 18th hole at the Dunes on Friday.

And Rick Dalpos, Cook's roommate for the week, shot 85 on the fourth day to finish tied for dead last in the field at 308 with Perry Moss. They were 22 shots off the number and 34 shots behind the co-leaders. A year earlier, Moss had tied for first at the school.

Now he and Dalpos and the other ninety players slamming their trunks as the sun went down Saturday night all had to go home and figure out what to do next with their lives.

Brian Henninger stood in the middle of the 15th fairway at the Nicklaus Course, hands on hips, his eyes locked onto the pin, which, according to his caddy, Chris Mazziotti, was exactly 194 yards away. "It's no more than a four-iron shot," Henninger said for a third time.

Mazziotti knew that, but he also knew it was a four-iron shot to an island green, over the same little lake that had swallowed Mike Donald alive four days earlier. Henninger was playing well, two under par through 14 holes on his fifth round, but he was frustrated because he had been hitting the ball close all day and not making any putts.

"It's not very far," Henninger said, looking at Mazziotti again.

Mazziotti wasn't answering. He didn't want to tell Henninger not to hit the four-iron, but he wasn't going to encourage him to hit it either. The first rule of Q-School is "don't make any big numbers," and attempting a long iron shot to an island green was one way of making a big number.

Henninger's playing partners had already laid up in front of the green and were down the fairway waiting for him to make his decision. Henninger felt as if he had a little devil sitting on one shoulder saying, "Go for it, you chicken," and an angel on the other shoulder shaking his head, clucking, and saying, "Remember, Brian, no big numbers; do the right thing and play safe."

Henninger shook his head in disgust and put the four-iron back in the bag. He wanted to be the devil but he didn't feel he could face the angel if he splashed one now. He pulled a nine-iron, took a half-hearted practice swing, and then chunked a mediocre layup shot that left him with 100 yards over a bunker to the pin.

"Good play," Mazziotti said, trying to sound upbeat.

Henninger wasn't buying. The devil had been right. His gut had told him to go for the green. He had been so unenthusiastic about playing the layup shot that he had hit it carelessly and now he wasn't in very good position. Sure enough, his wedge spun back, ending up 18 feet short and he missed the birdie putt. Henninger walked off the green fuming.

He *knew* he should have gone for the green. He was hitting the ball so well that the worst thing he would have done was hit it in the bunker and from there he would have still had a good chance to make birdie. Instead, he had overthought, been too cautious, and made a par on a hole where he might have made an eagle given how far he had hit his drive. Still muttering to himself, he pulled his second shot left at the next hole and made a bogey there.

In a matter of minutes, Henninger had gone from a good chance to be three under to one under. His mood was black even after he saved par from the sand at the 17th. That brought him to the 18th, a treacherous hole with water all the way down the right side and bunkers to the left and behind the green. Henninger stood and watched as both his playing partners hit second shots that drifted right and ended up in the water.

He took a six-iron and aimed left. The ball sailed left and kept going left. It ended up in the back bunker, with very little green between the ball and the pin. Henninger tried to get cute with his sand wedge, hoping to pop the ball close and somehow make par. Instead, he ended up leaving the ball in the bunker. His shoulders sagged. He played a more standard shot the second time, knocking the ball 20 feet past the pin. From there he two-putted for a double bogey. In four holes he had turned what should have been 68 or 69 into 73.

He felt sick to his stomach. "Standing on the 18th tee I remember thinking how hungry I was," he said later. "I went to Taco Bell as soon as I was done, thinking my stomach would feel better if I got some food in it. Then I just sat there for an hour and stared at the food. I couldn't touch it. I couldn't believe what I had done."

What he had done was put himself in jeopardy of not getting his card. Never once had it crossed Henninger's mind that he might not get through the school. After his 69 Friday, he had honestly believed he had a chance to finish first. Now, with only one round left, he was tied for fifty-first place, meaning he had to pass people on the final day. That hadn't been the plan.

Goydos, after a nervous 72 — "I started the day feeling awful" — was still comfortably in fourteenth place and Jeff Cook, after a 70, was in the group one shot behind Henninger.

Cook was in one of the last groups to finish that day. When he heard what had happened to Henninger he went looking for him. He knew his friend would be in a serious gloom-and-doom mood, and he didn't think that was the right way to feel with one day left to play at the school. "Brian has a tendency to pout," Cook said. "This wasn't the time for that."

He found Henninger half-heartedly hitting balls on the range. Henninger put down his clubs, sat on the cart with Cook, and told him what had happened. Cook listened and shrugged. "It's aggravating, I know that," he said. "But look where we are. If you shoot seventy tomorrow, you'll get your card back for sure, even seventy-one will probably do it. I've got to go one shot lower than that. Are you telling me we can't do that?"

"Of course we can," Henninger said. "But still . . ."

"I know," Cook said. "But you know what, no matter what happens tomorrow, we're both going to play golf next year. You're still going to have Cathy and Carlin, right? Look, Brian, I *know* golf isn't life and death because I've seen life and death."

Henninger knew that Cook was right, but he didn't buy all of it. There was only one place he wanted to play golf next year: the big tour. That was where he thought he belonged. Cook wasn't as driven as he was. He liked playing golf, and he worked to get better at it, but his real goal in life was to go back to Indiana someday and become the golf coach at his alma mater. Henninger's goals were different. He wanted to be a star on tour and he believed he had the talent to do it. Even so, he appreciated what Cook was trying to do. They sat in the cart until it got too cold to sit on the range and talk anymore.

Cook went home feeling good about the next day. "All I want to do is get a good start and put myself in a position where I have to choke to not get my card," he said. "If I can do that, I'll take my chances." He slept soundly.

Henninger didn't. He tossed and turned and spent most of the night wishing he had told the damn angel to mind its own business. It had been a long week.

The last day is the longest one at the school. Nerves are completely frayed. Amazingly, play gets even slower. Players seem to hear every noise, every chirping bird, every squeaking shoe. Disasters seem almost routine by the time the last putt has dropped.

Bill Murchison, who had traveled the big tour in 1993 with his wife and their eight children — all of them home-taught — made a triple bogey on the last hole to miss keeping his card by two shots. George Burns, at forty-five the oldest man still playing, bogeyed three of the last four holes to miss getting his card back by one.

Brian Henninger returned to the 15th hole, the scene of his Sunday crime, early the next day, since he played the back nine first. He was even par for the day to that point. The hole was playing into the wind so there was no question about laying up this time. But his third shot came up a little short, hit the front of the green, spun backward, and ended up in the water. Now Henninger had made the big number — a seven — he had been trying to avoid the day before.

Disgusted, he parred the next three holes, but three-putted number one to go to three over for the day. He had dropped to just one under for the tournament and, since the consensus was that the number would be at least six, he had no choice but to fire at the flag on every hole.

Playing boldly because you are way behind can do one of two things: it can loosen you up and draw you out of your lethargy, or it can cause the roof to fall in on you completely. Henninger, who had been tight as several drums since the 15th hole on Sunday, suddenly loosened up. He birdied the fourth, the fifth, the seventh, and the eighth.

From being absolutely nowhere with six holes to play, he found himself standing on the last tee — the ninth — needing one more birdie to have a good chance to keep his card.

The ninth hole at the Nicklaus Course is not a birdie hole under any conditions. Never was it less a birdie hole than on this day. The hole is a long par-four, with a second shot over water. The pin was tucked front left, about as close to the water as was possible. The players call this a "sucker" pin because only a real sucker will aim at a flag that is so close to water. The smart play is to knock your ball to the middle of the green, take your par, and get out of there.

Henninger didn't have that luxury. Even though he couldn't know for certain, he was convinced that the number was going to be six. From the middle of the fairway he took dead aim at the flag. A swirling wind made the shot even tougher. The ball climbed high into the air, headed right at the pin, and then began drifting ever so slightly left. Henninger's heart went into his knees. The ball splashed just to the left of the green, and as it sank so did Henninger's hopes. He bogeyed the hole to finish at 428 — four under par for six rounds of golf.

It was too early in the day to know yet what the number would be, but Henninger knew it wouldn't be four. "The only thing I was hoping was that it wouldn't be five," he said. "Because then I would have to kill myself for going for the flag on nine."

Paul Goydos had no such problems. Having survived his "throw-up" day, he was three under par through fourteen holes before he made seven on the notorious 15th. "The amazing thing is I did it without going in the water," he said, able to laugh when it was all finally over. He had finished with a 71. That left him at 422 — ten under par. He had cruised after the 65, ending up in a tie for eighteenth place.

"You know, it really didn't seem all that hard this time," he said.

"Speak for yourself," Wendy Goydos said.

Cook was the last member of the triumvirate to finish. He had gotten the fast start he had hoped for, getting to three under after four holes, but was back to one under by the turn. That put him at five for the tournament. Like Henninger, he played the back nine first, so he knew he needed to play the front in one under to keep his card. It was late enough in the day now that word had filtered around the course that no one was tearing the place up. That meant the number was almost certain to be six.

Cook got to six at number one, holing a 20-foot birdie putt after knocking his tee shot into the right fairway bunker and hitting a beautiful recovery. He was exactly where he needed to be. The question was, could he hang on?

He parred two from another bunker. Then, at the par-three third, he caught a horrendous break. His four-iron off the tee was pushed right and appeared headed for a bunker. Given the way Cook was playing from the sand, that didn't seem like such an awful place to be.

Only the ball didn't get there. It took one bounce, hit a rake, and stopped just outside the bunker. When he reached the ball and saw where it had stopped, Cook threw his head back in anguish. "Oh no," he said. "No, no, no. Why did that have to happen?"

He had to call for a ruling since the ball was leaning against the rake. He ended up dropping behind the bunker, the ball stopping on an impossible downhill lie. He was lucky to make bogey from there. Now he was back to five.

The fourth was a par-five, meaning it was a birdie hole. Cook finally hit a drive in the fairway and hit a huge three-wood onto the green. Two putts from 40 feet and he had the birdie and was back on the bubble at six. He parred five, then missed a makeable 10-foot birdie putt at six. Cook stood with his eyes closed, not moving for several seconds after the putt missed. He knew he had lost a chance to give himself a critical piece of cushion.

All the work had now come down to a few swings for everyone. Cook's two playing partners had gone in opposite directions the last few holes. Like Cook, both had been one shot off the number after nine holes. But Mike Emery had made a pair of double bogeys to knock himself out of contention. Mike Heinen, however, had made two birdies, and when he birdied the par-five seventh, he had given himself the cushion Cook lacked by reaching eight under.

Cook couldn't reach the par-five seventh in two and ended up in thick rough in front of the green. From there, he couldn't get a wedge close and two-putted. He was still at six.

Now they had reached the eighth hole. Cook had talked about the eighth the night before. "You sure don't want to be in choke position playing *that* hole," he said.

He was in exactly that position. The eighth is a par-three with water in front and to the right and bunkers to the left. The pin, naturally, was up front, near the water. There were two groups waiting on the tee when Cook, Heinen, and Emery arrived. Not only would Cook have to play the hole with no margin for error, he would have to sit and wait for twenty minutes before playing the shot.

Two players in the group before Cook's splashed their tee shots. Two more groups had now arrived on the tee. Everyone was pacing around nervously, talking in whispers, comparing scores, trying not to look at the water. It was Steve LaMontagne, who was also sitting on the bubble, who finally cracked.

"What a hole to have to sit and wait on," he said, his voice echoing off the trees. "I mean, can you believe this, can you fucking believe, we have to sit and wait on *this* goddamn hole!"

Everyone laughed nervously. Up ahead, on the green, someone turned around and said, "Hey!"

LaMontagne lowered his voice, but he continued to pace around in circles. "Okay, all you have to do is hit the goddamn ball onto the goddamn green, right? I mean, it's only a golf ball, right? If it goes in the water, so what?" He sat down in his cart and said it again, "What a hole to have to wait on."

The group ahead had cleared the green. Cook took a long time selecting a club. The wind was coming at him and he certainly didn't want to be short. He had 153 yards to the hole. He chose a six-iron and took a deep breath. His gallery — eight other players and their caddies — was silent. Cook's swing was as good as any he had made all day. The ball flew right at the pin. It had plenty of distance. It landed safely behind the pin and looked for a split second as if it might suck back and end up very close. It stopped twenty feet above the hole.

Cook shook his head. "Can't complain," he said. "I hit it pure."

His birdie putt was straight downhill. Cook wasn't about to do anything bold from this spot. He trickled the ball down the hill, then watched in horror as it slid past the cup and somehow kept on rolling until he had four feet left coming back.

He lined it up carefully, stroked it carefully, and watched it hit the side of the cup — and bounce out. The knot in Cook's stomach seemed to explode. He couldn't believe the putt had stayed out of the hole. Sitting behind the green, Mike Emery's father shook his head. "Poor guy," he said. "Probably just lost his card."

Cook was now in the same boat Henninger had been in earlier. He had to somehow birdie the ninth. Forced to wait again, he stood behind the tee staring into space.

His tee shot was perfect, but he still had 174 yards to the pin. This time the shot was downwind, so he took the six-iron again. And, just as at the eighth, he "pured" it. The ball flew right over the pin, landed 20 feet long, and slammed to a halt.

"No!" Cook screamed. "You can't go that far! Goddamn you ball, you cannot go that far!"

The ball had already gone that far. Cook's 20-foot card-or-no-card birdie putt slipped just past the hole. The six-inch tap-in was the one extra shot he simply couldn't afford to hit.

Cook picked the ball out of the cup and walked over to Heinen, who had finished at eight under. "Congratulations," he said. "Well played."

He signed his scorecard and joined Henninger and Goydos at the scoreboard. Nothing was definite yet. A few players who had been ahead of Cook had backed up. Maybe, just maybe, five would get in. But hope didn't last very long. A number of players had rallied. Steve Brodie, a twenty-eight-year-old who had traveled the Nike Tour in 1993 with his wife and four children — they were known as the Brodie Bunch — had shot the day's low round, a 65, to go from one under to eight under.

Rob Boldt, who owned a dog named Titleist, had shot 68 to get to six. A friend of Cook's, Shaun Micheel, like him an Indiana graduate, had shot 67 to get to six. When Micheel finished, he was congratulated on all sides and told he had earned a card. In the middle of his celebration, he heard a PGA Tour official say, "All of those at six under par please be on the tenth tee for the playoff in fifteen minutes."

Playoff? What playoff? Micheel had heard all week that the low forty players — and ties — got their cards. Now he was going to have to play off? How could that be? "I went from the best feeling I could remember to the worst in a few minutes," he said.

And back to the best, seconds later. The playoff was merely to determine the card number for each of the ten players who had tied for thirty-seventh place. Micheel was so relieved he birdied the first playoff hole and got card number thirty-seven.

The most harrowing story of the day belonged to Brad Lardon, a veteran of five finals. Fittingly, Lardon's caddy was his older brother Mike, who was a *paid* psychiatrist the other fifty-one weeks of the year. Lardon came to the 18th hole needing a par for a 69 that would put him at six. He played safely down the left side and to the back of the green, wanting to stay away from all the trouble on the right and up front.

His 40-foot birdie putt came up five feet short. Knowing exactly what was at stake, Lardon stalked around the putt forever before putting. Like Cook's putt at eight, it hit the hole. Only, instead of bouncing away, it bounced into the air and came down in the middle of the cup. Lardon had his card.

"That putt was probably worth $50,000," he said. "That's what being on the big tour is worth before you hit a ball."

Goydos, Cook, and Henninger all knew that. Goydos was going back to the big tour. Henninger, having finished two spots out of the top 125, would get into some tournaments on the big tour in 1994, but would have to play in Nike events to supplement his schedule. He was in limbo. And Cook was back to square one.

"Maybe I'll go back and play in Asia," he said, dreading the idea of a return to the Nike Tour.

Inside the clubhouse, the forty-six players who had reached the promised land were being briefed on the orientation program that the first-timers would have to go to in Florida the next week and on details that had to be taken care of before the new season began five weeks later in Hawaii.

Goydos had to go inside for his briefing. Cook and Henninger left without going inside again. They had no desire to see the happy, smiling faces of those who would make that trip to Hawaii in January.

Several hours later, after darkness had fallen, a lone couple stood in front of the scoreboard, staring at the numbers that meant nothing to them. Mike Emery's father, walking to his car, stopped in front of the board.

"Lot of golf," the man said to him.

"Lot of stories there," Mike Emery Sr. said. "My son" — he

pointed to Mike Jr.'s name — "had a chance, but he faded down the stretch." He pointed at Jeff Cook's name, which was just below the red, felt-tipped line that had been drawn between the survivors and the nonsurvivors. "Poor guy three-jacked it on the second-to-last hole," he said. "I'm not sure I ever saw anything sadder."

He walked away. School was out.

6

TALES OF TOMMY, JOHNNY, BILLY, AND DEANE

THE 1994 PGA TOUR began on January 6 — Paul Azinger's thirty-fourth birthday — at the La Costa Resort in Carlsbad, California, with the Tournament of Champions, an event that brought together — surprise — all the tournament champions from the previous year.

Only it wasn't the Tournament of Champions anymore. It was now the Mercedes Championships, so-called because Mercedes, in agreeing to take over the title sponsorship for five years, had insisted that the Tournament of Champions part of the name be dropped so that the media would have no choice but to call the event by its corporate title.

When Commissioner Deane Beman made the deal with Mercedes he knew he would take a beating for having sold one more traditional tournament name down the river to corporate America. The PGA Tour, as reinvented in the twenty years Beman had been commissioner, was, for all intents and purposes, owned and operated by two entities: corporate America and television.

That didn't make golf terribly different from every other sport. The only real difference was that golf had quit pretending that TV and the corporations weren't in control years ago. What had once been the Crosby Clambake was now the AT&T Pebble Beach Pro-Am. The Bob Hope was now the Bob Hope Chrysler Classic. There was a Buick Invitational in San Diego; a Buick Classic at Westchester; a Buick Open in Grand Blanc, Michigan, and a Buick Southern Open at Callaway Gardens in Columbus, Georgia. Arnold Palmer's Bay Hill Classic was now the Nestle Invitational in Orlando, Florida.

The venerable Western Open had been, in a period of ten years, the Beatrice Western, the Centel Western, the Sprint Western, and for 1994 would be the Motorola Western. If you could name all the Western's corporate sponsors you would win a year's supply of peanut butter, two telephones, and a television. For that matter, the Tournament of Champions had been the MONY Tournament of Champions and the Infiniti Tournament of Champions even before Mercedes showed up.

"I didn't invent corporate involvement in sports or in golf," Beman liked to remind people. "I just recognized the potential it had to help us build the game."

What Beman did was marry corporate America to television in order to get his sport on TV on a regular basis. Since the four majors — the Masters, the U.S. Open, the British Open, and the PGA — are run by separate governing bodies, the tour does not own their TV rights. Selling a TV package for all the nonmajors wasn't the easiest thing in the world to do.

"Imagine baseball trying to sell its TV package without the World Series or football trying to sell itself without the Super Bowl," Beman said. "That is exactly what we're asked to do every year."

Golf ratings for nonmajors on TV have never been terribly high. They are consistent and they reach the kind of audience sponsors like — people with money to spend — but they have never been high enough to warrant the TV networks' taking a chance on selling enough advertising to make money. So Deane Beman eliminated the risk factor for the networks by making the Western Open into the Beatrice-Centel-Sprint-Motorola and inviting every other corporation he could find to stick its name onto any tournament it was willing to pay for.

The way it works is this: If you want your name on a tournament and you want that tournament on network TV, you have to ante up about $1.7 million. A large chunk of that goes toward the purchase of thirty-two to thirty-six thirty-second commercials — sixteen to eighteen during your tournament and sixteen to eighteen more spread throughout the year on the rest of your network's TV package. You then spend about another $1 million for expenses and other advertising.

With half the tournament's spots sold to the title sponsor and a bunch more sold to the title sponsors for other tournaments, the networks found themselves in a position where they had to do very little work to sell out their advertising package. In addition, cable outlets looking for programming were willing to pay the networks for production costs, so many tournaments are now seen, not just on Saturday and Sunday, but also on cablecasts on Thursday and Friday. With corporate America paying the freight, Beman got golf on television almost nonstop. In 1994, thirty-five of the forty-one official PGA Tour events were on national television — twenty-eight on the networks, six on ESPN, and one on TBS. There were also twenty-five senior tour events on national TV and seven made-for-TV events in November and December. Not to mention the four majors and a twenty-four-hour Golf Channel planned for 1995.

That's a whole lot of golf on TV. Beman was justifiably proud of that, even though some people worried that it was getting to be too much of a good thing. Others, also justifiably, made fun of the corporate CEOs who insisted on introducing the telecasts by staring into a teleprompter and saying things like "We are so proud to be a part of this historic event, the Shell Houston Open." They also insisted on being "interviewed" at the end of the Sunday telecast. Without fail, regardless of who was leading or by how much, the CEO would shake his head and say, "Vern [or Jim or Mark or Andy or Bob], this has been about as exciting a week of golf as I can ever remember seeing."

Beman shrugged off those who thought the CEOs would be well advised to stay behind the cameras. "They pay the freight, they get to make the call on that."

Which was exactly what Beman's critics harped on. Sure, he had greatly increased golf's TV exposure and there was no doubt purses had gone sky-high during his tenure. But, they said, he had also sold golf's soul and history to Mercedes and Kmart and Buick and Federal Express and just about everyone in the telephone business.

The Crosby is a favorite example for some of what's wrong with golf sponsorships. "I don't care what Deane Beman wants to call it, the Crosby will always be the Crosby," said Dan Jenkins, golf's funniest and most eloquent writer.

The Crosby had been invented long before Beman reinvented the

tour. It had come into being as a week-long party — or Clambake —
that Bing Crosby threw for his pals along the shores of Carmel Bay.
Golf-playing celebrities got to play with the pros in professional/ama-
teur pairings. The golf tournament was the sideshow back then; the
presence of the stars in the Pro-Am the main event.

The Crosby continued to be the Crosby after the singer's death,
but in 1985, Beman and Crosby's widow, Kathryn, got into a dispute
when Beman went out and got AT&T to buy the title sponsorship.
Kathryn Crosby took her husband's name to North Carolina and
created a nontour event. In 1986 the original Crosby tournament
was rechristened the AT&T Pebble Beach Pro-Am. Keeping Pebble
Beach in the name was a way of reminding the world that this was
the tournament and the golf course with all the history and all the
lore.

The celebrities kept coming and the tournament continued to
flourish. In 1994, Pebble Beach was the fifth stop on the West Coast
schedule, coming after La Costa, Hawaii, Tucson, and Phoenix. Or,
as Beman and the tour might put it, after the Mercedes, the United
Airlines, the Northern Telecom, and (whoops) Phoenix. (This space
available, call 904-285-3700 and ask for Deane.)

The format at Pebble Beach is the same as it has always been.
Each pro is assigned an amateur partner and they play three rounds
at three different golf courses. Until 1991, the three courses were
Pebble Beach, Spyglass Hill, and Cypress Point. But when the tour
insisted, in the aftermath of the 1990 Shoal Creek racism controversy,
that any club wishing to host a tournament have at least one minority
member, Cypress Point dropped out of the rota. It was replaced by
Poppy Hills, an inland course with none of the drama or romance of
Cypress Point.

After three days' play, the field is cut to the low sixty pros and the
low twenty-five pro/amateur teams. They all play Pebble Beach the
last day. The AT&T Crosby is the only tournament on tour in which
amateurs play on the final day. This makes for some strange pairings
because some Pro-Am teams qualify even though the pro hasn't made
the cut and — obviously — a number of pros make the cut without
their amateur partners.

Since the last round invariably takes more than five hours to play because of the presence of the amateurs on a very difficult golf course and since the final putt must be struck by 3 P.M. local time so that CBS can be off the air by 6 P.M. on the East Coast, the final round at Pebble Beach can be, to put it mildly, a mess.

The Sunday pairings at Pebble were the least of Deane Beman's concerns in February 1994. For years, Beman had always looked forward to the tour's West Coast swing. He and his wife, Judy, would fly west the first week in January on the tour's corporate jet — known as Air Beman — and set up headquarters in the large, comfortable tour-owned condo in Palm Springs. Staffers called it the Western White House. Beman would play some golf, ride his motorcycle with Judy, and occasionally make his way up and down the coast and to Hawaii and Arizona to press the flesh at each tournament. Some sponsors complained he played too much golf and often didn't press enough flesh.

This year was a little different. Beman was fifty-five, and for the first time since he had accepted the job, he was wondering if it wasn't time to move on. Even though he was making $2.2 million a year, he often felt underappreciated, not only by the players, who he knew often sniped at him behind his back, but by media and those always demanding sponsors. Beman looked at what he had wrought and thought he had done a hell of a job. He had turned the PGA Tour from a mom-and-pop candy store into a thriving corporation with millions of dollars in assets. And what did he get in return?

Bill Murray.

Actually, Beman had thought about quitting to take a shot at playing the senior tour long before Bill Murray and Pebble Beach came along to ruin the month of February for him.

Murray had become one of the stars of the AT&T event in recent years. The actor brought his wacky sense of humor to the golf course and just about everyone loved the act. Murray danced with marshals and he did his "Caddyshack" routine routinely — and hysterically.

Murray's antics, Jack Lemmon's never-ending quest to make the cut (zero for twenty-one and counting), Joe Pesci cracking one-liners through an ever-present cigar, and the presence of celebrities throughout the field were what set the Pebble Beach event apart from others on the tour. Sure, there was serious golf being played, but there were also some real live laughs during the first three days. Murray leading 5,000 people in a wave to the Blimp in 1993 was going to be remembered a lot longer by most people than Brett Ogle winning the tournament.

Beman knew that and he had no quarrel with it. But in the process of promoting the 1994 tournament, CBS kept showing a 1993 shot of Murray spinning an elderly lady around in a sand trap and finally letting go of her as she fell over in the sand.

It was a funny scene and one that CBS correctly thought sent the message to viewers that this golf tournament wasn't like all other golf tournaments. But there was a problem. The woman in question, although unhurt, had felt embarrassed by the incident and had complained about it to tour officials. Now her embarrassment was being shown over and over again. Beman couldn't — and wouldn't — try to stop CBS. But he felt he had to do something to rein Murray in — at least a little bit.

And so he asked the local organizers if they would talk to Murray before the tournament started and ask him if he could make his act just a little bit less outrageous. The message was supposed to be "Bill, we love you, we think you're great for the tournament, but could you please not dump any more women in sand traps this year."

Somewhere in the translation the part about "Bill, we love you and we think you're great" didn't reach Murray. The part that reached him was "Cool it." Murray didn't take this well. He was furious. While many of his fellow celebrities accepted complimentary spots to play in the tournament, Murray always paid the $3,500 to play even though he didn't have to.

Who was complaining? he wanted to know. Certainly not his playing partners. Certainly not the gallery. Certainly not CBS. Beman had hoped his request to Murray would stay private. No chance. Murray played, but he blasted Beman. He called him, among other things, a Nazi and, half-jokingly, called for his resignation. He said he would not return to play in the tournament after 1994 even if he was asked. When his group reached the 18th hole at Pebble Beach on Saturday, long after the TV cameras had been turned off for the night, Murray announced to the gallery, "This is my final shot ever in this tournament."

*　　*　　*

Lost in all the head-shaking and hand-wringing over L'Affaire Murray was the fact that a very good golf tournament was taking place. Since a lot of the big-name players skipped Hawaii and the Arizona tournaments, Pebble Beach was the first event since the Mercedes Championships in which the stars came out to play.

The leader board on Saturday night was a reflection of that fact. The leaders were Dudley Hart and Johnny Miller. Hart was not exactly a household name, but was one of the tour's better young players. Miller *was* a household name, but for the past five years it had been because of his work for NBC as golf's most outspoken commentator. His last win on tour had come in 1987, in this same tournament. One shot back was Tom Watson. Two shots behind Watson was Tom Kite.

This was time-warp stuff. Miller was forty-six, Kite and Watson forty-four. Miller had been *retired* for five years and played at Pebble Beach only because he had grown up on the course, had won the tournament twice, and still lived nearby. Watson hadn't won a tournament in seven years and had spent more time the last two years answering questions about the Ryder Cup than about his golf. Kite was a different story. His career had crested after forty. He had finally won a major title in 1992 at the age of forty-two, and in 1993 he had started the year by winning back-to-back at Los Angeles and the Hope, been sidelined for three months by back problems, and then come back to play superbly in the Ryder Cup.

There was more. All three players had spent transcendent moments in their career at Pebble Beach. Miller had grown up playing the golf course and, while coming into his own as a young star, had lost a playoff here to Jack Nicklaus in 1972 when he hit a dead shank on the 16th hole during the last round.

Watson and Kite had won their U.S. Opens at Pebble, Watson making the memorable chip-in at 17 in '82, Kite making a remarkable chip-in of his own at the seventh in '92 while winning on a day so brutally windy that many in the field failed to break 80.

Watson and Kite and their amateur partners would tee off at 9:20 in the second-to-last group of the day, with Hart and Miller and their amateurs right behind. At most golf tournaments, the leaders don't tee off on Sunday until close to 2 o'clock. This wasn't most golf tournaments.

And, if you needed one last element to make the story complete, the weather Sunday turned up windy and rainy, the kind of day that had built the legend of both the Crosby and Pebble Beach. "When we come around that bend at number three and hit the water, we'll get the full force of it," Watson said, sounding as if he relished the thought.

Watson may be the best bad-weather golfer in history. Growing up in Kansas City, he became accustomed to playing in cold and wind and rain. Even as an adult, he was one of the few pros who didn't find himself a warm-weather winter home. That meant a lot of practice time in less-than-perfect conditions. Throughout his career, Watson has played some of his best golf — witness his record in the British Open — under the worst conditions.

Each of the four leaders went into Sunday's round with an entirely different attitude. Hart, who had been in position to win before but had never gotten to the finish line first, wanted to take the step from contender to winner. Kite was a little surprised to be so close to the lead because he didn't feel comfortable with his swing. Watson was hitting the ball better than anyone. He had survived his third round at Poppy Hills, normally a bugaboo course for him, with an even par 72 and thought he had put himself in position to win. Miller was just having a good time and thought playing in the last group was a kick for someone who made his living as a television announcer.

Miller wasn't the only television personality in the final group. His amateur partner was Bryant Gumbel, the *Today Show* host, who had never dreamed that he would end up in the final pairing on Sunday when he and Miller — who had worked together on NBC's golf telecasts for two years — decided to team up.

"It just occurred to me that I'm going to be on TV tomorrow," Gumbel said as he walked to his car Saturday afternoon.

That was a funny line coming from someone who made a career of making being on television look easy. "Yeah, but this is different," Gumbel said. "This is golf. I'm not so hot at golf."

Gumbel really wasn't bad — an 11 handicap — but his trepidation was understandable. While CBS built its Saturday telecast around the celebrities, Sunday was for the pros. Gumbel wasn't likely to get a lot of camera time — unless he made a hole in one or killed someone. Or something.

Watson's reaction to Miller's presence on the leader board was a bit different than Gumbel's. "What'd he do, go see the Dalai Lama?" he asked jokingly on Saturday night. "Whatever it is, I hope he gives me some of it."

Ironically, Miller had been driven from the game, at least in part, by the same thing that had made Watson miserable: putting. "Mine was different though," Miller said. "Tom has trouble from six feet in. I had the reverse yips. I was fine from twelve feet and in. It was the longer putts I couldn't handle."

Miller also had serious leg problems. His joints were so creaky that he played only about twenty-five rounds of golf a year in retirement and almost never practiced. About the only thing that got him on the golf course at all was the chance to play with his five children.

It was already starting to rain hard when Watson and Kite reached the first tee. Kite's amateur partner was Rudy Gatlin, the country music singer, who was a good player, a six handicapper. Watson always played with Sandy Tatum, a former president of the U.S. Golf Association and a lifelong friend. This was the first time in years that they had made the Pro-Am cut.

"Boy it's nice to be out here together on a Sunday, isn't it?" Watson said to Tatum as they shook hands on the first tee.

"It's even nice to be here and get rained on," Tatum answered.

"Rain?" Watson said, grinning. "What rain?" The rain was coming down sideways at that moment.

One of the tour's unspoken and most unnoticed little traditions is for players to wish each other luck on the first tee. It isn't necessarily anything so formal as a handshake or going from player to player saying "good luck." It is more subtle than that, almost a murmured aside after the first player in the group has been introduced.

And so, when Kite had been introduced, he stood behind his ball for a moment staring down the fairway and said softly, "Tom, let's have a good day."

"Yes," Watson said. "Let's have fun."

Neither man could possibly know what lay ahead over the next five and a half hours.

Watson's prediction about being hit full-bore by the wind coming around the corner at number three was accurate. By then, Kite had already bogeyed number one and Watson had missed a four-foot birdie putt at number two.

It is at number three that Pebble Beach starts to become Pebble Beach. The first two holes are ordinary, inland holes. Number three begins a stretch in which the players go back and forth to the water for four holes. They then play right at the water at the tiny seventh, one of the most dramatic par-threes in golf. The next three holes are, in Watson's words, "the three best consecutive par-four holes in the world." They are long and difficult, almost always windy, and have the beach, the rocks, and Carmel Bay all the way down the right side.

The course turns inland at number 11 before coming back to the water at 17 and 18, which may be the two most famous finishing holes in golf.

On a day like this, scores would not be low. Anyone who could get under par would probably be in good shape. It was Watson who broke through first, birdieing the par-five sixth. Kite was already four over par for the day by then and shaking his head while saying to Gatlin over and over, "Sorry, partner."

Watson gave back the shot he had picked up at the sixth when he blew a three-iron over the ninth green, chipped back to eight feet, and missed the par putt. It had taken them just under three hours to play nine holes. Watson, Miller, and Hart were tied for the lead.

Almost every round of golf on tour follows a distinct pattern. It begins — unless you are playing with Nick Faldo — with chatter and small talk on subjects ranging from family to appearance fees to hunting and fishing to last night's ball game to movies. Watson and Kite spent several minutes during a delay on the third tee peppering Gatlin with questions about the country music business.

Sooner or later, the talk dies. On Thursday, it is apt to last longer than on Friday, especially if someone in the group is grinding to make the cut. Saturday tends to be more like Thursday (unless disaster strikes someone early), and Sunday almost always gets very serious by the 10th tee.

Kite had managed to stay fairly cheery in spite of his play through most of the front nine, although he admitted at one point that "it's hard to keep smiling through all the bogeys." Watson was still loose enough on the fifth tee to compliment the amateurs in the group ahead on their tee shots. When the wind died briefly going up six, Kite and Watson joked about how balmy it had gotten. Five minutes later, when the wind and rain slapped them in the face on the seventh tee, they both laughed and broke out the rain gear again.

Watson's bogey at nine, combined with a glance at the scoreboard, ended the day's chatter.

While the rest of the group waited on the 10th tee for the fairway to clear, Watson walked into the tent behind the tee and asked a volunteer if he could have two Twix bars. She handed him one. "I need two," Watson said patiently. "Two Twix bars. Please."

He didn't raise his voice and he could not have been more polite. But the edge was there. You could hear it in the word "please." There were nine holes left in the golf tournament and Watson was tied for the lead with a television announcer and a kid. He knew the tournament was his now. To win. Or to lose. It had been a very long time since Tom Watson had been in such a position so late on a Sunday.

He parred 10, then hit a monstrous drive at 11 that started to veer right. "Don't go right!" he hissed angrily. The ball seemed to listen. It stopped in the fairway but caught the edge of a divot. Undeterred, Watson hit a pitching wedge to 15 feet and drained the putt. He was nine under par and had the lead.

Pumped, Watson absolutely airmailed the 12th green with a four-iron and made bogey. Now he and Miller were tied again. Hart had dropped back to six under. It was a two-man tournament, a duel between two men whose rivalry went back twenty-five years. "Down the stretch I kept thinking, I never beat Tom Watson, he always makes a putt somewhere to beat me," Miller would say later.

That seemed a likely scenario when Watson made a 10-foot birdie putt at 13 while Miller was bogeying 12. Suddenly, Watson led by two and there were just five holes to play. "Nice putt," Kite said softly on the 14th tee.

Watson smiled his thanks and said nothing. This wasn't the time to talk. He was on a roller coaster now. Fourteen is a par-five, a potential birdie hole. Watson's third shot, a wedge straight at the flag, just caught the bunker in front and rolled back into the sand. From there, he made another bogey.

Miller, standing in the fairway, saw Watson catch the bunker. "That's a trick pin placement," he said. "You can't aim at the pin. You have to aim twelve feet left."

Local knowledge. Advantage Miller, who parred the hole. That left them tied again, since Miller had birdied 13. They were still tied when Watson reached 16. But as he walked off the tee, with the 15th green to his left, he could see that Miller had just blown his second shot way over the green, an almost certain bogey. Watson was leading again. Three holes left.

His second shot, a gorgeous five-wood into the wind, stopped 12 feet short of the pin. Watson's heart was going a million miles an hour. Make this, he thought, and you're two shots up with two of your favorite holes in golf left. He took longer than usual lining the putt up. Then, just as he was about to draw the putter back, he noticed some grass on the blade and stepped away.

Again, he lined the putt up. For a split second, it looked as if he had made the birdie. The crowd screamed, then groaned. Too charged up, Watson had rolled the ball four feet by the hole. He was in the throw-up zone, right at the distance that had bedeviled him the last few years. "That first putt was a speed putt," he said later. "I got caught up worrying about the line and forgot about the speed."

In the tower behind 16, CBS's Jim Nantz said, "I don't even want to watch this."

He knew what he was talking about. The putt never touched the hole. Bogey. Instead of leading by two, Watson was tied again.

They had to wait on 17, the long par-three that goes to a tiny finger of land with water crashing in on all sides. The wind was howling by now and, even at 2:30 in the afternoon, it was almost dark because of the scudding rain clouds overhead.

Watson stood in front of the tee during the wait, hands jammed in his back pockets, staring at the green as if trying to conjure up 1982 in his memory. When it was finally his turn to hit, he peeled off the jacket and blasted a four-iron safely over the bunkers and onto the green, but a good 35 feet right of the pin.

In 1982, Watson had been off the green, left. On that day, in one of golf's more memorable exchanges, his caddy, Bruce Edwards, had instructed him to "knock it close."

"Close?" Watson answered. "I'm going to knock it in."

And so he did. Now, as Watson lined up the long birdie putt, Edwards, who had rejoined Watson in 1993 after an unhappy two-year sojourn with Greg Norman, whispered in his ear, "Let's do something special from *this* side."

Watson certainly tried. The putt actually nipped the cup, slowed down briefly, and then stopped three feet past the cup. Not a tap-in, but not in the throw-up area either. Except now, with all the pressure crashing in on him, it was more than Watson's shaky stroke could handle. He jabbed, the ball went around the cup and stayed out. Standing on the tee watching, Miller knew he now led the golf tournament.

Torturously, Watson's group had to wait again on the 18th tee. They could easily have watched what was happening on 17 since the green was only a few yards from the tee. Watson didn't even turn his head.

By not watching, Watson missed one of the more tragicomic moments in golf history. Hitting first, Bryant Gumbel sent his tee shot sailing toward the green, only to see it intercepted by a seagull. The seagull and the ball both dropped like stones. The ball had apparently caught the poor gull square in the head. It was dead before it hit the ground.

Gumbel was truly shaken. So was Miller, who felt bad for his partner and for the innocent bird. He also had a bit of a club-selection problem. Since he carried a seven-wood, Miller had no three-iron in his bag. The shot was a perfect three-iron. "I had to try and hit a four-iron as hard as I could," he said later. "Believe me, I was having trouble concentrating on that shot. When it hit the green, I'm not sure if I was more surprised or relieved."

Miller was in almost the same spot as Watson had been. But he managed to two-putt. Watson heard the applause for the par as he walked off the 18th tee, having split the fairway with his drive.

Watson knew he had to birdie the hole to have any chance to catch Miller. Standing in the 18th fairway, he had dropped from being alone in first place on the 16th green to a four-way tie for second with Corey Pavin, Kirk Triplett, and Jeff Maggert, all of whom had finished at six under.

The 18th at Pebble Beach is not normally reachable in two except on those rare occasions when the hole is playing straight downwind. To have a chance to get home in two, a player must play his tee shot over the water and beach and rocks that parallel the hole all the way down the left-hand side and then play another long, risky shot that can also end up in the paws of the seals who like to frolic on the rocks below.

Having hit a perfect drive, Watson went for the green, although he was careful to keep the ball far enough right that, if he didn't reach, he would end up in the front bunker. That's where his ball landed. For Watson, up and down from most bunkers in the world is, at worst, very possible. In the TV tower Ken Venturi, who very rarely makes a demeaning comment about a player, said, "The only way he can make birdie is to hit this ball about an inch from the cup." Any other putt, Venturi reasoned, was out of Watson's range at this point.

Watson hit a good bunker shot, not a great one. It bounced toward the hole, then past it, stopping 8 feet away. The birdie putt was dead center but two inches short. Halfway there, it appeared to bounce, as if it had hit a spike mark. That didn't matter. Watson made par, and par wasn't good enough.

On a day when he had hit the ball superbly, he ended up shooting 74. He had taken 34 putts, including eight on the last three holes. He had made just two putts longer than five feet and had missed *six* inside 10 feet. Once upon a time, he would have made at least five of those — and thrown in a 20-footer and a 30-footer for good measure. Not anymore.

Miller, watching every move Watson made from behind him, played two conservative shots, wedged on, and two-putted for an improbable victory.

"This didn't really happen," he said later. "I'm not a golfer, I'm a television announcer. I'm a grandfather, for crying out loud."

No one would have blamed Watson if he had signed his card, gone through his postmatch interview, and fled. But that isn't Watson. He waited for Miller to finish, a blank look on his face, except for the smile he forced when Linda came up to give him a hug. Miller was so dazed and overcome by what he had done that he almost walked right past Watson on his way into the scorer's tent.

"Johnny," Watson said, getting his attention. "Congratulations."

Miller had tears in his eyes. Watson put an arm around him. "Now get your butt back up in the booth."

Miller laughed. Somehow, Watson had found the right words. After leaving Miller, he made the long walk to the interview room and patiently went through the round, shot by shot, with the media. He was composed, smiling at friends, trying to sound upbeat. He had hit the ball well all day and he still believed he would win again very soon. When he tried to talk about his putting, though, the words came more slowly.

"I lived by the putter early in my career, I'm dying by it now. I keep tinkering, looking for an answer. Maybe I tinker too much." He shook his head and said very softly, "I could have won fairly easily today if the flat stick had even been mediocre."

Walking out the door, he forced one more smile. "Now I have to go call my kids," he said. "The first thing Michael's going to say to me is 'Daddy, why did you have to three-putt?' "

If Watson had known the answer to that question he wouldn't have been walking out with an empty feeling in his stomach while Miller sat in the interview room saying over and over, "This isn't right, this is a fluke."

The tour had launched a series of public service announcements at the start of the year with the slogan "On the PGA Tour, Anything's Possible."

If they had been thinking fast in Ponte Vedra that night, a new PSA would have hit the airwaves that week showing the final leader board at Pebble Beach. Anything *was* possible.

7

STRUGGLING

THE TOURNAMENT with the smallest purse on the tour's annual West Coast swing is the Los Angeles Open. Or, as it is now called, the Nissan Open, the car sponsor demanding that Los Angeles be taken out of the title in 1995 for the same reason that Mercedes wanted Tournament of Champions to disappear in 1994.

To the players, whatever the tournament's official name is, the week means one thing: Riviera Country Club. Fred Couples calls it his favorite golf course, and a lot of players agree or rank it somewhere in their top five. That is why L.A. annually draws one of the tour's best fields even though it had a 1994 purse of "only" $1 million. During the first six months of the year, $1 million was the lowest purse on tour.

No matter. Riviera will always draw a quality field, although if there was a year when it might not have, it was '94. To begin with, word had spread among the players that the course's new greens, put in because Riviera would host the PGA in 1995, weren't ready. They were slow and bumpy and really not in the kind of shape you would expect at a quality golf course.

Beyond that there was the not-so-little matter of the earthquake that had rocked the region on January 17, 1994. Aftershocks were still being felt regularly and traffic in the city, always awful to begin with, was even worse than usual. All of that caused a few players to skip L.A., but not many. Most players showed up because it was Riviera, because they wanted to see the new greens for themselves no matter how bad they might be, and because most players, once they commit to playing the West Coast, want to play at least two or three weeks in a row.

One player who wouldn't think for a second about skipping L.A. was John Cook. For most of his career, the West Coast had been Cook's time to cook. In 1992, his best year on tour, he had started the season with wins in Hawaii and at the Hope and never looked back, going on to win more than $1 million.

The West Coast was also home. He and his wife, Jan, and their three children lived in Mission Hills, a few miles from the four golf courses where the Hope was played, a two-and-a-half-hour drive from L.A., and less than two hours from the last stop on the western swing in San Diego.

That was important to Cook, who, like a lot of tour players in their thirties and forties, found himself fighting a constant battle between his need to be at home so he could be the kind of father he wanted to be and the need to be on the road so he could be the kind of golfer he wanted to be.

This is a problem that occurs more often in golf than in any other professional sport for the simple reason that golfers peak later than other athletes and often continue to play competitively until well into their forties. Athletes in other sports are often near or at the end of their playing careers by the time they start a family. What's more, team sports have off-seasons of four to six months *and* home games. Golfers and tennis players have virtually no home games and almost no off-season. Of course most tennis players are retired at the age when most golfers start to make serious money.

Tom Kite, who had a thirteen-year-old daughter and twin eight-year-old boys, explained the golfer's dilemma most succinctly: "When you're home, you feel like you ought to be on tour; when you're on tour, you feel like you're missing something important at home."

Ask any golfer with a family about the toughest part of the job and, without exception, you will get the same answer: walking out the front door. "It was tough enough when they were babies," Paul Azinger said late in 1993. "Now they wrap themselves around my legs and say, 'Daddy, please don't go, please don't go.' How brutal is that?"

Very. No one felt the tug of home more acutely than Cook, whose children were twelve, ten, and seven at the start of the new year. Those are ages when it becomes very difficult to take kids on the road, even if you have the money to afford it. They have school, they have friends, they have activities going on all summer long. They miss their dad, but they also don't want to miss out on their friends.

Cook, who grew up with a father who traveled often, was one of the few players on tour who actually talked about the possibility of quitting at forty. He was thirty-six, he had achieved a lot in the sport, and if he walked away to be with his kids during their teenage years, he didn't think he would lose his mind being away from the tour.

Then again, he wasn't sure. After all, golf had been at the core of his existence for as long as he could remember. On his first date with Jan — they had been high school sweethearts — he took her to a golf match he was playing in. "I shot thirty-four, we won the match, and then we went to eat," he remembered. Jan still isn't quite sure why she hung around that long. Then again, she's still hanging around waiting for John to finish playing so they can go eat and it is now twenty years later.

Cook was one of a handful of players on tour who seemed to have been bred to play golf. His father, Jim, was a good player and, after giving up a career in coaching, he had run the World Series of Golf in Akron for several years. When John was seven, the family moved to California, where he played all sports throughout high school, although it was apparent the one he had the most talent for was golf. In high school, Cook met Ken Venturi, and the 1964 U.S. Open champion took him under his wing. The relationship still exists today. When Cook is having trouble with his swing, he still goes to see Venturi.

Cook chose Ohio State over a bevy of collegiate suitors and won the U.S. Amateur title in 1978, just before the start of his junior year. He returned to school, picked up a copy of the *Cleveland Plain Dealer,* and saw his picture with a caption that said, "The Next Nicklaus?"

Cook wasn't the first or last person saddled with that label. He found it flattering and amusing and never really let it bother him. He decided to turn pro at the end of his junior year and was one of those fortunate few to clear the Q-School hurdle the first time and never have to go back.

He won a tournament in his second year out and seemed on his way to stardom. Then, in 1982, he began to feel pain in his right wrist. He had it checked and was told it was probably tendinitis. Rest would clear the problem up. It did, and he won twice more in 1983. But the pain came back. Rest would help; then it would come back again.

Every doctor Cook saw told him the same thing: rest will make you better. "I played seven years waiting for my wrist to start hurting again," he said. In those days, there was no protection for an injured player on tour. If you were hurt, you had to play your way back from square one like anyone else.

In 1989, with the pain worse than ever, Cook saw a hand specialist who did an MRI — still a new procedure back then — on his hand and wrist. The MRI turned up a small break that X rays had been missing for years. "When I would rest, the break would heal, but as soon as I started playing again, I would rebreak it," Cook said.

He had surgery that spring and sat out six months, under orders not to pick up a golf club until his right wrist was stronger than his left. When he came back late that fall — by then the tour had created medical exemptions for injured players — the pain was gone and didn't come back. "I went from wondering if my career was over, to having a new life in the game," he said. "It was an unbelievable feeling. After that, it was a matter of rebuilding my game."

His breakthrough year came in 1992, when he started out hot and stayed that way almost the entire year. Like Azinger in 1987, he should have won the British Open. And, like Azinger in 1987, he handed the tournament to Nick Faldo on the last two holes at Muirfield.

Cook had come from way behind on the last day and had a two-shot lead on Faldo when he played the par-five 17th. Faldo, two groups behind him, was struggling, having blown what had once been a four-shot lead. Cook hit two perfect shots onto the 17th green and almost holed the eagle putt. If that putt had dropped, he could have waltzed down 18 to victory. Even so, he had only two feet left for the birdie that would give him a three-shot lead.

Somehow, he missed. To this day, Cook isn't certain what happened, other than the fact that he got a little bit nervous over the putt and didn't hit it solidly. At almost the same moment, Faldo birdied the 15th. With his lead down to one, Cook pushed a two-iron second shot at 18 and made bogey. Faldo, given a second life, birdied 17 to get even and, thanks to Cook's bogey, needed only to par 18 to win — which he did.

Cook was devastated. He had committed to playing in the New England Classic the next week, so he flew straight there, still brooding about what had happened. He walked into the locker room Tuesday morning, turned the corner, and bumped smack into Paul Azinger.

Azinger grabbed him by the arm, sat him down in a corner, and told him exactly how he was going to feel about what had happened during the next few days, weeks, and months. "Running into Paul that way was the best thing that could possibly have happened to me," Cook said. "It reminded me that I wasn't the only guy in the world by any means who had lost a chance to win a major. It still hurt, but I knew it was a hurt I could deal with."

Three weeks later, Cook made another run at a major, finishing tied for second behind Nick Price at the PGA. That wasn't as disappointing, though, because it had been Price's tournament to lose. The British had been *his*.

Cook began 1993 thinking he would build on what he had done in 1992. Only he didn't. His success had made him one of the most visible players on tour. Everywhere he went he was in demand, and that wasn't easy for him. He had also added some overseas events to his schedule because the money was too good to turn down.

By the time he missed the cut in the British Open a year after he had almost won it, Cook was a burnout case. He was drained, physically and mentally, and he felt out of sorts with his life.

"I just wasn't used to the attention," he said. "I'm the kind of guy who likes to come to the golf course, play my round, and slip away unnoticed. But I couldn't do that. Even if I didn't play well, I still had to talk to people, because they wanted to know why I wasn't playing as well as I had in 1992. Hell, if I knew the answer, why would I be playing this way?"

For the first time in his life, Cook began to see and hear people criticizing him. He had become a disappointment, a one-year flash who couldn't sustain his good play, a guy who *almost* won the British Open and then disappeared. The criticism stung, especially since it was something brand-new. Cook had never had a chance to develop anything resembling a hard shell because he hadn't had to. Now, all of a sudden, he was reading that he was going to be the weak link on the Ryder Cup team.

That really hurt. The thing Cook was most excited about at the start of 1993 was the prospect of making his first Ryder Cup team. When his place on the team appeared to be in a little bit of jeopardy in July, he dug down and played his best golf of the year, finishing strong at New England and Memphis, then finishing sixth in the PGA to clinch his spot by a wide margin.

Even then, he still heard whispers that Watson wished someone else had qualified. After the PGA he was so fried he probably should have taken a break. But he had made commitments, so he played. A mistake. At the World Series of Golf he suffered the humiliation of being disqualified along with Australian Peter Senior when they hit one another's balls early in the third round and didn't realize what had happened until it was too late to go back and replay the shots. When they reported what had happened at the end of the round, the rules officials shook their heads sadly and said, "Sorry, guys, we've got no choice."

Two weeks later, Cook made a last-second decision to play in the Canadian Open, thinking he needed one more warm-up tournament before the Ryder Cup. The weather was awful and Cook shot 81 the first day, the worst round he could ever remember shooting as a pro. He thought about withdrawing, decided against it because he had never done *that* in his life, then found himself in the middle of a rain delay Friday afternoon.

"Get out of here," Fred Couples told him in the clubhouse. "You did the right thing, you showed up to play today. Don't miss your plane. Get your clubs and get out of here."

Cook knew Couples was right. He bolted. Still, he hated doing it. "My last two tournaments before the Ryder Cup and I produce a DQ and a WD," he said. "Nice preparation."

Then came the White House flap that Cook was smack in the middle of, after he publicly blasted President Clinton's economic plan. "I'm a ditto-head," he said months later, referring to the term for conservative bigmouth Rush Limbaugh's most loyal fans. "I said

I didn't think it was right to tax the most productive people more for being productive," Cook said. "I'm not sorry for feeling that way, but I probably would have been smarter to keep my mouth shut."

Once again, Cook found himself getting ripped in print. By the time he arrived at the Belfry, he was tired and frustrated and his golf swing wasn't in very good shape either. He wasn't surprised when Watson sat him out on Friday, but he was shocked when he still didn't crack the lineup on Saturday morning. His wife and oldest daughter had made the trip along with his parents, his sister and her husband, and several friends. And they were doing the same thing he was doing: spectating.

Cook hated every minute of it. Here he was at the pinnacle of his career and all he wanted to do was go home and climb under a rock. He felt humiliated. When his chance finally came Saturday afternoon, he and Chip Beck emerged as heroes with their victory over Nick Faldo and Colin Montgomerie. That salved a lot of wounds, but the loss in singles to Joakim Haeggman the next day left Cook with an empty feeling about the whole experience even though he kept hearing Watson and the others say that the match he and Beck had won had been the key to the victory.

"That part was wonderful," he said. "And I knew we had contributed to the win and I was glad to be part of the whole thing. But it bothered me to lose to Haeggman because I should have won the match on the fourteenth hole. When we left the team in New York and got on the plane to fly home, people kept coming up during the flight and saying, 'Great job' and 'Thanks for bringing the cup home.' I loved all of that but I still felt odd about it, like I had been there, but I hadn't been there."

Cook finally took a break after the Ryder Cup and came back to finish the year well. He dropped precipitously on the money list — from fourth with just over $1 million to forty-fifth with $342,321 — but he felt as if he had learned a lot of lessons during the year and that he had found his game again in the fall. He was excited about 1994, so excited that he decided to add Phoenix, a tournament he normally skipped, to his schedule. He hadn't played in all the made-for-TV stuff at the end of the year the way he had in 1992, so he was rested, fresh, and eager when he flew to Hawaii to start the year.

"I felt great about my game," he said. "The one good thing about not having such a good year in 1993 was that I knew I could go back to my old routines, just play golf, and go home. I was really looking forward to it."

The problem was he was going home too soon each week. He missed the cut in Hawaii. Disappointing, especially on a course where he had won before, but it was just one week. Then he missed the cut in Phoenix. Aggravating. Probably should have stuck to the original plan and not played. Then he missed the cut at Pebble. Three tournaments, three misses. He had played seven rounds of golf in 1994 and hadn't broken 70 yet.

What the hell was going on here? "I'm not hitting the ball badly," he kept saying to Jan and his friends. "I just can't score to save my life."

By the time he arrived in Los Angeles, Cook was in a sour mood. In addition to the troubles with his golf, his best friend's father had been in a serious automobile accident over the weekend. He was upset about that and wondering where his game had gone. Then, on Thursday, things finally got a little better. He shot 70, one under par. It wasn't a brilliant round, especially with Tom Purtzer leading the tournament after a 64, but it was a start. He had been paired for the first two days of the tournament with Mark O'Meara, his closest friend on tour, and with Mike Hulbert, one of the best-liked players in the game, someone who was as easy and comfortable to play with as anyone you could draw.

"As good a pairing as you could possibly hope for," Cook said.

Friday dawned sunny but cold, with a blustery, gusting wind that was so strong that the walking scorers who carried the little boards showing player scores were ordered not to carry the boards because they would be blown over in the wind.

Riviera was playing considerably tougher than it had under perfect conditions on Thursday, but that was still no reason to shoot 40 on the first nine holes of the day. That, though, was what Cook shot. By the time he three-putted the 18th for his fourth bogey of the morning, his face was contorted with anger and frustration, a look that he had worn so often in the recent past that Eric Hilcoff, the tour's on-site travel agent, had started calling him "Mr. Happy."

"I can't even argue with him," Cook said. "It's been a while since I've felt real happy out here."

From a distance, John Cook looks like the most mild-mannered man in golf. He has long, straight blond hair, blue eyes, and a quick, easy smile. He is soft-spoken, always friendly and polite, the classic golf gentleman. In the 1980s, when media critics of the tour started claiming that all the pros were faceless clones, they probably had Cook in mind.

But they were wrong about Cook, the way they were (and are) wrong when they claim that the tour is made up of a group of bland guys who all have the same perfect golf swing. If they all had the same perfect golf swing, no one would ever have a bad round. The truth is, Cook was going through the same kind of stretch that almost everyone on tour goes through.

Losing the edge that makes you a hot player is a whole lot easier than finding it. More than any other sport, golf is a constant battle with yourself because *you* are the only one who controls your performance. That means there is no rationalizing failure. Sure, golfers can crank out excuses as fast as anyone, whether they are about spike marks, divots, unraked traps, sudden gusts of wind, or faulty equipment. At the end of his first year on tour, Paul Goydos decided there was one sure way to tell the difference between a star and a nonstar. "The star is the guy who, whenever he misses a putt, the first thing he does is tap down a spike mark that was in his line," Goydos said, laughing. "It's never *his* fault."

But when golfers go home at night — stars and nonstars alike — and look in the mirror, they know it wasn't the spike mark or the divot or the equipment. After his final round in the PGA last year, someone asked Nick Faldo if his failure to win a major in 1994 was a problem with his putter.

"The problem," Faldo said, "was with the puttee."

Slumps are a part of all sports, but in golf there are enough examples of players going from the top or near the top to completely out of the game in almost no time that any player going through tough times worries that he is about to become one of those guys whose name is whispered around the locker room in the way people talk about the recently dead.

Wayne Grady. Ian Baker-Finch. Mike Donald. Kenny Knox. Brian Tennyson. Grady almost won the British Open in 1989, did win the PGA in 1990, and in 1993 and 1994 virtually disappeared from sight. Baker-Finch won the British in 1991 and was, without question, one of the ten best players in the game. Three years later, he couldn't break par. Donald went from almost winning the U.S. Open to Q-School in less than two years.

Knox had won three times on tour and had played in the last group at the 1991 PGA with John Daly, finishing third. He won $423,025 that year. Two years later, he made two cuts all year in twenty-two tournaments and won a grand total of $3,630. His stroke average of 74.74 per round was more than a stroke higher than David DeLong's, whose 73.53 ranked 189th and last among those who played at least fifty rounds for the year. Knox played forty-eight rounds and was thus mercifully absent from the official rankings.

Tennyson won $443,508 in 1990 at the age of twenty-eight with *eight* top-ten finishes. Three years later, he wasn't even on tour.

There were other examples. Curtis Strange hadn't won on tour since his second consecutive U.S. Open title in 1989. Greg Norman, probably the most consistent player in the game in the last ten years, had gone more than two years without winning, 1990 to 1992.

It happened to everybody somewhere, sometime. The question was, would you bounce back and how long would it take? Most good players would turn their game around. But until the turnaround comes, the question lingers. When Billy Andrade hit the worst slump of his career in 1993, missing seven straight cuts, his wife, Jody, remembered the phrase she had heard another player's wife use to describe what she was feeling: "the silent terror."

"There are enough examples of players who don't come back that everyone wonders," Jody said. "But it isn't something you talk about. He knows he's a good player, you know he's a good player, but deep down, until he starts to play well again, you both worry."

Billy Andrade broke out of his skid at the Southern Open in 1993, finishing second after losing in a playoff to John Inman. "It was a relief," he said later. "I kept telling myself that I was too good a player to be playing the way I was, yet every week I would go out there and, before I knew it, I was beating myself up again."

By the time John Cook reached the first tee at Riviera on that cold Friday morning in February, he had beaten himself to a pulp. He was now three over par for the tournament and figured he needed to play his second nine holes of the day in no worse than one under if he wanted to make the cut.

He missed a five-foot birdie putt at number one, then proceeded to par the next four holes. He was still thinking he needed one birdie when he reached the sixth hole. The sixth at Riviera is a narrow par-three, a pretty, tree-lined hole. The wind was swirling when the players reached the tee, and O'Meara, hitting first, took a long time before deciding on a seven-iron.

He had 190 yards to the flag and figured the swirling wind was, at that moment, behind him. He was right. The ball took off like a rocket and sailed over the green on one bounce. Seeing that, Cook decided to hit a seven himself and ease up just a little.

And then the wind died. Cook knew it as soon as the ball left his club. "Where the hell is the wind!" he screamed in anguish as the ball began to descend well short of the green. He slammed the club into the ground as he walked off the tee, knowing he now had to figure out a way to get up and down for par and then make a birdie on one of the last three holes.

When he arrived at his ball, more bad news awaited. The ball had come up even shorter than he had thought, just past the first bunker, leaving him a long, tough chip. "What!" he screamed at everyone and no one. "How could the wind die like that? Hit a seven-iron 190 yards — right!"

He stood there shaking his head for several seconds, then played his chip 10 feet past the cup. He stood off to the side talking to himself while O'Meara and Hulbert played their shots. His par putt looked for a moment like it might dive in the hole, but it trickled a foot past. Cook's face turned red. He walked up to his ball and carelessly backhanded it into the hole.

Only he missed. Cook had committed golf's mortal sin: he had stopped trying. Every golfer does it at some point in his career. The best ones do it once and never do it again. Cook had never done it before in his life. He was so shocked at his behavior that all the anger seemed to run right out of him. He played the last three holes in complete silence, making routine pars to finish with a 77.

He had never in his life felt like this on a golf course. Helpless. Humiliated. Embarrassed by both his play and his behavior. When a neighbor from back home walked up to commiserate, Cook couldn't even make small talk. "I'm really sorry," he said. "I've just got to get out of here."

It was a wise decision. Because if Cook had been around late that afternoon he would have learned that the wind and cold had sent scores soaring in the afternoon. The cut had not come at two over, as he had thought, or even three or four. The cut was five. He had finished at six. Had he not backhanded the one-foot bogey putt at the sixth, he would have played on the weekend.

John Cook had hit bottom. He hoped.

Jeff Sluman could relate to a lot of what John Cook was feeling. He arrived in Los Angeles having played in the same three tournaments Cook had played with results that were depressingly similar. Sluman had made a cut — in Hawaii — where 70–71 had put him right on the number and 72–70 on the weekend had left him tied for fiftieth place, earning him the princely sum of $2,818.67.

"I'm saving the sixty-seven cents," he said. "The way things are going, I may need it."

Hawaii had been the highlight so far since he hadn't even come close to making the cut in either Phoenix or Pebble Beach. Pebble was the worst of all: 77–75–79. He missed the cut by fourteen shots.

Sluman knew he was a better player than that. Loads better. At thirty-six, he was one of the most respected and best-liked players on tour. He was a bulldog competitor, who had all the shots and had proven his toughness in 1988 when he produced a 65 in the final round of the PGA to win his first major and his first tournament.

For the next four years Sluman was good, very good, and at times brilliant. He was one of those players who seemed to save his best golf for the best golf courses and the most important tournaments. In 1992, he had finished fourth at the Masters, second at the U.S. Open, and fourteenth ($729,027) on the money list. He made tons of money, both on tour and overseas. He married a beautiful, brilliant young doctor, was elected to the tour's policy board by his peers, began building a dream house in Hinsdale, Illinois, and living happily ever after.

Only it wasn't quite that simple. Sluman is one of those people who has a knack for making life look easy when it isn't. The fact that he had grown up to become one of the best golfers in the world was, in itself, a remarkable story. He grew up in Rochester, New York, the youngest of three sons. Like a lot of people in Rochester, his father worked at the Kodak factory, often on the overnight shift. "Trick work," they called it, since the hours were never the same from week to week. The good news about those hours was that he often had afternoons free to play golf with his sons.

Jeff was a classic little brother, always working to keep up with the big boys. By the time he was ten, he was precociously successful at both bowling and golf.

It was at the age of ten that he was diagnosed as having a rare kidney disease known as nephritis. He had to take a steroid called prednisone for the next eight years to keep the disease under control. Although the prednisone worked, it also prevented him from growing. As a high school freshman he was 4-foot-6. It wasn't until he was in college and off the prednisone that he finally caught up with his peers — or at least almost caught up with them — in stature.

A bad kidney or being forced to take a steroid or a lack of height wasn't about to stop Sluman. He was breaking 80 in golf by the time he was twelve and was a scratch player in high school. When he wasn't recruited by anyone to play golf, he enrolled at Monroe Community College in Rochester and kept working on his game. After a year there, he transferred to Tennessee Tech, where he was on the golf team.

That was the good news. The bad news was that because of a lack of dorm space, he had to sleep in the back of the pro shop at the course where the team played. That didn't seem too awful until the pipes froze halfway through the winter and trips to the bathroom meant a trip outdoors, no matter how cold it might be in the open-air lavatory.

Still, he worked at his game. And when a friend told him that summer that he was going to Florida State, Sluman decided to go with him. He had no scholarship, hadn't applied to school there, and hadn't been invited down by anyone. "But at least I knew the weather would be warm," he said. "I've never heard of any pipes freezing in Tallahassee."

The pipes didn't freeze, and Sluman somehow talked himself into school and onto the team. If there is one thing Sluman can do as well as play golf, it is talk. He isn't a rapid-fire talker like his buddy Mike Hulbert, who can turn the answer to "how are you today" into twenty minutes on any subject from the weather to the economy. But he has about him a direct manner that makes people believe he is 100 percent sincere about everything he says.

On serious matters, he is. But there is always a joke lurking with Sluman. When Florida State's arch-rival Florida was upset by Auburn to lose the number one ranking in football 1994, Sluman called Dudley Hart — as fanatic about Florida as Sluman is about Florida State — and left a message from Florida coach Steve Spurrier apologizing for the loss.

"I threw my voice," Sluman said. "He'll never know who it was."

Want to bet?

By the time Sluman got to Florida State, he was off the medication and was all of 5-foot-7 and 140 pounds. But he could hit a golf ball a long way and he could hit it a long way straight. He graduated with a degree in finance and decided to give the tour a shot for a few years. If it didn't work out, he could always go back to business school.

He still hasn't gone back. The first three years were a struggle. He got his card in 1983, lost it and went to the mini-tours for a year, then got back on tour again in 1985. He decided that if he ended up back at school at the end of that year he was going to have to seriously consider another line of work. But he broke through in 1985, winning $100,523. After that, he just kept getting better and better.

In 1987, he should have won the Players Championship. He was lining up an eight-foot birdie putt that would have given him a playoff victory over Sandy Lyle when a fan jumped into the water that fronted the green. Sluman had to back off and wait for officials to collect the young man — a former Florida State cheerleader — and remove him. Shaken, he missed the putt. Lyle won the playoff one hole later.

Sluman was upset about what had happened, especially when he found out later that the swimmer had dived into the water earlier in the day, had been given a warning, and was allowed to stay on the premises. Eventually, though, Sluman found a way to laugh about what had happened. "I always tell people that the guy picked one hell of a time in *my* life to have an identity crisis," he said with a wry smile.

That is Sluman's way. He takes golf very seriously but doesn't take himself too seriously. Perhaps because it has never come easily to him, he doesn't seem to back off when the pressure is greatest.

"I still remember playing the last nine holes at the Players that year and starting to feel nervous," he said. "But then I reminded myself that this was what I had been working for my whole life. I always wanted to play the last nine holes of a big tournament and be in contention with great players around me. Well, there I was in the last group, playing with Norman and Lyle. If I couldn't enjoy *that,* what was the point of being out here? I just told myself to have fun."

Although Sluman comes across as quiet and shy — "I would describe myself as vanilla," he says — he is probably as good at having fun as anyone on tour. Having fun is one of the tour's most underrated skills. Sluman does it.

He leads the tour in inventing nicknames. Billy Andrade is "Chachi," in honor of the dark-haired, baby-faced *Happy Days* character. Davis Love is "Slick," since he is anything but. Steve Pate, the consensus choice for the tour's worst temper, is "Volcano," and Dudley Hart, probably a close second to Pate, is "Volcano Junior." Steve Lowery is "Yogi" because he looks just like Jellystone Park's famous bear.

Sluman is the guy who goes to the range to hit one bucket of balls and needs three hours to get it done. He knows everyone and everyone knows him. If there is a joke to be told or a story to be recounted, Sluman is right in the middle of it. Late afternoon on the range is the tour's version of happy hour at Cheers, and Sluman is the tour's miniature Norm. When he walks on the range, people do everything but stop and yell, "Slu!"

Most of the time, Sluman travels alone, which is both lonely and grueling. Linda is an oncologist, which makes it impossible for her to up and leave for two or three weeks at a time in order to travel with Jeff. That fact has always made working at the relationship that much more important.

"It's never been easy," Sluman said. "When we first started dating [in 1987] she was in medical school, and it was very hard because I couldn't just invite her to come out and spend time with me on tour. I had to get to Chicago to see her when she had free time, which wasn't very often, and then she would try to sneak away for weekends when she could."

They had met at the golf course when Linda joined a group of friends on a day off from school to go to the Western Open for an afternoon. Sluman was on the putting green when he spotted her. "Now there's someone I'd like to meet," he said to Russ Cochran, who was also putting at the time.

"So, why don't you go over and introduce yourself?" Cochran said.

Sluman shook his head. He was too shy. Cochran wasn't. He walked across the green and told Linda that the little blond guy on the other side of the green would really like to meet her. Linda thought that would be just fine, so Cochran walked her over to Jeff and the rest is history. They were married in July 1992 in Las Vegas. "If it was good enough for Michael Jordan, it was good enough for me," Sluman said of the setting.

Later that year they bought an old house in Hinsdale and decided to renovate it. That was fun, exciting, and aggravating. It also meant that they spent most of 1993 living out of a suitcase at Linda's parents' house while the work on their house was being done.

Sluman says that had nothing to do with his problems in 1993. Neither did the fact that he was spending as much time dealing with policy board politics as he was or the fact that he had a brief health scare — that turned out to be just a scare — early in the year. Neither did the fact that he had encouraged his caddy, Tony Navarro, to leave him at the end of 1992 to work for Greg Norman. Navarro didn't really want to leave, but Sluman pushed him out the door because he thought it would be unfair to Tony not to push him in the direction of the kind of money he could make working for Norman.

Any or all of those things might explain why Sluman's earnings dropped by more than $550,000. Sluman says none of them was a factor. "I just didn't play very well," he said. "I didn't hit the ball very well and I didn't think very well on the golf course. That's a bad combination. I remember in 1988, when I missed two cuts all year, I never seemed to hit a bad shot. And, even when I did, I knew exactly what to do to get out of trouble. In 1993, I always seemed to take a bad situation and make it worse."

It is probably not a coincidence that Sluman's two worst years on tour — 1989 and 1993 — followed his two best — 1988 and 1992. At the end of both those big years, he had offers to play all over the world. This is the successful golfer's constant dilemma: how much do you cash in when you have success? If you overdo it, chasing the short-run cash, you may ultimately damage your long-run potential. The list of golfers who have been hurt by overplaying and overtraveling is almost endless. IMG, the largest and most powerful of golf's management companies, has its tentacles in so many places around the world that it can get a good player work — and guaranteed money — almost any time he wants it.

So many players have gone this route and been damaged by it that players on tour often refer to the malady as "being IMG'd" into mediocrity. That's a little unfair, since IMG can't force players to overplay and other management companies send their players overseas whenever they can too. But the point is well taken. Agents, no matter who they work for, rarely worry about how much money a player might make ten years in the future. They worry about the here and the now and the offers that are on the table.

A perfect example is Lee Janzen, the 1993 U.S. Open champion. After his stunning victory, Janzen was transformed from an up-and-coming young player into an instant star. By the time his agent, Ken Kennerly, got back to his office the week after Janzen's win, he had a stack of offers that seemed to take up every inch of space on his desk.

If Janzen had accepted everything offered him, he could probably have made $5 million in the ensuing twelve months and would have spent the rest of his days happily residing in a sanitorium somewhere. "Your job as an agent is to present everything offered to your client," Kennerly said. "You also have an obligation to tell him what you think is worth the effort and what isn't. But you also know that when your bosses sit down to analyze your work at the end of the year that they probably won't be too thrilled if you tell them you recommended that a client turn down offers that could have been worth $500,000 to the company's bottom line."

The smart agent, the experienced agent, knows you don't overrun your horse. Most aren't that smart or experienced. Sluman overplayed at the end of 1988 and again in 1992.

"No doubt about it," he said. "I dead overplayed in '88 and, even though I tried to be more disciplined in '92, I still played too much. The dropoffs those year-afters probably weren't a coincidence."

Sluman's life changed forever in 1988, when he shot 65 on the last day of the PGA, caught and passed Paul Azinger, and won the title. Suddenly, he had gone from being a nonwinner on tour to being the winner of a major. He played a practice round with Tom Watson two weeks later at the World Series of Golf. "You know, you probably don't even realize what you've accomplished," Watson said to him. "Heck, I'd trade you a couple of my [five] British Opens to have one PGA."

Sluman thought that was very nice, but while winning the PGA was lots of fun, well, how big a deal could one golf tournament really be? He found out a couple of days later when he was introduced on the first tee.

"Now on the tee," Sluman heard the master of ceremonies say, "the new PGA champion, Mr. Jeff Sluman!" As the applause washed over him, Sluman understood what Watson was talking about. What he had done really *was* a big deal. He stepped on the tee, smiled at the crowd, took a casual practice swing, and stood over the ball thinking, Boy, you better not blow this, Mr. PGA champion.

He took the club back, swung — smoothly he thought — and watched in horror as the ball trickled off the tee and bounced and rolled a grand total of 30 yards down the fairway. "There was this *oooooohhh* sound from the crowd," Sluman said, "as if they couldn't believe what they had just seen. I mean, I'm not exaggerating when I say the ball went thirty yards. I don't think I've ever hit a shot like that in my life. I hit my second shot on the run, just so I could get out of there as fast as I could."

Overplaying and injuries — a torn shoulder muscle in March, an emergency appendectomy in May — ruined 1989, but he came back to steadily improve the next three years, culminating in his superb 1992. Still, for all his good play, Sluman hadn't won again, and when he struggled in 1993, he began to doubt himself. He told friends, half joking but half serious, that he was worried that he was going to go down in history as the worst player to win a major since Orville Moody, the ex-army sergeant who had won the U.S. Open in 1969 and then hadn't won another tournament until he reached the senior tour.

He missed Linda, who wanted to be out more but just couldn't. Every night he would call home and she would answer the phone sounding upbeat, just knowing that he was going to have good news about his day. "And then I would have to say, 'Honey, I shot seventy-five again,' " he said. "That was the hardest part because I knew how much she believed in me and how much she wanted me to play well and it seemed like I was always calling home to tell her I'd shot another seventy-five — unless it was seventy-six."

Sluman didn't want to coast through life on tour. Having won the PGA, he was exempt through 1998. He had made a lot of money and invested well. Even in a bad year, he was still at an income level that made him subject to the Clinton surcharge. That was not, however, Sluman's goal in life. He wanted to play well, to compete, to have a chance to win. Even though he didn't win in 1992, he had chances to win and he played very well at times. That wasn't the case in 1993, and he knew he wasn't going to be happy unless he turned that around.

"My goal out here is to play as hard as I can every day, no matter what I'm shooting, and to play well," he said. "I am not going to become one of these guys who starts thinking about what plane he's going to catch when things aren't going well on Friday. I can't stand guys who do that out here. I still remember hearing the story about Nicklaus playing the last hole on a Friday with no chance to make the cut. He got up over his drive and heard a noise. So he backed off. He went through his routine again, played the hole as hard as he could, and made birdie.

"He still missed the cut by a mile, but that's not the point. If the greatest player in history still works at it on one of the rare occasions when he's going to miss a cut, who am I not to follow that example?"

Sluman was determined not to spend much time slamming his trunk on Fridays in 1994. The house — which was only slightly larger than Wrigley Field — was finally finished as the year ended and Sluman hired Jim Walker to caddy for him. Walker is one of the tour's best-liked and most respected caddies, an outgoing, upbeat man who knows the game and knows the players. Almost as important, he was a Florida State alum, just like Sluman, meaning they could spend hours boring everyone else on tour with their analysis of Seminole football.

Sluman wasn't just an alumnus, he was a fanatic. A couple of years earlier, when he had been in Japan for a tournament on the weekend of the Miami–Florida State game, he had called his father and had him put the telephone next to the TV set so he could listen to the entire game through the phone. The call cost about ninety zillion yen. When Florida State's last-second field goal sailed wide right, his father picked up the phone and said, "Doesn't look good, Jeff."

The phone line was dead. Sluman was so devastated he had slammed the phone without saying goodbye to his father.

Walker and Sluman were a perfect match. They enjoyed one another's company, and Walker wasn't the least bit disturbed by the long hours Sluman wanted to put in on the range. In fact, he was delighted. "I've watched the guy for years," he said in January. "And I know he can play. It's just a matter of him believing that again."

Sluman was having trouble believing very much of anything when he arrived in Los Angeles. Pebble Beach had been a disaster, and thoughts of Brian Tennyson and Kenny Knox were occasionally sneaking into his thoughts. Thursday was a strange day for Sluman. He bogeyed two of the easier holes on the course — 10 and 17 — then birdied one of the toughest — 18 — to finish at 72. But there was a lot more to the back nine than birdies and bogeys.

As Sluman and his playing partners, David Toms and Dick Mast, walked onto the 12th green, they saw an Emergency Medical Systems cart racing past them with two paramedics hard at work on someone who appeared to be in cardiac arrest. One of them was pounding on the victim's chest. "Jesus," Sluman said to Walker, "that doesn't look very good, does it?"

Later, when they finished the round, Sluman and Walker checked with the EMS unit to find out if the man was all right. They were told he had died on the way to the hospital.

Shaken by what he had seen on the 12th, Sluman snapped his drive into the trees on 13. He pitched out and hit a gorgeous chip to three feet. The 13th at Riviera sits right beneath a cliff that has several huge old houses on it. Some of the houses had smashed windows, battered roofs, and many other signs of serious earthquake damage.

Sluman shook his head. "Here I am, walking along moaning and groaning about my golf game and I see someone go by me who may be dying and then I see *this*" — he pointed at the houses — "and I start to wonder about my priorities. I mean, should I be here, trying to hit a golf ball, or should I be in Somalia? Or Bosnia? Or saving the gorillas? Sometimes, I really wonder."

Maybe seeing firsthand just how good his own life was helped Sluman that week. Or maybe it was just the hours on the range paying off. For the first time in a long time, he began to feel his swing coming back. He even made some putts. By Sunday night he had played four solid, unspectacular rounds and finished in a tie for 15th — worth $16,000. It was his best finish since early in 1993.

More important, it gave him some sense that the light at the end of the tunnel might be something other than a train. "At least now, I'm starting to hit the ball better on the range," he said. "For a while, I couldn't even hit it well *there*. I've still got a lot of scratching and clawing to do before I get where I need to be, but I feel like there's some hope now."

When the silent terror begins to creep in, hope is a giant step. John Cook left Los Angeles searching for it. Jeff Sluman didn't think he had found it just yet, but he did believe he had some idea of where it was. That was progress.

By the weekend, John Cook was home, Jeff Sluman was playing better, and Los Angeles had become a two-man tournament between Fred Couples and Corey Pavin.

That sort of matchup was ideal for television because Couples was one of *the* names in the game and Pavin was a member of the second echelon, a very good, highly respected player who was a notch below real stardom.

Beyond that, the contrasts between the two players were about as striking as you could find anywhere in the sport. Couples was the handsome, languid, reluctant superstar with the smooth, easy swing and the little-boy-lost smile that sent the groupies scurrying after him as he eased his way around the golf course.

Pavin made it look as hard as Couples made it look easy. He had a funny-looking swing, a scruffy mustache, and a demeanor that suggested he would just as soon lay you out on the green with his putter as let you beat him. He had played his college golf in Los Angeles — at UCLA — and had been referred to in print as "the Gritty Little Bruin" so many times that some people on tour thought his full name was Corey Gritty Little Bruin Pavin.

The GLB also had another title — best player never to have won a major — and like those who had come before him in that role, he carried a little chip on his shoulder to go along with the title. "I don't think I have to apologize to anyone for my record," he said.

No one was asking him to apologize. But when you reach a certain level in the game, the "major question" is going to come up. Tom Kite had faced it for years, to the point where he had become so frustrated that for a while he referred to the four Grand Slam events as "the so-called majors." Paul Azinger had walked into the interview room at Westchester in 1993, still walking on air after blasting in from a bunker on the last hole to win the Memorial two days earlier, and was immediately asked, "So Paul, what do you think you have to do now to win a major?"

"All the joy I felt from winning at Memorial drained right out of me," Azinger said. "It was as if I couldn't escape it no matter what I did."

Whether a player wants to admit it or not, the majors are what make golf — and golfers — special. They are played on great courses, and virtually all of the game's great names build their years around preparing for them. If you want to be thought of as a great player, you have to win at the majors.

"A lot of great players haven't won majors," Greg Norman insisted one night.

He was asked to name one truly great player who had never won a major. He thought for a moment. "Okay then," he said finally, "a lot of *good* players haven't won majors."

That is no doubt true. It is the majors that set the great players apart from the good ones. That doesn't mean that every winner of a major is a great player. It just means that the Sunday leader board at the majors tends to weed out the less than great more often than the leader boards do on other weeks.

The majors are about tradition and pressure and memorable moments. If Tom Watson's chip-in at Pebble Beach had come in the AT&T Pro-Am instead of the U.S. Open, it would have been a terrific shot. Instead, it became a part of the game's history. A part of forever.

The only answer to the major question is to win one. Azinger's win came later that year at the PGA. Kite had done it a year earlier at the U.S. Open and had been so relieved and drained that he cried walking up the 18th fairway. "I waited so long," he said. "For me to have the career I've had [nineteen titles and more than $9 million in prize money] and not win a major would have been brutal, really unfair. I know guys have to talk about who the best player is who hasn't won a major, but why can't they say *yet?* Hasn't won a major yet. That's more fair."

Okay then, Pavin hadn't won a major *yet.* He had been fourth at the British Open in 1993 but had no chance to win in the face of Greg Norman's 64 on the last day. Pavin is the sort of shotmaker who should have a chance on the kind of golf courses where majors are held. Riviera is one of those courses, a past and future PGA site, a course where a player needs imagination to win. Couples had won the tournament in 1990 and 1992.

He and Pavin had remarkably similar records. Both were thirty-four — Couples was forty-three days older — and both had won ten tournaments coming into 1994. The difference was that one of Couples's ten had been the 1992 Masters. That had answered the "major question" for him and had transformed his image from that of a player with great potential, but not enough drive, to that of a great player.

All the attention that had come with being considered the best player in the world had not been easy for Couples. He is warm and funny when he is with friends and shy — very shy — around strangers. When he made the mistake of telling *Sports Illustrated*'s Rick Reilly that he didn't like to answer the telephone at home "because someone might be on the other end," the line was destined to follow him around forever.

Couples was actually quite different from his image. He did love to go to ball games and he did love to sit at home with a clicker in his hands and watch them too. But he had a wry sense of humor that rarely came across in public, and the notion that he didn't care very much about his golf was sheer myth. His frustration at the Ryder Cup had been evidence of that but that wasn't all.

Couples had been unhappy and distracted during most of 1993. He was going through a very messy and public divorce with his wife, Deborah, who had become something of a legend on tour herself after she had literally wrapped herself around Couples at the conclusion of the 1983 Kemper Open. Couples won a five-man playoff there for his first tour victory and here came Deborah Couples, blond hair flying, racing across the green to leap into her husband's arms and wrap her legs around him. The scene was there for all those watching on national television to see and the picture made just about every newspaper in America the next day.

The better Couples played, the more attention Deborah got. Which was fine with him since he didn't want the attention himself. Their final act had been played out at the British Open in 1992 when Fred missed the cut on Friday after Deborah had stayed out all night on Thursday partying. He left the tournament without her and never looked back, although it was costing him plenty to get on with his life without her.

Couples had still managed to win once in 1993 and finished eleventh on the money list — a great year for most, a mediocre one for him. He was now living in Dallas with his girlfriend, Tawnya Dodd, and his friends on tour couldn't remember when he had been so happy. A lot of people were predicting a monster year for Couples, and he had started strong, losing a playoff at La Costa to Phil Mickelson and finishing second behind Norman in a tournament in Thailand.

Los Angeles would become his third second-place finish when Pavin did his GLB routine down the stretch on Sunday. Freddy-mania always seemed to be at its zenith in L.A., but Pavin's local roots kept the crowd from turning completely against him and he made more putts down the stretch to win by two. That put him ahead of Couples in tournament victories, 11–10, but also served as a reminder to the world that there was no doubt about who was now the best player never to have won a major.

8

HOPE SPRINGS ETERNAL?

MOST OF THE PLAYERS headed out of Los Angeles Sunday night, driving east into the desert toward Palm Springs. The Bob Hope — now known as the Hope Chrysler Classic — was the tour's third February stop. That meant a week of perfect weather, easy golf courses, and four days of playing with amateurs.

Life is never perfect.

Except at the four majors and the Players Championship, tour players take part in a Pro-Am every week. Most weeks, the Pro-Am is on Wednesday. Fifty-six players, selected by the sponsor, play in five-somes, each joining four amateurs for 18 holes. Everyone who is asked must play in the Pro-Am. Each amateur antes up anywhere from $2,000 to $5,000, depending on the event, to play. The average Wednesday Pro-Am costs $3,500 to play in, and at that price, sponsors expect the likes of Greg Norman, John Daly, Fred Couples, Nick Price, and anyone else they ask for to show up and play.

The pros look at the Pro-Am as part of the job. Some even enjoy themselves and, as tour staffers point out to rookies at the mandatory seminar they attend the week after Q-School, Pro-Ams can be an excellent place to make business contacts that can be quite beneficial.

Some players actually enjoy Pro-Ams. Paul Goydos found during his rookie year that he was more relaxed playing with amateurs than with pros. "They think everything you do is great," he said. "It's an ego boost."

At Pebble Beach that year, Goydos arrived on the first day, looked on the board to see who his amateur partner was, and saw the name

Donald Trump listed next to his. "Must be another Donald Trump," he said.

It wasn't. When Goydos asked why he, Paul Goydos, tour rookie, would be paired with His Trumpness, he was told, "This way it will be Donald Trump's group. If we put him with a big name, then he would be shoved into the background."

Trump doesn't like background. And he isn't a bad player. He even made a hole in one during the tournament and later told friends that 5,000 people had seen the shot. Goydos figured it was somewhere between 50 and 500, but he didn't mind. "It was fun," he said. "He seemed like a pretty good guy."

Trump even talked to Goydos about doing some kind of sponsorship deal with him but never followed up. A year later, Goydos got a new partner, Jack Olsen, the chairman of the board of Hertz. The two hit it off, and Goydos ended up with a $50,000 deal to wear a Hertz hat and carry a Hertz bag for the rest of the year. All that and a free rental car every week. Trump talked, Olsen produced.

Of course the Hertz hat and bag would cause Goydos some discomfort later in the year after O. J. Simpson's arrest. At the Western Open, one spectator jokingly asked Goydos if he knew where the murder weapon might be. Before Goydos could answer — or not answer — his caddy, Ken McCluskey, turned around and said, "Sure, the knife is in the bag." McCluskey was no longer Goydos's caddy the next week or for the rest of the year. But Goydos missed him, so he forgave him and rehired him at the start of 1995.

Many of the pros become close friends with amateur partners and stay at their houses when they return to the tournament in future years. Tom Kite has written a thank-you note to every one of his amateur partners over the years. Older pros counsel younger pros always to be patient with their amateurs because stories about pros who act out or won't talk to their partners never seem to die. What's more, the money the amateurs ante up, ranging from $400,000 to $1 million, produces a huge chunk of each tournament's revenues.

Several tournaments don't limit the amateurs to Wednesday. Pebble Beach is the most famous of them, the Hope is next. Like his old road partner Crosby, Bob Hope wanted to invite his celebrity pals down to play when he put his name on what had been the Desert Classic in

1960. The Hope is one of two tournaments on tour played over five days (Las Vegas is the other), and the 384 amateurs are divided into three-man teams and paired with the 128 pros for the first four days. On Sunday — the fifth day — the field is cut to the low seventy pros and the amateurs go home. The tournament is played on four different golf courses (until Sunday), and the celebrities in the field are paired with the best-known pros.

The defending champion — Tom Kite in 1994 — always plays the Saturday round on TV with Bob Hope, former President Gerald Ford, and a celeb to be named later. In 1994, for reasons no one ever quite understood, the designated fourth was singer Eddie Van Halen.

A lot of players won't play both Pebble Beach and the Hope. It is just too much hit-and-giggle golf to bear. At Pebble, the golf courses are extremely difficult and set up with the pros in mind. At the Hope, they are relatively easy and wide open, and the rough is cut low to make life easier for the amateurs. Kite had been 35 under par in 1993, meaning he averaged 65 for five rounds. The seventy-two-hole cut was usually somewhere between five under and 10 under, and anyone who couldn't break par didn't need to even think about hanging around until Sunday.

Tuesday is the most relaxed day of the week on tour. Most players arrive either Monday night or sometime Tuesday and usually show up at the course to play a practice round with friends sometime during the day.

Regardless of what happened last week, this is a new beginning. Everyone will start at zero Thursday morning and the guy who won on Sunday may be slamming his trunk on Friday night. There is also the possibility that someone who hasn't played the weekend for months will end up holding an oversized check over his head on Sunday. Hope does spring on tour, if not eternally, certainly every Thursday morning.

Tuesday is also shootout day on tour. The shootouts have become a staple at most tournaments in recent years. It is a way to draw people to the golf course to see something resembling a competition on what is usually just a practice day.

Each week, ten players compete in the shootout for a purse of

$15,000 put up by a sponsor, usually — but not always — Merrill Lynch. One player is eliminated on each hole, either by having the highest score or, in cases where there is a tie, by a shootout. For instance, if three of the ten players are tied for high score at bogey on the first hole, one of the players chooses a shot — a chip, a blast from a bunker, a long putt — and the player who finishes farthest from the hole is eliminated. This goes on until the winner is left standing with a $5,000 check on the ninth green.

Players are invited to play in the shootouts based on where they stand on the money list and their marquee value. Some players say no almost every time they are asked; others almost always say yes. The shootout field at the Hope was a pretty good one: Pavin, John Cook (local hero), 1984 Masters champion Craig Stadler, the effusive and popular Peter Jacobsen, Ryder Cupper Jim Gallagher Jr., up-and-coming youngster Bob Estes — the BPOTWHWAT . . . Y (best player on tour who hadn't won a tournament . . . yet) — solid veterans Dan Forsman and John Huston, and two men who had won the U.S. Open: Scott Simpson and Curtis Strange.

Strange had not won a golf tournament on tour since 1989. He had finished ninety-ninth on the money list in 1992 and sixty-third in 1993. He had seriously considered an offer from ABC to become its top commentator at the end of 1992. He had gone from the world's best player to the invisible man in what seemed like the blink of an eye.

"I'll tell you how low I've been," he said one night. "I've actually had people come up and *congratulate* me on the year I had in '93. I'm sixty-third on the money list and they're telling me, 'Great job.' Are you kidding me?"

They weren't kidding. Strange had been the best player in the game for the second half of the 1980s, a player who won seventeen times on tour and, after wearing the best-player-never-to-have-won-a-major label for three years, shed it emphatically in 1988 and 1989 when he became the first player to win back-to-back U.S. Opens since Ben Hogan. The cover of *Sports Illustrated* the week after his second victory had a picture of Strange over the caption "Move over, Mr. Hogan." If Mr. Hogan was moved by the feat, Strange never heard about it.

A year later, Strange went into the final round of the Open two shots off the lead and shot 75 to finish tied for twenty-first. He drove away from the golf course that day feeling drained and empty. He won a grand total of $48,064 the rest of that year and didn't come close to winning again for the next three years.

And yet, as he stood on the first tee waiting for the shootout to begin, he was easily the best-known player in the group. Strange has always been easy to pick out of a crowd even before his hair turned prematurely gray in his early thirties.

In many ways, the story of the courtship of Sarah and Curtis Strange is like most stories involving Strange. There is a part of the story where Curtis doesn't behave very well. He eventually comes to his senses and manages to put things right because he is bright, charming, funny, and if you look hard enough, a person who cares deeply about the people in his life.

Sarah swears she knew she was going to marry him even before she met him. "I was walking into a Wake Forest basketball game one night and I looked across the court and there was this guy walking down to his seat," she said. "It was as if bells went off in my head. I just *knew* he was the man I was going to marry."

Sarah was a freshman at Salem College at the time. A few weeks later, at a Wake Forest mixer, she came across the young man she had spotted at the basketball game sitting in a corner of the room. She worked her way over to him, started talking to him, and . . .

"The rest was not history," Strange says, picking up the story later. "I almost screwed it up."

Curtis and Sarah dated for the rest of that school year. At the end of the spring semester Sarah asked Curtis if he would escort her that summer at her coming-out party. (This was 1974 and girls from New Bern, North Carolina, still made their debut back then.) Curtis said no. "I have to play golf," he said.

And off he went. He played amateur tournaments around the country all summer, putting in the time and the work that was vital if he wanted to be a pro. He never called; he never wrote. Sarah went home to New Bern and had no trouble finding another escort for her debut. But she missed Curtis and was saddened by the apparent end of the relationship. He missed her too, and he knew he had, as he put it, "messed up big time." But there didn't seem to be anything to be done. The boat had sailed and he had stood on shore and watched.

It was David Thore, another member of the golf team, who told him to quit being a jerk and persuaded him to call Sarah again at the end of the summer. "At first I told him, no way, I blew it, it's over," Curtis said. "But he kept bugging me, telling me I was crazy if I didn't call her. Finally I told him I would call her but only if he and his girlfriend would go along with us the first night."

Thore agreed. Strange made the call. Sarah wasn't sure. She had been hurt by Curtis and there was this other guy back in New Bern . . . But there was also the memory of that feeling she had that first night at the basketball game. Okay, she finally decided, one last chance. Curtis got it right this time, and they were married in the summer of 1976, shortly after Curtis had dropped out of Wake Forest following his junior year to turn pro.

"I proposed on the phone from the British Open," he said. "I figured it was safer from 4,000 miles away. I was less likely to choke."

Sarah Strange spent the first night of her marriage in the Watergate Hotel, the second in Arnold Palmer's guest room because Curtis played in an exhibition that afternoon with Palmer. After that, her honeymoon consisted of one golf tournament after another, from Europe to Indonesia to Japan — with a brief stopover in Moscow. She was nineteen, she was in love; if this was what her husband wanted, it was what she wanted. She had known she was marrying a golfer, a star golfer at that, so this was part of the deal.

Only she hadn't realized just what was at stake. She hadn't quite understood the depth of her new husband's intensity about his work. "It all came clear to me in Tokyo one night," she said. "You see this alarm clock hit the wall traveling very fast . . ."

Curtis was the son of a golfer, Tom Strange, who had met his mother, Elizabeth Ball, while he was in the coast guard. She had heard from a friend that he was a scratch player and invited him to play with her brother and father, who were also excellent players. Tom Strange and the Ball family became good friends — on and off the golf course.

Shortly after they were married in 1953, he turned pro. Allan and Curtis were born in January 1955, Allan arriving four minutes before

Curtis. Both boys began playing with cut-down clubs when they were five. By the time they were seven, they had created their own par-five putting course that wound through the living room and dining room. At nine, they both started going to the golf course with their father. It was Curtis who stayed, though, Curtis who loved leaving the house with his dad at 7 o'clock in the morning and coming home with him at 10 o'clock at night.

He worked around the golf course, picking up balls, cleaning clubs, running golf carts, anything his father wanted. And when he wasn't working he hit balls. Hundreds and hundreds of balls. Then hundreds more. There was no better feeling than to look at his hands and see the blisters and cuts that came from working on the range for hours and hours. To this day, he can't sleep at night if he hasn't spent time on the range during the day.

Allan had talent too, but he never wanted to spend the time on the range or at the golf course the way Curtis did. He was a good baseball player who might have been a great baseball player if he hadn't hurt his back in high school. Curtis played baseball too, but gave it up at twelve when he had to choose between a Little League game or playing in the Virginia State junior championship.

A year later, Curtis almost won the Norfolk City Amateur Championship. That was one of the few times his father saw him play in a tournament. Most of the time, it was his mother who drove him to tournaments because his father had to work. But when Curtis shot 30 on the front nine during the second round of the Norfolk City, someone called the pro shop and told Tom Strange he better get over to see his kid because he was doing something special. Curtis looked up on the back nine and saw his father out there watching. He didn't win the tournament, but he remembers the look on his dad's face that day when he shot 65 and led all the grownups after two rounds.

Curtis was a star by then, but didn't really know it. His parents never made a big deal of his ability. His father just told him to keep working, whether he was playing well or playing poorly. "Hard work may not pay off today or even tomorrow," he would say, "but it will pay off somewhere down the road."

That was the way Tom Strange had always lived, working hard to provide a living for his family after making the decision to become a club pro rather than trying the tour. In the 1950s, the life of a touring pro was anything but glamorous; making a living was tough and it meant long stretches away from your family. Older players who knew Tom Strange, including Arnold Palmer, told Curtis later that his dad had the game and the temperament to make it on tour if he had decided to try it.

Tom Strange stayed home. And worked. He didn't play a lot with Curtis because kids weren't supposed to play with adults, they were supposed to play with other kids. But when Curtis came in one day in tears because he had figured out that he hadn't figured out the game, that he *didn't* know everything there was to know about the golf swing, Tom dropped what he was doing and spent the afternoon working with him, first on the range, then on the golf course. By the end of the day Curtis figured he had it figured out again. At least for a little while.

By the time Curtis was fourteen he was winning junior tournaments all over Virginia and entering tournaments against adults. His father had saved enough money to buy the golf club where he had been working since Allan and Curtis had been in the second grade and was in the process of making the deal. But that spring, he got sick. Mononucleosis, the boys were told. It lasted a long time, three weeks, four weeks, five weeks. Tom Strange had always been a smoker, two or three packs a day, so the coughing and hacking the boys were hearing was nothing new.

But then they began to hear other sounds. Their mother talking in a whisper on the phone, then hanging up and sitting quietly with tears welling up in her eyes. They figured it out — "around corners, overhearing whispered conversations, seeing Mom upset all the time." Tom Strange had lung cancer. Curtis was told later that he got it from licking golf balls that had fertilizer on them, but he can't remember ever seeing his father lick a golf ball.

The summer of 1969 is mostly a blur to Strange. Men were landing on the moon, Ted Kennedy and Mary Jo Kopechne were going for a drive on Chappaquiddick Island, and thousands were driving to Woodstock. Curtis Strange was watching his father die. One day the two boys were taken to their father's hospital room. He was in an oxygen tent a lot of the time by then. He told them he was very sick.

Cancer. They knew what that meant, but they didn't really know. They knew it was bad enough that after he told them he broke down, couldn't talk anymore, and told them to get out of the room.

Tom Strange came home shortly after that. They stopped the cobalt treatments and he went out and played a few rounds of golf. A few weeks later, on a Saturday afternoon, Curtis had just finished playing his third round at the state open, a tournament his dad had won several times, when someone came up to him and told him there was an emergency phone call from home. He went home that night. All he remembers about the next few days is hearing the word "gentleman" over and over again.

Years later, during a practice round at the PGA, Jay Haas, Curtis's closest friend since college, asked Arnold Palmer what he remembered about Tom Strange. "He was a gentleman," Palmer answered, "and he was a damn fine player too." He pointed at Curtis, who was then thirty-seven, a year younger than his father had been when he died, and said, "This one, at his best, is exactly like him."

To Curtis Strange, that may have been the highest praise he ever received.

The numbness began to wear off the next summer when he found himself playing in tournaments, but didn't have Dad to go home and talk to when they were over. He won the state junior on the same course where he had been playing the state open on the day his dad died. By then he was able to smile, knowing how proud his father would have been.

If he had ended up working for a Wall Street brokerage the way Allan did, maybe his father's memory wouldn't have burned quite so brightly through all the years. But being in golf, it seemed as if his father was always there. To this day, he hears about his father, and to this day, when he does something he knows would make his father proud, he thinks of him.

That's why, when he won his first U.S. Open in 1988, he talked about his father and how much he had wanted to win for him and he broke down and cried and showed the world a side of himself it had never seen. He had first thought about dedicating a victory to his father during the last round of the Masters in 1985, when he had led the tournament, only to let it slip away on the back nine at Augusta.

"It was never anything I actually thought about or planned," he said. "Somewhere in the back of my mind, I always knew that if I ever won a major I was going to want to talk about my dad. But I never thought about what I was going to say or how I was going to say it. When the time came, it just came out of me. I guess it was always in there someplace."

Somewhere inside Strange there was always a need to live up to what his dad had been. He wanted to be a great player and a gentleman too, and neither one was very easy. Maybe there was some anger because his father wasn't there to see him as he climbed the golf ladder, although he insists that it was his father who was cheated more than anybody.

But there was no question about the anger. No one could put on a game face on the golf course like Strange. He always has taken golf personally because it has always been so important to him. "I've heard guys say they wouldn't want golf to be that important to them," he said. "Well, it is that important to me and I'm not going to sit here and BS you and tell you it's not. It's my livelihood but it's also my passion."

His passion was evident whenever he played. His temper was a part of his persona growing up, all through college, and then on tour. He jokes today that Deane Beman always found him *before* he finished a round to tell him he was being fined for cursing. The parabolic microphone became his mortal enemy. When tournaments began to expand TV coverage to Thursdays and Fridays, Strange's fine budget went up. One tour official remembers receiving a call from Strange after a first-round tirade to complain about a fine. "You mean to tell me I can't get away with 'goddammit' on *Thursdays* anymore?" he asked.

Strange isn't proud of his temper. He was a good basketball player in high school, but he also led the team in technical fouls. He constantly tells his two sons, now twelve and nine, that Dad isn't always the best role model in the world. He was chagrined and embarrassed when Palmer dressed him down publicly ten years ago after a female walking scorer at Bay Hill complained about his profanity throughout the round. There have been incidents with cameramen and photographers and days when he stalked away from the media and autograph seekers.

He has worked very hard to get better. Once, he told Palmer that he was sick and tired of people sending him twenty requests for autographs in one envelope. "I just sign one and send the rest back," he said. "What do you do?"

"I sign them all," Palmer said. "Those are the people who keep us in business out here."

Now Strange signs them all. He still can't understand adults who ask for autographs, and he goes crazy when people ask his children for autographs — "Kids, are you kidding? That's sick," he says — but he always signs for kids. He has actually become a media favorite in recent years because he is blunt and funny and totally incapable of handing out pabulum.

During the last two years he has enjoyed golf more than at any time in his life. Some will tell you it is because he has accepted mediocrity, that the hunger to be the best is gone. Maybe some of the anger is gone. But the desire to do the work, hit the balls on the range, and compete is still there. Only now, perhaps for the first time in his life, he appreciates how lucky he is to be able to practice his passion day in and day out.

That appreciation was hard-won. In 1992 Curtis felt so sick that Sarah worried that something was seriously wrong with him. She could deal with the struggles he was having on the golf course, but not with him feeling weak and helpless all the time. The doctors had run tests for everything. They had suggested he might be fighting depression or that he might be allergic to something that didn't show up in allergy tests. They thought it might be stress or just exhaustion.

There were lots of questions, very few answers. A trip to the Mayo Clinic turned up nothing. Sarah's sister-in-law had told her that Allan talked often about being almost the same age his father had been when he died. Curtis never talked like that, but maybe he had the same thoughts and fears and this mysterious malady was their manifestation.

The doctors finally decided it was some kind of virus that had gone undiagnosed. Slowly, Curtis began to feel better. Then came the offer from ABC. The network was looking for someone to be its lead golf analyst. Dave Marr had been fired a couple of years earlier, and Steve Melnyk hadn't really worked out. Strange had been a nonfactor on tour in both 1991 and 1992; maybe he would be willing to make the move.

He was tempted. The money was excellent and he suspected he would be good at the job. He had always been comfortable in front of a camera, and although he knew he couldn't say *everything* he was thinking, his straightforward style would probably work well. It had certainly worked for Johnny Miller on NBC.

But deep down, even though the ABC people pointed out that he could play all he wanted to on the weeks they weren't on air, he knew that taking the job would mean conceding that he was finished as a player. For one thing, if he committed to being on the road for ABC for fifteen weeks, he wasn't going to want to be away from home for another twenty to play in tournaments. He would probably end up playing at most half as much as in the past and that meant he would be a part-time golfer.

Was he ready to do that? He was about to turn thirty-eight, hardly an age where a golfer is through, but the fact was he hadn't won since the 1989 Open and hadn't been playing very well even before he started to feel sick.

It was Palmer who answered his question. Late one night, at an exhibition in Mexico, Strange pounded on Palmer's door. He needed to talk. Strange had gone to Wake Forest on an Arnold Palmer golf scholarship, and Palmer has tried, since then, to look out for him. Often, that has meant lecturing and cajoling him in a way no one else can. Palmer is the same age Tom Strange would be, and all three of his children are girls. It may be a stretch to call him a father figure, but there is no question that, when Palmer talks, Strange listens.

He sat up that night with Curtis and told him he thought he was crazy if he took the ABC offer. "If you do it, then you have to accept the fact that you aren't a player anymore," Palmer told him. "You're a commentator and a spectator and that's it. If you're ready for that, fine, do it. But I don't think you are."

Allan said the same thing. So did Sarah, although deep down, she wouldn't have minded seeing him stop playing because that would have meant more time for her and the boys. But if quitting meant he was going to be unhappy and unfulfilled, that was the last thing she wanted.

Strange finally said no. He held a telephone press conference with the nation's golf writers to tell them that rumors of his retirement had been greatly exaggerated. He felt better and he still wanted to play.

Once that decision was made, he felt as if he had been given a new lease on his golf life. It wasn't as if his game magically came back or even that he thought he was twenty-two again. There were still times on the road when he felt lousy in the morning and wondered if he would make it through his round. And, for the first six months of the year, he wasn't exactly tearing up the tour.

But a lot of the old feeling had come back. For one thing, he wasn't sleeping well. That was a good sign. From the very beginning of his career, Strange had been a restless sleeper. He would lie awake in bed, replaying every shot he had hit that day, questioning himself, wondering how he could do better the next day.

Sarah thought at first it was the tension of trying to break through, to reach a point where they weren't staying in $22-a-night motel rooms because that was all they could afford. In 1980, he finished third on the money list and still didn't sleep well. He went through a major swing change that year, convinced he had to hit the ball straighter with more consistency even if it meant giving up distance if he wanted to take the next step from good player to great player.

Sarah didn't really understand. He was playing well, improving all the time, why make a change now? Because, he told her, *good* isn't good enough. He needed more.

He got it. By 1985, he was the leading money winner on tour. That was the year of the Lost Masters, the year he came back after shooting 80 the first day to shoot back-to-back 65s to lead the tournament. Then he put a ball in the water at 13 and sank another one at 15 and lost to Bernhard Langer. "The worst shot I hit all day wasn't the one into the creek at thirteen, it was the one out of the creek," he said. "I still could have made par there and I didn't. The shot at fifteen, I swear to this day, I hit the ball just the way I wanted to. I still don't know how it ended up in the water."

Sarah was home because their second son had been born a week earlier. On the phone that night, he kept saying, "When will I have a chance like this again?" When he got home the next day he walked in through the garage, collapsed in her arms, and cried. For an hour, they both cried about it without saying a word. So close. So painful.

That was why winning the Open at Brookline in 1988 had been so important. Leading Nick Faldo by one shot, Strange three-putted 17, then had to get up and down from a bunker at 18 just to stay even with him and create a playoff. "If I had lost that one that day, I'm not sure I ever would have come back," he said. "I'm not sure I could have taken another disappointment as devastating as that Masters was."

He won the playoff the next day, playing near-perfect golf. Then he collapsed in Sarah's arms again, only this time it was joy and relief and all those thoughts about his father. The next year at Oak Hill was almost like a bonus. It was Tom Kite's tournament to win until he triple-bogeyed the fifth hole on Sunday. Two holes ahead, Strange heard word drifting along the ropes that Kite had made triple. He asked someone from the USGA to check and find out if that was true. Moments later, the word came back: Yes, Kite had tripled. Suddenly, he was tied for the lead. "The game was on," Strange said. "I remember when I was in high school, whenever we were in a close game, I wanted the ball. I wanted to take the last shot.

"There are a lot of guys who don't want to take the last shot. Sometimes, the most talented players you'll ever see don't want the ball. Michael Jordan *always* wanted it. I think I'm that way. I've always been someone who, when I get in the hunt, I usually know what to do. I may not have had as many chances to win as some guys, but when I've had chances, I've usually played pretty well."

He was absolute steel down the stretch at Oak Hill that day, making one key putt after another to win. He was the King of Golf after that. And then, almost overnight, he was gone. Once he shot that 75 on the last day of the Open at Medinah in 1990, all the anger, all the desire, all the need to work and win and compete disappeared.

"When he won in 1988, there was never a time when we sat back and said, 'Wow, we climbed the mountain, look where we are,' " Sarah said. "It was work and more work and more pressure. He traveled more and he did more and he never seemed to have the chance to stop and take it all in. He worked all his life to get to the top and then when he got there, I'm not sure he liked it up there very much."

It wasn't until years later, on a winter night before Christmas in 1993, that Sarah expressed that view to Curtis. When she did, it brought him up short. The notion that he didn't like being the best player in the world had never occurred to him. But when he thought about it and looked back at what had happened, he wondered if it might not be true.

"I was never comfortable with being a public figure," he said. "I can't be Arnold, I just can't. After I won at Brookline, everything changed. Everywhere I went, I was recognized, I mean everywhere. Instead of being an occasional thing, it became a constant thing. I began to rebel against it. Sometimes I wouldn't sign autographs just because *I didn't want to.* Maybe I was wrong, but that was the way I felt. And after I lost at Medinah, it was as if I had been flushed clean. I was totally empty."

"Medinah," said Sarah, "is when it was over. That's when he stopped grinding and grinding."

And when he did, he wasn't the same player. And then he got sick and then he decided not to quit and then in the summer of 1993, it started to come back. He had gone back to grinding, back to all the hours on the range, the sitting up at night going through the round shot by shot, the room service most nights on the road. He could see improvement but it wasn't as if he woke up one morning and started putting back-to-back 65s on the board.

There was a good last round at the 1993 Open. Then there was a seventh place at the Western. A week later, home at Kingsmill for the Anheuser-Busch Classic, he looked up on Sunday with nine holes to go and found himself one shot out of the lead. It had been so long it was almost a shock. But he hung in. He birdied the 14th hole and walked to the 15th tee thinking he was tied for the lead. Then he heard a huge roar from down in the trees where the green is and he knew something had happened and he probably wasn't in the lead anymore.

He was right. Jim Gallagher Jr. had rolled in an eagle putt. He followed that with a birdie at 16, and no one in the field, including

Strange, had answers for that. Strange finished third, three shots behind Gallagher, but the feeling he had being back in the hunt energized him. "I didn't back off when I had the chance," he said. "I handled the pressure. I was a little surprised by that."

A week later, he was fifth at New England, then came a sixth at Memphis. Four weeks, four top-ten finishes. That was a roll for anyone who wasn't named Nick Price or Greg Norman. Home for a week before the PGA, Strange picked up a newspaper and saw a story speculating about who Tom Watson might pick for the last two spots on the Ryder Cup team. Lanny Wadkins, Raymond Floyd, Fuzzy Zoeller, and John Daly were all mentioned. So was Curtis Strange.

And why not? Watson had said repeatedly he wanted to pick two players who were playing well. On that list no one was playing better than he was. But he had been gone for so long, would Watson really take him seriously?

Yes. The night before the PGA began in Toledo, Watson called him in his hotel room. He wanted him to know he was considering him for the team and he asked for an honest analysis of his game and of the other players he was thinking about. They talked for an hour. Strange told him he was playing well but wished he was putting better. Did he want to be on the team? Damn right he did.

Maybe he wanted to be on the team too much. He knew that Sarah had always enjoyed Ryder Cup and he had always enjoyed the team aspect of the competition. If he played well in the PGA, Watson would almost have to pick him, especially since Wadkins and Floyd, who had been the two likely choices all summer, hadn't been playing well.

But he missed the cut. "I was thinking about making the team," he said later. "You can't do that. You have to let those things happen. I had come from nowhere to [being] in contention in four weeks just by going out and playing. When I started to think about it, to really want it, I didn't perform."

There was still a chance, though, because Floyd had missed the cut too. Strange was flying to Japan on Sunday night to play in a tournament there. Watson had told him to call him in his hotel room that night to find out if he was on the team. Changing planes at O'Hare Airport in Chicago, he found a phone and called Watson. He was surprised at how nervous he was.

"You're out," said Watson, never one to mince words.

"I understand," Strange said. "If there's anything I can do to help, let me know."

He hung up with an empty feeling in his stomach. He was glad Watson hadn't done any beating around the bush or fed him any lines about how tough a decision it had been. He called Sarah and told her. It was a downer but, as Sarah pointed out, "A month ago you wouldn't even have been making that phone call. You've come a long way."

They both knew that was true. The three years of constant struggle seemed to be over. But then, two weeks later, Sarah began to feel tired, very tired, while taking her morning walk. She took a nap and woke up feeling worse. It was time to drive her car pool, so she got in the car to pick up the kids. On the way back, she saw a youngster in front of her, knew she had to stop, but couldn't. Her body wouldn't do what her mind was telling it to do. She just missed the child.

That was it. She went straight to the hospital. The doctors ran all sorts of tests. She didn't have "any of the bad stuff." That was the good news. The bad news was they couldn't figure out exactly what she did have. This was 1992 all over again only now Sarah was the one with the mystery ailment.

Curtis, baffled and scared, offered to stay home for as long as she was feeling sick. She didn't want that. He was playing well, he should be out playing. He went to play at Disney in early October, and by the time he came home she was completely exhausted. Back to the doctors. They had been doing blood work for weeks. Some kind of virus had gotten into her and the result, they thought, was something called Chronic Fatigue Syndrome.

Curtis knew what it was as soon as the doctor said it because it had been brought up to him a year earlier. He knew that couldn't be Sarah's problem, though, because Sarah was the most energetic, up-beat person he knew.

"That's exactly the kind of person this usually hits," the doctor said.

The scariest part was that there was no cure and no way of knowing if it would get better, get worse, stay the same. Curtis sat the boys down and explained to them that Mom wasn't feeling well and that it was up to all three of them to take care of her. He drew up charts with work assignments for everyone. Dishes were broken on a daily basis, but there was no questioning the effort. Sarah would lie in bed, hear the crash, and know the dishes were being done. "We were down to plastic after a few weeks," she said.

Sarah had good days and bad days. Some days she couldn't even get out of bed. On others, she would make it to the bottom of the steps to see the boys off to school. When Curtis was home he brought her lunch in bed every day, drove the boys' car pools, and even did some cooking. In a sense, Sarah loved what she was seeing. He was bonding with the boys in new ways, and she felt closer to him than she ever had.

He didn't want to travel, but she kept pushing him out the door. They worked out a plan with her parents and her sister so that someone would come up and stay whenever he had to go away. "I felt so guilty," Sarah said. "I couldn't do anything. I knew Curtis needed to play and if he had stayed home because of me I would have felt awful."

She told him that, so he played. He went to Australia in late November and won a tournament, his first victory anywhere in the world since 1989. That qualified him for an elite, big-money, made-for-TV tournament in Jamaica two weeks later. He didn't want to go. Sarah pushed him out the door again. He finished fifth.

Curtis was torn. Finally, he was playing good golf again, but he hated the idea of Sarah sitting at home feeling so lousy while he was out playing. She felt well enough to make the trip to the Phoenix Open in January at the start of the '94 tour, but was completely exhausted by the time she got home. Curtis shot 64 on the last day there to tie for eighth. He was starting to get hot. But Sarah felt so rotten he knew he had to go home. He stayed for two weeks. When Sarah felt better, he decided to play in the Hope.

He arrived in the desert not knowing what was going to happen next. He told a few close friends what was going on so that if he disappeared suddenly, they would know why. He couldn't stand seeing Sarah sick and he felt helpless and angry watching her suffer. Some days she was better. Other days weren't as good. He knew that if he stopped playing or starting playing poorly again, she would blame herself and that was the last thing he wanted.

So he did what he was most comfortable doing: he went back to his routine. Hours and hours on the range, trying to get back that feeling he had when he was a kid, pounding balls until dark. Then it was back to the hotel for room service and a phone call home. Every night he would say the same thing: "Are you okay?" And she would say, "I'm fine." He knew she wasn't all that fine but at least she wasn't any worse.

"She's taken care of me for twenty years," he said one night. "If I take care of her for the next twenty years, that's fine with me. Except I know she'll hate every minute of it."

He lasted five holes in the shootout that day at the Hope, trading barbs with master of ceremonies Gary McCord and the others, showing the crowd a Curtis Strange they didn't think existed. McCord, the ex-player turned very funny TV announcer, makes the shootouts work with a steady stream of cracks and one-liners that sets a loose tone for the afternoon.

Strange should have been out on the first hole but survived; should have been out on the second but survived; then became the first player to make a birdie on the third.

"Is this some kind of a round of golf or what?" said McCord, who had pronounced Strange dead on the first two holes only to see him squirm free.

"Least I'm playing," Strange shot back, a reference to McCord's relatively brief career.

It was a joke, a throwaway one-liner that got a good laugh from the crowd. But if he had thought about it for a moment, Strange would have realized that his playing was, in fact, a very big deal.

9

WHO'S THE BOSS?

AS THE TEN PLAYERS taking part in the Hope Shootout made their way down the first fairway, Peter Jacobsen, one of three players wearing a wireless microphone, asked Scott Simpson — for the benefit of the crowd — if he had talked to his friend Bill Murray recently.

The quiet, dignified Simpson and the slapstick Murray might have seemed like an odd couple, but they had been partners the last two years at Pebble Beach. When the Murray–Deane Beman skirmish became public, Simpson had been asked if Murray's antics ever bothered him. Quite the contrary, Simpson answered. He said he enjoyed every minute of the experience and hoped that Murray would continue to play in the tournament. Of course Murray had left Pebble Beach vowing never to return unless Beman was gone. "I am demanding Deane Beman's resignation," he said as he departed the premises.

Simpson laughed when Jacobsen brought Murray up and told him he thought he was doing just fine. "By the way," Jacobsen asked, "has Deane resigned yet?"

Everyone got a yuck out of that one. What they didn't know was the answer was yes. Beman had resigned.

He had been under siege since Murray-gate at Pebble Beach. Most of his players had sided with Murray. Most of the media sided with Murray. Most of America, it seemed, sided with Murray.

Beman will always insist that the timing was a coincidence, but a week after Pebble Beach, during the Hope, he sat down with Dick Ferris, the chairman of the tour's policy board, and told him he was quitting. He had already hinted to the board that he might not return after his current term as commissioner expired at the end of 1995, but now he had decided he didn't want to wait even that long. He wanted out as soon as a suitable replacement could be found.

"I'm going to be fifty-six in April," Beman said. "If I want to play the senior tour, I need to get going as soon as possible."

No one doubted that Beman wanted to play golf. He had always been a very good player, a U.S. and British Amateur champion who had gone into the insurance business rather than turn pro after college. But at twenty-nine, even though he was making a lot of money, the itch was still there. He turned pro and spent six years on tour. He played well, winning four times, but was never as successful as he wanted to be — or thought he should be.

Beman had the same drive and fire that Palmer and Nicklaus had, but not the talent. It galled him that he couldn't play at their level, and he never completely gave up the idea that he was as good as they were. When Joseph Dey, then the commissioner of the still-young PGA Tour, approached him about the possibility of succeeding him, Beman said no. "I still had more to do as a player," he said. "I had been hurt and I wanted to come back and prove I could still play."

He did that late in 1973 when he won the now long-extinct Robinson Open. The commissioner's job was still open. He called Dey. "If you still want me," he said, "I'll take the job." They still wanted him, intrigued by his background as both a player and a businessman. On March 1, 1974, Beman became commissioner. He was thirty-five, an age when a lot of players still have their best golf in front of them.

"I only wanted to keep playing if I thought I could win major titles," he said. "If I had thought I was going to win a major that year and two the next year and another one the year after that, I would have kept playing. But I knew that wasn't likely. I decided if I couldn't be the best player, maybe I could be the best commissioner."

Almost from day one, he was a controversial figure. He made sweeping changes, moving the tour's headquarters to Ponte Vedra in a brilliant land deal (he bought several thousand undeveloped acres for one dollar) and built the first Tournament Players Club there adjacent to the new tour offices. He turned the tour from a small business into a big one, buying up land to build Players Clubs around the country, making corporate deals, and eventually expanding the regular tour while creating the senior tour and then the Hogan (now Nike) Tour.

He brought corporate America into golf in a big way, got his tournaments on television constantly, and increased purses in leaps and bounds every year. The tour grew, a lot more people made a lot more money, and Beman became a wealthy man himself, negotiating an annual $2.2 million compensation package for himself when he signed his last contract.

The fact that Beman was making $800,000 more annually than Nick Price had made as the tour's leading money winner in 1993 galled some players, but most of them grudgingly gave him his due, conceding that he had brought golf into the big time.

But it was always that — a grudging concession. Beman was bright, sharp-witted, and a smart, tough negotiator. But he simply wasn't comfortable with people. His humor always seemed forced and, even though he had been a very good player, he was never — *ever* — one of the guys.

As a player, Beman had been a grinder: someone not blessed with great ability, but a bulldog competitor with a work ethic that made him play better than he should have. To be called a grinder in golf is high praise because it means you have used all the talent you have.

Great players can be grinders. Tom Kite and Curtis Strange are probably two of the great grinders in history, men who got every last ounce out of their golf just by dint of hard work. Others, with less talent than Kite and Strange, also rose above what they should have been by putting in endless hours on the range.

In fact, most players who last a long time on tour are grinders to one degree or another. For every Palmer, Nicklaus, Watson, or Norman, there are hundreds and hundreds of grinders. The best of them are the ones who have long careers.

What Deane Beman did was make the PGA Tour safe for grinders. He created the all-exempt tour in 1982, meaning that instead of only sixty players being exempt for the entire year, 125 players were. That meant more than twice as many players started each year knowing they had a safe place on the tour. He gave older players a second life with the senior tour and a lot of players — young and old — a fallback place with the Hogan Tour.

That didn't always thrill the stars. Palmer and Nicklaus almost led an insurrection in 1983, thinking that the tour should just run golf tournaments and not be in the golf course and marketing business. Beman beat back that charge by creating — almost overnight — the tour's first annual report, which showed everyone else just how much money the tour's aggressive approach was making for the nonmillionaires. Nicklaus and Palmer backed off.

Beman fought a lot of battles, got nicked up on occasion, but usually emerged as strong as ever. Until he took on Karsten Solheim. The story of the tour's lengthy fight with Solheim over the square grooves he put into his Ping clubs has been the subject of millions of words of debate, not to mention millions of dollars in lawsuits. The best way to boil it down is this: Beman didn't want players using Solheim's square grooves on tour because he — and many others — believed they allowed players to put too much spin on the ball. He banned the grooves. Solheim took him to court and, after a long, bitter fight, the tour settled out of court in the spring of 1993 at a reported cost of about $7 million. The grooves stayed.

Beman and the tour tried to characterize the settlement as a compromise. Most compromises don't cost $7 million. Everyone else in golf chalked it up as a major loss for Beman. There were even rumors that one of the provisions of the deal was that Beman would resign within a year. Beman hotly denied that rumor whenever it came up. "That's a damn lie," he said on the afternoon of March 1, 1994. Beman almost never uses profanity, especially in public, unless he has been severely provoked. The notion that Solheim had something to do with his departure was severely provocative.

March 1, 1994, was Beman's twentieth anniversary as commissioner. The tour had finished its West Coast swing with Scott Hoch — the man best remembered for missing a two-foot putt that would have won the Masters in 1989 — winning at the Hope, and Craig Stadler — who *had* won the Masters in 1984 — winning the Buick Invitational in San Diego.

Florida was next for four weeks, beginning in Miami at the Doral Ryder Open. For most of the top players, the beginning of the Florida swing is the time to begin preparing for the Masters. That is one reason why Doral always draws a strong field, and 1994 was no exception: Nick Price, Greg Norman, Nick Faldo, and Fred Couples were all playing. About the only big name missing was Phil Mickelson, who had played San Diego since it was his hometown and was taking a week off to go skiing.

Doral was also the site of the first 1994 meeting of the tour's policy board, scheduled for Tuesday, March 1, at 7:30 A.M. The agenda was expected to take up most of the morning. It was all pretty routine stuff: a report from the golf course properties advisory board; three items on the subject of TV and marketing; a lengthy report on tournament administration and membership. Also to be addressed were three Nike Tour topics and two from the senior tour. That would be followed by an update on progress of the World Golf Village and reports from audit and treasury and, finally, PGA Tour charities.

They would probably be finished by lunchtime, meaning that the four players on the board — Jeff Sluman, Brad Faxon, Rick Fehr, and Jay Haas — would have plenty of time to get in an afternoon practice round.

Four men walking into the room knew that the meeting would not be as routine as everyone else thought: Beman, Dick Ferris, deputy commissioner Tim Finchem, and communications director John Morris. When the minutes had been read and approved, Beman stood up, cleared his throat, and said quietly, "There's something I'd like to say to you all before we continue."

He nodded at Morris, who began passing out copies of Beman's letter of resignation. Beman waited a few minutes to let everyone read what the letter said, then spoke briefly about why he was stepping down and how much he had enjoyed the job. Ferris had already put together a search committee, which he would head himself, to find Beman's replacement. Beman wanted Finchem, his right-hand man for five years, to replace him. But he knew it would not be an easy or simple process to get him the job.

By the time the meeting was over, word was beginning to spread around Doral that something momentous had taken place. Morris told his two on-site staffers, Marty Caffey and Wes Seeley, to assemble the media for a 1 o'clock press conference. The subject, they were told, was a nonagenda item that had come up during the policy board meeting.

"Deane's resigning," Iva Green of the Associated Press said as soon as word about the press conference came down. "What else could it be?"

Nothing. Shortly after 1 o'clock, Beman, most of the board, and quite a few staff members arrived at the upstairs ballroom that had been converted into an interview room for the week. Beman, dressed nattily in a blue blazer with a blue shirt and a red-and-white polka-dot tie, stood at the entrance to the room for several minutes awkwardly exchanging small talk and jokes with reporters and staffers. He looked tired, even a little bit nervous.

Morris went through a routine with the media similar to the one that he had gone through with the board. The letter of resignation was passed out, and Morris read it aloud. Beman took the microphone, applauded by the board members and staff members.

"I've enjoyed every minute of it," he said. "But I'm not getting any younger and, in my opinion — *and only my opinion* — it is time to get on to another phase of my life."

He went on to talk about what he planned to do — play the senior tour and design golf courses — and about how he had come to this life-changing decision. When he started to talk about his pride in what golf stood for, he began to get emotional. His voice caught just a tiny bit, but he went on. Someone asked him about what qualities the search committee should look for in a successor.

Beman got one sentence into his answer before Ferris interrupted. "Um, Deane, I think I should say a few words, um, right about now, if you don't mind."

Whether Beman minded or not clearly didn't matter to Ferris. He walked to the podium and did everything but shove Beman aside. Beman forced a smile, then stepped away. It was probably the first time it had occurred to him that he was no longer the man in charge. Ferris, all bluster and bombast, read a patronizing statement about Beman's accomplishments while everyone squirmed uncomfortably. Whatever anyone in the room thought about Beman, this wasn't fair. He should have been allowed to make his exit on his own terms without someone pulling a grandstand act and treating him like a hired hand.

When Ferris was finished, he and Beman answered a few more desultory questions and then they began a walk-through on the putting green and the range. By now everyone knew what had happened. The news wasn't shocking, but it was stunning. Twenty years is a long time. To almost every player on tour there had been only one commissioner: Beman. As Beman and Ferris approached, each player stopped what he was doing to shake Beman's hand and say thanks or good luck or we'll miss you. Ferris stayed close to Beman almost as if making sure nothing untoward was said by anyone.

This wasn't a day for that. The stubborn little grinder had never been able to compete with Nicklaus or Palmer on the golf course. But there was no doubting the fact that he had created a legacy for himself in the game anyway, one that would last for a long, long time.

The search committee gave no time frame for when it would come up with a replacement, but there was no doubt that Beman wanted the process to be as swift as possible. When a staffer walked up to him that afternoon and asked, "How long, Commish?" Beman said, "I'll be out of there within thirty days of the new guy being named." He smiled. "I've got a lot to do."

He had already done plenty.

Later that same afternoon, with players huddling in groups of three and four to discuss Beman's departure and what it would mean, Nick Price and his caddy, Jeff (Squeeky) Medlen, headed for a corner of the range to hit some balls. Price had played only one tournament so far in 1994 — an overseas event — and Doral would be his PGA Tour debut.

Price lit a cigarette, took a few quick drags, then handed it to Medlen. He took out his wedge and began lofting short shots in the direction of a nearby flag.

He had hit four balls when the first equipment representative walked up. He just wanted to say hi, congratulate Price on being player of the year, and tell him if he could help, to give him a call.

Price stopped what he was doing, leaned on his club, and chatted. How was the family? Did you have a good winter? Two kids now, right?

The man moved on. Price hit two more balls. A local TV reporter moved into his vision. He was sorry to interrupt, but would it be a problem to get him on camera for a live shot, just for a minute, even thirty seconds, in a little while. "How soon do you need me?" Price asked.

Thirty minutes. Fine. Where? The man pointed to a camera at the far end of the range. "Send someone for me when you're ready."

Price hit another wedge shot. Now a tournament rep was standing over him. Was Price planning to play in their event this year? No? What a shame, you know how much we love having you and our fans are crazy about you.

"You have a great event, I've always loved playing there," Price said. "It just didn't quite fit this year and I feel badly about that."

Maybe next year then?

"Oh, absolutely, very possible."

They would check with him later in the year, maybe call. Anything they could do, please let them know.

Price nodded again. "Anytime, Bob," he said, using the man's name for a third time. Price never forgets a name and never fails to use it so the person he's talking to knows that he remembers him.

By now Medlen was rolling his eyes. They had been on the range thirty minutes and hit eight balls. Someone from the tour approached wanting to know about a junior clinic at the Players Championship. Was it still okay with him for Tuesday afternoon with Greg Norman?

"Absolutely," Price said. "If there's anything I can do to help, let me know."

The staffer walked away shaking his head. "If they were all like that," he said, "this would be the best job in the world."

They weren't. No one in golf is like Nick Price. If you took a poll among everyone connected with the tour — players, sponsors, reporters, staffers — and asked who is the nicest man playing the game right now, the vote would be almost unanimous. If a few didn't vote for Price, it would be because they didn't know him or because they picked him second just to be different.

"My mother always taught me to treat people the way I would like them to treat me," Price said. "Most of the time, people mean well. There are times when you have to say to fans or people who really don't understand what we do, 'I'm really sorry but I've got to get my work done now.' When that happens, I try to make it clear that I'm not giving them the runaround, I just can't talk to them right that second. And I hope the day will never come when another golfer thinks he can't come up and speak to me. I would hate that."

Price wasn't the least bit shocked that afternoon at Doral when he found himself inundated by sales reps, tournament reps, corporate reps, media, and the inevitable autograph-seeking volunteers.

On any Tuesday or Wednesday on tour, the range looks like the exchange counter at Macy's on the day after Christmas. All the various reps know that most players will show up to hit balls sooner or later, so they camp out there and wait. They will check with players who use their equipment or wear their hats, visors, or shirts, to make sure they have everything they need. They will flirt with players they don't have, knowing that no contract is forever. Tournament reps do the same thing. They ask players who are committed to their event if there is anything they need help with and try to twist an arm or two among those who aren't planning to play. There are also local TV crews looking to grab players and set up a shot with golfers in the background.

For the big-name players, the circus atmosphere can be a problem. Most try to deal with all the various requests and well-wishers either at the beginning or end of their practice session, hoping most people will get the message to leave them alone when they're working.

Because Price has a reputation for being cooperative and easygoing, people are less hesitant about approaching him. And, having been away from the tour for four months, he knew Doral was going to be full of distractions. He had won four tournaments in 1993 and the player-of-the-year award. As the year went on, the demands for his time had increased. A couple of times, he crashed.

It happened first at the Masters. Having won the last major of 1992 — the PGA — and the first big nonmajor of 1993 — the Players — he had arrived at Augusta as the favorite and simply didn't handle the distractions and demands and pressure. He missed the cut. Then, at the Tour Championship in San Francisco, he went into the week with a slim lead over Greg Norman and Paul Azinger for both the player-of-the-year and the money titles.

He played poorly, never made a putt, and, uncharacteristically, blew up on the golf course Saturday when he couldn't even scare the hole with his putter. "The worst I've ever behaved in my life," he said later. "I wanted it so much and I saw it all slipping away. I handled myself very badly."

He still won both titles because Azinger didn't play any better than he did and because Norman, leading the tournament with three holes to play, collapsed, finishing 6–5–5 to lose to Jim Gallagher Jr. by one shot. That was the difference between Norman being player of the year and Price winning the award.

"To be honest, Greg lost it more those last three holes than I won it," Price said. "I was thrilled to win in the end, but not with the way it happened. That's one of the reasons why I want to really play well this year. I don't want to be a one-year wonder. I want to build on what I did in '93 and be a better player this year. I still don't think I've reached my potential as a player. That's what's driving me now, wanting to still get better."

It has always been that way with Price. His demeanor can be deceiving. For all of his kindness and gentility, Price is as driven as anyone in the game. He has never been satisfied with his status. He was good enough as an amateur to qualify for the British Open at eighteen and to reach the quarterfinals of the British Amateur that same year. He came home devastated he hadn't done better. He improved steadily in his early years on the European Tour but was convinced he needed a brand-new swing when he was twenty-five. He became a steady moneymaker on the U.S. Tour in the 1980s and was frustrated because he had won only one tournament. When he started to win tournaments, he thirsted to win a major. When he won a major, he wanted to be the best player in the world. Now, as the world's best player, he wants to win all four majors and be remembered as one of the game's greats before he is through.

Where that kind of drive comes from is always impossible to analyze. But Price's journey to the top of the game is completely different from that of anyone else playing golf. His parents were adventurers, both British citizens who volunteered for the Indian Army in World War II. He was a major in the infantry, she was a lieutenant in the nursing corps. They met in India, were married, and had a son, Kit, in 1946.

When war broke out on the Indian-Pakistani border in 1947, they got on a mail ship with their infant son, intending to go to Kenya.

But when the boat stopped in Durban, South Africa, for several days, Raymond Price ran into an old friend who had settled there after getting out of the military. He decided to stay and got into the clothing manufacturing business. A second son, Tim, was born in 1950 and Nick in 1957. Four years later, hearing stories about a brand-new "land of opportunity," Raymond and Wendy Price took their three sons to Rhodesia and opened a clothing factory.

It was Tim who introduced Nick to golf. He was fifteen and needed a caddy, so he took his little brother with him to the golf course. Since Nick was left-handed, he played with the one lefty club the boys could find. When their mother realized how much the boys liked golf, she decided to buy them a set of clubs — one set. Since all the new clubs were right-handed, Nick had to learn that way. For years, he held the club crosshanded.

Raymond Price died of lung cancer when Nick was ten. His memories of his father are vague, but he does remember the smoking. Everyone in Rhodesia smoked, or so it seemed, and Price became a smoker very young, following in the footsteps of his brothers. They have both now quit, as has his mother. Nick still smokes, which doesn't make anyone in his family happy. He constantly vows to quit, but hasn't yet. "I know I have to stop," he said. "I don't want to leave my kids the way my father left us. But I'm not quite ready."

Once he learned a proper grip and stance, Nick was a natural on the golf course. By sixteen, he was certain he wanted to be a pro. He was so certain that he took an extremely unusual step. This was 1973 and there were still two different-sized balls used in golf: the smaller ball, which was used in amateur tournaments around the world and in many pro tournaments in Europe, Asia, and Africa, and the larger American ball, which was always used on the PGA Tour. The smaller ball, naturally, traveled farther. A player using it against a player using the bigger ball had a distinct advantage.

Price abandoned the small ball even though he knew it would lessen his chances of winning junior and amateur tournaments. "I knew I wanted to be a pro and I thought this was the best way to prepare," he said. "At times, it was frustrating, but when I did turn pro, the transition was easier for me to make than for some others because I had already been playing the big ball for a few years."

His progress was interrupted, first by his disappointment in the British Amateur in 1975, which caused him to seriously consider quitting — "I just didn't think I would ever be good enough," he said — and then by twenty-one months of mandatory service in the Rhodesian Air Force. Civil war had been a part of life in Rhodesia since 1965, the country's blacks seeking independence from the British government, which had established apartheid in both Rhodesia and South Africa.

Price was drafted into the Rhodesian Air Force to fight for a cause he knew little about. "We were all brainwashed back then," he said. "The government told us we were fighting against communism, which I suppose was technically true since the other side was getting money from the Soviet government because they couldn't get it from anyone else."

Only later, when he began to travel the world, did Price understand why the Rhodesian blacks fought so fiercely for the independence they finally won in 1980 when Zimbabwe was created with a one man, one vote government.

Civil war was a part of daily life in Rhodesia for most of Price's boyhood. He remembers hearing stories about people he knew who had been killed and seeing war, and what it produces, all around him. He has often been described as a fighter pilot, but he says that is exaggerated. "I was trained, but I never flew operationally," he said. "The saddest thing about being in a war is that the idea of people getting killed becomes part of your life. I never really faced death. I was in places where people did die, but I never had to shoot a gun.

"Being in the military changes you forever, though. It gives you discipline like nothing else can. When you have to be up at four o'clock every morning, bed made, backpack ready for inspection, floor area around your bed shined and cleaned, you learn about self-discipline. What we all used to do was clean the area around our bed, then put newspaper on the floor and sleep on it so we would have fifteen extra minutes in the morning since our bed was already made. You became close to people in a way you'll never be close to anyone else ever again.

"The parties were the best parties you'll ever go to because you became fatalistic. There was a chance you were going to die young, so you wanted to enjoy every minute you possibly could because you just didn't know what was awaiting you the next day. That may sound melodramatic but there's something to it. It wasn't as if I was on the front line, I wasn't. Still, casualties were low in Desert Storm but people did die. Sometimes, people forget that. I look back now and what I think about is the waste. Guys I knew who aren't here who might have been great doctors or lawyers or scientists. War is a very great waste. You don't see it that way when you're young though. You think you're fighting for a cause and in the middle of a great adventure."

Later, when Price was asked during his early years on tour to talk about his military experience, he would dodge the question with a joke. "I tried to get out of the military by telling them I had a skin disease," he would say. "When they asked me what was wrong with my skin, I told them bullets went through it."

When he talks about the experience in a more serious vein, it is apparent that part of what he is today is because of what he saw growing up. When you have seen death up close, it gives you a greater appreciation for life. "I often stop and think about how fortunate I am, to have the family I have, the friends I have, the life I have," he said. "It didn't have to turn out this way."

Price was twenty-one when he got out of the military. He turned pro almost immediately and headed for Europe. His first year there, 1978, was extremely difficult. He had trouble adjusting to the cold weather and, even though he played well enough to finish fifty-first on the Order of Merit (the European money list), there were times when he worried about running out of money. At one point, after missing several cuts in a row, he was down to enough money to make it through two more tournaments. If he didn't play well in either, he would have no choice but to go home. He finished fourth the first week and third the next.

He improved rapidly the next two years and was eleventh on the Order of Merit in 1980. But he backslid in 1981 and went home to play the South African tour in the winter convinced he had to find someone to completely change his golf swing. Denis Watson, another Zimbabwan, had just finished his first year on the American tour. He had spent time that year working with David Leadbetter, also from Zimbabwe, someone Price had grown up with. Leadbetter had become a teaching pro and had set up shop in Florida. Watching Watson swing, Price could see he had made major strides.

Price called Leadbetter in January of 1982 and made plans to go see him in March. He ended up spending six weeks working with him. Leadbetter showed him his swing on tape, which horrified him — "I had about five different swing planes," he said. "I knew it was bad, but I never dreamed it was *that* bad" — and began working with him to find the swing he needed to compete.

By the time he left Leadbetter, Price felt like a new player even though he felt he still had lots of work to do. Friends were amazed at what they saw when he returned to Europe and, that July, he almost won the British Open. "Should have won it," he said. "I birdied ten, eleven, and twelve the last day for a three-shot lead. Walking on the thirteenth tee, I said to my caddy, 'Well, that's done it, now all we have to do is finish.' "

The minute he said that, Price was a dead man. He played the last six holes four over par and lost the tournament to Tom Watson by one stroke. It was a loss that would haunt him for years, but it also taught him a painful lesson about not taking anything for granted in golf, especially in a major.

He had already decided to take a shot at the U.S. tour before the British because he was convinced that he needed to compete with the world's best players on a regular basis in order to become one of them. He made it through Q-School on his first try and then won the World Series of Golf in 1983, a remarkable victory for a rookie and one that was critical to his development as a player.

Since the World Series carries a ten-year exemption, Price didn't have to worry about making the top 125 on the money list each year. He was already in. That meant he could experiment with Leadbetter and try new things without worrying that he was going to go into a slump that would cost him his card.

The next eight years weren't easy. Price had flashes of brilliance: a course record 63 in the third round of the Masters in 1986 and a number of tournaments where he led early or charged late. But he never won. "I always threw in one bad round," he said. "I hadn't learned yet how to shoot seventy or seventy-one on the day I was going badly. It was always seventy-five, and that would be the difference between first and fifth or eighth."

He had another chance to win the British in 1988, leading Seve Ballesteros by two shots going into the final round at Lytham and St. Anne's. He shot 69 the last day, which should have been good enough to win except for the fact that Ballesteros, in one of the last great demonstrations of his wizardry, made shots from everywhere all day on his way to a 65 that beat Price by two shots.

"I knew after that tournament that my swing was good enough to win," he said. "I hit the ball better than anyone that week but I was out-putted. After that I became much more conscious of my putting."

He finally broke through in 1991 when he won the Byron Nelson in Dallas. That was the boost he needed. He won again before the year was over (at the Canadian Open) and finished a career-high seventh on the money list. He won twice more in 1992 — including the PGA — and won more than $1.1 million. Then came the four victories and the player-of-the-year award in 1993. They were gratifying and enriching, but they left Price wanting more.

He knew that no matter how many times he won in Hartford or Dallas or Chicago or even Ponte Vedra that the measure of a truly great player is how he performs in the majors. While his good friend Norman sometimes rationalizes about his many near-misses in the majors, Price never hesitated to talk about the holes he felt still had to be filled. "A lot of guys win one major," he said. "I want more than that. That was the disappointing thing about '93, I was never in serious contention in a major. That's what I want to change this year."

Price was now living the life of a full-fledged superstar. He had bought Norman's plane in the fall when Norman decided to buy a bigger plane, and he was planning to rent private homes at all four majors so that he and his family and friends would have room to spread out in a way that is impossible in even the poshest hotel.

He was also considering leaving IMG, which had managed him almost since the beginning of his career. Norman had left at the end of 1993 to start his own company and Price was wondering if going out on his own might not be the right way to go.

"IMG has always been very good to me," he said. "We've had disputes, but they've been cleared up. They're a very big company, though, and someone like Greg feels that he needs more personal attention than they can give him. I'm not at that point yet."

That "yet" would turn out to be a key word.

Price didn't come to Doral with very high expectations, and he was right. He played four mediocre rounds, never breaking par, and ended up tied for seventy-second place. He wasn't panicking, though; this was only a warm-up. Faldo played even worse, missing the cut, and Norman, after barely making the cut, shot 69–67 the last two days to finish seventh.

This was the week when all the big news was being made off the golf course. Beman dropped his bombshell on Tuesday. Then, on Wednesday, while rain was washing out the Pro-Am (no refund of the $3,500 entry fee for the amateurs) came word that Phil Mickelson had broken his leg skiing. At twenty-four, Mickelson had been anointed as the Next Great American Hope. He had won a tournament while still in college and then had won twice in 1993, his first full year on tour. When he won at La Costa to start the year, he became the youngest player since (who else?) Jack Nicklaus to have won four times.

He would be out for at least eight to ten weeks, interrupting a year in which he had already won $315,645. That put him in second place on the money list ($5,000 behind the Gritty Little Bruin) at the end of the West Coast swing.

Mickelson's injury meant that two of the best American players were now on the sidelines, since Azinger was in Los Angeles that week for his fourth round of chemotherapy. By Sunday, the list of missing Americans had grown to three. As he warmed up on the range for the final round at Doral, Fred Couples felt a surge of pain in his back and collapsed in agony. He had to be helped off the range to the fitness trailer, where he was worked on feverishly in the hope that whatever had tightened on him might loosen up and allow him to play.

A few minutes before his tee time, rules official Jon Brendle came in to see if Couples was going to be able to play. Couples asked him to wait a minute so he could see if he could stand up. He got halfway up, let out a scream, and collapsed. No one knew when he would play again.

Couples's sudden absence meant that John Huston, his playing partner, would have to play alone. There was no time to re-pair and no one hanging around who could play as a marker for Huston. He ended up playing the first twelve holes alone before Brian Claar, who had played in one of the earlier groups, came back out to play in with him as a marker.

By then, the tournament had come down to two men: Huston and Billy Andrade. These two had followed similar career paths since joining the tour in 1988. Each had won two tournaments and been labeled a future star at one point in his career. Huston was almost thirty-three. Andrade had just turned thirty.

The phrase on tour for someone who shows great potential is "he's got a lot of game." (Conversely, if someone doesn't look like a player, the phrase is "he can't play dead.") Huston and Andrade both had plenty of game. Andrade also had the kind of personality that would quickly make him into one of the game's big stars if he could ever relocate the magic he had conjured up in 1991.

Andrade won twice that year — twice in a row. Once upon a time, players winning back-to-back tournaments on tour wasn't that unusual an occurrence. After all, Byron Nelson won eleven straight times in 1945. But as more and more good players began appearing, winning two tournaments in a row became a rarity. In fact, when Price won the Hartford and the Western back-to-back in 1993, he became only the fourth player in the 1990s to win two in a row on tour. Hale Irwin had done it in 1990, winning the U.S. Open and the Westchester in consecutive weeks, and Davis Love had done it in 1992 at the Heritage and Greensboro. Irwin was a three-time U.S. Open winner, Love a Ryder Cup hero, and Price was a PGA champion and a player of the year.

That was fast company for Billy the Kid — or Chachi Chacherelli, as Sluman called him — but it was exactly where he wanted and expected to be.

Andrade first signed his autograph in sixth grade. Actually he *practiced* signing his autograph, killing time when class got boring by repeatedly signing his name the way he planned to sign it when he was a big star. At that point in his life he wasn't certain what he was going to be a star in, only that he was going to be one.

By the time he hit high school he knew the answer: golf. He had played all sports until then, but kept getting hurt in football, couldn't hit a curve ball in baseball, and didn't have the size or quickness to progress all that far in basketball. He did continue to play basketball through high school, playing for a small Rhode Island prep school. At the end of his senior year, he was named all-state, which sounds impressive except for the fact that the "state" in question was a six-school prep league that, according to Andrade, "wasn't exactly full of stellar players."

Nonethless, the legend of his basketball prowess has followed him. To this day, the PGA Tour media guide mentions that he was an all-state basketball player in high school and most profiles of Andrade mention that he was quite a high school basketball player. "It got a little out of hand after a while," Andrade said. "One of my cousins, who remembered that we were 2–18 my junior year, called me after one story and said, 'What's all this all-state basketball player stuff?' "

Andrade did average 20 points a game as a senior. "I shot fifty times a game," he said. "Didn't throw a pass the entire year."

It was in golf where he really *was* a star. His grandparents had introduced him to the game as a kid and he fell in love with it, although he admits that for the first couple of years the game's main appeal for him was driving golf carts. By the time he was in high school, when he wasn't being an all-state guard, he was winning a lot of golf tournaments.

He chose Wake Forest over a bevy of other schools, partly because he loved the campus, partly because he was offered an Arnold Palmer Scholarship. There, he faced the first real crisis of his career when he finally decided he had to change his grip.

Although millions of dollars are spent every year on golf instruction and millions of words are written about the golf swing, there are really only two basics in the game: grip and stance. If you have a bad grip or a bad stance, your chances of playing the game well are severely diminished.

Almost everything else is based on feel, and small technical flaws really don't matter. Tom Watson's swing was always too long, Jack Nicklaus had a flying elbow, and Arnold Palmer looked like a corkscrew at the end of his follow-through. All three managed to play the game fairly well. The consensus among today's players is that the two purest swings on the PGA Tour in the last ten years belong to Tom Purtzer and Steve Elkington. Each is a good player, but not anywhere close to being great. Elkington has won five times in eight years on tour; Purtzer five in twenty.

But no one succeeds without a decent grip and stance. That's the first thing every pro teaches, and the best ones, once they see that a kid with talent has that right, will pretty much leave him alone. Sure, Paul Azinger's grip looks different, but his stance is perfect and his grip isn't so far awry that he can't get the club back into the proper position — although he has had a tendency to lose the ball to the left at times during his career.

When Andrade first started playing with his grandparents, he used a baseball grip because he didn't know any better and it was comfortable. Later, he took a couple of lessons and learned a proper golf grip but still had a very strong — too strong — grip that caused him to hook the ball a lot more than he wanted to. His natural talent and feel for the game allowed him to overcome that all through high school, but when he got to college he knew he was going to have to make a change.

To be that good a player, especially when you are thinking about a pro career, and make a radical change in your grip can be traumatizing. Andrade knew his golf would get worse before it got better and he was nervous, even though everyone whose opinion he respected told him he had to make the change if he wanted to have a future in the game.

His savior turned out to be Jesse Haddock, his college coach. Haddock is one of college golf's legends. He had been at Wake Forest for so long there are people who think the school's buildings were constructed around him. He can be as tough and mean as any coach around. When Curtis Strange was at Wake, Haddock spent three years telling him he wasn't any good, didn't work a lick, and never would be any good.

But when Andrade faced his grip crisis, Haddock stuck with him. He told him to make the change and not worry about his spot in the lineup, that he would keep on playing him no matter how much his game might suffer. Andrade made the change during the winter, spent a lot of time shoveling snow off the driving range so he could hit balls in January and February, and was relieved and amazed at how quickly he was able to make the adjustment. It was at the end of that spring that he began to think he had a realistic chance at a pro career.

"Until then, I just wasn't good enough," he said. "It would be easy for me to say, 'Well, my education was important so I stayed in school,' but the truth is I didn't have any choice. I'm pretty sure I wouldn't have left anyway because education was always very important in my family. My grandfather always used to tell me, 'You have to hit the books because that's the only way to find out what's in them.' I didn't find out until I was older that he had gone to Bates College on a baseball scholarship and flunked out and that's why it was so important to him. The odds are I wouldn't have left, but the fact is I never had to make the decision."

Wake won the national championship Andrade's senior year — coming from sixteen shots behind on the last day to do it — but Andrade decided to play amateur golf for one more year and go back to school for a fifth year to get his degree. That turned out to be a critical decision in his life because if he had turned pro that summer and not gone back to school in the fall of '86 he might never have met Jody Reedy.

Andrade was lonely that fall since most of his class had graduated in the spring. He was complaining to a friend about his lack of a social life and the fact that he didn't have a date for homecoming. His friend mentioned a sorority sister of hers who had just broken up with someone. She thought they might hit it off and, besides, she said, you two look a lot alike.

Sort of. They both have brown hair and brown eyes and they both have a gleam in their eyes that hints at a good sense of humor. Billy is boyishly handsome; Jody is girlishly pretty. Billy has a better golf swing; Jody looks a lot better in shorts.

Wake is a small school. Billy went to a football game that weekend and had someone point Jody out to him. Jody already knew who he was from a ceremony at which the golf team had been honored. A few days later, Billy was sitting in a local deli when Jody walked by.

"Hi, Billy," she said.

He turned around, smiled, and apparently not the least bit surprised that a stranger knew his name (he was, after all, a big golf star), said, "Hi, Jody."

He was leaving town in two days for a golf tournament in Venezuela. Was she, by any chance, free for dinner the next night? She was. Billy was elated until it hit him that that next night was game seven of the American League Championship Series between his beloved Boston Red Sox and the California Angels. He would have to miss the game or miss the date. He opted to miss the game.

"I knew if I went away for two weeks without going out with her that she would be going out with someone else by the time I got back," he said. "Wake is just that kind of school. I made a reservation at the best Italian restaurant I knew and figured I'd just have to deal with missing the game."

When he showed up to pick her up the next night, she was watching television. Specifically, she was watching the Red Sox and Angels. "You know, if you'd rather just order a pizza and watch the game, that would be fine with me," she said.

He was tempted — really tempted. But no, he had to make an impression. And watching a baseball game and munching on a pizza wasn't the way to do that. They walked to his car and, much to Jody's surprise, Billy opened the passenger door. "Since he was from the North, I wasn't really expecting that," she said. "I was impressed that he was such a gentleman."

She was less impressed when he got in, slid across the seat to the driver's side, and waited for her to climb in. "The door on this side has been stuck for months," he explained.

At the restaurant, Billy wanted to order linguine with clam sauce but decided against it because he didn't think that garlic on his breath on a first date was a great idea. Jody ordered the linguine with clam sauce.

"I was hooked," he said.

So was she. They made a date to go to a football game when he got back from Venezuela. Soon after that, Billy called his older sister and told her he thought he was in love. "Whatever you do, don't tell her that," his sister ordered. "You'll scare her off."

Right, he said. Absolutely not. That night he told her.

Billy went to Q-School the next winter and passed with flying colors. He returned from the second stage at Pinehurst and proposed. They were married the following summer and spent almost no time at home during the first few months of their marriage. Trying to hold onto his card, Billy played the last thirteen tournaments of the year. He missed — finishing 134th on the money list — but that stretch did answer one question for the Andrades: Jody was not going to survive slogging around after Billy every week.

"I think it took her about a month to be sure," Billy said. "But there wasn't any question that she wasn't going to be happy following me around a golf course every day or going shopping. I mean, this is someone who got her degree in economics and now has a master's. When she was a senior, she won some big economics award, and at the dinner, they asked each of the winners to talk a little bit about what they were going to do after graduation. One guy is going to Harvard for his MBA, another is going to Georgetown law school. Jody gets up and says, 'I'm going out on the PGA Tour with my husband.' Let's face it, something was wrong with this picture."

Billy knew Jody wasn't going to be able to deal with thirty weeks a year on tour. He also knew that their marriage wasn't going to work if they were apart thirty weeks a year. He came up with a compromise idea: what if she could work the weeks she was on tour? He had gotten to know Chuck Will, the associate producer of CBS's golf telecasts. Maybe he could find work for her.

He could. "You want to work for me?" Chuck Will said when Jody Andrade presented herself to him at the CBS trailer one afternoon. "Fine. You're hired. Get me a cup of coffee."

Jody's career with CBS almost ended at that instant, but she bit her tongue and quickly learned that Will's bark was a lot worse than his bite. Will figured out pretty quickly that this wasn't someone cut out for go-fer work, and Jody quickly was moved through the ranks to the job of announcer's assistant. She was so good that CBS asked her to work on tennis at the U.S. Open and if she would be interested in moving to New York to work full-time for the network in marketing.

Jody was happy with the part-time work. It was not the most intellectually challenging job in history, but she enjoyed the rush of live TV and the fun of the little soap operas that are a part of any traveling carnival.

"It wasn't something I wanted to do forever," she said. "But at twenty-two, it was terrific."

Most important, it meant that she could be with Billy on tour for fifteen to twenty weeks a year without losing her mind. That also made Billy's life easier because he didn't have to worry all day whether Jody was bored out of her mind waiting for him to get finished at the golf course.

He survived his return trip to Q-School, finishing third at the 1988 Fall Classic, and improved steadily the next two years, making more than $200,000 each year to establish himself as one of the game's future stars.

Then, in a two-week period in June 1991, the future became the present. Andrade hadn't even planned to play in the Kemper Open that year. He didn't like the Tournament Players Club at Avenel, the new golf course in Potomac, Maryland, that had replaced fabled Congressional as the tournament site in 1987. The course change saved the tour lots of money (since it owned Avenel it didn't have to pay neighboring Congressional's hefty rental fee) but angered a lot of players who considered trading Avenel for Congressional akin to trading Yogi Berra for Yogi Bear.

But Andrade changed his mind about playing the Kemper when he forgot to enter the Byron Nelson and had to sit out a week in May he hadn't planned to sit out. The Avenel golf course had been improved considerably in the four years since it had opened, and Andrade felt comfortable from the first day, when he shot 68. The course was playing fast and easy and scores were frighteningly low. Andrade shot 64–64 the next two days and was 19 under par with three holes to play on Sunday. That put him in second place, behind his pal Jeff Sluman, who was in the clubhouse at 21 under.

He birdied 16 and 17, then made par from the bunker at 18, to finish tied for first. Sluman was waiting for him when he came into the scorer's tent. "Make sure you add 'em up right, Chachi," he said, since Andrade hadn't signed his card yet.

In the playoff they went back to 17, a par-three with water in front of the green. Andrade had stuck a five-iron eight feet thirty minutes earlier. This time he hit it six feet. Sluman's shot also flew right at the flag and Andrade walked off the tee thinking one of them would make a birdie putt here and it would be over. The next sound he heard was an "aaahh" from the crowd. Sluman's ball had come up just short and gone in the water.

He had won the tournament and $180,000. His only concern was Sluman, who had been one of the players who had taken him under his wing almost from day one on tour — "Little guys have to stick together," Sluman said — and now had been denied his second tournament victory by his young pal Chachi.

Andrade lost sleep worrying about it that week. He was concerned that it might affect his friendship with Sluman. He walked into the fitness trailer at Westchester the next week and found Sluman lying face down on a rubdown table. Nervously, he tapped him on the shoulder. Sluman picked his face up, looked at Andrade, and said, "I still don't know how that fucking ball went in the water."

Andrade breathed a sign of relief. Then he went out and won Westchester. "I was exhausted on Thursday, but somehow I shot sixty-eight," he said. "After the round I was out on the range and Jay Haas came up and asked me how I played. I told him and he said, 'You know, Billy, the best time to win your second tournament is the week after you've won your first.'"

That thought stayed in Andrade's mind all week. It almost made sense. Having won a tournament and all that comes with it — the two-year exemption, a spot in the Masters, the World Series of Golf, and the Tournament of Champions — he had absolutely no pressure on him to perform the next week. Some players are so exhausted and elated that they slam their trunks the next Friday without a second thought. Andrade realized after his good start Thursday that Haas might be right.

He hung around the lead the next two days and then got one more boost on the 18th tee Saturday afternoon when he heard Brad Bryant, who was leading by two shots at the time, say to his caddy, "All I want to do is make birdie on this hole and then hope for a rainout tomorrow."

In other words, Bryant — who had not won on tour — thought his best chance to win the tournament was to not play on Sunday. It didn't rain Sunday, and Andrade, pumped and full of confidence, roared past Bryant and everyone else, shot 68, and won by one. Two weeks, two victories, and $360,000 in the bank.

And a phone that wouldn't stop ringing. When Jody called in to check messages on Monday night, there were more than a hundred messages on the tape.

At first it was nice, wonderful in fact. Andrade went to the U.S. Open the next week, and as soon as he arrived he was approached by a U.S. Golf Association official. Could he come to the media tent for a pretournament interview?

He sure could. The official asked him what would be convenient. Andrade suggested the next morning at 9 o'clock. The official looked at his schedule. Sorry, Nicklaus is coming in then. Okay, how about 10 o'clock? No, we've got Faldo then. Fine, 11? Sorry, Watson.

Andrade threw up his hands. "You tell me when," he said. Well, could he come that afternoon at 4 o'clock, right after Seve and just before Palmer?

"Right after Seve and just before Palmer," Andrade repeated. "Yeah, I think I can handle that."

He missed the cut at the Open that week, but what the hell, he was on a joyride now. He and Jody took two weeks off and had a great time celebrating their sudden success. They laughed about that first date when Jody had asked Billy what he wanted to do after he graduated and Billy answered, "I'm going to be a professional golfer."

Jody's response had been direct. "That's nice," she said. "But what else will you do?" Now they had a definitive answer to that question: become rich beyond their wildest dreams. "The week after Westchester, the guy who handled Billy's money at IMG called and said, 'Jody, you guys have $360,000 sitting here, what do you want me to do with it?' And I said, 'I haven't the faintest notion.' "

Billy went to a Red Sox game one night during their vacation, and Sean McDonough and Bob Montgomery had him come up to the TV booth to do a couple of innings with them. His signature, now perfected, was very much in demand. It was all so much *fun.*

When Andrade got back on tour, everyone wanted a piece of him. His offers for outings and overseas tournaments and sponsorships quadrupled. Everyone wanted to talk to him or have their picture taken or just have him say a few words to their little corporate group.

Yes, yes, yes, Andrade said. And then yes, yes, and yes some more. He said yes in part because all sorts of money was being tossed in his direction. Beyond that, though, he didn't want to say no to anyone. "I'm a pleaser," he said. "I want everyone to like me. I mean everyone. I've always been that way. I don't like to say no and have people think I'm big-timing them or something."

Sometimes pleasers end up pleasing everyone but themselves. Andrade did so much the second half of '91 and early in '92 that he seemed to be constantly tired the next year. He changed club companies for big money and wasn't comfortable with the new clubs. The contract was voided and he went back to his old clubs, but the upward curve he had been on for three years had turned the other way. He wasn't awful in '92, but he slipped from fourteenth to seventy-sixth on the money list, had only two top-ten finishes, and went from $615,765 to $202,509 in earnings.

The kind of money Andrade was making at the age of twenty-seven, especially at a time when the economy in New England was in a deep funk, was bound to cause some jealousy. When Billy and Jody went north for the summer the next year, they began to hear wild rumors. One had them getting divorced, another had Billy's parents getting divorced. One day Billy even heard from a friend that his father was telling people that he and Jody were about to split.

"I don't know what it is about New England, maybe it's the curse of the Red Sox, but people can be very, very negative," he said. "When I first started on tour, people would ask me what I was going to do when I didn't make it and had to come home. Then, when I did make it, I started hearing all this crazy stuff about my personal life. It hurt — a lot. I mean, if you want to say I'm an overrated golfer or I can't make a putt, fine, I can deal with that. But leave my family alone."

The money and the jealousy and the wild rumors were the least of Andrade's worries by the end of the year. After his success in '91, he and Jody had bought a house in Atlanta (that was one way to spend some of the money) and had decided to start a family the following year. In the fall, Jody got pregnant and Billy stopped caring all that much about what was wrong with his golf game. Life was wonderful again.

Two days before Christmas, Jody didn't feel very well. They went to the doctor the next day. She had lost the baby. Like any young couple, the Andrades dealt with the trauma by trying to look ahead and by listening to all their friends and family and the doctors who told them this was not an uncommon occurrence and the next time everything would turn out all right.

Billy played better the first six months of '93, but by July, Jody hadn't gotten pregnant again. "I was freaking out," she said. "I was convinced I was never going to get pregnant again. I just wasn't handling it all very well."

Just before the British Open, Billy sat Jody down and told her he understood how she was feeling and her anxiety was understandable. But he was twenty-nine and healthy and she was twenty-seven and healthy and it hadn't been all that long and she needed to relax and not obsess about getting pregnant again. He knew that was a hard thing to ask her to do, but he thought it would be healthy for both of them if she made a conscious effort not to be so hard on herself every month.

She knew he was right, and she vowed to not freak out the next month if she wasn't pregnant. But when she did her pregnancy test the first week in August, she freaked out anyway — she was pregnant. She had to fly to Grand Blanc, Michigan, that afternoon to meet Billy at the Buick Open. When she told him the news that night, they both agreed that — unlike the first time — they wouldn't tell anyone until the first trimester had safely passed.

Times were tense during the next two months. After starting the year off well, with five top-ten finishes during the first four months of the season, Billy had hit the worst slump of his career. He missed seven straight cuts from July until late September and was more uptight on the golf course than he had ever been in his life.

"Every week I would start out saying, 'Okay, let's have fun playing this week,' " he said. "Then I'd miss a putt early, catch a bad break, make a bogey or a double bogey someplace, and boom! I'm not having any fun."

Very few golfers like to talk about slumps when they are in the midst of them. "It's as if talking about it makes it real," Jody said. "If you keep on saying, 'I'm hitting the ball okay,' you don't have to face up to the fact that you just aren't playing very well."

Jody could see that Billy was uptight, but experience had taught her not to push him. And yet, she remembered what one of her friends, Cathy Wiebe, had told her about her experience in 1991, when her husband, Mark, had played poorly and lost his card. "She finally sat him down and said, 'I can't *not* talk about this anymore.' I was certain Billy was going to come out of it because I wasn't ready to think, what if? It's the unspoken terror that everyone has out here."

Billy wasn't in danger of losing his card because he had played so well the first half of the year, but he was baffled by what was happening. Finally, late in September '93, Jody decided it was time for her to say something. She knew Billy respected a lot of people he had worked with on his game: his teacher, Rick Smith; his psychologist, Bob Rotella; his friends on tour like Sluman and Love and Brad Faxon. Maybe, Jody suggested, Billy should just be Billy Andrade for a while and not be all the things people suggested he should be. She wasn't putting down his friends and advisers, but she thought he had too many thoughts in his head, too much clutter.

"The Billy Andrade I know is a great player," she said. "Just be him for a week and see what happens."

Andrade left for the Buick Southern Open the next night with that thought in his head: "I'm Billy Andrade and I'm a good player." He made the cut with ease to end the streak, then shot 67 on Sunday to come from behind and tie with four other players for first place. John Inman won the playoff, but the streak was over. He was still a good player. Two weeks later, he finished third at the Texas Open. That put his earnings for the year at $365,759, his second best year on tour.

More important than that, the first trimester had come and gone without incident. Andrade could now tell the whole world that he would be a father in April.

At Doral, Jody was a month from her due date and in no condition to walk the golf course. But she was there with Billy's parents and he felt good from the very beginning of the week. Doral is one of the tour's traditional golf courses, the Blue Monster, so named because the courses are color-coded at Doral and the Blue becomes a monster when the wind kicks up.

It was brutal on Thursday, with gusts up to 50 miles per hour. Only three players broke 70. Andrade wasn't one of them, but he was right at 70, tied for fourth. A 68 the next day tied him for the lead, and a 66 Saturday sent him home with a two-shot lead on the field.

This was what he had been waiting for since the back-to-back wins. "I can't wait to win again," he said often, "because this time, I know I'll handle it better."

He handled the front nine just fine on Sunday, with a one-under-par 35, and still led by two. But an ugly bogey at 10, at almost the same moment that Huston was birdieing 13, suddenly dropped him into a tie for the lead, and another Huston birdie put him behind. Huston was brilliant, finishing with a 66, nailing a 10-foot par putt at the 18th to stay two shots ahead of Andrade.

Three groups behind, Andrade knew he had to birdie both 17 and 18 to tie. Difficult, but not impossible. When he hit a gorgeous eight-iron to three feet at 17, it looked like he was halfway there. Only the putt didn't go in. It slid left all the way and never touched the hole. Andrade stood there frozen in shock. He was still in a semi-coma when he hooked his tee shot at 18. That led to a closing bogey, which knocked him down to a tie for second with his old friend Brad Bryant.

It was a downer for Andrade even though he picked up a check for $123,200. He had wanted to win, to feel that rush again, to be back in that group that won golf tournaments. He had come close, but he still wasn't there.

Cameron James Andrade was born on April 5. It took an emergency C-section and a few scary moments to bring him into the world, but he arrived healthy and happy. Not winning Doral meant that his father didn't get into the Masters and was home that week. The Masters could wait until next year.

10

ARNIE ... AND FRIENDS

AFTER DORAL, the tour works its way north, stopping first in Fort Lauderdale for the Honda Classic, then moving to Orlando for the Nestle Invitational, before finally arriving at the House That Deane Built — the Tournament Players Club in Ponte Vedra for the Players Championship.

Most players either play all four Florida weeks or skip one stop — usually the Honda. Doral is a golf course most people don't skip and, at $1.4 million, it is one of the larger purses on tour. Everyone plays the Players because it is the tournament created by and for the touring professionals.

And everyone plays at Nestle because of Arnie.

Of course no one on tour ever says he is going to play "Nestle." They all say they're playing "Bay Hill."

Bay Hill is the golf course Arnold Palmer owns, it is the place where he lives during the winter months, and it has been the site of "his" golf tournament since 1979. If you are a golf pro and Arnie invites you to his tournament — Bay Hill is an invitational — you go play.

"We all grew up watching Arnie and rooting for him," Jeff Sluman said. "But the real magic comes when you meet him. There's just no one like him."

There are very few legendary figures in sports who actually measure up to people's expectations in person. Mickey Mantle used to slam bus windows on little kids' hands, and Joe DiMaggio isn't really all that interesting if he won't talk about Marilyn Monroe. Bjorn Borg used to kill time at tennis tournaments watching cartoons, and John Riggins once fell asleep under a table at a posh Washington dinner party after telling Supreme Court Justice Sandra Day O'Connor, "Loosen up, Sandy baby."

There is also O. J. Simpson and countless other tales about fallen heroes. Pete Rose was banned from baseball for gambling, and Michael Jordan was lucky not to be banned or suspended from basketball for some of his gambling escapades.

And then there is golf. Jack Nicklaus is respected, even revered, after winning eighteen Grand Slam events. Tom Watson is deeply respected after winning eight. Greg Norman makes countless millions, and Nick Faldo amazes people with his relentless obsession with the game.

But no one has ever been loved and revered and *worshipped* like Arnie. He was once a great player, good enough to win seven Grand Slam titles and a U.S. Amateur title. "I get mad when people say I won only seven majors," he said. "Because at the time I won the Amateur, it may have been the biggest one of all. It was certainly the most work."

Okay, give him eight majors. That means Nicklaus has twenty, since he won the Amateur twice. Palmer last won a major in 1964. Lyndon Johnson was president and Vietnam was just becoming a blip on the national consciousness. Nicklaus clearly surpassed him as a player and so have others. And yet no one, including Nicklaus, would argue with the fact that Palmer has been the single most important player in the history of golf.

Comparing his game or his swing to Bobby Jones's or Ben Hogan's or Walter Hagan's or Sam Snead's or Byron Nelson's or Nicklaus's, Watson's, Faldo's, or Price's is completely and totally irrelevant. Palmer made golf a sport people wanted to see, in person and on television. He brought big money to the game and, by sheer force of his personality, helped make golf a major sport. Later, he played a huge role in the development of the senior tour. Without Palmer there is no senior tour today — period. Without Palmer corporate America would not have come running when Deane Beman called. Without Palmer no one on tour would be flying his own plane today.

"You know, I was the first golfer to buy my own plane," Palmer said, smiling. "But when I bought my first one, I had won the Masters twice. Now these guys win *anywhere* and they buy a plane."

And that is because of Palmer.

The question is not *whether* Palmer is the most important figure in the history of the game, it is *why* he is. To simply say he had charisma and he hitched his pants and always charged is simplistic. The fact is, he charged backward almost as often as he charged forward. Who can forget the U.S. Open at Olympic in 1966? Up seven with nine to play, Palmer ended up losing a playoff to Billy Casper.

No, it wasn't just charisma or the corkscrew swing or even the drop-dead smile that still makes women sigh. It went beyond that. Palmer, it should be remembered, is the son of a club pro. He talks often about the influence his father had on him. Deke Palmer taught his son the game and the etiquette of the game. When young Arnold threw a club in a tournament, he was warned to never ever do that again. Since his father was an employee at Latrobe Country Club (which Palmer now owns) and not a member, Arnold swam, not in the club pool with his friends who were the children of members, but in lakes and streams near the club. He worked long hours like his father and he was taught that every member he came in contact with was an important person.

That was the beginning. To this day, Palmer approaches everyone he meets the way a club pro would. The club pro is the guy who has time to listen to his members go through their rounds shot by shot and smiles and somehow looks interested even if he's been at work for twelve hours that day. He is always patient, always courteous, always manages to give everyone the impression that their life is very, very important to him.

Walk the golf course with Palmer and you can see the club pro's son at work. When people call his name, he doesn't give them the Papal Wave the way most players do, he searches them out, makes eye contact — *every time* — and says something. "How are you today . . . Good to see you . . . Thanks for that . . . Sure is hot, got to keep on going, though . . . Yes, I remember you, Oakmont in '73? Right, of course . . ."

And so on. People leave the golf course feeling as if they talked to Arnie, touched him in some way. Of course it is he who touched them.

Players are not quite so easily impressed as fans. There is always a certain amount of jealousy directed at the wealthiest and most famous players. Many of the younger players will tell you that Nicklaus and Watson can be condescending. "I'm sure it's subconscious," Davis Love said one day, "but sometimes with those guys you feel as if they have to remind you how great they were because they can't show you anymore. They don't do it on purpose, but they do it."

Not everyone finds Nicklaus to be that way. Both Greg Norman and Nick Price remember the first time they spoke to Nicklaus as young, unknown players, and both say the exact same thing: "He treated me like an equal even though I wasn't anywhere close to being one."

There are also those who find Nicklaus's support for his sons' golf careers — especially that of Gary, the youngest and most talented of them — heavy-handed. In 1994, Nicklaus played at Pebble Beach, Los Angeles, and Doral to start the season. Jack Jr. and Gary were also at Pebble on sponsor exemptions, and Steve played there as his father's amateur partner. Gary also got into L.A. and Doral on sponsor exemptions.

When Patrick Burke, who had just missed keeping his card in 1993 and was in that 126-to-150 netherworld of wondering week to week if he would get into tournaments, noticed the presence of Nicklaus *père* and Nicklaus *fils* at three straight events, he thought he noticed a trend.

"I heard one of the caddies had a dream," he said. "In it, Jack had 144 sons and *no one* could get into Doral."

When that line showed up in *Golf World* magazine quoting an anonymous player, Burke, who has one of the tour's most wicked senses of humor, was incensed. "Why wouldn't they give me credit for the line?" he said. "What do I care if Jack gets upset. It's not as if he's going to invite me to play in the [Nicklaus-run] Memorial."

These days, it is Norman who is the subject of more backbiting in the locker room than anyone else. Part of it is jealousy, part of it is players wondering why someone who has won two majors (one less than Larry Nelson and as many as Andy North) is treated by the public and media as if he is Nicklaus, Watson, or Faldo.

Norman also has a tendency to say things that are meant innocently but come out sounding arrogant. At Doral, he mentioned in a press conference that he was helicoptering to the tournament each morning from his home in nearby Hobe Sound.

"Nice to sleep in your own bed and then just hop on the 'copter each morning, isn't it, Greg?" someone said.

"Yeah, but you know, it isn't quite as easy as it sounds," Norman said. "Today, we had a really windy, bumpy flight coming over, and if the weather were to get any worse I might miss my tee time altogether."

The reaction in the locker room to that comment was almost unanimous: "Oh boo-hoo, tough life having to worry about those winds."

Everyone in the spotlight has loyal subjects and critics. Except Arnie. No critics. He is the Teflon golfer. When some of his business deals went bad, he was seen by the public as a victim of IMG's mismanagement. Sure, he liked to party when he was younger and some of his drinking binges are still talked about, but, what the heck, that just means he was human, a man of the people. One of the guys.

The last four words are the key when it comes to the locker room: Arnie has always been *one of the guys.*

Virtually every player on tour remembers the first time he met Arnie. The story always is the same: a timid introduction by the young player, followed by a warm handshake from the legend, a look in the eye, and then questions: "Where are you from? Married? How are you playing? If there's ever anything I can do, please let me know," and, inevitably, "Thanks for taking the time to say hello."

In 1991, Palmer made the cut at Bay Hill at the age of sixty-one, a surprise to everyone, including Palmer. That night, Peter Jacobsen went to a nearby Winn-Dixie and asked for a sheet cake that could feed two hundred people and would be ready the next morning.

"The guy looked at me like I was nuts," Jacobsen said. "He just shook his head, laughed, and said there was no way. I said, 'But it's for Arnold Palmer.' He never blinked. All he said was 'Do you need it tonight?' "

The next day, during a rain delay, all the players gathered in the locker room and Jacobsen presented the cake to Palmer. "We just wanted to say thanks, Arnie," Jacobsen said. "It's a great week here every year, and we're thrilled you're playing on the weekend."

Then everyone clapped. Palmer tried to talk, but couldn't. He managed a thank you, then began cutting the cake. "He cut every single piece," Jacobsen said. "And thanked every single guy."

Palmer remembers the afternoon well and becomes emotional even now talking about it. "I was overwhelmed," he said. "It meant a lot because the message was that I was still one of the guys, that I did still have a role to play in this game. And that's important to me. I want to feel like if I have something to say to a younger player, they'll listen to me. I don't want to be some old man going on and on about the old days, but I still have some strong opinions about the tour and the game and the players in the game today. That cake and the way the players acted that day said it was okay for me to still tell them what I think."

And what did he think, sitting in his Bay Hill condo on a warm March Sunday morning in 1994?

"I think the players have almost become too friendly with one another, especially here on our tour," he said. "There's no reason why foreign players should dominate the majors but the last few years they have, except at the U.S. Open. I just think our tour has become too comfortable. When I played, we were friendly, sure, but when it was time to play we went out there to whip one another. You shouldn't walk away from a week that you finished second feeling good because you made a hundred thousand dollars or whatever it is. You should walk away mad because you didn't *win.*

"That's what I always did. That's certainly what Nicklaus did and what Watson did and what Curtis [Strange] did. I think Faldo does that, and probably Azinger too. I'm sure there are others, but there should be *more.*"

Palmer might have put himself in a position to be more of an influence on tour if his good friend Dick Ferris had succeeded Beman as commissioner. Ferris certainly acted as if he wanted the job at Doral on the day of Beman's resignation. Palmer talked him out of it.

"He was definitely interested," he said. "But I told him he was crazy. Right now, he gets to play with the best golfers in the world just about any time he wants to and to enjoy being around the tour. If he becomes commissioner, he has to be available twenty-four hours a day to answer any and all complaints. Why would he want to do that?"

Ferris apparently agreed with Palmer, because shortly after the two men talked he announced that he wasn't a candidate for the job. Palmer had, for the most part, excused himself from tour politics after he and Nicklaus had made their brief attempt to curb Beman in 1983. He was content now to enjoy the week at Bay Hill every year, to play in a few tournaments and a few senior events, and to design golf courses.

Although he had suffered some business setbacks, his one real frustration was the fact that he couldn't play better golf. He would be sixty-five in September, and he knew that his days as a serious competitor on either tour were behind him. And yet it aggravated him when he couldn't break 75 or sometimes even 80.

He still loved to practice, to work on his game, and to spend time in his little workshop tinkering with clubs and searching for the putter that would bring back the '60s (and scores in the 60s) even though he knew it was now the '90s and *he* was the one who was in the 60s.

"Realistically I know where my game is," he said. "But when I walked off the golf course here [at Bay Hill] Friday after missing the cut, I was really angry. What I really wanted to do was go out and pound balls until dark to figure out what the hell was wrong."

As Palmer sat and talked there was a light tap on the screen door in the back of the condo. In walked Curtis Strange. He was playing fairly early that day, and he wasn't sure if he would be around at day's end to see Arnold and Winnie and thank them for the week, so he was dropping by in the morning. Sarah had come to the tournament — her first time out since Phoenix — and had walked the golf course Thursday and Friday. She was starting to feel better.

Palmer looked at Strange, so different from him in so many ways and yet someone he felt a bond with, and smiled the famous smile.

"You aren't that far back," he said. "You start strong today, you could make a move."

Strange laughed. "I don't think I've got that many birdies in me."

"You never know, though, do you?" Palmer said. "That's why we still tee it up."

Strange hugged Winnie Palmer and left to get ready to play. Palmer watched him leave. He had spent a lot of time with Strange, trying to convince him that he owed the public more than just good golf shots. "Players complain to me all the time about how hard it is to constantly sign autographs or talk to the press or spend time with amateurs," he said. "I tell them all the same thing: *'If you don't like it, don't walk out the door. Quit. No one is forcing you to do this.'* "

He sighed. "A lot of players just don't understand how lucky we all are to be doing what we do. I look at my life and all I can do is be thankful for everything I've been given by so many people over so many years."

Maybe that is the key to Arnold Daniel Palmer. After all these years; after playing golf with six presidents; after having signed every autograph; after granting every interview request; after making several thousand golfers wealthy men; he looks back and talks not about what he did for golf, but about what golf did for him.

"Everyone talks about how different Curtis and I are," he said. "And we are in a lot of ways. But there's one way we're exactly the same: we'll both never stop playing. It's just too much damn fun to ever stop."

For many players, Bay Hill means a week at home. A small colony of tour players has sprung up around Orlando in the last ten years. The weather is warm all year, but not quite as stifling as south Florida; there is an abundance of courses; the theme parks are wonderful for young children; and the airport offers connections to enough places that travel is not too difficult.

Lee Janzen lived in nearby Kissimmee, but he hadn't moved there after turning pro. Janzen's family had moved to the area when he was thirteen, and it was there that he had blossomed as a young golfer.

What was most amazing about Janzen was that he arrived at Bay Hill as the U.S. Open champion the world had forgotten. The previous June at Baltusrol, he had taken the lead on the 13th hole on Friday afternoon and never given it up. When Payne Stewart caught him briefly on Sunday, he responded with three birdies on the last five holes, including a chip-in at 16, and became the Open champion.

His victory stunned everyone in golf. Not because they didn't think he had talent. There was no doubt about that. Janzen was twenty-nine and had the kind of short game that makes other players drool. He had won his first tournament in 1992 and finished ninth on the money list for the year. He had won again early in 1993 and was a virtual lock to be the youngest player on the Ryder Cup team even before Baltusrol.

What surprised everyone, even his friends, was that Janzen — or anyone else — could go from never having made a cut at the Open to winning it. His goal when he arrived at Baltusrol was simple: play the weekend. He not only played, he played in the last group on both Saturday and Sunday.

On that last day, Davis Love had sat in the fitness trailer with Rocco Mediate, Janzen's best friend since their days as teammates at Florida Southern, and watched the final holes unfold on television.

"Can Lee Janzen really win the U.S. Open?" Love asked Mediate. "I mean can he really *win?*"

"What do you mean?" Mediate said. "Of course he can, Lee's a great player . . ."

Love shook his head. "That's not what I'm saying. I know that. But he's one of us, he's twenty-nine, this is his first time in contention in a major. He shouldn't really be *ready* for this."

Janzen was ready. Then again, he wasn't. When he rolled in his eight-foot birdie putt at 18 to wrap up a two-shot victory over Stewart, he looked up and saw Mediate standing behind the green with tears in his eyes. "That was the first time I lost it," he said later.

A few minutes later, when his wife, Bev, four months pregnant with their first child, came into the scorer's trailer, he broke down completely. He had to fight his way through an acceptance speech — "every word was an effort" — and from that moment on his world started spinning.

It wasn't any one thing. If it had just been all the offers for outings and overseas tournaments and endorsements, he could have handled that. If it had just been the media requests from around the world, he could have handled that too. If it had just been impending fatherhood, fine. If it had only been dealing with the pressure of playing in his first Ryder Cup, okay. But all of it put together was just too much. And there was one other thing too. "You feel like you should play up to a certain level when you're the U.S. Open champion," he said.

"When I think of the kind of player who wins U.S. Opens, it isn't me. I think of someone on another level. Then, when you don't play well, you start to feel embarrassed."

This is not a new phenomenon by any means. Sluman's 30-yard top on the first tee at the World Series of Golf in 1988 may be the most tangible example of feeling the pressure to prove that you are worthy of the major title you have won. When Larry Mize holed his miraculous chip shot in 1987 to steal the Masters from Greg Norman, he spent a long time feeling he had to prove to people that he hadn't just made a lucky shot but that he really did deserve to win. Nick Price, after winning the 1992 PGA, felt that he wouldn't be validated as a player until he proved he could do it more than once.

Pressure is a relentless thing in golf. It follows you up the ladder, nipping at your heels no matter how high you go. Players start out saying that if they can just get their card and get on tour they will be happy forever. Then it becomes a matter of keeping the card. But just making money isn't enough for a competitor; he wants to win. Winning Phoenix or Hartford or Memphis is awfully nice and brings a lot of money and benefits, but if you want to be considered a special player, you have to win a major. And, as Price points out, if you do win a major, you almost feel as if you have to win another to prove the first one wasn't a fluke.

Janzen leaped from thinking about keeping his card to winning a major in a little more than two years. In 1990, he was 115th on the money list, scrambling until year's end to avoid a return to Q-School. Thirty months later, Davis Love was shaking his head and saying, "Lee Janzen *can* win the U.S. Open."

For several years, Janzen has been an avid reader of Tony Robbins's self-help books. He began keeping a journal shortly after he came on tour, although he doesn't always write in it on a regular basis. Robbins encourages setting goals for yourself, whether for a day, a month, or a year. Janzen's goals for 1993 had been to win a second tournament, to finish in the top ten on the money list, and to make the Ryder Cup team. When he left Baltusrol, he had accomplished those goals and far, far more. That meant setting new goals.

"What you have to do is try and pretend that you haven't really done anything yet," he said. "You have to tell yourself that if you don't keep playing well, you aren't going to have a good year. But deep down, I knew that wasn't true. I knew that if I didn't make another cut, I had already had a great year and that took something out of me. I wasn't playing with the same kind of intensity that I had before the Open."

It wasn't that Janzen wasn't trying. In fact, he may have been trying too hard. At the British Open, knowing that the eyes of the golf world were focused on him as the U.S. Open champion, he started out with solid rounds of 69 and 71. When he got to the golf course on Saturday, he felt flat, wiped out. He had worked so hard to make sure he made the cut that he had nothing left for the weekend. He finished tied for forty-eighth.

It was hard for Janzen to really feel bad about not playing his best golf during the summer. He had decided after the British Open that the most important thing left for him to do was get ready for the Ryder Cup. That was something he had been working toward for a long time, and he wanted to be certain that his game peaked during the last weekend in September.

It didn't work out that way. The most disappointing aspect of the week was Bev's absence. Since her due date was less than a month away, the doctor told her she couldn't even consider a transatlantic flight.

The Janzens are not your typical golf couple. Bev Janzen is ten years older than Lee, and Lee is ten years older than Bev's daughter, Mendy. Lee and Bev met while Lee was in college. Bev was divorced and working in a golf shop in order to support herself and her young daughter. When they started dating, a lot of Lee's friends were skeptical. So was his family. They all changed their minds when they met Bev. The consensus was that they were meant for each other.

Going to the Ryder Cup without Bev was not Lee's idea of a good time, especially since every other player on the team would be traveling with his wife or (in Fred Couples's case) girlfriend. "There was no sense getting upset about it because that was the way it had to be," Janzen said. "But it was lonely."

It became lonelier when Janzen had a terrible week with his putter. He hit the ball fairly well, but his putting — normally his strength — let him down. He got to play only twice: Friday afternoon in the four-ball with Jim Gallagher and Sunday in the singles. He and Gallagher lost an excellent match to Peter Baker and Ian Woosnam on the 18th hole on Friday. Janzen figured he would play at least once on Saturday, especially with Couples struggling. But trailing by three points after the morning matches, Watson felt he had to leave Couples in the lineup even if he was playing poorly.

That hurt Janzen. He understood Watson's feeling the way he did about Couples, but he thought his play on Friday had merited another shot Saturday afternoon. He was so dispirited that when word first began circulating that Sam Torrance wasn't going to play Sunday, he was convinced he would be the name in the envelope. Lanny Wadkins kept Watson from having to make a decision like that and Janzen got to play Colin Montgomerie.

He lost the first two holes of the match, but fought his way back to even through fourteen holes. Then on 15, the reachable par-five, he drilled a three-wood from the fairway to within eight feet. Finally! That was a U.S. Open champion's shot. His teacher, Rick Smith, jumped five feet in the air when the ball landed on the green. "Now he's got him," he said.

Montgomerie got his ball on the green too, but he was 30 feet from the hole. The crowd was as quiet as it had been all day when Montgomerie lined up his long eagle putt. Seconds later, it was as loud as it had ever been when the putt rolled straight into the hole. Janzen was stunned. Convinced he was about to go one up, he now had to make his putt — which suddenly looked about twice as long — to stay even. "All I could think as I was standing over it was if you miss, you're going to hear an unbelievable roar."

He missed. The roar was unbelievable. They halved the next three holes. Montgomerie won, one up, on the strength of the putt on 15. Janzen was devastated. At the moment he shook hands with Montgomerie on 18, things didn't look good for the Americans. They turned around in the next two hours and he found himself back on the 18th green celebrating with his teammates.

It was, though, a little bit of an empty feeling. When the awards ceremony was over, everyone gathered on the putting green to take pictures — first the official team pictures, then the unofficial ones that everyone was taking of each other. Janzen spent a lot of time being the team's unofficial photographer since he was the only player who didn't need to have his picture taken with his wife.

When that was over, they all went back to their rooms to get ready for the victory dinner. Janzen was all by himself, and the fact that he had been the only member of the team who hadn't scored hit him hard. He felt very lonely and let down and, at that moment anyway, not really a part of the victory.

It all changed when he got home. Most people didn't notice who had and who hadn't won matches. All they knew was that the Americans had gone to England and come home with the Ryder Cup. Janzen couldn't turn around without being congratulated. That felt good. So did being home. And when Connor arrived on October 20, complete with Lee's long, curly hair, the disappointments of the summer seemed a long way off.

Janzen could sit in his living room with Bev and look at Connor, then look up on his mantel at the Open trophy. "Sometimes, none of it seemed real," he said. "I would look at Connor and look at Bev and look at the trophy and think I had to be the luckiest guy in the world."

Janzen walked off the 15th green at Bay Hill on Thursday afternoon with a confused look on his face. An old friend walked up as he was on his way to the 16th tee and Janzen stopped to shake hands.

"How's life?" his friend asked.

"Life is good," Janzen answered. "It's my golf that stinks."

He had just birdied the 15th hole, which meant he was now only three over par for the day. He was disgusted. Every week, it seemed, he started out thinking things were going to turn around, and every week the ball started flying in a million different directions on Thursday, usually the wrong ones.

The only exception had been at Phoenix. There, as the defending champion, he had shot 68–69–68 to put himself in position to win the tournament on Sunday. Instead, he shot 74 and faded all the way to thirtieth place. Since then he had gone cut–cut–34th–cut. For the year, he had earned a grand total of $37,453.

He had ended 1993 thinking that the new year would give him the fresh start he needed. He sat down and wrote out a set of new goals:

win again, finish in the top ten on the money list, play well in all the majors.

But it wasn't quite that simple or easy. Janzen was making a lot of changes. He had new clubs, having signed a lucrative deal with the Hogan Company to play the new irons it was marketing. The deal also called for Janzen to carry the Hogan bag and wear a Hogan cap. It made Janzen quite wealthy. He had also changed caddies, dropping Dan Huber, whom he had worked with in '92 and '93, and hiring the more experienced David Musgrove, an Englishman who had worked for Sandy Lyle during his glory years in the late 1980s.

There was one other change that Janzen hadn't contemplated. His agent, Ken Kennerly, had left Advantage International to take over the player-management division of Golden Bear Inc. Jack Nicklaus had decided he wanted his company to manage golfers and had hired Kennerly to recruit them.

Kennerly's profile in the game had greatly increased after Janzen won the Open. Like Janzen, he was twenty-nine and suddenly he found himself managing one of the most-sought-after players in the world. The decision to leave Advantage for Golden Bear had been a big one, especially since it meant that, in their first six months of marriage, he and his wife would be moving into an apartment in Washington then out of it and into a house in Florida.

Naturally, Kennerly wanted his top client to move with him from Advantage to Golden Bear. Just as naturally, Advantage didn't want Janzen to leave. Janzen had only had one agent and that was Kennerly. He wanted to stay with him. Advantage's answer was, in essence, see you in court. As the year began, Advantage, Golden Bear, and Kennerly were still negotiating.

Through it all, Janzen managed to keep his sense of humor. In February, at the Nissan Los Angeles Open, he had been the only one of the 1993 Grand Slam winners in the field. The tournament took out a large ad in the *Los Angeles Times* to sell tickets. There were huge pictures of Jack Nicklaus and Tom Kite, who was the defending champion. Under their pictures, it said, "And there's more: Couples, Watson, Pavin, Mickelson, Stewart, Jacobsen, Crenshaw, Cook, O'Meara — and other top pros!"

The defending U.S. Open champion was one of the 132 other top pros not named in the advertisement. Janzen noticed, but laughed it off. "The only way I'll say anything about it," he said, "is if I win."

Unfortunately, he missed the cut. He really had become the invisible U.S. Open champion.

Janzen wasn't comfortable with his new clubs, and every time he thought he had hit rock bottom, he seemed to find a way to go a little bit lower. Bay Hill was no different: 77–76 and out. That was four missed cuts in five weeks. As he walked off 18 on Friday, Bev was waiting for him.

"What are you going to do?" she asked.

"Go hit some balls," he said. "I mean, I can't keep playing like this forever." He paused and forced a smile. "At least I don't think I can."

The U.S. Open champion kissed his wife and began walking toward the driving range. Not a single person stopped him to ask for an autograph.

Janzen wasn't around for the weekend at Bay Hill, but most of the game's big names were. Nick Price, who had rebounded after his sluggish performance at Doral to win the Honda Classic with a 66 on Sunday, was the leader after two rounds. Greg Norman was in contention, and so were Tom Watson and Fuzzy Zoeller. Vijay Singh, the graceful Fijian who had made a name for himself on tour the year before by winning at Westchester, finishing third at the PGA, and most of all by spending more hours on the range than anyone else, including (gasp!) Tom Kite, was the third-round leader.

The final day was wild. Singh led briefly, then Andrew Magee took command for a while. Norman shot 67 to put himself into the hunt. Watson, just one shot back starting the round, had another tough Sunday with the putter, shooting 73 to finish eighth. He was so aggravated walking up 18 that he decided to do something he had never done in his life. "I was going to throw my putter in the lake after I holed out," he said. "I just figured it was time to do something like that."

He never got the chance, though, because he chipped in from the fringe, meaning that the putter never got out of his bag. It lived to yip another day.

For a long while, late in the afternoon, it looked as if Fuzzy Zoeller was going to win the tournament. That would have been — to put it mildly — a popular victory. Zoeller had won two majors: the 1979 Masters and the 1984 U.S. Open, but his career had been curtailed by recurring back problems. He was forty-two now and hadn't won since 1986, although he had finally found himself virtually pain free after a New York doctor, early in 1993, manipulated his back in such a way that, for some reason, he felt better.

Frank Urban Zoeller — FUZ, or as the golf world called him, Fuzzy — was one of the tour's characters, a genuinely funny man who walked around the golf course whistling regardless of how he was playing. If Zoeller was angry or upset about something, he was the only one who knew about it.

At Bay Hill, Zoeller walked into the locker room one afternoon and saw Janzen sitting at one of the card tables in the middle of the room with a long face. "Hey, Lee J., why the face?" he asked. Without waiting for an answer, he plowed on. "Look outside, man, it's a beautiful day, we're healthy, and these people are actually *paying* us to play golf. Life is a beautiful thing."

Janzen laughed. Zoeller walked around a corner, spotted Curtis Strange and Billy Andrade, and paused to tell a couple of off-color jokes. By the time he reached his own locker, everyone he had come in contact with was laughing.

Zoeller had played well late in '93 and had started '94 much faster than usual. Late Sunday, he arrived at the par-three 17th hole leading the tournament by one shot. He pushed a three-iron shot to the right and appeared to catch a break when the ball conked a spectator on the top of the head.

The spectator was unhurt. Zoeller wasn't. The shot ricocheted from head to (under) tow, ending up in the water. Zoeller's chances sank with the ball. He made five.

Paul Goydos had an adventure of his own at the 17th. He put his tee shot in the water there but arrived to find the ball right on the edge of the hazard. With the crowd urging him on, he took off his shoes and socks, rolled up his pants, and waded into the water. He chopped the ball out onto the green to about 15 feet and then made the putt for a miraculous par.

That shot and routine got Goydos not only his first moments on national TV but also onto sports reports everywhere that evening, including ESPN's Sportscenter. It also earned him a new nickname, courtesy of Janzen: Aquaman.

Aquaman shot only 73 on the last day but finished tied for thirteenth — his fifth top-twenty finish of the year. He earned $19,950 for the week, putting his earnings for the year at more than $135,000. That meant he had already clinched a spot in the top 125 for the year. He had come a long way from his days as a substitute teacher in Long Beach.

When the water and dust and divots finally cleared at the end of the day, the winner was not any of the big names in contention. It was Loren Roberts. At thirty-eight, Roberts held the unofficial title of number one grinder on tour because he had won more money (slightly more than $2.2 million) in his career than any other player who had never won a tournament.

As recently as 1987, at thirty-two, Roberts had been forced to go back to the Fall Classic. He had finished in the top forty on the money list once in his life (twenty-fourth in 1990) and had often told friends that he would never feel complete as a player until and unless he won a tournament.

This, then, was his day of completion. While everyone else was finding people's heads or bunkers or some other form of disaster down the stretch, Roberts held together, shot a solid 67, and walked off with the victory.

Twenty-four hours earlier, after finishing the third round at eight under par, Roberts had been asked to come to the interview room. At that moment he was only one shot behind the leader. However, Singh went on a birdie binge, and by the time Andrew Magee was finished doing his stint with the media, Roberts was three behind the leader.

Sheepishly, Chuck Adams, who had asked Roberts to come in, told him he really wasn't needed. He knew that late on a Saturday afternoon, with deadline fast approaching, the writers weren't going to sit around and listen to anyone who was three shots behind the leader unless his name was Norman, Price, or Palmer. Rather than put Roberts through the embarrassment of talking to an empty room, Adams sent him back to the locker room.

The next night, when Roberts was playing to a packed house with a $216,000 check and the trophy sitting in front of him, a few people couldn't resist teasing Adams about sending the tournament winner away the previous evening.

"Well, if I had known," Adams said.

No one had known, including Roberts. "Until you win out here, you're just a day worker," Roberts said.

The last man out of the locker room each week on tour is the winner. By the time he receives the trophy, does all the requisite post-tournament interviews, poses for pictures, signs all the autographs, and works his way back to clear out his locker, everyone else has moved on.

When Loren Roberts finally left the Bay Hill locker room on that Sunday, the sun had been down for quite a while. After fourteen years on tour, he was no longer a day worker.

11

SHARK ATTACK

BEFORE HE TURNED IT OVER to his successor, Tim Finchem, last June, Deane Beman's office at PGA Tour headquarters in Ponte Vedra was the kind of large, comfortable office you would expect to find if you were looking for the man who is arguably the most powerful person in golf.

Behind the big desk was a large, framed picture taken at dusk on a golf course. Given Beman's position in the sport, it is probably fair to say that he could have hung just about any picture of any hole in the world — the 12th at Augusta, the 18th at Pebble Beach, the Road Hole at St. Andrews — on his wall. The picture is of the ninth at the TPC/Sawgrass.

That should surprise no one, though, because the Tournament Players Club is Beman's creation. Pete Dye designed the golf course, but the concept, the plan, the *dream* was Beman's. He wanted a home for another of his babies — the Players Championship.

When it began in 1974, it was the Tournament Players Championship and, as with the U.S. Open, British Open, and PGA, the plan was to take it around the country to top golf courses. Beman envisioned the tournament as golf's fifth major, maybe even as a fourth major, because it certainly wouldn't have bothered him one little bit if his tournament supplanted the PGA, run by his rivals at the other end of the state, the PGA of America, as major number four.

Beman's problem, just as it later became Jack Nicklaus's problem when he created the Memorial, was that you don't create majors. For one thing, no sport can handle more than four majors in a calendar year. When Butch Buccholz created *his* Players Championship for tennis ten years ago, he hoped it would become that sport's fifth major. The tournament has done just fine in spite of numerous site changes and political battles, but it is a long way from becoming a major championship.

When Beman made the deal to move the tour's headquarters to Ponte Vedra in 1976, he decided to take his tournament there with him. The tournament was played across the street from the under-construction TPC for five years before moving permanently to the new course in 1982.

And then the screaming began. Beman had ordered Dye to deliver a difficult, different golf course, one that would be as unique in its own way as Augusta. Dye had done that, and the players went crazy. It was too hard, it was too tricky, all those big mounds — built for spectators to create "stadium" golf — were ridiculous.

Players called it everything from screwy (Tom Watson), to awful, to the Marriott Muni (John Mahaffey) in honor of the Marriott Hotel that sits a few yards behind the 13th tee. When Jerry Pate won the tournament that first year, the first thing he did after holing out on the 18th green was grab Beman and Dye and toss them into the water (he went too) in a mock show of solidarity with his fellow pros. He was joking. Sort of.

What must be understood about professional golfers is that they are creatures of habit and exactitude. You will never hear a caddy (at least one who wants to stay employed) say to a player, "You've got about 150 to that bunker and, oh, I'd say 175 to 180 to the hole." No. What you hear is, "It's 154 to the bunker, 167 to the front, and 181 to the pin, and the wind is across but helping you slightly, except that once you get above the trees it may help you more than you think."

The TPC wasn't exact. It was like riding a roller coaster. You hit and hoped. Golfers hate that. The first two years the tournament was played there, no one broke 280.

Time has changed a lot of things. The course has been redone over the years and it has matured, as golf courses do. It has become more predictable and the scores have gone down steadily, as has the yelling. In fact, when the players began gathering for the twenty-first version of the tournament — the thirteenth at the TPC — there was some talk that maybe the course was too *easy*.

"It used to be pretty brutal," Nick Faldo said. "Now I'd just say it's demanding, but fair."

Tom Kite was more to the point. "If you're trying to build a major championship, you can't have the golf course play this easy," he said. "The way this course is set up, you're going to have very low scores, too low in my opinion."

Beman had long ago given up on the notion that this was going to be a major championship. He had come to understand that the Players (it was renamed in 1988 so that when people used the term TPC, it would be only in reference to golf courses) had grown up to be a respected title, a tournament that always had a superb field on a golf course that had slowly but surely earned a good deal of respect. It was the only event run by the tour that Beman would *never* slap a corporate name on. The Motorola Players? No way.

The Players would not be a major, and the TPC would not be Augusta. But both would be creations about which Beman could feel proud.

This would be his last Players as commissioner and, on Tuesday night, March 22, he presided over his final player meeting. Only he really didn't preside, Finchem did. Beman turned most of the meeting over to his deputy because he wanted to build support among the players for Finchem as his successor.

Technically, the players had no say in who the new commissioner would be. A four-man search committee that included Jay Haas and Rich Fehr, both player-directors on the policy board, would recommend a candidate to the full board. In fact, when he met with the players at a hastily called meeting on the evening of Beman's resignation at Doral, Ferris had told them that the search would be conducted in secret, that a list of candidates wouldn't be released. "You will know who the new commissioner is when we name him," Ferris said.

Clearly, it wasn't going to happen quite that way. A number of names had been floated, some legitimate, some not so legitimate. What's more, if a lot of players had a serious problem with a candidate, they would let Haas and Fehr know. That could severely handicap anyone who wanted the job.

Like Beman, Finchem had enemies. Part of it was simply the role he played as the number two man. Often, he was the one who handed down discipline to players, and often he was the one who delivered bad news — like the Karsten Solheim settlement — at meetings. His closeness to Beman would hurt him with some players.

But not with the majority. Most of the players were quite happy with the life that Beman had created for them. They were making good money and they were well treated. The tour was prosperous, and the bottom line was, if you could play, you could become quite rich. Most players didn't really care about the game's politics as long as the money and the courtesy cars were there each week. When ballots were sent out to elect a new player-director to succeed Jeff Sluman (self-addressed and stamped) only 86 of 200 players bothered to vote.

Some people were always going to be unhappy. Already, Larry Rinker, a veteran tour grinder, had posted a petition in the locker room at Bay Hill demanding that the players have more input into the decision on who the new commissioner would be. Five players had signed the petition, and one of them was John Daly, who, the joke went, probably thought it was a sign-up sheet for a paid outing.

Finchem handled the meeting smoothly. Unlike in some past meetings, there were no confrontations or shouting matches. When all the business had been taken care of, Jerry Pate, the man who had pulled Beman into the water with him twelve years earlier, stood up.

"Deane," he said, "I know there have been times when people have disagreed with you over the years, but I'd like to say that I think you've done a great job for all of us over the last twenty years, you've helped us all make a great living and I just want to say thank you and wish you all the best."

They started to applaud as Pate was finishing and then everyone in the room stood, with two exceptions: Bob Gilder and John Inman, both players who were under contract to Ping and had been on the other side of the dispute with Solheim. Even so, it seemed petty not to give Beman his due. A lot of players who joined in the standing ovation had done battle with Beman over the years but put those feelings aside.

"What Jerry did was great and the right thing to do," Peter Jacobsen said the next day. "Look, I was on the board and I disagreed with Deane on more than one occasion. That's not the point. The guy worked his butt off for twenty years and this was the time to acknowledge that. Those guys who didn't stand up, well, that just stunk."

It didn't take long for Tom Kite's comments about the golf course to make their way back to the tour's agronomists and to Fred Klauk, the TPC's course superintendent. By the time Kite had finished talking to the media, Klauk was waiting for him outside the brand-new TPC media center.

Klauk is not a confrontational man and neither is Kite, but there was very definitely a disagreement here. Klauk, acting under orders from his bosses at the tour, had to create a golf course that was challenging for the pros one week a year but playable for amateurs the other fifty-one. The TPC was, after all, a very profitable cash cow for the tour.

Kite really didn't want to hear it. All he knew was that the golf course was playing like one of the desert courses in Palm Springs and that didn't seem right to him. He and Klauk talked for forty minutes before finally agreeing to disagree. When a couple of reporters asked Kite what he and Klauk had been discussing — as if they didn't know — Kite said it was between the two of them and that he had really said enough for one day.

"Kite in the Middle of Controversy" is not a headline seen often during Kite's twenty-three years on tour. It is man-bites-dog stuff. But then Kite is someone whose image has never been a true reflection of the man.

To most people who follow golf, Kite is the ultimate overachiever, the pasty-faced little guy who has to swing out of his shoes just to keep up with the big boys, but somehow has managed to compete all these years just by putting in hours and hours and hours on the range.

As with any cliché, there is some truth to be found. Kite is only 5 feet 8, he does weigh only 155 pounds, and he does usually look as if he's spent the last twenty-three years in a cave. And he does work very hard. But the notion that he has won nineteen tournaments, more than $9 million in prize money, and the 1992 U.S. Open just by spending a lot of time on the range is ludicrous.

Kite was a natural when he first began to play as a five-year-old, he was a star throughout his junior career, and he was a star at the

University of Texas, where he and Ben Crenshaw tied for the NCAA title in 1972. He was rookie of the year on tour in 1973 and has twice won the Vardon Trophy for low scoring average and twice been the leading money winner. One doesn't do all of that just by working hard.

"I think a lot of it gets back to appearance," Kite said. "I don't *look* like someone who should be a star. I'm not tall, I wear thick glasses, I'm kind of pasty-faced, and I don't hit the ball nine miles. People looked at someone like Tom Weiskopf and they saw a person who *looked* like a star. He was tall and good-looking, he had a good-looking swing, and everyone expected great things of him. The fact is, Tom had a good career. But because he didn't win more than he did, a lot of people labeled him an underachiever. I've been labeled an overachiever. Probably, we both have achieved pretty close to what our ability has allowed us to achieve."

There is no doubt that people look at Greg Norman, six feet one, with broad shoulders and flowing white-blond hair, and see a star. Years ago, the same comparison was true of Palmer and Nicklaus; one movie-star handsome, the other nicknamed "Ohio Fats" until he lost weight in his thirties. Nick Faldo looks like a movie star: Harrison Ford. Colin Montgomerie does too: Mrs. Doubtfire. But in 1994, Montgomerie was a better player.

If Kite has a secret, it is the Kite family competitiveness. His dad, Tom Sr., who worked for the Internal Revenue Service for thirty-five years, didn't take up golf until he was an adult. When he first started playing, his friends laughed at him because he simply couldn't keep up with them. For the next couple of years, Tom Kite Sr. got himself out of bed at sunrise and sneaked off to the golf course before work. A few years after taking up the game, he was a two-handicap and was consistently beating his no-longer-laughing buddies.

"Family trait," Tom Kite Jr. says. "My grandfather was the same way."

Given that, it is not surprising that once he discovered he had talent for the game, Tom Kite Sr.'s only son became addicted to it. The golf course became his playground, and he and his friends spent all their afterschool hours and all their summertime hours there. When he was eleven, Tom went to his first pro tournament, the old Dallas Open.

By the time he got home that first day, he knew this was what he wanted to do for a living.

"I loved everything about it," he said. "Of course a lot of kids announce what they want to be at eleven and then change their minds fifteen times, so my parents didn't take it all that seriously."

Maybe not, but when they moved to Austin two years later they took Tom, by then a single-digit handicap, to Austin Country Club and put him in the hands of Harvey Penick. If you lived anywhere near Penick and didn't go to him for lessons, you were missing out. Everyone connected with golf knew who Penick was back then. But it wasn't until he came out with *The Little Red Book* in 1991 at the age of eighty-nine that he became a nationally known figure.

By then, Kite had gone on to Texas and stardom on the tour. But there was one giant void in his record: no major titles. Kite had become the PGA Tour's all-time leading money winner in 1988, but he still hadn't won one of the four majors. He had been close, agonizingly close, on numerous occasions, but had never closed the deal. He had worn the best-player-never-to-have-won-a-major yoke for so long that it almost seemed as if he had been born with it tied around his neck.

Publicly, Kite bore the burden with a kind of resigned shrug of the shoulders. Yes, he said, he wanted to win a major. No, he insisted, it didn't keep him awake at night. Yes, he thought people made too big a deal of it, but what the heck, that's the way life is.

Inside, he burned. The inside of Tom Kite is a lot different from the outside. Peter Jacobsen does imitations of most of the tour's stars and has had Kite in his repertoire for years. Jacobsen puts on a panama hat, pastes a wide grin on his face, and waves happily at the crowd. Then he hits a good shot and awkwardly shakes his fist and smiles some more.

Kite is a hail-fellow-well-met, always polite, always trying to make sure he says the right thing and doesn't offend anybody. But, as with any great player, Kite has a mean streak, an edge that isn't seen often but can spring up in the heat of the moment.

During the Ryder Cup, his good friend Davis Love was shocked when Kite, thinking that Seve Ballesteros and José María Olazabal were being given a drop they didn't deserve, went ballistic. "All of a

sudden he started running over to where they were dropping, screaming, 'No, you can't do that, that isn't right!' " Love remembered. "I
never heard Tom curse like that in my life. He was calling these guys
every name in the book, his face was red as a beet, I mean he
was *mad*." Love paused. "I was standing there thinking, I'd hate to
be one of his kids and have to come home and tell him I cracked up
the car."

Kite will never start throwing clubs around a golf course or get
caught cursing with a boom mike around. But he will walk off to the
side of a tee and quietly dress himself down for a mistake or, if he
thinks his longtime caddy, Mike Carrick, has made a mistake, dress
him down.

"Mike's been with me thirteen years," Kite said. "Which is definitive proof that he is a very patient man."

The questions about his lack of a major title haunted Kite. He even
became snappish occasionally when the subject came up, which it
inevitably did, especially during major weeks. "That all should have
ended in 1989," he said. "But I gave the golf tournament away."

The golf tournament in question was the U.S. Open at Oak Hill.
Kite had a three-shot lead early in the final round and looked to be
in complete command until he triple-bogeyed the fifth hole and then
went completely off the deep end, shooting a horrific 78 to finish in
a tie for ninth place, five shots behind the winner, Curtis Strange.

Kite was devastated. He felt he had failed, let everyone who cared
about him down, and wondered — briefly, he says — if perhaps he
just wasn't meant to win a major. He knew he had given the golf
tournament away. If someone had shot 65 the last day to go past him,
that would have been disappointing but not in the same way. To shoot
78 with a major title in sight was not the way Kite wanted to be
remembered.

"A lot of people helped get me through that," he said. "Christy,
Mike, Bob [Rotella], Mr. Penick. They just kept telling me that I had
to look at this as part of the learning curve, a painful part, but to
understand that no matter what people said or wrote, the dream was
still out there."

Kite managed to bounce back at the end of that year to win the
season-ending Nabisco Championships, which gave him the money-

winning title for the second time. Unfortunately, it also sharpened the focus on his ability to play well with money on the line but not with a major on the line.

The next two years were difficult ones. He dropped out of the top-ten money winners in 1990 for only the second time in ten years and then went all the way to thirty-ninth in 1991, the lowest he had finished on a money list since his rookie year on tour. It was the first time since 1976 (when he was twenty-first) that he was out of the top twenty. He did win a tournament in each of those years, but he wasn't the same Tom Kite, the one who seemed to be on the leader board every week.

His low moment came early in 1992 when he wasn't invited to the Masters for the first time in fifteen years. Kite has more top-ten finishes at the Masters (ten) than any active player on tour. But, since he hadn't won in the year between the 1991 Masters and the 1992 Masters and was not a Masters champion, he wasn't invited.

"I understood why I wasn't invited," he said. "But it was disappointing. If I was a foreign-born player, they simply could have given me an invitation as a foreign player. Greg Norman hadn't won during that year either, but because he's foreign-born, even though he's a member of our tour, they invited him. I can't say that I thought that was fair."

Kite was forty-two, an age when most players are beginning to wind down. It certainly looked as if his days on top were behind him. A couple of months later, the week before the U.S. Open, instead of practicing or playing in a tournament to get ready, he took his family to Baltimore for the World Gymnastics Championships. His daughter, Stephanie, then ten, is an avid gymnast, and the Kites built a family vacation around the gymnastics championships.

Kite did sneak away to hit balls a couple of times that week at Cave Valley, a club near Baltimore where a good friend of his, Dennis Satyshur, is the golf pro. But most of the time was spent at the Aquarium or the Inner Harbor or getting his twin boys onto the field before a baseball game at Camden Yards. No grinding. Just fun.

Kite went from there to Pebble Beach and, as usual, hung around the lead for the first three days. For a while it looked as if Gil Morgan might run away with the event, but by Saturday night the field had bunched and Kite was in a three-way tie for second, one shot off the lead.

And then the wind came up Sunday. It wasn't just blowing or swirling, it was howling, ripping through the golf course, making it close to unplayable. Twenty of the sixty-six players in the field didn't break 80 that day. No one broke 70. Three players broke par: Colin Montgomerie with a 70 and Jeff Sluman and Nick Price with 71s.

When Montgomerie, playing in one of the earlier groups, holed out at 18 to finish at even-par 288, Jack Nicklaus walked up to him and said, "Congratulations, I think you may have just won the U.S. Open." The conditions were so bad that Nicklaus was convinced that none of the ten players who had started the day at even par or better would be able to beat Montgomerie's total.

He wasn't far wrong. The conditions became more brutal as the day wore on. When Sluman somehow got to the clubhouse at one under, that looked like a potential winner too. But Kite was having one of those "zone" days when your concentration is so good you just don't notice anything. He knew the wind was there, but it didn't matter. He was just playing. At the tiny seventh, a torture test in the wind, he hit his tee shot way left of the green and looked like he would be lucky to make bogey. Instead, he chipped in.

The shot was as brilliant and unlikely as Watson's chip at 17 in 1982 and, like Watson's shot, it turned out to be the one that won the Open. Unlike Watson, Kite still had eleven holes to play. "Look at me on the replay sometime," he said. "All I do is smile, then go get the ball and walk to the next tee. That was the mode I was in. It was, okay, that was good, now what do I need to do next."

He kept doing it all day, keeping the ball in play, getting it in the hole. His lead on Sluman dwindled to one for a while, but a late birdie gave him a two-shot lead walking onto 18. Three very careful shots later, his ball was on the green and Kite was walking down the fairway knowing he had finally, finally won a major. He looked up and saw Christy and his parents by the green and began to cry.

"To have the career I've had and to finish without ever winning a major would have been brutal," he said. "I mean, think about it. I'm a good player. I watched a lot of guys, who, well, I didn't think were as good as I was, win majors. And I still hadn't won one. That was tough to take. People talk about me being the leading money winner of all time, but I guarantee you what I want to be remembered for first and foremost right now is winning the U.S. Open."

Two days later, Christy returned home to Austin while Tom flew east to honor a commitment. At Tom's request, Christy took the Open trophy to Harvey Penick and handed it to him. "Tom wanted you to have this," she said. "He never would have won it without you."

The Open victory changed Kite and it changed his life. Winning a major changes any player's public profile, no matter how well he might have been known beforehand. TV ratings for major championships are about double what they are for week-to-week tournaments and media coverage goes up a hundredfold. Curtis Strange says that winning the Open in 1988 changed him from someone who was occasionally recognized to someone who couldn't get through a meal in a restaurant without being interrupted for an autograph.

Kite had a similar experience. He became a major celebrity, recognized wherever he went. He was invited to play in the Skins Game for the first time, and he was amazed at the number of people who wanted to come up and congratulate him.

Unlike a lot of players who find their newfound celebrity a burden, Kite didn't mind. He is a private person and he wasn't going to spend a lot of time doing Letterman and Leno if he won ten U.S. Opens. But the victory was such a relief, such an unburdening, that he didn't care if a thousand people a day came up to him and wanted to tell him where they were when he chipped in at number seven. He reveled in it, and he started 1993 playing the best golf of his career. He won back-to-back at Los Angeles and the Hope and looked like he might turn the entire tour into a mockery.

But then he hurt his back and needed disc surgery. That put him on the sideline for three months. Amazingly, he almost won his first tournament back — the Kemper Open — in early June, finishing one shot behind the winner, Grant Waite. He also played superbly in the Ryder Cup, especially in the singles, where he hammered Bernhard Langer, shooting six under par for fifteen holes to close Langer out with ease.

That made him a spectator during most of the late drama, but that was fine with Kite. When someone pointed out that he should stop winning his matches so easily so he could get some more attention, he shook his head and laughed, "The sooner I get it over with the better," he said. "I don't need any more attention than I'm getting."

He finished the year eighth on the money list, remarkable for someone who had missed three months. He turned forty-four in December but didn't seem to be anywhere close to being finished.

"I hope not," he said. "I still feel like I have a lot more to do."

After all, he was probably the best player in the world who had never won a Masters, a British Open, or a PGA . . . yet.

"Well now, isn't this a surprise. Look at these scores. Who would have predicted it?"

Tom Kite was sitting in the interview room after playing his first round at the Players Championship. He had shot a seven-under-par 65. That was one shot off the previous course record. It was also two shots off the lead. The course record was now 63. Just as Kite had predicted, the TPC was taking a beating.

The new holder of the course record was one Gregory John Norman, also known as the Great White Shark or, when he was striding the fairways listening to the shouts from his gallery, simply, Shark.

Low rounds were nothing new for TGWS but they seemed to come more often at the end of tournaments, when Norman would come roaring out of the pack to close a nine-shot lead to two or, on occasion, to catch the leader. In 1989 at the British Open, he had shot a masterful 63 on the last day at Royal Troon to pull even with Wayne Grady and Mark Calcavecchia and force a playoff.

He then birdied the first hole of the playoff. Only that didn't make him a winner, because the British had gone — that year — from a sudden-death playoff format to a four-hole playoff. So Norman birdied the second playoff hole. So did Calcavecchia, though, and when Norman bogeyed the third hole (number 17 on the golf course) he and Calcavecchia stood on the 18th tee dead even. Grady was two shots back.

Calcavecchia, not wanting to gamble on finding the fairway bunker that yawned on the right side, played a three-wood shot safely into the short rough on the right. Norman, living up to his macho, go-for-broke image, pulled out his driver. In the TV booth, his good friend Jack Nicklaus was stunned.

"I can't imagine what Greg is thinking taking out a driver here," he said as Norman stood up to the ball. "The only thing he can do by hitting a driver is bring the bunker into play, which is the one place out there he wants to avoid."

The Shark took a mighty swing, the ball flew well past Calcavecchia's, and landed smack in the middle of the bunker. Nicklaus sighed. "Well, what he has to do now," he said, "is play a wedge of some kind safely onto the fairway and hope he can pitch the ball close enough from there to make par. If he goes for the green from that lie, the best he'll do is knock it in the bunker in front of the green. If he does that, he's in serious trouble."

No wedge for the Shark. Another mighty swing, another groan as sand flew near the green. Nicklaus was two for two. Calcavecchia, seeing where Norman was, played a perfect five-iron shot to eight feet. Now the Shark had to come up with a miraculous bunker shot, somehow make par, and hope Calcavecchia missed.

Miracles were the man's specialty. His bunker shot flew from the bunker in the direction of the pin. It went over the pin, over the green, over everything until it got to the base of the clubhouse wall. The Shark was out of bounds. He never finished the hole. Calcavecchia rolled in the birdie putt, and it was over. On a day when Norman had played twenty holes about as brilliantly as anyone had ever seen, the lasting memory he would leave behind would be of that 18th hole: a hacker's X.

Later, when Norman heard what Nicklaus had said on the telecast, he was upset because his friend had second-guessed him. But Nicklaus hadn't second-guessed anything, he had first-guessed, questioning Norman's shot selection before the disasters had occurred.

In many ways that day at Troon was a microcosm of Norman's career. He has had moments of untouchable brilliance, days and weeks when his golf left everyone — including his fellow players — breathless and in awe of the shotmaking he produced. And yet, he has also had moments — like the final hole at Troon — where he has left even his staunchest supporters wondering what went wrong.

He has won a staggering sixty-five tournaments around the world during his career, but only twelve of them have come on the PGA Tour, along with two British Opens. Twelve tournament victories in twelve years on tour is nothing to be ashamed of by any means, but it is certainly not a record that causes the heavens to shake, especially when one considers the fact that Norman's good friend Nick Price has won eleven times on tour in the last three years (and a British Open) while Norman, who has played extremely well since he ended his twenty-seven-month victory drought in 1992, has won three tour events during that period, plus the 1993 British.

Nevertheless, it is Norman who has parlayed white-blond hair, the Crocodile Dundee accent and devil-may-care attitude, and a memorable nickname into millions and millions of dollars. The only players in the history of the game who have made more money than Norman (on and off the golf course) are Palmer and Nicklaus, and he may yet surpass them.

Norman is almost always spectacular, whether winning or losing. In 1986, he led all four majors after three rounds and won only the British. He has lost a playoff in each of the four majors. When he won his first British Open, at Turnberry in 1986, the victory was built around an extraordinary 63 in near-hurricane conditions on the second day. When he won his second British seven years later, he did it with a final-round 64 that swept him past Nick Faldo, Bernhard Langer, and Corey Pavin. It was an almost perfect round of golf.

Norman can be charming when he wants to be, with a wise-cracking, boys-will-be-boys sense of humor. He always seems to say the right thing when the little red light is on and is every TV producer's dream. After all, if the Shark is in the hunt on Sunday, you know you're going to have a show one way or the other. He is so close to CBS executive producer Frank Chirkinian that Chirkinian's own people often tease him about the relationship.

Early in 1994, when CBS was about to go on the air for a second-round USA Network cablecast at Greensboro, associate producer Lance Barrow was sitting in the producer's chair since Chirkinian had the day off.

"Okay, everybody," Barrow said into the earpieces of his on- and off-air crew, "when we come on the air, we're going to pick Greg up and follow him into the clubhouse."

There was a long silence. Finally, somebody bit. "But Lance, Greg's not playing here."

"Okay then," said Barrow, who had been hoping someone would

fall for his setup, "in that case, we'll find some tape of Greg and follow him into the clubhouse that way."

Norman takes a lot of hits in the locker room and with the media (print, that is) because of his tendency to flop at the wrong moments and because the wrong thing will occasionally sneak out of his mouth. After his fabulous last round in the 1993 British Open, he said all the right things about how thrilled he was to win against a leader board filled with great players and about how much it meant to him to win golf's most historic tournament for a second time.

But he couldn't resist adding, "You know, I'm not usually one to brag, but I was in awe of myself out there today."

Among the thousands of words Norman spoke that day, those were the ones that were repeated over and over again. Unfair? Sure. But when you have made millions being a public figure, you pay a price. Intellectually, Norman understands that, but emotionally he has had trouble dealing with it at times.

"I get in trouble because I say what I'm thinking too much of the time," he said. "I've been burned a few times, and there have been times when I've found myself getting cynical, pulling back. Then I catch myself because I don't want to be that way. That's just not me."

Price says that to understand Norman you have to remember that he is Australian. "I don't want to stereotype," Price said, "but Australians, generally, are very outgoing and friendly, very opinionated, and usually convinced that they are 100 percent right in every opinion they have. If you think about it, *that's* Greg."

Maybe that's why he told a friend, "I'll bet you I marry that girl," the first time he set eyes on his wife, Laura. He had just boarded a flight in Toledo after the 1979 U.S. Open and she was working as a flight attendant. By the end of the flight, Laura had gone into the cockpit and told the captain, "I think I've just fallen in love with a golfer."

"A golfer," said the captain, an avid fan. "Which one?"

"I think his name is Greg Norman," she said.

"No way," the captain answered. "There's no golfer named Greg Norman."

Norman loves to retell that story, even adding a kicker about watching that same pilot almost lose control of a plane on a snowy runway while Norman waited in the terminal to meet Laura several months later. "I said to him, 'You know, I may not be a famous golfer — *yet* — but I could probably land a plane better than *that*.' "

And of course he did marry Laura.

And yet Norman admits that behind all the brashness and swagger and arrogance, there is still a little boy who was afraid of walking into dark rooms, who woke up in the middle of the night screaming, convinced there were snakes under his bed.

He didn't start playing golf until he was fifteen and then it took a family move to Brisbane to get him to the golf course in the first place. His mother, Toini, was an excellent player, a three-handicapper. When Merv Norman took a job in Brisbane and moved his family there, young Greg, without his friends from home, was a little bored and a little lonely, so he went to the golf course a couple of times to caddy for his mother.

He loved it there and began to play on his own. Seeing his interest, his mother bought him two Jack Nicklaus instructional books — *55 Ways to Play Golf* and *Golf My Way.* He devoured them and set out to learn the game. Within two years, he was a scratch player. He had played team sports when he was younger but found that he loved the individual nature of golf. *You* succeeded or *you* failed. You weren't dependent on anyone else.

At eighteen, he announced to his parents that he was abandoning his idea of joining the air force and training as a fighter pilot to pursue a career in golf instead. He played in amateur tournaments for the next couple of years before becoming an assistant pro for $28 a week. At twenty-one, he won his first tournament and $7,000. He thought he had hit the lottery. He won another tournament in Japan shortly after that and got paid in cash. "I remember sitting on a bed in this hotel room with like a zillion yen all over the room," he said. "I thought I'd never need to work another day."

He played the European Tour after that, working to hit the ball lower than he had hit it in Australia. He was very long back then — "John Daly long," he says — but he knew he hit the ball too high, so he worked in Europe on hitting the ball lower in the swirling winds that often prevail on courses there. In 1982, after five years in Europe, he decided he was ready for the American Tour.

He already had his nickname by then. Early on, the Australian media had started to call him the Golden Bear Cub, because of his young Nicklaus-like length and a friendship with Nicklaus that had started when they lockered next to one another at the Australian Open in 1976. But that never caught on. In 1981, he led the Masters after two rounds and they brought him into the interview room.

Everyone wanted to know his life story and Norman was only too glad to tell it, complete with stories about going shark fishing off the Great Barrier Reef in Australia. The next morning, Norman picked up the newspapers and there were the headlines: "Great White Shark Leads Masters."

A logo had been born. Norman had played in the States often enough by the time he came over full-time that he wasn't as intimidated as he once was by all the big names. He quickly became friends with both Nicklaus and Palmer, who saw greatness in him and offered to help him in any way they could.

He lived at Bay Hill for several years before moving to the Palm Beach area near Nicklaus because, according to Norman, "Barbara Nicklaus convinced Laura that the schools were better down there."

He made his first big splash in 1984 when he won twice and lost a playoff for the U.S. Open title to Fuzzy Zoeller. Even though Zoeller killed him in the playoff, winning by eight shots, a lot of golf fans remembered the three spectacular saves Norman made coming down the stretch on Sunday to force the playoff.

Two years later, he was the dominant player in the world. He was in position to win at all four majors. Nicklaus caught him on Sunday at the Masters, he faded at the U.S. Open, won the British, and lost the PGA in dramatic fashion when Bob Tway holed a bunker shot at 18 to beat him by a shot.

Tway's shot was the first in a series. Eight months later, Larry Mize holed his 100-foot chip to beat Norman in a playoff at the Masters, and in 1990 Robert Gamez eagled the 18th at Bay Hill from the fairway and David Frost knocked one in from a bunker at New Orleans to turn Norman wins into Norman near-misses.

Those four shots became a part of any Norman chronicle. When people wondered why Norman hadn't won more majors, Tway and Mize immediately came up. No doubt both shots were once-in-a-lifetime propositions. But it should be remembered that Norman had a five-shot lead on Tway with nine holes to play and shot 40 on the back nine. He had to let Tway back into the tournament for Tway to win. And, in both 1986 and 1987, Norman bogeyed the 18th at Augusta, first to give Nicklaus his win, then to let Mize and Seve Ballesteros get into a playoff with him.

Chokes? Perhaps. But to be fair, when a player gets into position to win as often as Norman, there are going to be times when he succeeds and times when he fails. Norman always seems to save his most spectacular failures for the moments when the most people are watching.

And, while some of his fellow pros whisper that Norman is a choker and point out — accurately — that he almost always comes up with some rationalization for his failures, his constant presence in the spotlight has made him a very wealthy man.

When a management company sits down with a corporation to sell a client, the question asked is not "How much has he won?" but "How visible is he?" That is why you can't watch golf on television for five minutes without having John Daly's face pop up on your screen. Daly has won three tournaments in his life, but anyone with even the mildest interest in golf knows who he is: he's the guy who hits the ball nine miles.

And Norman was (and is) the Shark. There he was, every Sunday, smiling that killer smile for the cameras, win or lose. He didn't always win, but he always got noticed. Corporate America loved him.

By 1990, Norman was a multimillionaire with a very good playing record, even if it didn't match his notoriety. And then, for more than two years, his game virtually disappeared. He went from winning $1,165,000 (and the money title) in 1990 to $320,000 in 1991, a precipitous drop that landed him fifty-third on the money list.

Norman says now that he let down mentally, stopped working as hard as he had in the past, and kept trying to find something new in his swing that would "take me to another level." He laughs when he says that and adds, "I succeeded brilliantly. I found a level about five levels down from where I'd been."

He went from March 1990 to September 1992 without a victory. His obituary as a player was written several times during that period. The headline might have been "Golfer, 37, succumbs to *too much.*"

Norman wanted everything: he wanted to win all over the planet; he wanted a hand in all his business ventures; he wanted to cash in on the easy $75,000 a day that corporations were willing to pay for outings, and he wanted to be a father too.

It was all too much. By late in 1991 he was at wit's end. Another Australian player, Steve Elkington, had been trying to get him to see his teacher, Butch Harmon, for months. When Norman went to the range one afternoon in Houston and couldn't even come close to hitting a decent golf shot, he turned to Elkington and asked him if Harmon was anywhere to be found. Since Harmon lives in Houston, he was found easily and Norman asked him to take a look at his swing.

"No need," Harmon said. "I've seen you swing. Just take out a two-iron, move a little closer to the ball, and swing as hard as you can."

Normally, Norman takes orders about as readily as a cat in heat. But he was in such a state of shock about his game — "If I tried to hit the ball left, it went right; right it went left; straight, forget it, completely out of the question" — that he simply followed Harmon's instructions. He stood on the practice tee drilling shots for several hours.

"I just wanted him swinging at the ball," Harmon said. "We worked later on shortening his swing a little bit for accuracy, but the important thing was to get him taking a crack at the ball again. He wasn't swinging like Greg Norman."

What he had been trying to do, even though he would never admit it, was swing like Nick Faldo. Beginning with his British Open victory in 1987, Faldo had become the game's best player, winning five majors titles — two Masters and three British Opens — in five years. Much was made of Faldo's complete rebuilding of his swing in mid-career with David Leadbetter. The key to Faldo, or so the thinking went, was mechanics. He understood every single inch of the golf swing. Norman tried to be more mechanical. It didn't work.

By the next summer, Norman was beginning to feel better about his game. He had made a decision at the end of 1991 to rededicate himself, physically and mentally, to the sport. He looked in the mirror and saw a man who had not yet lived up to the vast potential everyone had seen in him and decided that rather than walk away, wealthy but unfulfilled, he would work harder than he ever had in his life.

He started a conditioning program that took off fifteen pounds and turned him into the closest thing to a hardbody that you were likely to see on tour. When Davis Love went to work out with him one day early in 1994, Norman picked up a medicine ball and suggested they play catch with it. Love isn't exactly a pushover at 6-foot-4 and 180 pounds, but when Norman began throwing the ball to him, he felt completely overmatched. "It was like in those cartoons, where the guy throws you the ball and it knocks you through the wall," Love said. "I knew Greg was in shape, but I didn't really know just how strong he had gotten."

Norman stayed up late less and got up early more. He forced himself to be less involved with business and he went back to the regimen of his youth, hitting balls on the range for hours and hours. Slowly, his game came back. At the British Open in July 1992, he finished in 18th place while Faldo was winning, but he walked off the 18th green after a 68 in the last round (no one shot lower that day) and announced to Harmon, "I'm back. I was making the ball talk out there today."

Six weeks later, he won the Canadian Open, and he started 1993 by blowing the field away at Doral. "I played the best golf I think I've ever played and I lost by four shots," Paul Azinger said. There was no doubt then that the Shark was back trolling.

Still, Doral ain't Augusta, and when Norman started out with 74 at the Masters five weeks after Doral and went on to finish thirty-first, it looked like the Shark was back but up to his old card tricks — the ones where you fold under pressure. When he missed the cut at the U.S. Open it was more of the same.

It was Tom Watson who had counseled Norman to stay patient after the Tway-Mize-Gamez-Frost series of miracles. Watson hadn't been beaten quite as dramatically or as often as Norman, but he could remember leading the U.S. Open at Winged Foot in 1974 after three rounds and shooting 79 the last day, and Larry Nelson's 60-foot putt at the 1983 U.S. Open that had stolen a chance for back-to-back titles from him.

"You know something, Greg," Watson said one day, "when you bite that snake's head off, the SOB will stay dead forever."

For Norman, who still had those memories from boyhood of snakes under his bed, the metaphor was just right. Over and over again he told himself that someday he was going to bite the damn

Greg Norman
Still without the trophy he wants most.

Lee Janzen
The Open champion whom
golf fans forgot.

Davis Love III
A Ryder Cup hero hoping for heroics
in the majors.

Billy Andrade
So close at Doral but convinced his
time will come again.

Paul Azinger
An inspiration to golfers and nongolfers around the world.

Mike Donald
Nothing comes easy, but he never
quits trying.

John Cook
Mr. Happy searches for the joy of
victory once more.

Curtis Strange
After all the questions, he has finally
found a lot of the right answers.

Tom Watson
The Man in the Arena forges on.

Brian Henninger
Finding success and happiness on the
big boy tour.

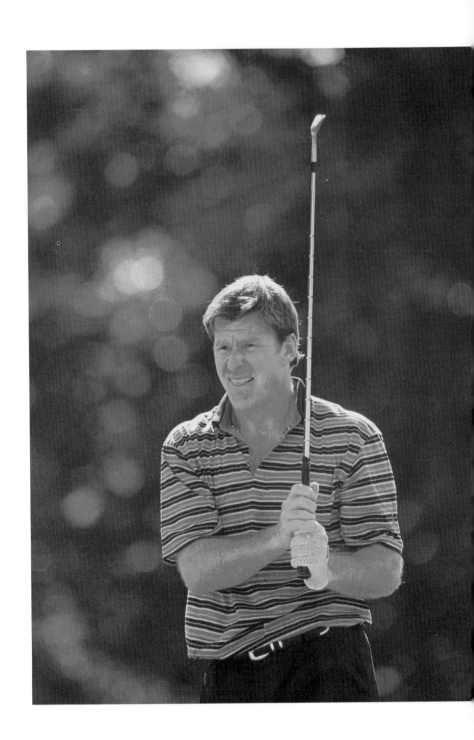

Nick Faldo
Golf: his magnificent obsession.

Bruce Fleisher
Four years to the senior tour
and counting.

Jeff Sluman
''I hate this game — and I can't wait
till tomorrow to play again.''

Tom Kite
The most talented grinder
in the game.

Jeff Cook
Still in search of the perfect swing.

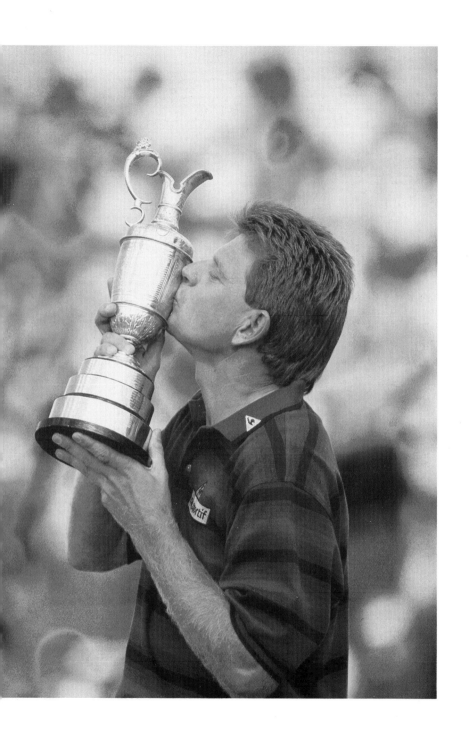

Nick Price
The best for all of 1994, just as for 1993.

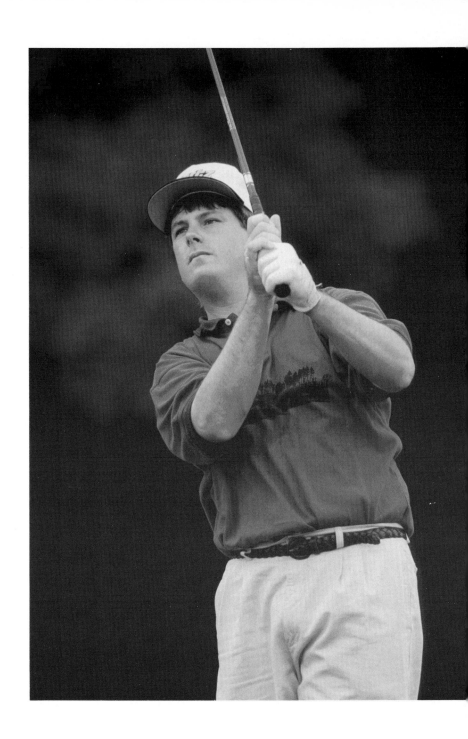

Paul Goydos
One of the most improved players
on tour in 1994.

snake's head off and then never have to deal with the wretched thing ever again.

The snake finally died at Royal St. Georges. Norman started the tournament with a double bogey the first day but, for once, didn't get ruffled. He played the last seventeen holes six under par and stalked Faldo through the first three rounds. He was one shot back of him and Corey Pavin starting the final round, a familiar position. The consensus that morning was that Faldo was the man to beat because he had proven in the past that he didn't let majors get away when he had them in his sights. The snake, it seemed, never bit Faldo.

This time, the Shark did. Faldo played superbly — shooting 67. So did Bernhard Langer, who was tied with Norman one shot back starting the day. But that wasn't good enough. Norman was in the zone all afternoon. He walked onto the first tee and decided, instead of trying to hit a fade or a draw the way he normally did, just to hit the ball as straight as he could. "The ball took off like it was on a clothesline," he said, smiling at the memory. "After that, I just knew that nothing was going to bother me."

He was perfect for eighteen holes, except at the 17th green when he somehow missed a one-foot putt. Even so, he still had a two-shot lead on the 18th tee. Did any of the old memories creep back into his mind? He swears no. He hit a perfect drive and a perfect four-iron to the green. No one would catch him this day, no one would hole out to steal a victory from him. He had shot 64, the lowest final round ever by the winner in British Open history. At thirty-eight, he had unwritten the obituaries. The snake was dead.

"I honestly believe this is only the beginning," he said. "I think I can play great golf until I'm forty-five."

He almost added the PGA title to the British, losing on the second hole of sudden death to Paul Azinger. Twice he rimmed the cup — "paint jobs," the players call such putts because they hit the painted cup and spin out — on putts that would have ended the tournament. They hit paint but didn't drop. Azinger won. No one called Norman a choker though. He had put that label to rest at St. Georges.

At least for a while.

When Norman began the first round at the Players, he had no idea that he was about to do something special. He had played well at Bay

Hill, finishing sixth, and thought his game was rounding into shape for the Masters. Even though the Players is an important tournament, Norman saw it only as a warm-up for Augusta.

"If I'm going to be honest with myself, the thing I want to do most before I stop playing is win Augusta," he said. "I love everything about the tournament. I love the course, the clubhouse, the way it's set up, everything. I've been so close so many times that I'll really feel as if I've missed something in my career if I don't win there at least once."

Norman was paired for the first two rounds at the Players with Tom Watson and Davis Love, a glamorous grouping. He was comfortable playing with Love. They often played practice rounds together and both worked with Butch Harmon. With Watson, it was more of a competitive thing. Watson had done a lot of the things in golf that Norman hadn't.

There was mutual respect between the two men, but there was also a simmering rivalry. Watson was as shy and private as Norman was outgoing and gregarious. Each probably wished he could be a little more like the other, but didn't quite understand the other's chosen lifestyle. Norman could no more shut down and go off to spend winters in Kansas City than he could fly to the moon with a jetpack.

It was already sticky and humid when the three men teed off on the back nine at 9 o'clock in the morning, and Watson made it clear right away that he had come to play, birdieing the first two holes. There was little of the usual Thursday morning chatter. Watson and Love talked hunting, comparing guns briefly, and Norman and Love talked airplanes for a while. That was it. Like Watson, Love birdied the 11th and Norman found himself staring at a 10-foot birdie putt of his own wondering if his playing partners were both planning to shoot 60.

"It was like, 'Whoa fellas, wait for me,'" he said later. "You start out Thursday morning, you're just trying to clear cobwebs, get your footing, and post a decent score. These guys came flying out of the gate."

Norman made that birdie putt. At their fourth hole — the 13th — Norman hit a mediocre six-iron onto the green way right of the pin. The putt was over hill and dale and seemed to take twenty minutes to reach the hole. It went in. Suddenly, Norman was energized. This day might turn out okay after all. He birdied the next three holes.

Now it was Watson and Love who were wondering what was going on. When he birdied 18, Norman was out in 30 and the large gallery that had started the day with the group had doubled. Was 59 possible on this golf course?

Maybe. Norman birdied one and two, giving him seven birdies in eight holes. While they waited on the third tee for a group to clear the green, Love, who wasn't exactly hacking it around at four under, sidled over to Watson, who had slowed down and was just one under.

"You may not have noticed this, Tom," Love said. "But Greg's playing pretty well."

Watson just rolled his eyes. Norman was human the last seven holes. He made just one more birdie, but he never came close to a bogey and finished with 63. There was just one small problem: this was Ponte Vedra, not Augusta. If he could bottle the feeling he had and hang onto it for two weeks, life would be perfect.

"You can't really worry about peaking too soon," Norman said. "Your job is to get your game on-song before the majors so you don't go into them searching for something. If you do that, then it's just a matter of having things go your way that week."

Norman was certainly on-song. He was hitting the ball as long as he ever had and more accurately. He was putting with complete confidence, and he never seemed to miss a green. In fact, en route to the 63, he missed exactly one green, catching a greenside bunker at number seven. He blasted to four feet for the easy par.

Often, when a player shoots a spectacular first round, he will come back to the field the next day. At the Players, Lee Janzen had his best round of the year on Thursday — a 65 — then came back with 75 the next day. Any golfer will tell you that the toughest round to play is the one after the great one because, no matter what you tell yourself, you are going to be disappointed when you aren't making birdie on every hole the way you did the day before. Everything seems hard and frustration comes faster.

Norman would have had every right to be frustrated Friday. A lengthy rain delay in the morning meant the afternoon players wouldn't get to finish their rounds before dark and would have to wake up early the next morning to finish and then come back after a break to play the third round in the afternoon.

Nothing was going to shake the Shark though. He followed the 63 with 67–67–67. By the time he was through on Sunday evening, he had shot 264 — a staggering 24 under par — and Tom Kite, who finished tied for ninth, fifteen shots behind Norman, was no doubt saying, "I'm not going to say I told you so, but I told you so."

To be fair to the golf course, Norman might have run amok anywhere in the world during this week. He made one bogey in seventy-two holes and that didn't come until the 14th hole on Sunday when he had left the field in his wake. It is also worth noting that only two other players, Zoeller at 268 and Jeff Maggert at 271, were *way* under par. Hale Irwin was fourth at 276 — 12 under. Nonetheless, having the tournament record broken by six shots certainly lent legitimacy to Kite's claim.

For Norman, it was another week of superlatives. The media went gaga over his performance, as usual, and even the most cynical players had to shake their heads and concede that he had put on a clinic. Then again, some of them couldn't resist one last comment. "Great performance," several of them said. "Let's see how he does at Augusta."

Even Norman had to agree that was a fair question. He was convinced, however, that he had the answer.

While Norman was making a mockery out of the final hours of the Players, the rest of the field was attempting to accomplish some less spectacular feats.

Nick Price, the defending champion, showed up sick and played sick, missing the cut by five shots. Janzen followed his uplifting 65 with three mediocre rounds and finished thirty-fifth. Paul Goydos, who had sneaked into the field on the strength of his play during the first ten weeks of the season, was in the last of the dog groups Friday afternoon and had to grind until the last hole on Saturday morning to make the cut. He did — right on the number at 144 — and looked at that accomplishment as a huge bonus.

"I'm so exhausted I can't even see," he said. "I've played eight straight weeks now and I've made every cut. I need a break to catch my breath."

Part of Goydos wanted to play the next week in New Orleans — he had even been asked to play in the shootout there — but he knew he couldn't handle it. He missed his family and knew he needed two weeks off. When he had made his schedule at the start of the year, he had figured on a four-week break in late March and early April since he wasn't in the Players, the Masters, or the Heritage Classic. New Orleans came between the Players and the Masters, but he had decided to skip that too rather than fly cross-country for one tournament.

But because he had played so well, Goydos had gotten into both the Players and the Heritage. That meant his break would be two weeks. The good news was he was playing well enough to get into top-drawer events. The bad news was he was spending more time away from home than he had planned. Without Wendy and the two kids, Goydos was lonely and he felt guilty about not being home when Courtney or Chelsea had a sore throat or an ear infection. But he knew it was part of the deal on tour.

If he wanted to know more about dealing with the loneliness, Goydos might have consulted Bruce Fleisher. Ten years earlier, Fleisher had dropped off the tour during what should have been the prime of his career. He was thirty-five, but he was totally burned out by the life, he hated leaving his four-year-old daughter, and he had never fulfilled the dreams he had brought to the tour thirteen years earlier.

"I could never really adjust to the idea of being mediocre," he said. "I realize, intellectually, that being on the tour means you're one of the best players in the world. But emotionally, when you go week after week finishing tenth or twentieth or fiftieth, it beats you down. I came out thinking I would set the world on fire, I think most guys do. When you figure out that isn't going to happen, you have to adjust your thinking. I had trouble doing that."

Fleisher had left home at seventeen to find a way to play golf for a living. He was the son of immigrant Jews, his father having escaped Austria in 1939 while he was studying to be a rabbi. According to Bruce, Herbert Fleisher never really recovered from what he saw during the Holocaust. His own father, a rabbi, was killed by the Nazis, and he and his mother fled to England. Although he eventually built a successful life for his wife and four children as an engineer, he had seen so much suffering as a boy that he never seemed to find joy as an adult.

"I remember having him up to visit and play golf a few months ago," Fleisher said. "We played eighteen holes on a beautiful course on a perfect day. Dad never said a word until the end of the round when he looked at me and said, 'I remember you used to hit the ball much longer.' I just said, 'Yeah, Dad, but now I hit it straight.' "

Fleisher was a phenom as a kid. Although his father kept the family moving — "always searching for the perfect job" — it was in Wilmington, Delaware, that Bruce and his older brothers discovered golf. They all caddied and played at a club called Pine Valley (not *the* Pine Valley). Bruce was the star. He eventually was able to parlay his golf skills into a scholarship at Furman. He lasted less than a year there before flunking out. "I hadn't done enough work in high school to deal with real college work," he said. "I knew what I wanted to do — play golf."

He found a place where he could play golf and do the classwork, at Miami Dade Junior College. His game got better and better, and in 1968 he shocked the golf community by winning the U.S. Amateur, wearing the same pair of frayed dungarees through all four rounds. The runner-up that year was Vinny Giles, one of the most distinguished amateurs in the game's history. Fleisher, at nineteen, ragged pants and all, was just a little too good for Giles and everyone else.

A year later, he turned pro, and after losing out in a playoff at his first Q-School, he made it the second year. He had just turned twenty-two, he was a newlywed, and stardom was definitely in his future. "I had a lot of game," he said, shaking his head. "I just couldn't quite figure out how to use it on tour."

He wasn't exactly a washout, but he wasn't a star either. He struggled to keep his card through the 1970s, always having to play in Monday qualifying since he never cracked the top sixty. Those weren't easy days, driving from one tournament to another, wondering from week to week whether he would be playing. But at least he had Wendy with him wherever he went and they had a core group of close friends who shared the trials and tribulations with them.

Then, in 1979, Wendy got pregnant. Their daughter, Jessica, was born in March 1980 on the last day of the Tournament Players Championship. Fleisher finished his round that afternoon, called home, and was told Wendy was in labor. He raced down I-95 to Miami as fast as he could and arrived shortly after Jessica was born.

She was doing fine, the doctors told him. There was some concern about Wendy, though, a problem with the anesthesia. The situation quickly went from bad to worse to near-tragic. Something had gone wrong in the delivery room, the doctors weren't exactly sure what it was, but Wendy was very, very sick. The day after Jessica was born, she was brought into her mother's room and laid on top of her because the consensus was that Wendy wouldn't live through the night.

She did live, but for four months she was never completely conscious. By the time she came home from the hospital she weighed sixty pounds. It was a year before she could walk and talk normally. The trauma all but knocked Fleisher off the tour for the next year, and when he came back it was difficult to get motivated even though Wendy and Jessica were both doing fine by then.

"I just couldn't put my heart and soul into the game the way I had," he said. "To succeed out here you have to go out every week and think that it's life and death. I knew after what happened that it wasn't. I had seen life and death, lived with it for weeks and weeks. That first year, psychologically, was brutal for both of us. Now I look at Wendy [who has recovered completely] and I see a walking miracle. But it took a long time for both of us to get to that point. It was a long, tough haul."

In 1984, Fleisher was offered a club pro job in Florida. The money was good, he would be able to stay home, and he thought the time was right. He would have had to go back to Q-School that year if he wanted to play the next year anyway, so he decided to hop off the merry-go-round.

For most of the next six years, he stayed home. Occasionally, during the quiet summer months in Florida, he would play mini-tour events or, when he was offered a sponsor exemption, a tour event. By 1989, though, he was starting to feel itchy. Whenever he did play in a tournament, he played pretty well. Jessica was going to be ten, Wendy was back working . . .

"It was Wendy who pushed me to try it again," he said. "She just knew it was something I wanted to do, that I still felt I had the game to compete out here. I finally decided, what the heck, let's give it a shot."

He played in some tournaments overseas in 1990 and in some

Hogan Tour events, trying to get sharp for Q-School. He didn't make it through the school, though, and had to play on sponsor exemptions in 1991. He was taking a week off in July when he got a phone call on a Wednesday afternoon from Jon Brendle, one of the tour's rules officials. There had been some last-minute withdrawals from the New England Classic. Fleisher was on the entry list, so if he could get a flight, he could play in the tournament. Fleisher arrived late that day and, without benefit of a practice round, led the tournament after two days.

On Saturday, he shot 73 to drop back in the pack. "All I wanted to do Sunday was have a good round and make a decent check," he said. "I wasn't even thinking about winning. Then everything started dropping. The whole thing was almost mystical."

When his last birdie putt dropped on 18, he had shot 64 and had a one-shot lead. Ian Baker-Finch birdied 18 to tie him, and the two men went to a sudden-death playoff. Back and forth they went, Baker-Finch missing putts that could have won for him; then Fleisher missing chances. By the time they got to the seventh playoff hole — the 11th at Pleasant Valley — dusk was starting to close in.

Fleisher hit his second shot left of the pin, about 50 feet away. Baker-Finch, 15 feet away, had the much better birdie chance. Fleisher's putt rolled in; Baker-Finch's rolled just right. Twenty-three years after winning the U.S. Amateur, seven years after retiring, Fleisher had won his first PGA Tour event.

In addition to being worth $180,000, the victory gave him a two-year exemption and turned him into a full-time touring pro again. Two years later, with his exemption coming to an end, he returned to Pleasant Valley and finished tied for second, behind Azinger. For the year, he earned $214,279, which kept him comfortably in the top 125 at eighty-first.

He was off to a good start in 1994, having made eight cuts in a row coming to the Players. A tie for fourteenth at the Hope and a tie for ninth at the Honda had pushed his earnings to close to $66,000, about halfway to the $130,000 most players thought would be needed to make the top 125 in '94. His goal at the start of the year had been to make $400,000. That was a long shot, but the start was encouraging. He would be forty-six at the end of the year, and each year he kept his card put him one year closer to the magic fifty mark when he could take his game to the senior tour.

On the regular tour, Fleisher was never a long hitter and, with each passing year, it becomes tougher and tougher for him to keep up. He was ranked 176th in driving distance during 1994, his average tee shot coming up 45 yards short of John Daly's average tee shot. That puts him at an extreme disadvantage. But on the senior tour, where the courses are considerably shorter, Fleisher would do just fine averaging 244 yards off the tee, and with his accuracy (fifth on tour in '94) and his touch around the greens, he stands to make a good deal of money in the future.

But that is still four years away, and Fleisher would very much like to stay on tour during that time. He knows it will not be easy.

The Players is one of the richest events on tour. It has a purse of $2.5 million, more than double the payout at the average event. Making the cut is worth a minimum of $5,000 and a top-twenty finish is worth at least $30,000. Fleisher started out on Thursday with a comfortable 70, two under par. The cut looked as if it would come somewhere around even, so he had some cushion to work with on Friday.

By the time he reached his last hole of the day — the par-five ninth — the cushion was used up. He was two over for the day and even for the tournament. Fleisher was almost certain even par would make the cut, not so sure about one over. The ninth is a birdie hole, a long par-five that isn't always reachable but should, at the very least, provide the chance to hit a wedge from close to the green to set up a short birdie putt.

Fleisher had been working with a new caddy in '94 because Tommy Mascari, his longtime caddy, had decided he had seen enough of the road and gone home. At the ninth, he and his new caddy, Rick Wynn, took a long time deciding what club to hit. Fleisher thought he might be able to get home with a driver. He had a good lie on the fairway, and he was thinking a birdie would not only cinch the cut, but give him a leg up on the weekend. Wynn agreed.

But Fleisher pulled off the driver in mid-swing, hit the ball way left, and ended up making a bogey on the hole. He then had to sit around and wait until Saturday morning to find out officially what he had been fairly certain of unofficially on Friday: he had missed the cut by one shot.

A bogey at a par-five is one of tour golf's greatest sins. Any six on a scorecard is considered a crime against yourself. To bogey a par-five to miss the cut is pretty close to being a capital offense.

Fleisher was devastated. He had let a potentially big payday, one that could have (with a good weekend) just about erased any doubts about the top 125, slip away. He was angry with Wynn, who he felt should have counseled him to be more cautious, given the situation.

"I made the decision, I hit the shot, I ultimately have to take the blame," he said. "But one of the things your caddy is there for is to call you off when you have a mental lapse. I had a mental lapse there, and it was his job to say, 'Whoa, let's back off a little bit here. Make sure we get par and then make our move on the weekend.' I was struggling a little bit that day and a bold play wasn't the right play."

Fleisher knew blaming the bogey and the missed cut on Wynn was unfair. But he couldn't get it out of his mind. He stewed about it the next two weeks while he was at home, trying to decide whether or not to fire Wynn.

"I should have fired him after the Players," he said. "I hadn't been all that comfortable with him to begin with and, whether it was fair or not, I lost confidence in him after that. In my position, any distraction is going to create a problem."

Fleisher missed three more cuts before he fired Wynn. He had now dug himself into a rut and he couldn't seem to climb out. He made only two cuts from March through July and added only $7,705 to his earnings. Ten years after retiring, Fleisher didn't want to retire again. He would need a strong finish if he didn't want to find himself back at school at the age of forty-six.

12

THE MEN OF THE MASTERS

TRADITION is one of the most important words in the lexicon of golf. There is no doubt that tradition is a key element in explaining what draws people to the game. If you walk the Old Course at St. Andrews and are not moved by the tradition that is spread out before you every step of the way, then the sport has not connected with you or you with it. If you don't hear, at least faintly, the footsteps of Old Tom Morris and Young Tom Morris, then you are wasting your time from the moment you arrive in Scotland.

The same can be said — and is often said — of the Augusta National Golf Club. But while there are hundreds of years of tradition and memories at St. Andrews, there are only sixty at Augusta. While it was the Scots who invented golf, it is the men who wear the green jackets of Augusta National who believe they are the ones who got it right.

The Masters is the greatest golf tournament in the world. Ask the men in the green jackets. If you do not treat the Masters with a reverence that goes beyond all other golf tournaments, it is quite possible you will be asked not to return. Jack Whitaker learned that in 1966 when he referred to a crowd around the hallowed 18th green as "a mob." The Men of the Masters told CBS he would not be welcome the following year and CBS meekly complied with that request. Twenty-eight years later, Gary McCord commented that the greens were so slick they looked like they had been bikini-waxed. The MOTM again made their displeasure known to CBS and, again, the network did as it was told. McCord was not invited to return in 1995.

The Masters *is* all about tradition. The only green jacket that ever leaves the premises is the one worn by the current champion. The members and past champions wear theirs only at the club. Every year, Masters week at Augusta is the same, from the champions dinner on Tuesday to the par-three tournament on Wednesday, to the ceremonial tee-off on Thursday, to the four minutes per hour of commercials on Saturday and Sunday, to the members dinner with the new champion on Sunday night.

Every April it is the same, and every April the Masters is seen as a signal of rebirth. The gorgeous azaleas and Georgia dogwood are in bloom, the huge pine and oak trees are as stunning and sturdy as ever, and golf is at its most poetic, especially during those final nine holes on Sunday when, as the TV voices are required to say at least 4,567 times each year, "The golf tournament really begins."

There is no doubting the greatness or the beauty of the golf course that Bobby Jones created as his legacy to the game. The back nine, with two reachable par-fives and water in play at five of the first seven holes, is a perfect setting for the final holes of a major championship.

But there is also no doubting that Augusta National is not a comfortable place for most people. It is a place golf people go every April because (of course) it is a tradition. Players know that a Masters victory ensures them a hallowed place in the pantheon of the sport. It also means you can come back and play in the tournament for the rest of your life and that you will be treated with an extra measure of respect wherever you go in the golf world.

To some extent, this is true of any major. Not like the Masters. Andy North won the U.S. Open twice and some people still point to those victories as proof that the Open isn't as great a championship as it is cracked up to be. A British Open champion is a hero in Europe but often unnoticed in the United States. And to this day there are players who claim that the PGA shouldn't be considered a major because it allowed forty club pros into the field each year (until dropping the number to twenty in 1995) and is almost always played in brutal August heat.

Jeff Sluman, who won the PGA in 1988, has heard the arguments that his victory shouldn't count as a major. "Fine," he says, "I'll accept the fact that I can't count mine as a major when you go and tell Nicklaus that his *five* don't count."

No one questions a Masters champion whether he is Nicklaus or Palmer, Tommy Aaron or Charles Coody. You have worn the green jacket, you have selected the menu for the champions dinner and dined with the members. You have driven up Magnolia Lane to the clubhouse instead of coming in the main gate off Washington Street the way mere mortals do.

Tradition means rules, and Augusta has more rules than anyone. There is no running allowed anywhere on the grounds, and while you may ask for autographs on the parking lot side of the clubhouse, you may not do so on the golf course side. On the practice days, a sign posted on the first tee instructs players to play "only one ball please." If you want to play two or three balls from a certain spot, you are more than welcome to do so — next week at Hilton Head.

The chairman of the club, currently Jackson Stephens, meets with the media every Masters Wednesday at precisely 11 A.M. That is the only time he speaks to the media and he speaks briefly. The same two club members — Charlie Yates and Dan Yates — have moderated the press conferences for as long as anyone can remember. Both men were excellent golfers in their day, especially Charlie, who won the British Amateur in 1938; Dan's son, Dan Jr., was once the runner-up in the U.S. Amateur and a member of the U.S. Walker Cup team and has played in sixteen Masters.

The Yates brothers are both well into their seventies now. They still address female reporters as "pretty little ladies" and, on occasion, will babble on for a while at the start of an interview while a player and reporters sit fidgeting uncomfortably waiting for them to finish. It was Blackie Sherrod of the *Dallas Morning News* who hung the nicknames "Big Silly" and "Little Silly" on them years ago.

Race and gender are still uncomfortable topics at Augusta — as they are at almost all golf clubs worldwide. Augusta has no female members and admitted its first black member four years ago, after the Shoal Creek debacle forced everyone in golf to make *some* attempt to open doors previously closed to blacks. During the 1994 tournament there was talk that Augusta might be getting ready to admit a *second* black member.

There is no shortage of black faces around Augusta National however. Blacks work as waiters, caddies, and members of the grounds crew. Most of them come in through gate seven, on the far corner of the grounds, report to their work stations, and leave through gate seven in the evening. Once a year, the club invites them all to a barbecue and picnic.

There are even rules for television at Augusta. Unlike any other sports event in the world, the Masters is paid far less than market value for its television rights. On an open market, during a time when NBC is paying the U.S. Open $13 million a year for the next three years, the Masters would be worth at least that much — perhaps more. Instead, CBS, which has televised the tournament for the last thirty-nine years, pays in the neighborhood of $4 million a year.

Why? So that the Masters can remain in complete control of the telecast. That means not only having the right to fire announcers like Whitaker and McCord, but the right to approve any announcer before he (no women announcers here either) is handed a microphone. It also means that someone from the club (the chairman until 1994, when vice chairman Joe Ford did the honors) asks the champion the first question on the air when he arrives at Butler Cabin to receive the green jacket.

And it also means that there are only four minutes of commercials per hour — two minutes for Cadillac and two minutes for Travelers Insurance — because the Men of the Masters don't want their telecasts glutted by commercials. Naturally, they have final approval of all commercial copy. You aren't likely to see any Miller Lite commercials on the Masters anytime soon. Since CBS pays a lower rights fee, the lack of commercial time doesn't create a problem.

The members' approach is simple: This is *our* tournament. If you do not like the way we do business, you are free not to do business with us. If you find our past policies on race or our current policies on gender offensive, you need not attend the tournament, televise the tournament, write about the tournament, or, for that matter, play in the tournament.

If you doubt the power of the Men of the Masters, consider the column that appeared in *Golf World* magazine a couple of weeks after the announcement that McCord had been banned from Augusta. "I applaud their decision," it read. "In the contract with CBS, they have the right to evaluate the announcers and decide who personifies the muted rituals of restraint. I am a loud wail."

The author of the column was Gary McCord.

No one is above the laws of Augusta. Several years ago, Pat Summerall, who did his twenty-sixth and last Masters for CBS in 1994 and was given what amounted to a royal sendoff by the MOTM (a gold badge, which grants him lifetime access to the tournament), was about to climb the steps to the tower behind the 18th green, when a Pinkerton guard stopped him.

"You need a pass to get up there," the guard said.

Summerall had left his pass in the CBS trailer. He explained that to the guard, noted that he had taken these same steps every day all week and for many years. The guard didn't care. No pass, no passage. The argument got heated, and Summerall was dragged off to the proper authorities. There, he had to be freed by a great deal of apologetic pleading by his boss, Frank Chirkinian.

Chirkinian has produced the Masters telecasts for thirty-six years. For twenty of those years he lived at Augusta. He has been friends with all the club chairmen, plays the course every year, and produces the pictures and sounds that make America wax poetic about the Masters each year.

In 1994, Chirkinian arrived for the tournament and was told that CBS's ticket allotment had been cut by twenty-five, a disaster since the network flies in all sorts of clients as a major perk. When Chirkinian asked why, he was told "because."

"Arbitrary decision," he grumbled later in the week. Then he caught himself. "Of course, it's their ballpark."

It sure is. That's why when Summerall's partner, Ken Venturi, parked his car in a space where he wasn't supposed to park, Chirkinian got another call. Venturi could move his car — within the next fifteen minutes — or it would be moved — towed — for him.

"If I can just get into the truck and do my job, I can enjoy the week," Chirkinian said. "Until then . . ."

Until then, he was like everyone else, a guest of the Men of the Masters — as long as he behaved.

No one on tour was looking forward to the Masters more than Davis Love III. A week shy of his thirtieth birthday, Love had already accomplished more in golf than 95 percent of the players in the world will accomplish in a lifetime. He had won eight tournaments, been a Ryder Cup hero, and made enough money on and off the golf course to guarantee his family's future *and* buy an $800,000 airplane.

But none of that was what he had set out to do in golf. He was nine when he told his father he wanted to be a golf pro. He was eighteen when he and his father began plotting his future with one thought in mind: how to someday be the best player in the world.

The best player in the world is not someone who wins in Las Vegas and Greensboro. He wins at Augusta and at Oakmont and at St. Andrews and Turnberry. Love had never done that. His record in the majors, especially considering his accomplishments elsewhere, was awful. He had never finished in the top ten at any major, his highest finish being a tie for eleventh at the 1991 U.S. Open. His best finish in the Masters had been a tie for twenty-fifth in 1992 and, in all, he had three top-twenty finishes in majors in his career.

Love did not sit around making excuses for his failures in the majors. He didn't rationalize and point to his other accomplishments because that is not his way. His goal for 1994 was simple and direct: play better in the majors.

"I'm very proud of the fact that I won the Players Championship [1992] and of all the tournaments I've won," he said. "But the fact is, when I'm done, I don't want to be introduced as the winner of eight tournaments or a former Ryder Cupper. I want to be introduced as the champion of a major."

In a sense, winning major championships is what Davis Love was bred to do. His father, Davis Love Jr., was talented enough to play in the Masters at sixteen as an amateur. He never made it to the tour, but he did become one of the most renowned golf teachers in the country. His two most important pupils were Davis and his brother Mark, who is two years younger.

Davis Love Jr. never forced golf on either son. Both boys played other sports. When Davis played peewee hockey, his father got up at 5 A.M. to drive him to practice. When Davis showed an interest in fishing, Davis Jr. found out which member of the Atlanta Country Club (where he worked at the time) knew the most about fishing and introduced him to his son.

He never told Davis or Mark that he had to play golf, but his attitude always was "if you're going to do something, you do it all out and you do it right." When Davis made it clear that golf was what he wanted to do, it became as much his father's obsession as his — maybe more.

"Dad always told both of us that if he had our natural talent, he would have been a star," he said. "His talent was for work. He always talked about hitting balls until his hands bled when he was a kid. Some days I would go out and hit all these balls and I'd say, 'Dad, when will my hands start to bleed?' And he would just look at me and say, 'Not for a long time yet.' "

Mark was more of a natural, according to the father/teacher, but Davis had the patience that is a prerequisite for success in golf. If Davis Jr. challenged the boys to hit a certain kind of shot, Davis III would stay on the range for hours until he could hit the shot. If Mark couldn't figure it out in fifteen swings, he would just say, "This can't be done," and leave.

The family moved to Sea Island, Georgia, when the boys were teenagers, after Davis Jr. was hired as the pro at the resort there. Davis grew to a lean 6-foot-4 and began hitting the golf ball frighteningly long distances. His father had never been able to hit the ball very far but had always scored well because of his short game. He focused constantly on Davis's long game, perhaps because that had been his weakness.

Whenever Davis worked on the range or played with his father, there would be a complete review of the day when they got home that night. Davis Jr. would write down all his thoughts on yellow legal pads and then go over them at dinner. Penta Love was a golfer too, a five-handicapper, so she never objected to all the golf talk at her dinner table. Sometimes it would get to be too much for Davis. He would be relaxing in front of the TV set and his father would walk in with the legal pads and a look on his face that said "there's still more to talk about," and Davis would wonder if there would ever come a time when there wasn't more to talk about. He still has a lot of the yellow pads in boxes in his house. His only regret is that he didn't save them all.

He was a prodigy in high school, as much for his length as for his scoring. He chose the University of North Carolina because he wanted to get out of Georgia and had met three other recruits that he liked during his visit to Carolina and they all decided to go to school together. He never really hit it off with coach Devon Brouse, and by the middle of his junior year he had decided to drop out of school and turn pro.

"I was getting to a point where I was just kind of hanging out waiting for the next thing in my life, which I knew was going to be turning pro," he said. "I wasn't working very hard in school, mostly it was just going to parties and playing golf. It was definitely time to move on."

He did make himself a part of golf history at Carolina by giving Michael Jordan his first golf clubs. After Jordan's golf-gambling problems became the subject of so much public scrutiny, people often asked Love about Jordan's beginnings as a golfer. "Sometimes," he said, "I feel like the guy who gave John Dillinger his first gun."

Love dropped out of Carolina after his junior year without taking final exams and began preparing to play the Q-School in the fall. While he was home, he spent a lot of time at night hanging around a place called Brogan's Bar. Most nights, a friend of his from high school, Robin Bankston, was there too.

Love had dated Robin on and off in high school, but never for very long. "She was the five-foot-ten blonde everyone wanted to go out with," he said, laughing. "I would go out with her a couple of times and then some surfer would show up and I would be history. But we were always friends."

Love wasn't thrilled with the crowd his old friend was running with during that summer of 1985. He didn't like — "actually hated is a better word" — any of the guys she was dating. He asked Robin out again, partly because he wanted to go out with her, partly because he didn't want her going out with the guys she was seeing. They began dating regularly and by the time the Love family set off for Greenlefe, Florida, in the fall for the Q-School finals, Robin was along for the trip. She never went back to hanging with the crowd at Brogan's again. Neither did Davis.

He shot 66 the first day at Q-School and cruised to a seventh-place finish. "It may be the best week of golf I've ever played," he said. "The stakes were so high. I had turned pro, so I couldn't go back to college; there was no Nike Tour back then. It was make it or head for the mini-tours."

Mark caddied. Robin and his mother walked the fairways. And Davis Jr., as always, kept looking for trees to hide behind. Davis always laughed at his father's superstitions. He always knew where he was, and he was amused when his father would pick up a rock or a stick and hold onto it as long as Davis was playing well. At Greenlefe, he picked up a stick early on the first day and hung onto it the whole week. Davis's mother still has the stick.

There were only two potential problems the entire week. The first came when his father almost rammed into a semi-truck while trying to analyze Davis's first round and drive at the same time. "He could never drive and talk golf at the same time," Davis said. "He just got too wound up."

The second problem came on the 18th hole the last day. Davis was comfortably in, and when he reached the last hole, a par-five, he hit a driver and a one-iron to the green. Just short, he chipped up and made par. When he came off the green, his father was pale. "Why in the world did you hit one-iron with out-of-bounds on the left there?" his father demanded.

"Dad, I was in all the way," Davis answered. "I was fine."

"I know *you* were fine," Davis Jr. answered. "I was dying."

Love played well enough his rookie year to keep his card with ease (seventy-seventh on the money list), and early the next year he won the Heritage Classic, the week after his twenty-third birthday. With his exceptional length and a tournament victory so young, the star label was placed on him. Naturally, he struggled, dropping from thirty-third in 1987 to seventy-fifth on the money list in 1988. He was still trying to become consistent with his short game, and he could still get wild with the driver.

The weekend after the official season had ended in '88, Davis was home in Sea Island. He and Robin were leaving the following Tuesday for the tournament in Kapalua, one of their favorite events since it was unofficial, pressure-free, and in Hawaii. They would be leaving their five-month-old daughter, Lexie, with Davis's parents. It would be their first trip together since her birth.

On Saturday afternoon, Davis was about to get into his truck to go pick up a boat motor. His dad came out of the house and casually asked him if he had practiced that day. Davis hadn't. "Don't you think you should practice before you go to Hawaii?" his father asked.

"Dad, it's Kapalua," Davis said. "I go there for fun."

His father said nothing. "You mind if I tag along with you?" he said. Davis immediately knew something was up, but he said fine.

Davis Love Jr. was always very direct. "Do you still love golf?" he asked as they bounced down the road.

"Absolutely."

"No, I mean, do you really love it? Are you as enthusiastic now as when you were a kid? Or is it more of a job?"

Davis thought about that for a minute. It was more of a job, no doubt, but he loved his job. He told his father that. There was a long silence.

"I just wonder if you shouldn't be working with someone else besides me," his father finally said. "I just don't feel like I'm getting you where you should be as a player. I don't see the enthusiasm you once had. I don't see you improving as much as I think you should, and I wonder if someone else might do better."

In many ways, that was typical of Davis Love Jr. If working with someone else would make Davis a better player, then he wanted Davis to do that. His ego wasn't such that he thought he was the only one who could help him. When Davis had first mentioned the idea of talking to Bob Rotella, the sports psychologist, Davis Jr. had been all for it. Some of Rotella's ideas — like not continuing to practice with any one club once you hit a few good shots with it — blew his mind; but if it would help Davis, that was what mattered.

Davis was touched by his father's concern, but didn't give it much thought. He and Robin flew to Maui three days later. Shortly after they arrived, they got a phone call from an old family friend who was also on Maui and suggested they get together for dinner. They were about to leave to go snorkeling when Davis suggested calling home. His mom would be happy to hear they had hooked up with their friend and they could check on Lexie.

As soon as his mother answered the phone, Davis knew something was terribly, terribly wrong. She had just hung up the phone with the Federal Aviation Administration. Davis Jr. and two other golf pros, both friends of Davis and Robin, had been flying a private plane into Jacksonville Airport that night en route to a clinic. Something had happened. The plane was down. No one knew yet if anyone had survived.

Davis and Robin repacked their bags and headed for the airport. Twice en route Davis had the cab stop so he could phone home. No word yet. At the airport, he called Jim Griggs, a friend who is a member of the tour's Golf Course Board, and told him what had happened. Griggs told him he would be waiting for him in San Francisco with his private plane. That way, they wouldn't have to wait until morning for a commercial flight.

When they landed in San Francisco, Griggs was waiting. He and Robin collected the luggage while Davis went to a pay phone to call home again. The plane had been found. No survivors.

The next few days are a blur to Love. He remembers thinking about Mark on the plane flight home and what he must have gone through sitting there with his mother waiting for word. The other two men in the plane had young children — five altogether — who would be without fathers for Christmas. When they got home that day and had gone through all the rituals and made all the plans, the Loves fell into bed exhausted. Several hours later, Davis woke up screaming, swinging at something so violently that he frightened Robin.

For the next few months, as he tried to help his mother piece her life back together and dealt with all the golf people who had known his father coming up to tell him how sorry they were, Love felt like he was in a bad dream. His worst dreams came at night, though, especially when he was on the road without Robin. Many of the dreams ended with him crying intensely. He would bolt awake and find tears running down his face. Then he would cry again. He thought often about his last conversation with his dad, about how much it meant to him to see Davis reach his potential and how willing he was to blame himself if that didn't happen.

Everywhere he went, the media would ask the same question over and over again: How was he dealing with his dad's death? "I suppose when you win the U.S. Open you get asked every week how it feels to win the U.S. Open," he said, looking back at that year. "That's fun. Being asked about my father's death every week wasn't."

He played remarkably well in 1989 under the circumstances, but it wasn't until he won his second tournament — the International in August 1990 — that he felt as if he could just be a golfer again, rather than a golfer who was dealing with the loss of his dad. He was trying so hard to prove that he could still play well without his dad and the yellow legal pads that he made everything that much more difficult for himself.

Now he thinks about his dad all the time, especially on the golf course. He can still hear his voice telling him what to do or, on those rare occasions when he and Davis would argue, saying, "You know I've been a pretty good teacher for a long time, I may know more about golf than you do."

Now, though, he can smile at those memories, even though he misses his dad. When he made the putt to beat Costantino Rocca at the Ryder Cup, his first thoughts weren't about his dad, but when he did think about him later, it made him feel good to know how much the day and the week would have meant to him.

Occasionally, there are twinges. Whenever he flies into Jacksonville Airport, he can't help but look at the trees where the plane went down. That's become a reflex, but being prepared for it, he can handle it. Only on rare occasions does the grief sneak up on him again. Late in 1993, he and Tom Kite flew into San Francisco Airport for the Tour Championship.

As they came down the escalator to the baggage claim, it occurred to Love that he hadn't been in the airport — except to change planes — since his father's death. A moment later, he walked by the phone booth from which he had made the call. His knees suddenly felt wobbly and the memories flooded back. He started to say something to Kite, a close friend of his father's, but decided to keep it to himself. No need, he thought, to make Kite share the sadness he felt at that moment.

When he threw both arms into the air after making the putt to beat Rocca at the '93 Ryder Cup, it was as joyful a gesture as Love had ever made on a golf course. While he was thrilled to have made the putt and to have helped win the cup, he also came out of that week thinking — and hoping — that he had taken a giant step forward in terms of his ability to play in the majors.

"There isn't any pressure I'm going to face that's more intense than the Ryder Cup was," he said. "I would hope that what I did there can give me a boost toward playing the way I want to in the majors."

His start in 1994 had been solid, not spectacular. He had had one superb round, a 60 in the second round in Hawaii, but had played mediocre golf on the weekend and finished a disappointing second to Brett Ogle. He led at Pebble Beach after two rounds, but faded to twenty-fourth on the weekend. He was within two shots of the lead after three rounds at Honda, but, like everyone else, couldn't stop Nick Price on Sunday and finished fourth. Two weeks later, he tied for sixth at the Players.

Three top tens in eight tournaments and winnings of $320,000 before the end of March. A great year for a lot of players, an ordinary start for Love. Still, he felt good about the Masters. His agent and longtime friend, Vinny Giles, had told him at the Players that he wanted him to buy something very expensive before the Masters to give himself incentive to play well there.

Love, who had been campaigning with Robin to buy a bigger plane ever since their second child (named Davis IV, but called Dru — for quaDRUple — just as Davis had been Trip for triple as a kid) had been born in December, thought that was a great idea. Robin didn't. "You always said you'd do something like that *after* you win a major," she said. Davis agreed . . . for now.

He was delighted with the way he was hitting the ball during his practice rounds but wary of the way the golf course was set up. The Men of the Masters had been a bit disturbed by some of the low scores that had been put up in recent years and they had shaved the greens (bikini-waxed them?) to lightning speed. When Love and everyone else showed up Thursday morning, they found that the pin placements, always critical on Augusta's large, undulating greens, were in the most difficult places possible.

"It's just this side of being ridiculous," Greg Norman said.

"Mickey Mouse–type stuff really," Nick Faldo said.

Love was two under par for eight holes on Thursday, but the back nine — which is where you are supposed to score — beat him up and he finished with a 76. Tom Kite, who had played with him earlier in the week, had seen potential trouble. "He's hitting the driver great," he said on Wednesday. "But he's not real confident with his irons.

You have to hit your irons great on this golf course or you're in big trouble."

Love was aggravated Thursday evening, but not despondent. No one had gone very low that day; Larry Mize was leading with a 68. Only three players — including Kite with 69 — had broken 70. "I hit the ball well, I really did," he said. "I'm so close." He brightened. "If I can shoot 67 or 68 tomorrow, I can get right back into it."

He was right about the numbers. José María Olazabal, who shot 74 the first day, shot 67 the next day and was right back in it — two shots behind Mize, who was still the leader. If Love had shot 67, he would have been only four shots back. He didn't shoot 67, though, or 68. He shot 78 — with a birdie at 18. He hit a six-iron to within a foot there. Sadly, that was about the only iron shot he got close all week. Kite's concern had been well founded.

Love walked off the final green as angry and upset as he had ever been on a golf course. He hadn't missed a cut all year. Now, in one of the four tournaments that his year was built around, he was trunk-slamming on Friday.

There is probably no one on the PGA Tour with a better demeanor, win or lose, than Love. He is the guy who walks off the course after a bad round and still makes sure to thank the woman who has walked 18 holes keeping score and then gives his golf ball to the kid who has been holding up the signboard with the players' scores. He asks names and remembers them. At Las Vegas the year before, leading the tournament on the back nine Sunday afternoon, he had turned to the youngster carrying the scoreboard.

"What happened to Sean?" he asked.

"Oh, we switch off after nine holes" was the surprised answer.

"What's your name?"

"Ben."

"Okay, Ben, I hope you do as well for me as Sean did."

Love couldn't handle any small talk now. He walked briskly to the locker room and began throwing things into a bag. "I just can't believe it," he said. "There's so much luck involved here. If you're off by one yard, you're dead. I was off by one yard for two days, that's all. Honest, one yard. I hate to whine but . . ."

Several reporters from Georgia rounded the corner. Could he talk for a few minutes? Love didn't want to talk. He wanted to bolt. He wanted to get in his car and let out a primal scream. He took a deep breath and sat down.

At the other end of the small locker room, John Daly — who had made the cut but was ten shots back — was surrounded by reporters as he took things out of his locker. Daly never looked up at anyone. Questions were asked, he didn't respond. He loaded the bag, turned, and walked through a path that magically appeared and went out the door without a word.

While Daly bolted, Love sat quietly answering questions. He never snapped at anyone. Finally, when there was a lull, he stood up. "I'm sorry, guys," he said. "I've just got to get out of here."

He got halfway to the door and stopped. "Damn," he said. "I forgot to tip the locker room guys."

He went back to write out a check. He could be forgiven for forgetting. He hadn't planned to leave on Friday.

The best moments of every Masters are the first ones. They come early on Thursday morning when Gene Sarazen, Byron Nelson, and Sam Snead make their way to the first tee. This is one of the traditions that makes the Masters unique. All three are past champions, each a living, breathing legend. Snead, the kid in the group at eighty-one, played in forty-four Masters, winning three times. Nelson is eighty-two, also a three-time Masters champion. More than anyone, though, it is Sarazen, now ninety-two, who helped make the Masters what it is.

It was his historic double eagle at the 15th hole in 1935 — the second year the tournament was played — that not only won the title, but put the Masters on the map. To this day, when you talk about "the shot heard 'round the world" to golfers, they think not of Bobby Thompson at the Polo Grounds in 1951, but Gene Sarazen at the Masters in 1935.

It is quite possible that these are the only three men in the world that Jackson Stephens ever waits for. Shortly after 8 A.M. Stephens stood on the first tee, wearing a floppy white golf hat that looked incongruous with his green jacket, and waited for the threesome that was scheduled to begin the tournament at 8:15.

To his left, on the board where the players' names are posted before they tee off, the three slots read: Sarazen–92; Nelson–82; Snead–81. The number usually tells the fan what number a player's caddy is wearing on his white overalls. The defending champion is always assigned number 1 and Jack Nicklaus is given 86 in honor of the year he won the last and most extraordinary of his six titles. The first threesome's numbers need no explanation.

Sarazen played his last nine holes at Augusta in 1991. For several weeks, prior to the '94 tournament, he had been concerned that shoulder miseries would make it impossible to take his one swing. A year earlier, Nelson, bothered by hip and knee problems, couldn't take his turn, and Sarazen was concerned he would be the spectator in the group this time.

At 8:12, he walked resolutely onto the tee, dressed in his trademark knickers and floppy hat, carrying a walking stick. The spectators, most of whom had ignored the Pinkertons' "no running" pleas when the gates opened at 8 o'clock, in order to jockey for position around the tee, burst into loud applause when Sarazen appeared.

Sarazen rubbed his left shoulder and, noting the breezy 51 degree temperature, said, "Cold out here for these old guys."

He took a driver out of the bag he had borrowed from Rick Fehr and began swinging easily to get loose. Nelson appeared a few moments later, followed by CBS's Ken Venturi, who once led the Masters after three rounds as an amateur. "I don't know if I can hit the ball," Nelson said, "but I found me a good boy here to tee it up for me."

Snead was the last to arrive, bursting onto the tee right at 8:15. "Jack, how is everything," he said, shaking hands with Stephens as if the chairman were his caddy.

They posed for pictures, then Stephens grabbed a hand microphone and introduced the three men. The other eighty-six players in the field would each receive exactly the same introduction on the first tee: "Fore, please, [fill in a name] now driving."

Period. Sarazen, Nelson, and Snead did considerably better. Stephens, whose voice always quavers a bit, went through their accomplishments in detail. ". . . In 1945, when Byron won eleven straight tournaments, his scoring average for the year was, I believe, 68.33."

"That's correct," Nelson confirmed, smiling.

". . . And Gene Sarazen won the U.S. Open in 1922 and 1932, the British Open in 1932 . . ." He paused. "Don't forget the PGA," Sarazen said.

Sarazen, whose ball had been placed on the tee for him before he arrived, hit first. He lofted a shot about 120 yards down the left side. As the applause washed over him, he smiled, relieved that he had been able to get his shoulders turned.

Nelson, after his "boy," the 1964 U.S. Open champion, had teed the ball for him, hit a short, low line drive down the middle. He was clearly thrilled at being able to swing the club again.

Snead needed no help. He teed the ball himself, took that picture-perfect swing that produced eighty-one tournament victories, and hit the ball well down the fairway. He grinned and looked around as if to say, "Anybody looking for a game?"

"The fifty-eighth Masters is now officially under way," Stephens said.

Everyone headed for the warmth of the clubhouse, although it was hard to believe it would feel any warmer in there than it had felt on the windswept tee for those brief, sweet moments.

"How come," Sarazen said to his partners as they walked off, "I'm the only one who gets older every year?"

The cool morning gave way to a picture-postcard afternoon. By the end of the day it was apparent that no one was going to challenge the tournament record of 271 co-held by Nicklaus and Raymond Floyd. The breezes and the greens were turning everyone into grinders.

Larry Mize had the lead at 68 when everyone was finished, with Tom Kite and Fulton Allem one shot back. Tom Watson shot 70 in spite of chipping into the water at the 15th and making a triple-bogey 8 there. Greg Norman also went into the water at 15, but saved par and also shot 70.

The 15th was the talk of the locker room. The embankment in front of the green just over the water had been cut so short that any ball that landed in front of the green was going to roll back and get wet. In fact, some balls that landed *on* the front of the green and spun also ended up wet.

If Norman was the favorite going in, favorites 1-A and 1-B were the two Nicks: Faldo and Price. Both struggled, Price to a 74, Faldo to a 76. Faldo came off the course mumbling about his putting and, after a brief chat with the media, went directly to the putting green.

There are two places at the Masters where players talk to the media. One is the interview room, where the leaders are brought in each day and put through their paces by the Yates brothers. The other is underneath the giant oak tree that stands just outside the entrance to the clubhouse.

Exactly how this particular tradition has grown up, no one is quite sure, but almost every player knows it and follows it. When you finish a round and you know you aren't going to be asked to the interview room, you march up the hill from the 18th green, step inside the ropes that stop the public from going farther, walk about five more paces, and find a spot under the oak tree. The tree is so huge that there is room for at least half a dozen players to spread out in different places and talk.

Occasionally, a reporter or two will follow a player into the locker room once he is finished under the oak tree, but most players do their talking there. The exception to this rule and tradition was John Daly, who walked past the oak tree each of the first three days (76–73–77) pursued by a bevy of reporters and never stopped to talk to anyone.

Only on Sunday, after finishing with a triple-bogey 7 at the 18th to shoot 76, did he pause to talk. He had been paired, by luck of the draw, for four straight rounds with Ian Woosnam, the Welshman who had won the tournament in 1991.

"Me and Woosie are talking about getting married," joked Daly, who was in the middle of an ugly divorce. "He told me this was the longest relationship I've ever had."

Standing at the bar inside the clubhouse, he sipped a Diet Coke. Someone asked if he could feel the support of the fans. "Sure could," he said. "Can't understand it."

He was asked if he had perhaps rushed a little bit on the back nine, gotten careless. He shrugged. "I'm damn sure not going to play slow when nothing's going right. At twelve, I hit me a seven-iron I thought was in the hole and it went in the water. That'll make you impatient.

Tell the truth, all I was trying to do today was get me some crystal."

The Masters gives out crystal to any player who makes an eagle during the tournament. Jeff Maggert had made a double eagle that day at the 13th, the third in tournament history. "Knowing this place," Daly said, "they'll probably tell him a double eagle doesn't count."

He put down the Diet Coke and headed for the door. He had been funny and charming and antsy all at once. Being near him gave one a sense of discomfort, as if a wrong question or comment might set him off. He had played the last round as if getting some crystal and getting out of Dodge were the only two things on his mind. The enigma grew.

By Friday evening at most majors, the list of contenders and pretenders has shrunk. The Masters is the only major tournament that repairs after the first round, meaning that the Thursday leaders go out last the way the leaders normally do at other tournaments only on Saturday and Sunday. By the time Larry Mize got to the clubhouse in the late-afternoon gloaming on Friday, he had shot 71 for 139 and he still had the lead. The list of those chasing him had changed considerably.

Norman was still there, one shot back after shooting 70 again. Tom Lehman, who had finished third in his first Masters a year earlier, had also shot a second straight 70. The two biggest moves of the day had been made by two men who knew what it felt like to contend on Sunday and come up short: Dan Forsman, who had led the tournament in 1993 until he knocked his ball into Rae's Creek at the 12th hole and made an eight, had produced a 66, the low round of the tournament, to tie Norman and Lehman. And José María Olazabal, who had stood on the 18th tee tied for the lead in 1991 only to bogey the hole and lose by one shot to Ian Woosnam, had come back from an opening 74 — identical to Forsman — to shoot 67. He was two shots back of Mize along with the rising young South African star Ernie Els and a trio of forty-something Americans: Hale Irwin, Kite, and Watson.

Olazabal's presence on the leader board was intriguing since he had become golf's version of the invisible man in 1993. He had been labeled the "next Seve" when he first began making a name for himself by winning two tournaments on the European Tour in 1986 at the age of twenty. A year later, he had started his famous Ryder Cup partnership with Ballesteros. He wasn't as classically handsome or charismatic as his older countryman, but he did have the same sort of magic touch around the green and a similar ability to extricate himself from seemingly impossible spots. When he won the World Series of Golf in 1990 at the age of twenty-four by a stunning twelve shots, it seemed to be only a matter of time before he began winning major championships.

Then he lost the 1991 Masters to Woosnam and his ascendancy stopped. He was still a good player, but he was not the same. In 1993, he failed to win on the European Tour for the first time in six years and dropped out of the top ten on the Order of Merit. In fact, he didn't even qualify for the Ryder Cup team and made the team only as a captain's pick.

He went from shy but charming to angry and aloof. He was constantly telling reporters to leave him alone and, during the Ryder Cup, Ballesteros did virtually all his talking for him. People wondered if all of the "next Seve" pressure had gotten to him the way all the "next Nicklaus" rhetoric had gotten to many young American players.

Olazabal said no, he just needed to tinker with his swing a little. He worked over the winter on his consistency and switched to a metal driver. Right from the start, he had played better in 1994 and had finished second in New Orleans the week before the Masters. When his name popped onto the leader board Friday, eyebrows went up all over the grounds.

The same was true of Els, the tall twenty-four-year-old South African with the long, dreamy-looking swing and easygoing manner. Els had already won seven times around the world, but more important than that, he had shown a knack for playing his best golf in the majors. This was his eighth major and he came in with four top-ten finishes. He had length comparable to Daly's, only he made it look much easier. And he had the good fortune not to be called the "next Gary Player," if only because, at a shade under 6-foot-4, he was almost nine inches taller than Player and played a game so different that the only thing they had in common was South African birth.

The real surprise, though, was who *wasn't* on the leader board: the two Nicks. Price and Faldo both struggled in with 73s on Friday, meaning both would play on the weekend — Price at 147 and Faldo right on the number at 149 — but neither was likely to contend, barring a miraculous round on Saturday.

Price, who had never won the Masters and knew that the lightning-fast greens probably would make it the most difficult major for him to win, was disappointed but sanguine. He knew, the way the course was set up, with the pins practically sitting on cliffs, that he would have to be at his very best with the putter and he just wasn't. "It's not as if I'm hitting the ball badly," he said. "I just can't make any putts on these greens."

Faldo wasn't quite as philosophical. He had won the Masters twice, in 1989 and 1990, and knew he was perfectly capable of making putts on Augusta's greens. Only he wasn't. Each day he walked up the hill from 18 to the oak tree, stood with his arms folded, and in a voice that couldn't be heard by anyone standing more than five feet away, kept saying, "It's horrible, terrible. Can't make a thing." The inquisition finished, he would find his caddy, Fanny Sunneson — one of a handful of female tour caddies — and head for the putting green.

To most players, Faldo was an enigma, the last person in the world you wanted to be paired with because the odds were good that the round would be played in complete silence. When he and Greg Norman played in one of the new Shell's Wonderful World of Golf matches that summer, the kind of exhibition where no one is uptight and everyone is supposed to have fun, Faldo didn't say a word for 18 holes.

"A barrel of laughs," Norman said later.

What Norman — and most others — couldn't understand was that golf wasn't *ever* a laughing matter to Faldo. He was the modern version of Hogan, the man the Scots had nicknamed the Wee Ice Mon, a superb, singularly obsessed player who had first played the game twenty-three years earlier at the age of thirteen and had thought of very little except the game since then.

It was the Masters that first brought golf to Faldo's attention. Sitting at home on Easter Sunday in 1971, he had flipped on the television — something his parents never had until he was ten years old — and had seen this great green place with huge trees, long shadows, and this large blond fellow who, at least to Faldo, seemed to dominate the proceedings.

"Big Jack," Faldo said, laughing. "I just remember watching him hit the ball and thinking, I'd like a go at this." Nicklaus finished one shot behind Charlie Coody that day, but he was the one the English teenager remembered. The next day he told his mother he wanted to take lessons. George and Joyce Faldo were usually willing to accommodate their only child's requests, so Nick was taken to a nearby club and introduced to a pro named Wayne Connolly. A lesson was arranged for the next day. The next day! That meant waiting twenty-four hours. "Patience was never my strong suit," he said, grinning at the memory.

Once Connolly had shown him a grip and a stance and — *finally!* — let him hit balls during the third lesson, the youngster was hooked. He had always been a superb athlete — a swimmer, a cyclist, a cricketer — and he was already well on his way to being one of the biggest truly great golfers in history. At 6-foot-3 and 195 pounds, with the broad shoulders of a swimmer, Faldo is a big man in a sport where most of the best players have been either small or average in size. "Big Jack" is under 6 feet and so is Long John Daly. Norman is 6-feet-1 and 185, but Faldo is taller and heavier.

The first time he went out on a course and played, Faldo three-putted the second hole and laughed at himself. That was a stupid thing to do, he told himself. I'll certainly never do *that* again.

He played by himself that day and remembers hitting the ball seventy-eight times but figures he lost at least three balls and hit a couple more out-of-bounds. It was a beginning. Day after day he went back, happy to play and practice alone, never once bothered by the solitary nature of the sport. As an only child, he was used to spending time alone, *enjoyed* spending time alone, so why shouldn't he be happy spending hours and hours alone at the golf course. He was, after all, doing exactly what he wanted to do.

Within a year of taking up the game, his schoolwork had gone completely to hell. Golf was his best friend, his constant companion. He didn't need anyone else to play or to practice and he could make every single shot interesting and fun to play. Teachers warned him that he was getting into trouble at school, but Faldo just shrugged. "I'm going to be a golf pro," he said. Didn't he understand, they told him, that one in ten thousand who try to be golf pros succeed? "Right, good," he said. "That one is me."

At sixteen he announced to his parents that he saw no point in wasting even a few hours a day going to school, that the time would be better spent on the practice tee. George and Joyce weren't thrilled, but Connolly had told them their son clearly had potential, and they knew trying to stop him was pointless anyway. He could go to work as an assistant pro for £4 a week but that would mean his father would lose the £4 a week the government gave him in national child benefits.

So Nick stayed home and spent the next two years practicing. Neither rain nor sleet nor snow stopped him from his appointed rounds — or practice. At eighteen, he won virtually every important amateur tournament there was to win, and a year later he turned pro. In 1977, his second year on the European Tour, he finished eighth on the Order of Merit and, two months after turning twenty-one, played on the Ryder Cup team. He won two team matches and beat Tom Watson in the singles. Watson was only the Masters and British Open champion at the time.

That weekend made him into a celebrity. Clearly, this was the man who would succeed Tony Jacklin as Great Britain's next champion. He played well the next few years, winning the Order of Merit in 1983 and winning a tournament on the PGA Tour, the Heritage Classic, that same year. But, much like Davis Love in the 1990s, Faldo never seemed able to come up with his best play in the majors. He would contend, then fall back. The British tabloids, gentle as ever, began referring to him as "Foldo."

By 1984, he was an unhappy man. His marriage had fallen apart. "The only time in my life I can ever remember shouting is during my first marriage," he said. "No one in my family ever shouted. If we disagreed, we just walked away and left it. But I found myself screaming and yelling at my wife and it was horrible. I said, 'This isn't me, something's gone very wrong here.' "

The split was, of course, grist for the tabloid mills, and Faldo earned less than half what he had earned in 1983. He was convinced, though, that there was more to his problems than the breakup of his marriage and bad publicity. He wasn't happy with his swing. When he had first played in the United States he had stood on the back of the range and watched Big Jack and Tom Weiskopf and others practice. He memorized their swings and compared them to his. His didn't measure up. "I was fooling myself," he said. "I was okay, but I wasn't close to where I wanted to be."

It was as if he had reached a certain level and couldn't go any further. Winning Heritage and the Haig Whisky and Sun Alliance championships put money in your pocket, but it wasn't what he had started playing golf for. He wanted to play in those long shadows late on a Sunday afternoon underneath those huge trees and be like Big Jack. It wasn't happening.

Late that year he was playing in Sun City, South Africa, when he bumped into David Leadbetter, who was just starting to forge a reputation as a teacher. Faldo asked him a couple of questions about his swing and his game, and Leadbetter answered at length about all the things that could be improved if he really wanted to think about it. Faldo didn't — at least not right away. But early the next year, after missing the cut at the Memorial (Big Jack's tournament), he saw Leadbetter again. Okay, he said, I'm willing to listen to what you have to say.

He went to Florida and Leadbetter told him he wanted to change the way he was rotating his arms on his backswing. Faldo went off to work on that. He came back — triumphant — and Leadbetter nodded and said it was very good, much better, and if you can keep learning at this pace it won't take any more than two years, maybe only eighteen months, to get it right.

Two years! Faldo didn't have two years to spend starting over. He was twenty-eight and the world was still waiting for him to win something worth remembering. He was making a very good living and, having been a Ryder Cupper five times and a winner of the Order of Merit, he was making lots of money off the golf course too. Leadbetter didn't care about any of that. If Faldo wanted to do the work, he was ready to dig in. If not, that was fine too.

Faldo dug in. If he had known then what the next two years would be like, he might not have agreed to go on. In July 1985 he watched Sandy Lyle become the first Brit since Jacklin to win the British Open. Even then, in the early stages, he was feeling the frustration of taking a swing that had been good and breaking it down, actually making it worse before it got better.

On Saturday, as he was slogging his way toward a thirty-eighth-place finish, he heard someone in the gallery comment that the trousers he was wearing were ugly. When the round was over, he went back to his room, took the trousers off, and tore them to shreds, piece by piece, screaming in frustration and anger.

By then, he had met Gill Bennett, a secretary in IMG's London office, and they were in love and getting ready to be married. Gill was patient and supportive and willing to put up with all the time on the range, all the sudden bolts for the door at dinnertime. "At seven o'clock I would think of something I wanted to try and I'd say, 'Back in half an hour,' " he said. "Of course, that was a golfer's half hour. I'd stay out there until dark. She never once complained."

He finished that year forty-second on the Order of Merit, his lowest finish since he had been fifty-eighth as a teenage rookie. The next year was better — fifteenth — but for the second straight year he didn't win a tournament. The corporate contracts were drying up quickly. Nick and Gill began calling John Simpson, Faldo's longtime agent, "the voice of gloom and doom." Every time he called, or so it seemed, it was to say that another contract wasn't being renewed or a deal he had been working on had fallen through. Only Pringle, the Scottish clothing company, stood by him. Simpson was sorry to be the bearer of bad news, but there was nothing he — or even his powerful employer, IMG — could do without results.

"Black days," Faldo remembered. "Sometimes I would just go into the garage and start throwing clubs or anything I could get my hands on against the walls. I wasn't going to show people how much it hurt at the golf course, so I would go off by myself and get it all out. I probably should have bought one of those Japanese shouting trees."

He went back to Leadbetter in the spring of '87, knowing that the two years weren't quite up but were getting awfully close. He had fallen so far he wasn't even invited to the Masters that year. Big Jack had won it again the previous year at the age of forty-six. Forty-six! And here he was in what should be his prime, about to be thirty in July, and he wasn't even invited. At twenty-one he had beaten Watson. Now he wasn't even allowed to play against him.

And then came The Click. It happens to the great ones, The Click, when all of a sudden the swing that is so damn hard becomes easy. Every time the club goes back you know what's going to happen.

Your brain tells your body what to do and your body performs. It can happen with one shot — Watson remembers hitting a sand wedge in Japan in 1976 and knowing he had found something special — or it can happen at the end of a long, brutal week in the Florida heat.

That was the way it was for Faldo. He flattened his downswing a little that week and found that he could fade the ball 100 times out of 100 if he wanted; 1,000 out of 1,000. Click!

He flew to Atlanta to meet Gill, who was flying over to join him. He was buoyant until he got to the airport and Gill came off the plane. He was thrilled to see her, but most of the British media that was en route to the Masters was also on the flight. The Faldos were going to Hattiesburg, Mississippi, for the Deposit Guaranty Classic, the tournament that ran concurrently with the Masters to give all those who didn't make the big event a place to play that week.

"The press guys turned right to go to Augusta," Faldo said. "We turned left to go to Hattiesburg. It was about as low as any moment I can remember."

He forced himself not to think about what was going on at Augusta and tried to focus on The Click. It was still there. He shot 67–67–67–67 at Hattiesburg and lost by one shot to David Ogrin. He didn't care. He had found *it,* the swing he had gone to Leadbetter in search of two years earlier. A month later he won the Spanish Open, his first win in almost three years. No one was running around screaming, "Faldo is back!" including Faldo. The old Faldo was gone, he thought. This was a new one, a Faldo who wouldn't fold under pressure.

The British Open — or as the Europeans call it, the Open Championship — was at Muirfield in 1987. They had played twelve Opens at Muirfield, the first in 1892. Big Jack had won the first of his three Opens there in 1966, then had lost by a stroke to Lee Trevino there in 1972. The last time the tournament had been played at Muirfield, Watson had been the winner.

On Tuesday night, Faldo stopped in the exhibition tent to pick up some putters. As he was walking back to the parking lot, he passed the 18th hole. It was 10 o'clock on a Scottish summer night and there was still some sunlight left, but not a soul around. He stood and stared at the huge yellow scoreboard for several minutes. It was blank at the moment, but he pretended it was late Sunday afternoon and the stands were filled and the name "Faldo" was on top of the board. He stared and smiled and finally went home.

By Saturday evening, Paul Azinger was leading the tournament with Faldo and several others one shot back. That night, Faldo dreamed that it was Monday morning and reporters were standing outside his home clamoring for the new Open champion to come out and talk to them.

The next day dawned cool and rainy, and clouds hung over the course like a damp shroud all afternoon. Faldo never saw them. He never saw anything but his clubs and the ball and the greens he was aiming for. He couldn't hear anyone or anything. He never made a birdie the entire round. But he didn't make a bogey either. One par after another, 18 of them in a row. Every time he missed a green, he holed a putt. At 18, he had one last birdie putt and missed it. He tapped in for par, a round of 71, and 279 for the tournament.

Behind him, Azinger had played the front nine in two under and led by three. But two bogeys cut the lead to one on the 17th tee. The 17th at Muirfield is a par-five, reachable in two as long as you don't hit your drive in one of the pot bunkers in the fairway. Ignoring the advice of his caddy, Azinger hit a driver. He found one of the bunkers and had to play out sideways. He missed the green with his next shot and made bogey. "Stupid mistake," he said years later. "I should have listened to my caddy. I was too pumped."

In the Royal and Ancient's tent, next to the scorer's tent, Faldo heard the roar when Azinger's bogey went up on the giant yellow board. They were tied. He couldn't watch. He sat with his head between his legs while his daughter Natalie, not quite a year old, romped around, oblivious to the tension.

Azinger's five-iron at 18 caught the front bunker. A huge roar — so loud that the captain of the club publicly apologized to Azinger during the awards ceremony — went up from the partisan crowd. Faldo still couldn't look. Azinger had an almost impossible bunker shot. Somehow, he got it to within 15 feet. He had to make the putt to tie. The BBC put up a split-screen shot of Azinger putting and Faldo with his head between his legs.

Faldo heard Peter Alliss's voice on the tiny television in the tent say, "The next few seconds will change the lives of these two men considerably." Azinger putted, Faldo heard a sympathetic groan, then wild cheers. Someone was pounding him on the back. A chill went straight through his body and he felt tears on his cheeks.

"All I could think was, I've done it, I've finally done it," he said. "It didn't matter how, all I knew was all the work and all the tough times had been worth it. I'd spent my whole life hoping for that moment and there it was."

Faldo went through the next few months in a fog of happiness. "It seemed like every fifteen seconds, no matter what I was doing, I would stop and say, 'I'm the Open champion. Is it really possible?' " Conversely, it took Azinger years to completely get over the loss.

That Open was Faldo's launching pad. No more Foldo. He was a national hero. Two years later he won his first Masters, and a year later he became the first player since — who else? — Big Jack in 1966 to successfully defend the title. Three months later at St. Andrews he shot 270 and blew the field away to win his second Open.

Naturally, all the winning brought far more attention than Faldo wanted. He was still the loner who, if he wasn't with his family, was happiest when he was alone on the range or the golf course. But national heroes, especially in a small country like England, aren't allowed solitude. Everything he did was news and sometimes things he *didn't* do were news.

He had never been comfortable with the media, and now he was decidedly uncomfortable. To him, it was a no-win situation. When someone asked him if he felt he had put his hometown, Welwyn Garden City, on the map with his stardom, he said, well, he supposed he had. The next thing he knew, everyone in his hometown was furious with him because he hadn't reminded the reporter that Welwyn City was already famous for being the birthplace of Samuel Ryder, founder of the Ryder Cup.

Any star is a target and Faldo was almost a sitting duck. He read stories that said he didn't have Seve's imagination, that he wasn't funny the way Trevino had been, and he couldn't communicate like Arnie. Watson brought romance to the game; Norman, sex appeal. Faldo was the mechanical man, the guy who could talk for hours about the swing plane but not for ten seconds about his emotions.

The more he won, the more brickbats flew his way and the more insular he became. When he won his third Open in 1992, playing four brilliant holes at the end to snatch the tournament from John Cook, he walked into his press conference and said, "I'd like to thank the press from the heart of my bottom." It was a line that would follow him for a long time.

He was never better than during the second half of '92, winning five times. Late that year, he was on his way to a Genesis concert in London with Simpson, when his agent — no longer Mr. Gloom and Doom — turned to him and said, "By the way, we've had a fax that says if you want to meet Ben Hogan, he'd be happy to meet you."

Faldo was stunned. He had heard earlier in the year from Dave Marr that the Wee Ice Mon had said the one golfer playing whose game he really liked was Faldo's. Faldo had told Marr that if there was any way for him someday to meet Hogan, he would be thrilled. Hogan was eighty-three and not in great health. He hadn't seen people often when he was healthy, now it was even more rare. But here was the offer.

"Do you want to do it?" Simpson asked.

"Want to do it?" Faldo answered. "Why don't we go to Heathrow right now?"

They did the next best thing and made an appointment to fly to Fort Worth the following week. Faldo was playing in Palm Springs in the made-for-TV Grand Slam of Golf. He could go from there to Fort Worth.

The night before the appointment, Faldo couldn't sleep. He had never in his life been so nervous about meeting someone. Finally, at 4 A.M., he got out of bed, pulled out a pad, and began writing down questions for Hogan. He had three pages of questions on the swing; four more on the mental approach to the game; three more on how to think like a winner.

The meeting was supposed to last an hour. They talked for two, then had lunch. Faldo asked Hogan to sign the first golf book he had ever been given, *Five Lessons: The Modern Fundamentals of Golf.* The author: Ben Hogan. He inscribed it "for better golf" and signed his name. His memory wasn't great, but he could still talk golf and answer Faldo's questions. Did his hands ever ache from hitting all those golf balls? Never, Hogan said. Your hands don't ache when you're doing what you love. Exactly! The perfect answer.

There were a couple of moments when Hogan started to answer a question, paused, then stopped. Had he forgotten something? Faldo didn't think so. "I think he was *still* holding back some of his secrets," he said, laughing.

When it came time to go, they shook hands, the Wee Ice Mon and the Strapping Young Ice Man. Hogan clasped Faldo's huge hands in his small ones. "You come back and see me," he said. Faldo felt a chill go straight through him.

When he got home, he took the autographed book and put it in his trophy cabinet next to the trophies from the Masters and the Open championship.

At that moment, Faldo was unquestionably the best player in the world. At thirty-five, he had won five major titles and still had the hunger to win more, to play even better, to dominate the way Watson had during his seven-year reign at the top of the game.

He came close to doing that in 1993. After a slow first half of the year — not that different from '92 — he had excellent chances to win at both the British and the PGA. He led the British after three rounds and shot 67 the last day only to watch helplessly while Norman shot 64 to beat him by two shots. The PGA was even more aggravating. This time, it was Norman who led after three rounds and Faldo who caught him on the back nine on Sunday. But, tied for the lead with Norman and Azinger, he missed a five-foot birdie putt at 16 that would have given him the lead, then parred 17 and 18. When Norman and Azinger each made a birdie coming in, Faldo finished one shot out of their playoff.

He finished 11 under par there, just as he had been 11 under par at the British. "If you think about it, in most years a total of twenty-two under par might win all four majors for you," he said. "To shoot twenty-two under at two of them and come up with nothing but silver medals is almost unheard of. It was aggravating and yet at least I knew I had played pretty well."

The ending of the PGA also produced yet another chapter in his ongoing battle with the media. As soon as he realized he couldn't win, Faldo said a series of quick goodbyes in the player lounge, hopped into his courtesy car, and drove off. He did not — surprise — pause to chat with the media at any great length about how he felt about the outcome. One newspaper described him as exiting "in a fury amidst a screeching blaze of tires."

When one of the London tabloids picked up the story and ran a back-page headline on it, Faldo really *was* furious. "I called the guy and I said, 'How can you write something like that without checking?' " he said. "If I storm off or if I do something wrong, I don't mind being called out on it. But I did not leave in a screeching blaze of tires. I was driving a *Buick.* How in the world can you leave in a screeching blaze in a *Buick?*"

It is worth noting that, even today, Faldo will call someone on the phone if he thinks he has been wronged in the media. He will often say that he doesn't read the papers, then quote from them. He is sensitive to criticism the way almost every celebrity in the world is, and is incapable of ignoring jibes he considers unfair. Even after all these years, it gets to him.

"I suppose it does," he said, shaking his head. "Sometimes, it doesn't seem fair. I mean, over the last few years there have been some long stretches where I was the best player in the world. But if I go through a year without winning a major, I get absolutely hammered, especially at home. I know people think I should smile more and wave to the crowd more; IMG have told me if I did that they could double the money I make. But that isn't me. I can't do it that way. Anyway, at this point, if I turned around and became sickly sweet, I'd get hammered for that because people would say I was being a phony.

"I think I've learned how to handle it [the media] through the years. First, you have to resist the urge to become a world authority on everything (see Carnac [Nicklaus] and Carnac Junior [Watson]) because people will make you that if you let them. Sometimes, I find myself rattling on about something and I have to say, 'Whoa boy, calm down here.' The best thing to do is make a few putts and then come up with some story about how you dug the putter you're using out of the trunk of your car and didn't even remember that you still had it. They love that kind of stuff. Doesn't matter if it's true or not. You give it to them and they're happy."

Faldo had played well at the Norman-dominated Players Championship, finishing fifth, and came to Augusta hoping he was ready to make a run at winning a third green jacket. He had worked with Leadbetter a couple of times in March and thought he was on the verge of hitting the ball the way he wanted to. Had he heard The

Click again? No. But it didn't seem that far off when he arrived at Augusta.

In the back of his mind, though, Faldo knew he wasn't 100 percent. He was tired, having played at Doral and Honda, then flown home for birthday parties, one for five-year-old Matthew, the other for one-year-old Georgia. "Matthew's party was twenty-eight five-year-olds," he said. "Completely wild. Georgia's was more sedate. Everyone sat around and drank tea."

Faldo was now reaching a point in his life where balancing his family and his golf had become difficult. Natalie was almost eight and was acutely aware of her father's extended absences and the fact that she sometimes had to share him with the public. One day when Faldo was at the market with Natalie and Matthew, someone asked him for an autograph. Confused, Matthew turned to Natalie and asked, "Why is Daddy writing on that piece of paper for that man?"

"Ssshhh," Natalie said. "Daddy's Nick Faldo, but we don't want anybody else to know!"

Matthew was now old enough that his father was beginning to see why people called him a driven perfectionist. He had always thought of that label as another media exaggeration. But when Matthew refused to leave for school in the morning until the length of his sweater *exactly* matched on both arms and his socks were at *precisely* the same height on each leg, his father groaned. My God, he thought, he had to get this from someone and it wasn't Gill.

Faldo loved spending time with the children and had, for the first time, started chartering planes to get him home from tournaments on the night they ended. At the same time, he heard the clock ticking on the years when he was still going to be a true threat in the majors.

He began 1994 almost convinced that he needed to play in the United States more during the first half of the year if he was going to be ready for the Masters and the U.S. Open. That was probably going to mean committing to play fifteen tournaments, since a non-PGA Tour member could receive only five sponsor exemptions to the nonmajors each year. If he did that, it meant a lot more time away from home. Faldo dreaded that.

"But I may have to do it," he said. "I just feel as if I have to do everything I can to win the big ones while I still have the chance.

That's still what it's all about, being out there on the back nine on a Sunday afternoon in a major with a chance to win."

He smiled. "Sometimes other players or even parents of youngsters ask me if all the hours of work are worth it. I look at them and say, 'If you even have to ask the question, then you won't understand the answer.' All the work is for that feeling you get in contention on the last day of a major. If you doubt for one second whether the work is worth it at those moments, then you shouldn't even be playing. I've played golf for almost twenty-five years. Never once has it bored me. When it does — if it does — I'll quit. But not until then."

Faldo certainly wasn't bored at Augusta. Frustrated, with two days to play and a lot of ground to make up. But never bored.

For most top players, the goal during the first two days of any golf tournament is simple: don't lose the tournament. That is especially true at a major, where the pressure on every shot beginning on Thursday seems to quadruple.

"You can always tell the first day of a major the minute you walk into the locker room," Jeff Sluman says. "The line for the bathroom is always a *lot* longer."

The great players rarely lead majors on Saturday morning. No one really *wants* to go wire-to-wire at a major because the pressure of sleeping with the lead for three straight nights can be unbearable.

It does happen. During the course of winning eighteen times, Nicklaus had to lead start to finish a few times. At Baltusrol in 1980, he shot 63 in the first round and led all the way, and he ran away with the Masters in 1965. Raymond Floyd led the Masters all four rounds when he tied Nicklaus's record in 1976 and also was in command for all four rounds when he won his second PGA title at Southern Hills in 1982.

More often than not, though, the real leader board — the one that will produce the winner — doesn't take shape until Saturday afternoon. Tom Watson never once led wire-to-wire on his way to eight major wins. In fact, even in 1977 at the British Open, when he and Nicklaus eventually lapped the field by 10 shots, they were not the leaders after two rounds. Roger Maltbie was one shot ahead of both of them.

"You want to play well on Thursday and Friday at a major," Nicklaus said. "But you want to save your best golf for Saturday and Sunday."

Most of the time, if you bet against the thirty-six-hole leader, you will win. In 1993 the only thirty-six-hole leader at a major who went on to win was Lee Janzen at the U.S. Open. That doesn't mean that no one took Larry Mize seriously after thirty-six holes at the Masters. After all, he had won the tournament before and had played the best golf of his career in 1993, winning two tour events and an IMG-run megabucks made-for-TV tournament in December. There, he had beaten an elite field by 10 shots to win $550,000. No question, Mize could win.

But not many people expected him to. The name that had been mentioned most often before the tournament began was Greg Norman. On Saturday morning, very few people had changed their opinion. Norman had done nothing to lose on Thursday and Friday and sat very comfortably one shot behind Mize.

"It's a little bit like going down the road with a ten-foot alligator running right behind you," Mize said.

Norman was trying to go the low-key route, refusing to get caught up in the hype that surrounded him. He had always liked little sayings; his first boss as a young assistant pro had always told him that the key to success in life came down to DIN and DIP — Do-It-Now and Do-It-Properly. He still believed in that. At Augusta, he said, the keys were the two Ps — Patience and Putting. Norman hadn't yet gotten on a roll with his putting, but he was patiently waiting for that to happen.

To most Masters veterans, there was something missing on this Augusta Saturday. For the first time in forty years, no one named Palmer or Nicklaus was around for the weekend. In one sense, this was no shock. Palmer hadn't made a Masters cut since 1983 and, at sixty-four, wasn't likely to make one again. Ironically, Nicklaus hadn't missed the last two rounds since that year. He didn't actually miss the cut in '83 either, but had been forced to withdraw Friday morning when his back began to spasm on the practice tee.

That was the first time that the media began speculating that his days as a serious contender were behind him. After all, he was forty-three. At forty-six, he won the tournament again. As recently as 1993 he had been tied for the first-round lead before finishing tied for twenty-seventh on Sunday.

But he had struggled with his game since January, when he started the year by winning the senior division of the Mercedes (don't call it Tournament of Champions) Championships. He hadn't made a cut on the regular tour in five tries, so missing at the Masters wasn't that surprising except for the fact that the cut at Augusta is probably easier to make than at any other tournament on tour.

Since the field is almost never more than ninety players (eighty-six in 1994) and everyone within 10 shots of the leader plays on the weekend, the cut is usually around 150. That was true this year — 51 players made the cut at 149 or better — but Nicklaus at 152 and Palmer at 155 were not among them.

Saturday is always called "moving day" on tour because it is the day when those who are way behind must make a move if they want to have any chance to win on Sunday. About once a year, someone will win a tournament after making the cut on the number, proving that it is worth grinding on Friday to make the cut because you never know when you are going to discover something on the range or get hot with your putter.

If you don't move on Saturday, your chances of winning on Sunday are nil. Not only are you going to be too many shots back, but you are going to be behind too many people. There is a big difference between being four shots behind the leader in third place starting Sunday and being four shots behind tied for fourteenth. If you have only two people ahead of you, the chances that both will falter are halfway decent. But if you have thirteen people ahead of you, there is no way that every one of them is going to collapse. You might shoot 67 and move up to third or fourth, but the odds are that at least one or two people will play well enough to stay ahead of you.

Norman was in the second-to-last group of the day Saturday, paired with Tom Lehman. José María Olazabal and Ernie Els were right in front of them and Mize and Dan Forsman behind. The day was warm and cloudy with enough breeze to toughen the course even more than on the first two days.

The Norman-Lehman pairing was intriguing, if only because they both were playing with the same irons — one for big money, the other for no money. Lehman had switched at the beginning of the year to the irons Cobra made for Norman even though it meant giving up some endorsement money from Cleveland Classics. He liked the Cobra irons better than Cleveland's new VAS irons and decided to play them even though the company wasn't going to pay him to do so. Norman appeared in commercials for Cobra all the time, pitching its King Cobra woods. He carried one King Cobra club — the driver — in his bag.

Norman was thirty-nine, a multi-multi-millionaire. Lehman was thirty-five, a veteran of every mini-tour there was, someone who had been off the tour between 1985 and 1992. He had gotten so discouraged at one point that he almost took the job as golf coach at the University of Minnesota for $29,000 a year. "I probably would have done it," he said, "but they wanted me to rent cross-country skis out of the pro shop in the winter."

Golf courses don't check résumés. And so it was Lehman who shot 34 on the front nine and Norman who shot 38. That tied Lehman for the tournament lead with Olazabal and Mize at six under. Norman had gone from one shot back to four back.

Still, there was no reason to panic. The back nine at Augusta is the place where players make their move. Once you get by 10 and 11, both long, difficult par-fours, the next six holes can be attacked. That is what makes Augusta the perfect setting for a major. Most years, the leader cannot play safe on the back nine because if he does someone will catch him.

When Bobby Jones built the course, he created the back-nine par-fives, 13 and 15, as par-four-and-a-halfs where a player in contention almost has to go for the green in two, but faces real peril — water and shallow, treacherous greens — in doing so. The kind of golf the back nine at Augusta can produce was never more evident than in 1991 when Tom Watson made a double-bogey five at the tiny 12th, then made eagle three at both 13 and 15 to tie for the lead.

Norman arrived at 13 on Saturday knowing that moving day was rapidly drawing to a close and the only move he had made was backward. He was now three over par for the day and trailed the leaders, Olazabal and Mize, by five. Lehman, having just bogeyed 12, was one shot behind them.

The 13th is the last hole of "Amen Corner," the three famous holes where water can turn the tournament around in one quick splash. The 12th, the par-three with the tiny green that almost never calls for more than a nine-iron but often decides the tournament because of Rae's Creek meandering along in front of the green and the bunkers behind it, is a hole where everyone just tries to make his par and escape.

The 13th isn't as simple. It is a dogleg left, with azaleas, dogwood, and the creek running along the left side of the fairway and trees most of the way down the right. The narrow slice of water in front of the green is almost invisible from where you play your second shot, except inside the mind.

Norman hit a perfect drive and, as is the case when you hit the ball straight off the tee at 13, had only an iron — a four — left to the green. He hit perhaps his best shot of the day and the ball checked up 18 feet beyond the flag. The huge crowd surrounding the green was going crazy. It was time for the Shark to stop this silliness and climb back into contention. An eagle would do just that. He would be three shots back with five to play, including the equally reachable 15th.

Norman was thinking the same thing. His goal on the tee had been to make a birdie — he hadn't had one all day — but now, as he surveyed the putt, he knew it was makable and he knew what it would mean to him — and to those he was chasing — if he made it. "I went for it too hard," he said later. "I wasn't thinking about anything except making that one, which was a mistake."

The putt was left of the cup all the way, the kind of pull that often comes off the putter when someone is trying too hard. Worse than that, it rolled a good six feet past. Now Norman had a tricky putt coming back just to make birdie. Still, if he could make this and get an eagle at 15 . . .

He couldn't. The putt slid just past the right edge. A three-putt par. In the meantime, Lehman made *his* birdie and moved into a three-way tie for the lead. Norman was deflated. He wasn't hitting the ball poorly, but nothing was happening with the putter.

Now he had to birdie 15. He parred 14 and hit a good drive at 15. But this time he missed the green, hitting his second safely over the water, but to a tough place to chip from. He got to within 10 feet, but again, the putter wouldn't work. He had gone 5–5 at two holes where

4–4 was an absolute must and 3–3 should not have been out of the question. Lehman, over the green in two, chipped to within two feet and made another birdie. He was now seven under. At 16, he had a 50-foot, curling birdie putt and somehow rolled that one in too. He was eight under and leading the Masters by two shots. The cheers echoing off the pines and oaks were for him, not for his far more famous and wealthy playing partner, who had started the day even with him and was now seven shots behind.

"When I heard the cheers walking off sixteen, my eyes got a little bit wet," Lehman said. "I mean, who would have thought a kid from Minnesota could lead the Masters?"

The kid turned human on 18, making a bogey from the middle of the fairway. That left him one shot ahead of Olazabal, two ahead of Mize, and three ahead of Tom Kite. Norman parred the last three holes, finishing with a birdie-less 75. Only once did he show his frustration. When he walked on the green at 18, knowing that most of the cheers were for Lehman, he marked his ball, then threw it to his caddy, Tony Navarro, who was still 100 yards down the fairway because he had just finished raking the fairway trap where Norman had put his drive.

It wasn't a heave, and Navarro scooped the ball up on a hop like a shortstop and cleaned it just as he would have done if Norman had calmly handed him the ball on the green. But the toss was telling. Norman wanted to get the round done and be gone. He had gone from a tie for second, one shot back in perfect position, to a three-way tie for eighth, six shots back.

While Lehman was being taken to the interview room to tell the gathered media his life story — a day earlier he had been asked four questions, now he was asked closer to forty — Norman stood under the oak tree and calmly told everyone he still didn't think he was out of the golf tournament, that he had hit the ball well and had every reason to believe he could go low on Sunday and catch the leaders.

As he started to walk away, with all the cameras and tape recorders still rolling, he spotted Tim Rosaforte of *Sports Illustrated,* who had just been elected president of the Golf Writers Association of America. Norman grinned and shook Rosaforte's hand. "Hey, Mr. President," he said cheerfully, "congratulations!"

He walked into the locker room and was about to make his escape when a freelance writer from Boston, who had been standing under the oak tree and had witnessed Norman's cheery analysis of the day, approached.

"Greg, I know this may be a bad time . . ." he began.

"You're certainly right about that," Norman said and kept on walking.

That was how Norman really felt about the day.

The four longest days of the golfing year are the Sundays at the major championships. The leaders have to wait until midafternoon to tee off on a day when they probably haven't slept very much and aren't likely to sleep very late even knowing they will have several hours to kill once they get out of bed.

Tom Lehman was up early on Masters Sunday to go to church. He had promised Ann Davis, the woman who ran the child-care center for the players at the tournament, that he would speak at her church that morning, and leading the Masters was not, in his opinion, any reason to back out.

Lehman spoke briefly to the congregation at Marks United Methodist Church. His message was simple and direct: He felt no pressure playing the last round of the Masters because he knew that because of his faith in God he was loved and eternally accepted whether he shot 70 or 80 or 90. Lehman is a devout Christian, but, like Paul Azinger, he doesn't talk about his faith publicly unless he is asked.

Lehman and José María Olazabal, who would make up the last pairing of the day, both arrived at the golf course shortly before noon. When Olazabal opened his locker, he found a piece of white notebook paper lying on the top shelf. It was a note from Seve Ballesteros.

Written in Spanish it said: "Be patient today. Remember, you are the best player. Wait for the others to make their mistakes and you will win . . . Seve."

Ballesteros had left the note just before he teed off at 12:06 — two and a half hours before Olazabal would tee off. He had arrived at the golf course that morning and remembered a note Gary Player had left in his locker before he played his final round in 1980. It had said approximately the same thing. Ballesteros won that day (and again in

1983) and never forgot the gesture. He thought he owed Olazabal, his longtime protégé and Ryder Cup partner, similar words of encouragement.

Olazabal picked up the note, walked outside the locker room, and sat in a rocking chair on the porch overlooking the first fairway. He read the note, smiled, read it again, then put it in his pocket. He sat in the rocking chair for several long minutes by himself, staring out toward the first tee.

Golf is the most solitary sport there is, never more so than on the last day of a major. There is no time for lessons or pep talks. You will be watched by thousands (millions on TV), but you and your game will be all alone on the golf course. Now, though, Olazabal wouldn't be completely alone. He would take Seve's note with him.

Most Sundays at Augusta are roller-coaster rides. Players race up the leader board, then fall back. Someone almost inevitably comes out of the pack to challenge, perhaps win. Player had shot 64 on the last day in 1978 to win, and Nicklaus had shot 65 on that amazing afternoon in 1986 when he shocked the world — not to mention Greg Norman — by stealing the green jacket. That is what makes the back nine of the Masters so special: the chance to go low is always there, especially when you get to 13 and 15.

But the Men of the Masters had outsmarted themselves this time. By setting up the golf course to keep players from going low, they had robbed the tournament of a good deal of its usual Sunday drama. On a golf course famous for yielding low Sunday scores, no one shot lower than 69 on this final day and only three players produced that score.

That meant the tournament would be decided by the players in the last three groups. Realistically, no one more than four shots out of the lead was going to win. By the time those final six players began to make their way to the back nine (where, as we all know, the tournament really starts on Sunday) the list of possible winners was down to three: Lehman, Olazabal, and Mize.

Norman's hopes for a Sunday charge had faded early. He three-putted the par-five second hole for a bogey, then hit his tee shot way left at number four and made another bogey. "It was over after number two," he said. "I walked on that green thinking I could make four and walked off it with a six. The thought crossed my mind right there that it wasn't going to be my day."

He slogged home with a 77. Standing under the tree again, he admitted that Saturday's round had hurt. "I lost all my spark," he said. "I tried to get it back going to the first tee today, but it wasn't there. The number I had in mind was sixty-six." He forced a laugh. "I guess I was a little off."

He started toward the locker room, pursued this time by Bob Drum, a veteran reporter and onetime CBS pundit who still did some work for the network. Norman's friend Frank Chirkinian had sent Drum to tell him that Chirkinian wanted him to sit in Butler Cabin with host Jim Nantz and analyze the last few holes of the tournament on TV. CBS often asks players — especially Norman — to do this when they finish early and, almost without exception, they comply — especially Norman.

When Norman heard Drum calling his name, he stopped and turned around. He listened as Drum repeated Chirkinian's request. For several seconds, he said nothing. Then, slowly, he shook his head. "No, Drummer, I can't," he said. "Tell Frank, I'm sorry. Next week, anything he wants, but not today. I just can't."

Drum didn't answer, he just stood there waiting for Norman to reconsider. "You sure, Greg?" he said, finally.

Norman sighed. "I'm sure."

"Any other tournament, I could have handled it," he said later. "But I just couldn't bear the thought of sitting there describing how someone *else* had won the Masters. It would have hurt too much. I just had to get out of there."

Several other players made brief moves on Sunday. Tom Watson, starting at two under (five behind Lehman) birdied number two, but promptly bogeyed three of the next four. Ernie Els, six shots back at the start, eagled the eighth to get to four under and birdied 12 to get to five. But he went for too much on his drive at 13, put it into the azaleas on the left, and made a bogey. Tom Kite got to five under with a birdie at the second, but bogeyed the fifth and never got closer than five under again.

And so it was left to the onetime champion (Mize), the onetime wunderkind (Olazabal), and the onetime mini-tour lifer (Lehman) to decide the tournament on the back nine. They were tied at eight under through 11. Then the 12th stepped in again. All three players — Mize was playing in the group right in front of Lehman and Olazabal — knocked their tee shots over the green trying to be sure not to get wet. Only Olazabal was able to chip close enough to make par.

He led by one. Mize was the only one to birdie 13, and that tied him with Olazabal again until he missed a five-footer at 14 to drop back. He never made another birdie and finished third. Olazabal and Lehman both parred 14, so they went to 15 with Olazabal still leading by one.

Lehman's drive was 25 yards past Olazabal's. Knowing Lehman would almost surely reach the green, Olazabal had to go for it, even though he had 215 yards to the hole and had to hit a three-iron as hard as he could to have a chance to clear the water. The ball hung in the air for what seemed like days, bounced on the upslope in front of the green, and seemed to hang there. Dozens of similar shots during the week had rolled back into the creek. But just as Fred Couples's ball had somehow not rolled into Rae's Creek at number 12 in 1992, this ball held on the front fringe 35 feet short of the pin.

"A foot shorter and he's in the creek," Lehman said. Undeterred, he hit a four-iron to within 15 feet.

If Lehman knocked in his eagle putt and Olazabal made a two-putt birdie, they would be even with three holes to play. Olazabal, off the green, left the pin in. His putt swooped left to right and headed straight for the cup. Five feet away, everyone knew it was in. Olazabal punched a fist in the air and, for the first time all day, smiled. He was ten under.

Now Lehman had to make his three to stay within one. His putt also looked perfect. But at the last possible second, it slid just over the right edge and stopped an inch away. Lehman stared in disbelief for a moment, then leaped into the air in agony, went to his knees and pounded the green in frustration.

"Sometimes," he said, "you put *so* much into a putt and when it doesn't go in, it just hurts."

Olazabal led Lehman by two, Mize by three. It was his tournament to lose now. On the 16th tee, Lehman said softly, "Great putt."

Deep down, he knew that Olazabal had just won the Masters. Not that Lehman stopped trying. He had birdie chances at 16 and 17, but couldn't convert. Olazabal bogeyed 17 (his second bogey in three days) to make the 18th suspenseful, but when Lehman made bogey there, all Olazabal had to do was two-putt from six feet to win. He didn't need the second putt. He shook his fist again, but didn't jump up and down or dance on the green. A number of people who remembered him dancing on the green after Europe had won the Ryder Cup in 1987 asked him why he had been so sedate.

"This is Augusta," he said, smiling. "You have to behave properly."

Here was a champion the Men of the Masters would happily dine with that evening. He was the sixth foreigner invited to Sunday dinner at Augusta in seven years. First, though, he needed a green jacket. After surviving the always-awkward TV ceremony, Olazabal walked onto the putting green shortly after 7 o'clock to join the assembled officials and fans. Jack Stephens introduced him as "Josay Marie Ola-Zabal," pronouncing the Z instead of the proper *TH*. The new champion didn't care. He gave Stephens a thumbs-up for trying.

The sun was beginning to set behind the oaks and pines when 1993 champion Bernhard Langer slipped the green jacket (a 41-long) onto Olazabal's shoulders. The son of a greenskeeper had a huge smile on his face as Langer led the applause for him.

It was a warm moment in a wonderful setting, a scene worthy of the Masters. Which, as the Men of the Masters would hasten to tell you, is saying quite a lot.

13

SPRINGTIME IN THE SOUTH

VERY FEW TOURNAMENTS can draw a strong field the week after a major. The MCI Heritage Classic is an exception to that rule. Harbour Town Links on Hilton Head Island in South Carolina is considered one of the best golf courses on tour, a beautiful setting on a resort island only about a three-hour drive from Augusta.

Everyone on tour takes a break at some point during the nine weeks between the Masters and the U.S. Open. The tour stays mostly in the South during those nine weeks, winding its way from Augusta to Hilton Head and then on to Greensboro, North Carolina. From there it goes into a Texas-boomerang mode, bouncing to Houston, then back to Atlanta; to Dallas, then back to Columbus, Ohio; to Fort Worth, then back to Washington, D.C.

By this time most players have played enough weeks to need a rest and with the hot summer months ahead, during which the last three majors will be played in a nine-week stretch, a spring break is an absolute necessity. A lot of players play Hilton Head and then take their break.

Davis Love III always played Hilton Head. He had won the tournament on three occasions, the first time in 1987, when he was a twenty-three-year-old second-year pro. He won there again in 1990 and 1992 and always looked forward to the week.

Not this time. Love had driven home from Augusta on Friday afternoon, still angry and puzzled by his performance. He couldn't understand why friends of his like Jeff Sluman and Lee Janzen could peak their games for majors and he couldn't. He hadn't been done in by nerves — he couldn't have been two under for eight holes on Thursday if that was the problem — so what was it? What was missing from his makeup that kept him from playing his best golf when he wanted most to perform?

He decided to avoid golf for the weekend and glanced only briefly at the tournament on Sunday. Watching Tom Lehman almost win started him thinking again about his own failure. Here was someone who had been in the Masters only twice and already had a third and a second.

Monday morning, he decided to go fishing. A little time alone would no doubt do him some good. He had been out on the water for about an hour when he got an emergency call to return to the dock. The news he received when he got in was sad but not shocking: his grandmother had died.

Mary Elizabeth Love had been in and out of the hospital for the better part of a year. She had suffered a small stroke that morning but had seemed fine when the paramedics arrived. They checked all her vital signs, decided there was no reason to drag her to the hospital, and left. An hour later she suffered another stroke. This one was massive.

"The only good thing was she had always told us she didn't want to be kept alive in some hospital," Love said. "She died at home, which is what she wanted."

Love had been scheduled to fly to Hilton Head on Tuesday morning. He called the tournament, explained what had happened, and said he would definitely miss the shootout and the Pro-Am but might still play on Thursday. "If it had been any other tournament," he said, "I would have just withdrawn right away."

Deep down, Love didn't want to play. The death of his last grandparent saddened him, much had to be done before the funeral on Thursday morning, and he had to deal with explaining to his daughter, Lexie, why she wouldn't be able to go over to her great-grandmother's house anymore. At five, Lexie had some understanding of death and had already been to the funeral of one of Robin's grandparents. But she had been close to her great-grandmother and loved spending time at her house.

"It was the one place where she not only had her own coffee table but was allowed to stand on the coffee table," Love said. "We had explained to her a couple times when Grandmother was in the hospital that she might not come out, but now we had to deal with the reality of her being gone."

The person pushing Love the hardest to play was his mother. This had been a recurring problem in the Love family since the death of Davis Love Jr. With her husband gone, Penta Love seemed to feel that the role of encouraging her son and pushing him to improve fell on her shoulders. Most of the time Davis understood what his mother was doing and it didn't bother him, but occasionally it did.

The previous fall, just before he had left to play at Las Vegas and San Francisco, the last two tournaments of the year, she had asked him about practicing more often.

"Why do I need to do that?" he asked.

"Well, these two tournaments are very important."

"More important than the last two I played or the two before that?"

"It's the end of the year."

"And then in January it will be the start of next year."

Love won in Las Vegas and called his mother from the locker room. "Do you see what can happen when you're comfortable and ready to play?" he asked her.

She did. But now with the Masters disappointment still on everyone's mind, Penta Love thought it important that Davis not miss a tournament he almost always played well in. The funeral would be in Hattiesburg, Mississippi, at 10 A.M. If Davis requested an afternoon tee time, he could make it.

Davis didn't want to do it. He didn't want to feel as if he was rushing to leave his grandmother's funeral. But Robin suggested that getting away to Hilton Head for the weekend might be healthy for them. Davis relented.

The plane landed at Hilton Head at 12:30 and was met by a police escort. Love changed into his golf shoes in the car on the way to the course, walked on the tee at 12:55 — five minutes before his tee time — took a practice swing, and hit his drive down the middle. He walked down the fairway and Frank Williams handed him a seven-iron. He could hear Williams talking yardage to him, but he couldn't focus on what he was saying.

"It just hit me that I didn't want to be here, that this was a joke," he said. "What was the big deal about playing? There was another tournament next week, and this tournament would still be here next year. I wasn't prepared, my mind wasn't on golf, and there were things I could be doing and should be doing if I had stayed home. All of a sudden I was really angry with myself for getting talked into playing. I understand what my mom was thinking and I knew why she wanted me to be there, but I should have made the decision and the decision should have been no."

He played most of the afternoon in an angry fog, shooting 78. The thought of withdrawing crossed his mind briefly, but he decided against that. He had never withdrawn from a tournament in his life and, like most players on tour, he believed that once you tee it up on Thursday, you should play as hard as you can until someone tells you that you can't play anymore. There are a handful of players on tour who will walk away after a bad first round, most notably John Daly, who was about fifty-fifty to show up on Friday if he had a poor Thursday.

Love not only played on Friday, he almost made the cut. He shot 67 and missed by two shots. "And I actually missed a bunch of putts," he said. "I could have made it."

He felt better after Friday because he had hung in when it would have been easy to quit. "Once I accepted the fact that I had made a mistake, I dealt with it better," he said. "I learned a simple lesson: sometimes you just stay home. You have to think long-term in this game, not short-term."

Paul Goydos had stayed home in Long Beach that week. As planned, he had skipped New Orleans and (not by choice) the Masters. He was going to fly East for Hilton Head and Greensboro on the Monday after the Masters. Sunday, he went out with some friends for an informal Beat the Pro (Goydos) round at the old Boneyard where he had grown up.

He was on the 15th hole when someone came out from the pro shop to find him. His daughter was in the hospital. Goydos panicked. He raced back to the clubhouse and called the hospital. There was no one registered there under the name Chelsea or Courtney Goydos. He called home to see if anyone was there. Wendy answered the phone.

The girls were fine. The message had gotten garbled: Goydos's father had been admitted to the hospital after going in for some tests. The tests showed a blockage around his heart. The doctors wanted to do surgery on Tuesday: seven valves.

Goydos called Hilton Head to say he wouldn't be playing. Then he called his older brothers. One of the benefits of being a golf pro was that all his frequent-flyer mileage made it possible for him to fly them into Long Beach for the surgery. The night before the surgery, Goydos asked the doctor if there was anything he or his brothers could do for their dad. The doctor nodded. "The best thing you can do for him," he said, "is pray."

Their prayers were answered. The surgery went well and, with his father's recovery going fine, Goydos decided he would play the next week in Greensboro.

The surprise winner at Hilton Head was Hale Irwin, the surprise being that, two months shy of his forty-ninth birthday, Irwin could still hit iron shots that seemed guided by radar as they honed in on the flag. Irwin had been written off a dozen times in his career. He had gone five years without winning a tournament between 1985 and 1990, then won back-to-back in June 1990, winning his third U.S. Open, then Westchester a week later.

He hadn't won since then and the consensus was he was biding his time until he turned fifty in 1995 and could make big money on the senior tour. Irwin wasn't thinking that way though. He was using new clubs — the King Cobras — and seemed more comfortable than he had been for years. He caught Greg Norman (Mr. King Cobra himself) from behind on the back nine on Sunday and won by two shots. It was a remarkable victory considering the fact that Irwin had won his first PGA Tour event on the same golf course twenty-three years earlier.

Irwin's victory underscored the success forty-something players were having on tour. He was the fourth player over the age of forty to win during the first fifteen weeks of the season. In addition to Johnny Miller's extraordinary victory at Pebble Beach, Craig Stadler (forty-one) and Ben Crenshaw (forty-two) also had won. Tom Watson (forty-four), Tom Kite (forty-four), Fuzzy Zoeller (forty-two), and Jay Haas (forty) had all been in position to win. Loren Roberts had won his first tournament a few weeks shy of turning thirty-nine, and Greg Norman and Curtis Strange would both be forty early in 1995.

The graying of golf is one of the biggest changes the tour has undergone during the past twenty years. Golfers had played well into their forties in the past — Sam Snead won a tournament at fifty-two, and Julius Boros won the PGA at forty-nine — but they were unusual. That is no longer the case.

New equipment — metal clubs replacing woods, irons (like the Cobras) with a larger sweet spot — better conditioning, and the lure of a second life on the senior tour have combined to keep players working at their games and playing successfully for much longer than they once did.

The tour is, without doubt, the most sedate of the professional sports when it came to nightlife. Most of the players are married and often travel with their families. Even when they don't, they all face early tee times at least once a week, sometimes as often as three times, and staying up late and being successful rarely mix.

What's more, it just isn't vogue to stay out late anymore. Most tour players are very health and diet conscious. More and more of them are using the tour-traveling fitness van supplied by Centinela Hospitals on a regular basis. Once a potbelly and a cigarette were almost as much a part of a touring pro's gear as a driver and a putter. Not anymore. When Lee Trevino began playing the senior tour — or, as 1965 PGA champion Dave Marr called it, "life's ultimate mulligan" — he began referring to the players on the regular tour as "flat bellies."

That isn't always the case. Players like Mike Springer and Steve Lowery and Craig Stadler (aka the Walrus) carry a few extra pounds, but they are exceptions now, not the rule. The same is true of smoking. If you look at pictures of Arnold Palmer and Jack Nicklaus during the 1960s, they always seem to have a cigarette dangling from their lips. Tom Watson was a lifelong smoker too, but had given it up in 1993 as part of a pact with a friend to get him to start wearing a seat belt. (Watson still sneaks some chewing tobacco into his mouth on occasion, but he readily admits that it is "a disgusting habit.")

Nick Price, Fuzzy Zoeller, Ben Crenshaw, John Daly, and Fulton Allem smoke, but they are very clearly a minority now. Price was trying to quit, especially on the course. He would grab a few quick drags and then hand the cigarette to his caddy, Jeff Medlen, who was also trying to quit, but would inevitably finish it.

With good players playing well longer, it has become tougher and tougher for young players to get on tour and stay on tour. The average age of the forty-six survivors of the 1993 Q-School was thirty. Only eight were twenty-five or less (and five of those were twenty-five on the nose). Once upon a time, top college players almost always got their cards the first time through Q-School, or at worst, the second. If you didn't make it in two or three tries, that was a strong hint that you might want to look for another job.

But now, with the Nike Tour providing a fallback position and with the money overseas having increased, players were less likely to give up the quest. They kept working at their games and, in some cases, improved enough that by the time they were in their late twenties or early thirties they could make it on tour. Tom Lehman, who had failed Q-School five years in a row before getting his card back at the age of thirty-two, was a perfect example.

Irwin's victory, by two shots over Norman (thirty-nine) and three over Roberts (thirty-eight) and defending champion David Edwards (thirty-eight), was more evidence that, while youth was occasionally being served on tour, the middle-aged weren't exactly going hungry.

From the resort of Hilton Head, the tour moved for the weekend of April 21–24 to the furniture and mill town of Greensboro, North Carolina. Although Kmart became the title sponsor of the Greater Greensboro Open in 1988 and, in doing so, made the tournament one of the richest on tour ($1.5 million in 1994, topped only by the three majors held in the U.S. and the Players, the World Series of Golf, and the Tour Championship), almost no one ever mentioned the discount department store when talking about the tournament.

It was, and always would be, the GGO. There may be no better example on tour of what a golf tournament means to a community than the GGO. The PGA Tour coming to town is fairly big news in Washington, Atlanta, Chicago, and Los Angeles; it is a somewhat bigger deal in New Orleans and Miami and Detroit. In places like Greensboro and Columbus, Ohio, and Endicott, New York, it is *the* story all week and, often, the week before and the week after the circus comes to town.

Traditionally, the GGO draws huge, knowledgeable crowds. People in North Carolina love golf and will come out to the GGO to see John Daly and Fred Couples but also to see Paul Goydos and Brian Henninger. The tournament organizers work very hard to put together their field every year, knowing that it comes during a time when many top players — especially those who go to Hilton Head — are looking for a break.

Daly was at the GGO, though not for long. He hit his first tee shot on Thursday morning out-of-bounds, made a triple-bogey seven, and went into a funk, finally finishing 78 shots after he started. Daly's mood was dark throughout the round. On the fifth tee — his fourteenth hole of the day — he hit a two-iron off the tee and when the ball came off the club less than perfectly, he stood staring at it for a moment, then turned to the assembled masses and said, "I swear to God I played better when I was drunk."

An uncomfortable titter ran through the crowd as if everyone hoped he was joking. There wasn't even a hint of a smile on Daly's face. Two holes later, at the short, par-four seventh, Daly pulled out his driver. The hole is a dogleg left, with water down the left side. If he absolutely crushed one, Daly might reach the green. The crowd was certainly whooping it up in anticipation of that kind of swing even though the smart shot was to pull out the two-iron, lay up, and try to get a wedge close. The shot was hooking the minute it left the tee. Daly didn't even watch. He just started walking, knowing it was wet. He finished the day tied for 151st place.

The next afternoon he showed up for the second round (no small thing in itself) without a single hair on his head. He had gone back to his hotel room and, feeling bored and frustrated, had decided to shave his head. It made for a great photo op and it gave TV something to talk about other than the smooth 84 Daly was in the process of shooting, which left him 18 shots outside the (not razor) cut.

Exactly how Daly felt about the whole thing no one knew, since he didn't hang around to discuss it. He finished his round, signed his card, and made a beeline for the parking lot where his van was parked. He signed autographs as he walked, but ignored reporters' questions and requests from photographers to take off his hat. The scene almost turned into a riot when a backpedaling photographer tripped over a cameraman and was nearly trampled by the mob pursuing Daly.

This was becoming a habit with Daly: when he played well, he was more than willing to hang around, do TV interviews, and chat with the media; when things didn't go well, you needed a stopwatch to clock the time it took him to get from the scorer's tent to the parking lot.

After being suspended by Beman late in 1993 for picking up his ball and quitting in midround at Kapalua, he had come back to the tour at the Honda Classic telling people he was a new man, that he was going to work hard on his golf, not give up when things went bad, and try to act like an adult. He started superbly, finishing fourth at the Honda, but it had been downhill since then. He had been back for only six weeks and already there were signs he was slipping.

After the head-shaving incident the whispers started around the locker room again. Clearly, John Daly was still a troubled young man. All you had to do was look at him on the golf course, chain-smoking, gobbling M & Ms, and drinking one Diet Coke after another. Exactly what pressures he was feeling, no one knew for sure. Something was eating at him. He wasn't drinking anymore, but a lot of the anger that had been there when he was drinking was still evident. Everyone on tour wanted to see Daly succeed. But there weren't a lot of them willing to bet on him.

The players who tee off early on Saturday and Sunday mornings are known on tour as "rabbits." Once, the term rabbit referred to players who had to take part in Monday qualifying, because they had to jump from one city to another, hoping for a place in the tournament field each week.

But with the coming of the all-exempt tour in 1982, Monday qualifying had become a minor part of tour life. Only four players got into the field through qualifying on Mondays and they were now known as "four-spotters."

Thus, the term rabbit was passed on to the weekend dew-sweepers. It had become especially true once the tour decided in 1988 to send the players out in twosomes on the weekend. It was not uncommon for players in the early groups to finish their rounds in less than two and a half hours. Certainly a rabbit-like pace. The leaders, starting later with more at stake, played considerably more slowly.

By the time he arrived in Greensboro, John Cook was beginning to feel as if he had been living on a diet of lettuce and carrots for two months. The good news was that he had broken his skein of missed cuts the week after Los Angeles, finishing twenty-first in the Hope. Since then, he had made seven straight cuts, which was more like the Cook of 1992, who had missed only three cuts the entire year.

The bad news was that Cook seemed to be playing rabbit every weekend. His highest finish was a tie for eighteenth in Hilton Head, and that had come on the strength of a 69–68 finish after he had made the cut with one shot to spare. Since the Hope, he had shot only one round under 70 on a Thursday or Friday, and that was way back in February in the second round at San Diego.

Even so, Cook was feeling much better about his golf and his life when he reached Greensboro. He was still waiting for his game to click in again, but he felt he had straightened out some things away from the course that made the return of his game only a matter of time.

As it turned out, Los Angeles had been rock bottom for him. He had been so discouraged after his Friday round there, when he had given up on a bogey putt and ended up missing the cut by one shot, that he had actually wondered aloud at dinner that night if he might not be able to get it done on tour anymore.

It was an outrageous thought, one that he knew wasn't likely, but it did cross his mind. "If something doesn't happen between now and the end of the West Coast swing [two more tournaments], I don't know what I'll do," he said to some friends he was eating sushi with. "I can't just go on like this. Who knows? San Diego might be it for me."

By the time he got home to Mission Hills the next day, he felt better. The Hope had always been one of his favorite events. He had won the tournament in a five-man playoff in 1992, going birdie–birdie–birdie–eagle to finally win on the fourth sudden-death hole. When he met his caddy, Pete Bender, on Monday morning to practice, Bender had one message for him: "You always light it up in the desert. Remember that."

Cook tried. He saw a glimmer of hope the next day when he finished second in the Merrill Lynch Shootout to Peter Jacobsen and felt even better after opening the tournament with a 68. It was his first round in the 60s all year, and the fact that it was on one of the relatively easy desert courses didn't matter. He played steadily throughout the week and his tie for twenty-first earned him $10,638.57. For a man who had made in excess of $1 million two years earlier, that was hardly a windfall. But for a man whose earnings for 1994 were zero, it was a start.

When his Sunday round was over, Cook found Mark O'Meara waiting for him. O'Meara is Cook's oldest friend in golf, someone he played with growing up. Like Cook, O'Meara was struggling with his game. An eight-time winner on tour, he hadn't won in more than two years and had struggled the last nine months of 1993, failing to finish in the top ten anywhere after a fifth at the Players.

Now, though, O'Meara wanted to talk about Cook. He suggested dinner that night. Jan came along and the two of them told him in no uncertain terms that he needed to change some things in his life. He had always been intense on the golf course, as capable of losing his temper as anyone on tour. But now it had become a hair-trigger. Cook knew O'Meara was right. Even that week in the desert, when he had played better, he had felt himself on the verge of exploding on more than one occasion.

"I had been a maniac for a few months," he said. "I still was at the Hope even though I played better. I was just angry and confused about a lot of things."

O'Meara suspected that a lot of it had to do with his father. Because of Jim Cook's involvement in golf, he had always been close to John and his career. In fact, he had always managed John's money and done a lot of his scheduling for him. Slowly, John had pulled back from that relationship, and he was ready to turn the bulk of his work over to Advantage International. But O'Meara thought John and Jim needed to sit down and talk about their relationship, that a lot of John's anger and frustration came from the pressure he felt from his dad. Jan, who had talked about this to John before, sat and listened.

Cook knew O'Meara was right. Two nights later, he and his father sat down for a talk he knew was necessary but that he dreaded. He was thirty-six years old, he told his dad, and he needed to put some distance in their relationship — at least on the business side. He wanted them to just be father and son rather than client and manager.

It wasn't easy for Cook to say those words to his father. He was afraid his father would be hurt and that he might be driving a wedge into their relationship. As it turned out, he underestimated his father.

Jim Cook understood how his son felt. In fact, he wondered how he had played as well as he had the last few years if this had been bothering him. All he wanted was for John to be comfortable and happy and play well. If letting someone else handle his money and his schedule would do that, then he was all for it.

"I don't think I realized just how much the whole thing had been bothering me until after I talked to my dad," Cook said. "Jan had been trying to get me to face up to it for years, but it wasn't until Mark sat me down that I realized just how right she had been. Then, after I talked to my dad, I felt as if this great weight had been lifted from my shoulders. It seemed like the minute we didn't have the pressures of dealing with each other in business, we were better dealing with each other as father and son."

Historically, Cook had never played well in Florida, and this year was no exception. He made the cut in all three tournaments he played in, though, including a tie for twenty-third at the Players. Considering the fact that two of the three cuts he had missed in 1992 had been in Florida, going three for three was a good sign.

He struggled — as always — at the Masters, making the cut but never breaking par. That was no surprise since Cook always struggled at Augusta — his highest finish in ten tries was a tie for twenty-first in 1981 — but finishing tied for forty-sixth was discouraging. Cook knew the golf course was never going to be easy for him, but he felt as if he was beating his head against a wall all week.

Some of the negative thoughts still lingering from the California swing crept into his head. Was he ever going to seriously contend in a tournament again? His highest finish in 1993 had been a fifth, in the first tournament of the year. There were days — far too many of them — when he felt as if chartering a plane to Mars would be easier than making a birdie. And two birdies in a row? That might as well be a day trip to Pluto and back.

He finally began to see some light — at least a glimmer — with his play the last two days at Hilton Head. His 69–68 finish earned him his first top-twenty finish of the year, a tie for eighteenth.

When he opened with 72–72 at Greensboro, Eric Hilcoff went back to calling him "Mr. Happy" in the locker room. The difference now was that Mr. Happy, while not exactly thrilled with his play, wasn't *un*happy.

A bit frustrated, yes. When he three-putted the 18th green Thursday evening, he walked out of the scorer's tent talking to himself. He went directly to the putting green and spent forty-five minutes there as if paying penance for the three-putt that had ended his day on such a sour note.

The next morning, playing the back nine first, he bogeyed 18 again, and when he pushed his drive into the rough at number one, he tossed his driver onto his bag in complete disgust. By the time he finished, he was pleased by the fact that he had hung in and made another cut, but mystified by his inability to get off his Saturday diet of lettuce and carrots.

"You do start to wonder when the payback comes," he said, eating a lunch that day that included no rabbit food. "I mean, I've really been grinding here these last few weeks, working and working, trying to get back to where I was in '92 and I don't feel like I'm getting the results I should be getting from the work I've been putting in. The hardest thing in the world out here is patience, especially for someone like me.

"I know it's going to come, though. It isn't as if I'm playing awful and there's no question I can see progress. It's just a lot slower than I want it to be. I just feel some days like no matter what I do I'm going to shoot seventy-one or seventy-two. If I hit the ball horribly, I'll shoot seventy-two; if I hit it great, I'll shoot seventy-one. I wonder where those sixty-fives I used to shoot have gone. They were fun. Heck, right now, I'd settle for a sixty-six or a sixty-seven. I'm not picky."

He laughed. At least he had progressed that far. He could laugh at golf again. In February, that would have been impossible.

While Cook was planning an early wake-up call for Saturday, Tom Kite, Davis Love, and Paul Goydos were all planning trips home.

Kite and Love missed the cut by three shots, and Goydos missed it by four.

Goydos's failure was the least surprising of the three. He was still exhausted and reeling emotionally from the week at the hospital with his father. He hadn't arrived in town until late Tuesday, and keeping his mind squarely on golf wasn't very easy. He had made eight straight cuts prior to his break after the Players, and he had hoped to pick up where he left off. But instead of coming back from three weeks off the tour feeling rested, he was actually more tired than he had been before. He thought briefly about skipping Houston the next week, then decided to play since he liked the golf course.

Love had been planning to skip Houston all along, and he almost seemed relieved when he finally finished his round of 77 on Friday. His mind still wasn't completely on his game as evidenced by the fact that he had twice hit *irons* out of bounds. He wondered if he was hitting bad shots or if he was hitting less-than-perfect shots that were turning out bad because of his equipment.

Like a lot of players, Love was going through doubts about his equipment. There are two kinds of irons that golf club companies manufacture: forged blades and, more recently, investment casts. The investment casts are made with the average player in mind. They have a bigger sweet spot and, generally speaking, give a player more distance. Most club manufacturers don't even try to sell forged blades to the public anymore because everyone wants the investment-cast clubs with their greater margin for error.

But to a touring pro, the larger sweet spot really doesn't matter. Players at that level will mishit a ball to the point where the larger sweet spot comes into play maybe one time in a hundred. If you look at a touring pro's irons, there is a worn area about the size of a quarter smack in the middle of the club face because that is where he always hits the ball. The forged blades may not get as much distance as the investment casts but, most players will tell you, they give you more control. At the level of the game where Davis Love plays, control is far more important than distance.

Love had been playing Tommy Armour investment-cast clubs for three years. He had, at times, had tremendous success with them, but now he was beginning to wonder if he didn't need the extra control of forged blades — or, as the players call them, blades — in order to hit the kind of crisp iron shots that he hadn't been hitting.

Tommy Armour had come out with a new investment-cast club at the beginning of the year — the Tommy Armour 855s — and Love had played several tournaments with them. He hadn't liked them at all and had gone back to the 845s he had been using. Now he wasn't certain about them either.

"I try very hard not to make excuses," he said. "If I play bad, I play bad. And I know if I'm really playing well, I can hit good shots no matter what I'm playing with. But sometimes the clubs can make just enough difference between a good round and a great one or a bad round and an okay one."

Love wasn't the only player unsure about his equipment by any means. Payne Stewart had signed a contract with Spalding to use a new set of irons and a new golf ball, and he was playing so poorly that he announced after the Masters that he was taking a few weeks off to try and get his head and game together. Two years earlier, Billy Andrade had signed a five-year contract with Maruman to use its irons. Halfway through the year, he asked out of the contract — which was for big dollars — because he was convinced he couldn't play with the clubs.

Some players changed companies because they had to. When Cleveland Classics decided that the best way to market its new investment-cast VAS irons was to pay a huge (and no doubt gritty) amount of money to Corey Pavin, many of their players found themselves looking at much smaller contracts or no contract at all. John Cook, who didn't like the VAS clubs anyway, ended up moving to Mac-Gregor.

Lee Janzen had signed a huge contract with the Hogan Company at the start of the year to play its new investment-cast clubs, the H-40s. At Greensboro he decided he had seen enough and asked Hogan to make him a set of forged-blade clubs. The company did, but wasn't happy. The investment casts were what the company was selling and what it was paying Janzen to endorse. If he won a tournament playing the blades, they couldn't put together a commercial or a magazine ad in which he explained how his Hogan H-40s had helped make him a champion.

Tom Kite was also under contract to Hogan, but for considerably less money. He played its blades and wore its cap but wasn't willing to risk making the switch to investment casts. With Kite, the only thing that mattered was his swing and how solidly he was hitting the ball. If he had to pay a company rather than have it pay him in order to ensure that he hit the ball well, he would make the deal in less time than it takes John Daly to escape after a bad round.

After shooting 75 in the first round of the GGO, Kite was wondering again about his swing. Kite is always wondering about his swing, day and night. He will ask almost anybody he sees to take a look at his swing. Several weeks earlier, Love had walked by on the range one day and observed Kite in the middle of a lesson — from an equipment salesman.

Thursday afternoon, Love had just left Gypsy's, the trailer where most of the caddies and some of the players eat lunch most days, when Kite spotted him and asked him if he would take a look at his swing.

Love would not be his father's son if part of him wasn't a teacher. He had given Kite lessons before and, by Love's count, Kite had won four tournaments immediately following their sessions. When Kite stopped him, Love told him he would be happy to look at him. But he would only do it if Kite promised to really listen and not ask twenty-five other people their opinions before the day was over. He reminded Kite of his past record as a Kite tutor. Kite nodded.

Love's theory on Kite's swing is simple and direct: since 1989, when he lost the U.S. Open after losing a tee shot way right, Kite has lived in fear of that shot. Clearly, he has done pretty well even with that fear, but Love believes that when Kite has a swing flaw it is because he is overcompensating to avoid the shot that flames right. He told Kite that and, after watching him hit some balls, suggested he lock his right knee so as not to let the ball ever go too far left on him.

The two men spent forty-five minutes together, Love talking and watching, Kite swinging and listening. Kite didn't win the next week at Houston, but he did tie for second. A week later, he tied for sixth at Atlanta. "I'm slipping as a teacher," Love joked.

Golf is the only professional sport in the world where players who are competing with each other on a daily basis regularly offer help and advice to one another. When Nick Price was struggling with his putter late in the spring, it was a tip from Greg Norman that helped straighten him out. Love often went to Kite for putting lessons. Players regularly point out flaws to one another on the range or the putting green.

One person who thought there was too much of that among the players was Arnold Palmer. "When I was playing, you might occasionally help a guy out who was having serious trouble, but you didn't do it all the time," he said. "Your goal was to *win,* and to win you have to beat everybody. I just think the guys on this tour don't put as much premium on winning because they don't have to win to make a lot of money. It bothers me because I sometimes think that winning is more important to the foreign players than it is to the Americans."

The current players would dispute that notion. They believe that your opponent every day is the golf course, not an individual player. And they also believe that the player you help one week may help you the next. In March 1992, Love was going through one of his periodic putting slumps. The week before the Players Championship, he asked Kite for a putting lesson. Kite got him — at least for a while — putting without moving his head. Love won three of his next four tournaments.

Love didn't ask Kite for a putting lesson in Greensboro. That would come later.

By the time the players' parking lot at Forest Oaks Country Club emptied out Friday night, the Greensboro Jaycees, who have run the GGO for fifty-six years, were looking at some significant empty spaces: Love — gone; Kite — gone; Lanny Wadkins — gone; Jim Gallagher Jr. — gone; Daly — long gone.

The only real "name" left in the field was Hale Irwin, whose irons still had some heat left in them after Hilton Head. The leader was Mike Springer, a twenty-eight-year-old fourth-year pro known in the locker room as "the Load," for the simple reason that he looked a bit larger than the 5 feet 11 inches and 210 pounds he admitted to. Springer wasn't fat by any means but he was, well, a load.

His nearest pursuers included players like Ed Humeník, Joel Edwards, and Brad Bryant, career nonwinners on tour, and John Huston and Gil Morgan, familiar names, tournament winners, but not players who would bring people in on a beautiful spring day to watch the golf tournament.

That was more a problem for CBS than the Jaycees. They wanted good TV ratings, but their gate was going to be huge whether the tournament leader was John Daly, Mayor Daley, or Mike Springer. On Sunday, the tournament drew about sixty more people than the Jaycees had hoped for. Midway through the final round, the uninvited sixty, all Kmart employees, staged a brief sit-in on the 10th fairway to protest wages and working conditions at Kmart. When the police showed up, the protesters were told that if they would get up and leave, no one would be arrested. They refused. So they were arrested, taken to jail, booked, and released.

No one was hurt, the story and pictures made the front page of the *Greensboro News and Record* the next morning, and most of the crowd didn't seem to care very much one way or the other about Kmart's dispute with its workers. The Kmart employees could have made much more of a scene than they did. By choosing to show up at 2 o'clock, they ensured that they would not be on the CBS telecast. They said their purpose had been to make a point, not cause a major disruption. That was exactly what they did.

By day's end, Springer had hung onto what had been a huge lead to beat Irwin by three shots for his first victory and $270,000. Irwin took home $162,000 for finishing second, giving him earnings of $387,000 for two weeks. Not bad for an old man.

The happiest man on the grounds Sunday evening — other than Springer — was John Morse, who had finished tied for third and had made $53,000 for his effort. Morse was a thirty-six-year-old tour rookie who had failed Q-School six times and had gone to Australia to play in the late 1980s. He stayed there for six years, coming home in 1993 to try the Nike Tour following the birth of his daughter. He had played well enough on the Nike Tour to finish fifth on the money list. That gave him a full exemption onto the big tour for 1994 without having to pass Q-School. No one on tour wanted to avoid the 1994 Fall Classic more than John Morse. The third-place finish at the GGO was an important step in that direction.

Springer, Morse, and Brad Bryant, who had been in contention for a while on Sunday afternoon, were not exactly Daly, Norman, and Couples. But on this Sunday on tour, they — along with Irwin — were the best players. They had put in the time and done the work. For them, the GGO was a big week in their lives. For the people of Greensboro — about 80,000 of whom came out to watch on Sunday — it was also a big week.

Not every week can be the Masters. Not every week needs to be.

14

GOLIATH BEATS DAVID ... BARELY

IT HAS BEEN SAID of the PGA Tour that all the stops begin to look alike after a while. Some ranges have more room than others, and some golf courses are more scenic than others. The jackets of the local organizers change colors every week, and some places supply Buicks as their courtesy cars, others supply Chryslers or Hondas or Cadillacs.

The two times of year when everyone must dig in and grind are the nine weeks between the Masters and the U.S. Open and the eight weeks between the World Series of Golf and the Tour Championship. None of the tournaments during that fall stretch are glamour events, but a lot of players are fighting for their golfing lives.

The spring grind is different from the fall grind. After the Masters the newness of the year has worn off and, unlike the winter stretch, when everyone feels privileged to be in warm-weather places like Arizona, Hawaii, California, and Florida, heat starts to become part of the drudgery. The weather gets hotter, tempers get shorter, and players who started slowly and thought it was just a bad start now must face up to the fact that their problem may be far more serious than that.

One player who was wondering where his year might be going as April drew to a close was Brian Henninger. After flunking Q-School in December, Henninger had gone home to Oregon and, in spite of his uncertain status on tour for 1994, had gone ahead with the plans he and his wife Cathy had made to buy their first house.

Henninger had made $112,000 on the golf course and roughly another $50,000 off it in 1993, so he wasn't in bad shape financially. Still, he wondered how many tournaments he would get into during the next year and how much time he should spend on the Nike Tour.

Henninger was in golf's version of the twilight zone. Having finished 130th on the money list, he was still a PGA Tour member and would probably get into fifteen to seventeen tournaments on the big tour in '94. Most golfers like to play between twenty-four and thirty-two weeks a year. Henninger had played thirty-one in 1993. That meant that if he wanted a full schedule he would have to play about a dozen Nike Tour events. That didn't thrill him. Once you have tasted the world of big crowds and fancy clubhouse meals and courtesy cars on the big tour, it is very difficult to return to the minor leagues.

Beyond that, Henninger also had to decide what was the best route back to a full exemption for 1995. Did he play every week he could on the big tour and hope he could make enough money on a limited schedule to make the top 125? Or did he make the Nike Tour his priority, knowing that if he finished the year in the top ten on the Nike money list that would put him back on tour? The only year he had been on the big tour — 1993 — it had been a second-place finish on the 1992 Hogan money list that put him there.

Henninger didn't have to make any decisions until March since there was only one Nike event during the first two months of the year. Until then he would play wherever his number came up on the big tour. That turned out to be Hawaii, Pebble Beach, and San Diego. He made the cut in the first two and earned a total of $6,883. Not exactly a flying start, especially since he knew he wouldn't get into any of the four Florida tournaments.

While the big tour made its way through Florida, Henninger headed for the Nike Tour. The only consolation about being back in Triple-A was that he was reunited with his pal Jeff Cook, who, after flirting briefly with the idea of going to play in Asia, had decided to give the Nike Tour one more shot.

Henninger's first venture back into Nike-land was a successful one. He finished second in the Monterey Open and made $22,700. Again, the question begged: grit your teeth and go the Nike route all year, turning down chances to play in big tour events, or keep going back and forth, hoping the half-baked approach would pan out somewhere.

Skip Kendall, who had finished one place ahead of Henninger on the 1993 money list, decided early in the year to make Nike his focus. He won the first tournament of the year and was never out of the top ten on the list all season.

Henninger had trouble staying enthusiastic. His next three Nike events produced two missed cuts and a tie for twenty-seventh. He knew that there were going to be chances for him on the big tour in May, June, and July. After playing Nike-Shreveport the same week as the GGO, he was told he would get into Houston and Atlanta the next two weeks. That would mean skipping Nike events in Alabama and South Carolina.

"I don't belong on the Nike Tour," he said during the week in Shreveport. "I really believe that my best golf is good enough to compete with the big boys and that's where I want to be. I may be wrong, but I'm going to play up there every chance I get."

Houston produced another missed cut. But Henninger wasn't discouraged. He was convinced that he was hitting the ball solidly enough to play well if — and this was always a big if — he could make some putts. Henninger is one of those players who changes putters the way most people change their shirts. He has a basement full of putters, and he is constantly down there pulling out old ones that have had success or looking at new ones that he is convinced will turn things around. After Houston, he decided to try a new putter — a Zebra — for the BellSouth Classic in Atlanta. "Maybe those stripes will straighten me out," he said.

Maybe. Or maybe it was Paul Goydos who straightened him out. Late Tuesday afternoon, he ran into Henninger on the putting green and they began talking about Henninger's frustration with the putter. Goydos suggested Henninger putt a few while he watched. What he thought he saw was Henninger moving the lower part of his body too soon — a common putting flaw. Goydos often practiced at home with his rear end up against the wall to force himself to get into the habit of not moving the lower part of his body. He told Henninger what he thought, and Henninger agreed to try to concentrate on keeping very still below the waist.

Whether it was the putting lesson or the stripes on the putter or biorhythms, Henninger came out putting like a demon on Thursday afternoon. Starting on the back nine, he birdied four of the first seven holes before missing the green at the tough 17th to fall back to three under. Undaunted, he birdied the par-five 18th to make the turn in 32.

His only scare came when he walked onto the 18th green and looked at the scoreboard on the far side of the lake that fronts the green. The board said he was seven over par, rather than three under. For a moment, Henninger's heart stopped. Then he laughed. "I figured that no matter what I had done, I hadn't picked up a ten-stroke penalty," he said. He double-checked with the walking scorer after making his birdie just to be certain there was no confusion.

After he had hit his drive at number one, Henninger walked off the tee and saw a leader board. Hal Sutton and Tom Kite were leading at six under par. At that moment, no one was at five under, and Henninger was one of several players at four under. Since he had reached four under most recently, his name was at the top of the four unders, meaning his was the third name on the board.

A chill ran through Henninger. *That's* where my name belongs, he thought. This is where I'm supposed to be and this is how I should play. He looked at Cathy, who had walked one hole with eleven-month-old Carlin, then taken her to the tournament day-care center so she could spend some time walking with her husband. Wearing sunglasses, Cathy betrayed no emotion. But Brian knew her well enough to know what she was thinking. He felt himself choking up. "I had to catch myself," he said. "I mean, it's only Thursday and I've played nine holes. But it had been so long since I'd put myself in position to be on a leader board that it really meant a lot just to be there."

Henninger knew he had to refocus quickly. In 1993, during the third round at Doral, he had seen his name pop onto the leader board right below the name Nicklaus. He had gotten goose bumps just looking at the board and he didn't get his concentration back until four holes and two bogeys later.

He was still fighting chills when he dumped his second shot into the right-hand bunker at number one. That turned out to be a blessing since it roused him from his reverie. He blasted to four feet and made the putt for par.

The rest of the day was all pars. Henninger made a couple of good saves and missed some decent birdie chances. His instinct about Cathy had been right. "When he plays this well, I get even more nervous," she said. At the sixth hole, she decided to go get Carlin so they could meet Brian when he finished. She made sure to tell Chris Mazziotti, Brian's caddy, that she was leaving so Brian wouldn't notice her absence and think something was wrong.

It wasn't as if she could blend in with the gallery. Henninger was in the second-to-last group of the day with Larry Silvera and Chris DiMarco and the course was virtually empty. When Henninger stepped up to hit his tee shot at the par-three sixth, he could clearly hear a woman holding a loud conversation about 50 yards away. He should have stepped back and asked for quiet, but opted not to. He ended up in the back bunker.

The emptiness of the golf course is just one of the things that makes playing in the late dog groups so difficult. The greens are spiky, the scoreboards seem frozen since so few players are on the course and the marshals are bored and tired. As Henninger found out, you can hear any conversation taking place in the same county.

It is a lot like being in a ghost town. That afternoon, when Tripp Isenhour, one of the players in the final group, had to return to the seventh tee after losing a ball, he found that the tee markers were gone.

Ghosts? No, the grounds crew, which follows close behind the last group, moving markers and pins and rolling and watering greens. Players in the last group learn that Satchel Paige was right. They don't look behind them because something is very definitely gaining on them.

It was almost six o'clock and the Atlanta Country Club was almost empty by the time Henninger and his playing partners walked off the last green. Henninger didn't care. He had shot 68, his best round of the year. "Three more like that and I'll be very happy." He looked at the scoreboard and pointed a finger at his name. "It looks good up there now," he said. "But the key is to still be there at this time on Sunday."

He was still there on Friday. In fact, he had moved up, into sole possession of second place after shooting a 67. He even made it into the interview room. "First time on the big boy tour," he said. "It was fun. I hope I get to go back."

If Henninger had walked off 18 that morning and announced that, yes, it was true, he really was Elvis and had started to sing "Hound Dog," no one would have noticed.

The reason was John Daly.

After the debacle at the GGO, Daly had gone on to Houston and, with his new haircut getting a lot of attention, had played extremely well, finishing in a tie for seventh. He started in Atlanta with a 69 and then, playing early Friday morning, he went on a birdie binge. By the time he was finished, he had shot 64 and had a two-shot lead on Henninger and three on everyone else in the field.

Daly had missed the Pro-Am Wednesday, excused by the tour because he had to be in Memphis for a custody hearing. He and his wife, Bettye, were going through a messy divorce, and some of Daly's friends believed that one of the reasons for his erratic behavior at the GGO was concern that he might not be granted visitation rights to his daughter, Shynah, who would be two in June. The judge had granted the visitation rights and Daly jumped into his van and drove straight through to Atlanta. Daly flies only when he has to, and the nine hours from Memphis to Atlanta was a piece of cake.

His Friday round electrified the tournament. When Daly is playing well, he is a joy to watch, not only because he hits the ball so far, but because he has a wonderful short game. He has soft hands and excellent feel around the green when he is working at his game. On a roll, he feeds off the gallery's enthusiasm, and the shouts and screams were echoing all over the golf course as he marched up the leader board.

Daly had been causing reactions like this ever since his fairy-tale victory at the 1991 PGA. He had gotten into the field there as the ninth alternate, finding out on Wednesday that he was in after Nick Price had to withdraw because of the birth of his first child. Daly made another all-night drive, pulled into Indianapolis without a practice round, hired Jeff (Squeeky) Medlen as his caddy for the week, and won going away.

He was twenty-five years old, hit the ball distances no one had ever seen before, and had an innocent charm that everyone latched onto. He also had a drinking problem that everyone on tour knew about. His victory thrilled and concerned Deane Beman and company. They knew they had a new folk hero, but they also knew they had a time bomb on their hands.

The explosions hadn't stopped since then. Early in 1992, Daly and his fiancée, Bettye Fulford, separated even though she was expecting their first child in June. At the Masters, Fulford had Daly served with palimony papers. A month later, they reconciled, got married, and Shynah was born in June. In December, police were called to their house in Colorado and Daly was arrested. Fulford opted not to press charges although she later alleged Daly had beaten her. Shortly after that, Beman suspended Daly from the tour, saying he could return after he had gone through alcohol rehabilitation.

Daly came back saying he was a new man and that he didn't need any aftercare like Alcoholics Anonymous or professional counseling. He had been befriended by Hollywood Henderson, the ex-football player and recovering substance abuser, and all he needed, he said, was Hollywood. He played superbly at the Masters, finishing tied for third, but the year went downhill from there.

He was disqualified from one tournament for refusing to sign his scorecard after the first round, and he quit another one after nine holes. In August, at Peter Jacobsen's charity event in Portland, he horrified Jacobsen and everyone else by turning around during a clinic and launching a drive over the heads of several thousand fans seated on a hillside. Jacobsen's entire life and career passed before his eyes as Daly's ball just cleared the heads of the amazed and frightened fans. For that stunt, Beman fined him $30,000 and told him there better not be another incident of any kind any time soon.

Daly lasted until early November, when during the second round of the Kapalua Invitational, he got disgusted with himself and, after missing a short putt, simply picked up his ball without putting out. That was an automatic disqualification. Worse, it came in the middle of a national cablecast and the entire country saw Daly blatantly give up in the middle of a round.

Beman had no choice now. He suspended Daly indefinitely. There are two unforgivable crimes in golf: cheating and quitting. Daly was one of the all-time recidivists when it came to quitting. That was the main reason Tom Watson never considered him for the Ryder Cup team.

Daly accepted his punishment, bought a condo in Palm Springs, and began preparing for his return. Everyone on tour wanted to see him get his life together. Jack Nicklaus and Arnold Palmer had both offered to let Daly stay with them if he so desired. On Christmas Day, Tom Watson, who had dealt with alcoholism among friends and family, called Daly to tell him if he wanted someone to talk to about what he was going through, he was there for him anytime, anyplace.

"I just wanted him to know I was thinking of him that day," Watson said. "We're all touched by alcoholism in our lives in some way, and I didn't want John to feel as if he was some kind of outcast because of what he was going through."

Quite the contrary, everyone on tour did everything possible to make Daly feel accepted. They knew what his potential was as a player and as an ambassador for the game and they didn't want to see him squander it before he turned thirty.

When Fuzzy Zoeller, his best friend on tour, visited him in Palm Springs shortly after New Year's, he reported that Daly was hitting the ball farther than ever, practicing harder than ever, and eager to return. Beman, who had initially planned to let Daly come back after the Florida swing, moved his return up three weeks, to the Honda Classic. It probably wasn't coincidence that the Honda traditionally drew the weakest field in Florida.

Daly said all the right things when he came back. He had learned his lesson and just wanted to work hard and play as well as he could. Still, his mood swings were mammoth. At Greensboro, two days before his 77–headshave–84 performance, he had held the shootout crowd in the palm of his hand all afternoon, signing autographs for kids, chatting with them, even asking one youngster for *his* autograph. It was two hours of warmth and fuzzies and Daly never stopped smiling.

Then came two days of whining and pouting. After that came seventh at Houston and now 69–64 at Atlanta. Who could figure Daly out? No one. Perhaps that was why Gary McCord had introduced him on the first tee during the shootout in Greensboro as "Fuzzy Zoeller's science project."

Henninger was sitting in the clubhouse finishing lunch when that afternoon's cablecast came on the air. Naturally, Daly was the big story for TV, and they showed tape of almost every birdie he had made in the morning. Then a leader board popped on the screen, showing Daly leading someone named Henninger by two shots. That was when it first occurred to Henninger whom he was going to be playing with on Saturday.

"Oh my God," he said, "unless someone gets to ten under, I'm playing with John." He leaned back in his chair. "My first time ever in the last group and I'm playing with John Daly. Boy, is this going to be an experience."

Henninger had played with Fred Couples at the Western Open the previous July, but that was different. Neither man was in serious contention to win the tournament, and they were five groups from the end. Even so, the gallery had been large and very pro-Couples.

This would be an entirely different experience. Not only was Daly leading the tournament, but his presence at the top of the leader board would bring several thousand people to Atlanta Country Club (aka the ACC) who would never think about buying a ticket to see any golfer in the world not named John Daly. "I guess I'll hear a few 'you-da-man's,' won't I?" Henninger joked.

"You-da-man" had become the battle cry of the boorish golf fan. It was a yell usually reserved for moments when the screamer knew a TV microphone was nearby. Sometimes, the screamer didn't bother waiting until a player had finished his downswing. The crowd that Daly brought out, many of whom had never been to a golf tournament before, would go bananas every time he drew the club back.

Henninger didn't want to think about any of that. He was playing well and putting superbly. Three times on Friday he had made long putts to save par. He would just focus on his own game and not worry about Daly or the crowds.

Easier said than done. Henninger is not someone who can suppress his emotions, as had been evident on the first fairway Thursday afternoon. When he went to bed that night, he had visions of Daly hitting tee shots hundreds of yards past him as thousands of fans wearing baseball caps turned backward screeched "You-da-man" over and over again. He tossed and turned, turned and tossed. Finally, exhausted by it all, he slept.

Fortunately, with a 2:10 tee time, he could sleep in. The day was warm and sticky, with scudding clouds overhead threatening rain.

When Henninger walked from the putting green to the first tee, he needed four marshals to get him through the crowd.

It would be that way all day. Fourteen marshals were assigned to Daly and every single one of them was needed. Watching them race down the fairways was a little bit like watching a president and his Secret Service detachment on the move. Walkie-talkies crackled: "Ten tee is secure, repeat, ten tee is secure"; two marshals walked stride-for-stride with Daly while others fanned out around the fairway to make sure no one jumped the ropes. Up ahead, the advance team made sure The Man would have a clear path to the next hole.

It was to the marshals' credit that they never forgot about Henninger. They made sure that he and Mazziotti were escorted through the masses from each green to each tee, no small task on a golf course where many of the tees are a good-sized hike from the previous green.

It took Henninger several holes to get his bearings. No matter how hard he tried to ignore what was going on around him, he couldn't. When Daly reached the par-five second hole in two and made a birdie to extend his lead to three shots, the massive gallery went stark raving mad. Daly just grinned his wide country grin, stuck his golf ball with the red Arkansas Razorback on the side onto a tee, and took another whack at the ball.

Henninger was shaken. He felt invisible. He was convinced that if he took all his clothes off, no one would notice. Occasionally, he heard comments like "*That's* the other guy? He looks fourteen." Or "This guy must feel like he's a marker for John."

But he hung in. Behind the baby face and the wide eyes, Henninger is a bulldog competitor. In 1992, he had won three events on the Nike Tour. "Any time he got into contention, he won," Goydos said. "Some guys know how to bear down when the pressure's greatest. Brian's one of those guys."

Under pressure like nothing he had ever felt in his life, Henninger bore down. He parred the first five holes, making tough up and downs on a couple of occasions. When Daly bogeyed the third hole and double-bogeyed the fourth after knocking a shot in the water, they were tied for the lead. Henninger got a second wind.

"I just decided that my support group were the people inside the ropes," he said. "The marshals were great all day and I knew Cathy was there somewhere even though I couldn't see her and I had [caddy] Chris too. That was all I needed. I knew all the others cared about was what John was doing. For a while, I got caught up in it, but then I found my comfort zone. I really didn't mind what was going on. Hell, if I came out to a tournament, I'd want to go watch John hit it three hundred miles too."

Daly and Henninger shared the lead until 16, when Daly rolled in a 25-foot birdie putt and Henninger missed the green and made bogey to fall two shots back. They both birdied 18 to shoot 69 and, when the long day was over, they were right where they had started: Daly at 202, Henninger at 204, and still 1–2 on the leader board. They would play together again on Sunday.

"It's different now," Henninger said. "I know now I can handle it, I've been through it. I know what tomorrow can mean to my career, but that's okay. I'm in position now. That's the hardest part."

Not exactly.

Shortly after Henninger woke up the next morning he got a phone call from Goydos, who was about to tee off. "Just remember you're a very good player," Goydos said. "Just keep on doing what you've been doing."

They talked about the overwhelming nature of the crowds. Goydos liked what he heard in Henninger's voice. No fear, no trepidation. Anticipation.

The first nine holes were not what Henninger had hoped for or anticipated. He just wasn't as sharp as he had been the first three days. With the crowds even larger and louder (if that was possible), Daly flew out of the box with birdies on the first two holes. At that stage, he led everyone by four shots. But, just as he had done on Saturday, he came back to the field, bogeying four and five. The problem for Henninger was that he bogeyed five and six and still trailed by four. What's more, the rest of the field had now caught them. Daly was at 14 under, David Peoples was at 13; Nolan Henke and Bob Estes were at 12, and Davis Love was at 11. Henninger was tied for sixth. Not only were his chances of winning fading, but his chances of making a big enough check to nail down a spot in the top 125 for the year — or at least come close to it — were fading too.

On the PGA Tour, a player simply cannot afford to go backward on Sunday. Every bogey literally costs thousands of dollars. Ask a player who shoots an over-par round on Sunday after starting on the leader board how he did, and he will shake his head and say, "I spent a lot of cash today."

Henninger couldn't afford to spend any cash. He needed it all. Even though his focus was on winning the tournament, he knew that second place was worth $129,600 and third would pay $81,600. That meant that second would wrap up the top 125, since $130,000 was expected to be the magic number. Even a third-place finish would at least get him about 70 percent of the way to the promised dollar figure.

Two bogeys and no birdies on the front nine put all of that in jeopardy. Henninger finally stopped his spending spree on the 11th when he rolled in a 10-foot birdie putt to get back to 11 under. Daly had bogeyed the 10th and was tied for the lead with Peoples at 13 under. Henninger went into his grinding routine. He saved several tough pars over the next six holes, including one at the 17th when he made a 10-foot putt.

Goydos, who had shot 69 himself to move up to a tie for eleventh place, was tempted to go back out on the course and join the gallery if only so he could be sure that at least one person would be cheering for Henninger. But the place was just too packed. There was no way to get out to the last group.

He settled for watching on television in the press room and was infuriated by what he saw and heard. The story of the day for the media was *not* Brian Henninger. It was John Daly. Jaime Diaz of *Sports Illustrated* had flown in because Daly was leading. So had Larry Dorman of the *New York Times*. Like everyone else, they were rooting for their story. Their story was *not* a Daly loss.

Goydos finally couldn't take it anymore. He left the press room and walked back to the 18th green to watch the last few groups come in. What he saw amazed him — and everyone else.

For a while, it seemed as if no one wanted to win the golf tournament. Love, after getting to 11 under, made two bogeys coming in and dropped to nine. Peoples, the co-leader for a while, missed a four-foot par putt at 18 to drop to 12 under.

When Peoples missed, Daly's girlfriend, Paulette Deane, who was standing a few yards from the green, clapped excitedly. Standing next to her, Mark Russell, one of the tour's rules officials, put an arm around her shoulder and said softly in his soothing southern accent, "Paulette, I think it would be better if you save your cheering for John."

Deane had met Daly while working at the Hope Chrysler Classic in 1992. She was one of the three women who walked around wearing halter tops that said "Hope," "Chrysler," and "Classic." Deane had been "Classic." So she did know something about golf etiquette. "Sorry," she said. "You're right."

Several minutes later, Nolan Henke — the defending champion — knocked his third shot at 18 to a foot and made a birdie. That put him in the clubhouse at 13 under. Peoples and Estes were at 12, and four players were tied at 11.

Standing on the 18th tee, Daly knew he needed a birdie to break the tie with Henke and win the tournament. Henninger was less sure about his situation. He knew he was two shots behind Daly and he suspected there was a logjam at 11 and 12 under because he knew 18 was a birdie hole.

The 18th hole at the ACC is considered one of the best finishing holes on tour. It is a relatively short par-five, a dogleg left that is reachable in two for most players. But there is danger all around the green: water to the front and left; bunkers left, right, and behind; and gnarly rough just about anyplace else. The green is huge and the Sunday pin placement is almost always the same: front left, meaning if you want to get anywhere close, both the water and the bunkers come into play.

Players must make all sorts of decisions at 18, which is why the hole is considered so perfect for the climax of a golf tournament. On the tee, Henninger saw Daly take out his driver and aim at a huge oak tree right at the corner of the dogleg. Even for Daly, hitting the ball over the tree seemed impossible.

Only it wasn't. The ball took off like a rocket, climbed over the tree, and landed on the left side of the fairway, 340 yards from the tee. Standing in what he thought would be the landing area, CBS's Gary McCord was stunned when he heard a *thump* 50 yards behind him and turned around to see Daly's ball.

Henninger knew he couldn't hit the ball there, but he had to get it far enough to take a crack at the green. He hit his driver solidly, not cutting nearly as much off the corner as Daly. For normal humans, he hit a fine drive. It ended up 50 yards behind Daly.

Up at the green, the crowd had become — with apologies to Jack Whitaker — a mob. They were screaming and hollering for Daly to be da Man and win the tournament. Frank Chirkinian, who has produced golf at CBS for several centuries, has always wondered why golf is the only sport in which most fans pull *against* the underdog. "I don't know what it is with golf fans," he said. "They want to see their heroes win. They want the stars to shine on Sunday. They don't mind if some unknown has the lead on Thursday or Friday, but by Sunday they want him out of the way.

"I looked out there in Atlanta and I saw this skinny little kid [Henninger] playing his heart out just trying to get a spot on the tour and I'm thinking, what a great story this kid is. No one out there knew he was alive. They wanted him out of the way for John Daly. Any other sport, they would have been for Henninger."

Maybe fans just want to root for someone they can *identify*. Whether it is Palmer with the hitch in his pants; Norman with his white-blond hair; Watson with his gap-toothed grin; or Daly with his Popeye forearms, shaggy blond hair (when it isn't shaved), and monstrous behind-the-ear swing.

Many people saw Daly as the Palmer of the 1990s, the blue-collar player to whom everyone could relate. He had none of Palmer's charm or humor, but he did bring the crowds out and rev them up to levels of fanaticism not seen since Palmer.

One thing made Daly unique: the ability to hit the ball farther than anyone had ever hit it. But he also came across as a sympathetic character, someone who had come from no money to huge money and was still fighting demons every single day — real or imagined. He looked more like someone you would bump into at the counter of a truck stop than in the grill room of a country club, and he sounded like it too. Daly would never say, "I had an eight-iron left to the pin" but, "I hit me an eight-iron."

Now, as he walked to his monster drive, the crowd was going berserk. After two days of this, Henninger finally had become immune. All he was thinking about was his second shot. He was 212 yards from the flag, and a lot of that distance would be over water if he tried to get the ball close. Sitting in the tower behind the 18th green, CBS's Ken Venturi watched Henninger study the shot and wanted to run down to him and yell, "Don't go for the pin!"

"He can't go for the pin here," Venturi said to his partner, Jim Nantz. "If he makes birdie and gets to twelve, he's going to make a big check and take a big step toward getting his card back. No one's been close to this pin all day anyway. He can't chance that water and make a bogey. He needs to think about his card."

Henninger wasn't thinking about his card. He was thinking about winning. The only way to win was to make an eagle, get to 13 under, and hope Daly didn't birdie the hole. What he didn't know was that no one had eagled the hole all day. Davis Love had tried to go at the flag an hour earlier and pulled his shot way left — behind the scoreboard — and made bogey. Getting close to the pin was an almost impossible task. No one had done it yet.

Henninger had to try. He was between a three-iron and a four-iron. Normally, he would have hit three, but he could feel his heart pounding and he knew he was pumping adrenaline all over the place. Three felt like too much. He pulled the four. Sitting in the clubhouse at Greenville, South Carolina, where he had just finished his last round in the Nike Tournament, Jeff Cook saw his friend take dead aim at the flag. "Oh my God, he's going for it," Cook said. He looked down and saw that his hands were shaking.

Henninger's were not. He swung as hard as he could, but stayed down through the ball all the way. The ball soared over the water and straight at the pin. Henninger held his breath. "Look at this shot!" Venturi yelled. The ball landed just past the pin, took one bounce, and skidded to a halt eight feet away.

Henninger heard the crowd roar — more in surprise than anything else — but he didn't need to. He knew he had nailed the shot as soon as it came off the club. "The biggest shot of my life and I never hit a ball better," he said.

Jeff Cook was on his feet. "Way to go, Brian!" he yelled, causing heads to turn in his direction.

All eyes now turned to Daly. He was only 172 yards from the flag and he decided to hit him an eight-iron. But the ball was left all the way and it flew into the left bunker. It was pin high, though, and not in that tough a spot to get up and down from.

As Daly marched to the green, the noise grew louder and louder. Henninger paused on the fairway to check the leader board. As he had hoped on Thursday evening, his name was still on it. He wanted to know exactly what the situation was. The board told him: if he made this putt and Daly didn't make a birdie, the two of them and Henke would play off; if he made his and Daly did make birdie, he and Henke would tie for second; if he missed the putt and made a birdie, he would tie for third with Estes and Peoples.

He finally turned to walk on the green with one thought: I have to make this putt to have a chance to win.

Henninger walked onto the final green the same way he had walked onto the first tee: virtually ignored. A few people clapped for his extraordinary shot, but 99 percent were focused on Daly as he dug his feet into the bunker. Henninger went and stood near the back of the green waiting for Daly to play his shot. He could feel himself shaking with nerves and excitement. He had to calm himself before it was his turn to putt. "I just went away for a few seconds," he said. In his mind's eye, he saw not the 18th green at the ACC, but a lake. He and his brother were fishing and it was very quiet and he was very calm . . .

Daly hit an excellent bunker shot to about four feet. Henninger knew he would probably make it. That didn't matter now. He lined his putt up carefully, took a deep breath, and rolled it dead center. Eagle! Venturi was shouting about how remarkable it was to make three on the hole, and Jeff Cook was jumping up and down and screaming at the television set. Henninger calmly walked to the side of the green to give the stage back to Daly.

Daly lined the putt up quickly, hit it perfectly, and shook his fist as the ball went in the hole. The green was shaking with noise. Henninger came over to congratulate him and the two of them hugged. They had played 36 holes together, and Henninger had shot 69–71 to Daly's 69–72. Daly's two-shot margin on Friday had ended up a one-shot margin.

While the pandemonium continued on the green, Henninger made his way through all the volunteers to the scorer's tent. Mark Russell stopped him. "That was as good a shot as I've seen in all my years out here, Brian," he said. "You should be proud."

Henninger was proud. He wanted to find Cathy and hug her and hug Carlin and collapse with exhaustion and joy. He had made $105,600. By making eagle instead of birdie he had earned an extra $43,200. He now had made $112,400 for the year, meaning he didn't have far to go to clinch his card. He could stop worrying about whether to play Nike events or regular tour events. He was back with the big boys.

Daly made the headlines and got the trophy and the biggest check and a hug from Paulette Deane. He told the throngs around 18 that he couldn't have done it without them and, his voice cracking, dedicated the victory to his daughter. "The most important thing about this," he said, "is that I know now I can win a golf tournament sober."

For the PGA Tour the idea of a sober John Daly winning golf tournaments was exciting to contemplate. There was no doubting the electricity he brought to a leader board.

Most people thought it would be remembered as the weekend when John Daly turned a corner. Very few gave much thought at all to the notion that Brian Henninger had turned a corner too.

15

WHO'S THE BOSS?

ON THE MORNING of May 19, 1993, Frank Chirkinian had arrived at the CBS trailer that is his office twenty-two weeks a year and found his phone ringing. The caller was Rudy Martzke, the sports television columnist for *USA Today.* John Daly had held a press conference the previous afternoon at the Kemper Open and had declared himself a new man, alcohol free, with all his troubles behind him. When, Martzke wanted to know, was CBS going to catch up with the rest of the world and do a feature on Daly's rehabilitation.

Chirkinian's answer was brief: "When I think he's rehabilitated." End of conversation.

"I'm like everyone else," Chirkinian was saying later that morning. "I want to see John Daly be the star we all think he can be. But just because he holds a press conference and says, 'I'm cured,' doesn't mean I buy it. I look at the kid and I see trouble ahead."

Chirkinian apparently sees quite clearly. The next day, Daly played poorly in the opening round of the Kemper Open and failed to sign his scorecard. When a tournament official chased him out of the scorer's tent to try and get him to sign the card, Daly ignored him and kept on walking. That same day, in a story in the *Washington Post,* Leonard Shapiro revealed that Daly's claim that his legal problems in Colorado were "basically taken care of" wasn't quite accurate. He had a court date the following Tuesday.

So much for features on rehabilitation. So much for questioning Chirkinian's judgment.

On tour, he is known as the Ayatollah, in part because he has a ferocious bark that causes people who don't know him to leap in sheer terror. But the title also comes from the power he wields as the executive producer of golf for CBS. Chirkinian has been producing golf at CBS since 1958 and there is almost no one on tour he doesn't know. And, since CBS televises seventeen regular tour events a year — more than the fourteen combined for NBC and ABC — no one in golf makes more decisions on who to give network airtime to, and how to give them that airtime, than Chirkinian.

The Ayatollah is sixty-eight, a short, round man who didn't play golf until he was twenty-four, but now keeps his handicap at about eight even though he can't hit the ball as far as he'd like to. *Nothing* gave Chirkinian more pleasure than shooting a gross 73 in a member-guest tournament early in 1994 that outgoing commissioner Deane Beman also played in. "Not only did my team win all the money," he said, laughing, "but I beat Beman *straight up*. Maybe I should go on the senior tour instead of him."

Like anyone who wields a lot of power and isn't afraid to tell people he wields it, Chirkinian has both detractors and enemies. They will tell you Chirkinian is arrogant (no one will argue that point) and that CBS's coverage of golf is fawning, that Chirkinian's announcers almost never say anything critical about anyone or anything in golf.

They will point out that, although it was Chirkinian who invented TV golf's version of the wheel — the concept of a player being under par and over par for the tournament — more than thirty years ago, CBS is behind ABC technically and the ABC concept of foot soldiers rather than tower troopers brings the viewer closer to the action. What's more, they will add, NBC, with Johnny Miller in the 18th tower, has the best commentator in the business.

Chirkinian doesn't dispute the differences in approach. In fact, he points them out. "One of the things that makes golf unique is that each network does take an entirely different approach," he said one morning at the 1994 Kemper (at which Daly managed to hang around for all four rounds). "If you turn on your TV and you are a regular watcher of golf, you will be able to tell almost immediately — even if the voices were somehow disguised so you couldn't tell who was talking — which network you're watching.

"I've always believed that our guys can see more and tell the viewer more from the tower, so I've kept them there. ABC is different, and that's fine — for them. I hear all this talk about Johnny Miller. What is the big deal about saying a guy choked? That's easy to say if you're not worried about going back into the locker room. Johnny Miller isn't welcome in any locker room on tour. We live with these guys twenty weeks a year. We need their cooperation and we get it. If we want someone in the tower after a round, or whatever it is we need, they do it for us. That doesn't mean we don't point out a bad shot or a mistake, but there's more than one way to do it. If you say, 'Oh boy, he didn't want to hit it over there,' the viewer gets the message."

If you watch golf on ABC, you often feel as if you are watching on ongoing tribute to Jack Nicklaus. The fact that Nicklaus works for ABC as an announcer and the fact that the executive producer of golf for ABC, Terry Jastrow, also runs the television arm of Golden Bear Inc. may have something to do with that.

If you watch golf on CBS, you aren't likely to miss anything Greg Norman or Fred Couples is doing. Why? Well, Norman and Chirkinian are such close friends that Chirkinian is often kidded by his friends and employees about it. When he and his wife separated last fall, Chirkinian moved out of their house in Augusta and bought a place in Hobe Sound, Florida — Norman's hometown. He also joined Norman's club there. And, since Couples and CBS anchor Jim Nantz were suite-mates in college and are still close friends, there isn't much in Couples-world that Nantz doesn't know about.

On NBC there's no doubt that Miller is the star. Unlike CBS, which had Pat Summerall as its voice on the 18th for more than twenty years, NBC has never really found an anchor it is comfortable with. It has gone from Jim Simpson to Charlie Jones to Vin Scully to Bryant Gumbel to Jim Lampley to Dick Enberg in 1995. Since 1990, Miller has been the constant, a lightning rod who attracts attention — and sometimes anger — with his bluntness. CBS's lead commentator for the last twenty years has been Ken Venturi, who isn't nearly as critical as Miller but does raise more questions than he is given credit for. At the Masters, when Tom Lehman, trailing by one shot, hit a one-iron off the 18th tee on Sunday, Venturi immediately said, "I don't understand that play. He's got to put pressure on Olazabal by hitting a driver."

Although it was Nantz who moved into the 18th tower after the Masters when Summerall departed to do football on Fox, the real star on CBS these days is Gary McCord. Chirkinian has always promoted a nonstar system. Ever since Brent Musberger became known as "the anchor monster" during his latter years at CBS, Chirkinian has vowed that none of his people would ever reach that point again. "If Jimmy Nantz ever starts to behave that way, I'll slap him down so hard he won't know what hit him," the Ayatollah said. "We don't have stars here. The show is the star. If there's gonna be a star, *I'll* be the god-damn star."

Even so, McCord has become a star. A journeyman player who never won a tournament on tour, he was plucked into the booth ten years ago by Chirkinian — after offering to work for him initially as a coffee fetcher — when he was looking for someone new with a sense of humor. McCord's sense of humor is off the wall and he sounds totally different from anyone else doing golf on TV, but he *is* a breath of fresh air. Sometimes his lines sound contrived — because they are. Occasionally, as the Men of the Masters would no doubt tell you, he goes too far. But he is clever, he is witty, and most important, he understands golf and the golf swing. He spends more time on the range and in the locker room than anyone else working TV today.

That's why he can give you a synopsis on the strengths and weak-nesses of almost any player who happens to show up onscreen and can usually tell you something about them that *isn't* in the media guide. He has the respect of most players because they know he works at what he does and knows what he's talking about.

He is a Chirkinian creation. If you are Tom Watson or the Men of the Masters, that is one more black mark for Chirkinian. If you are CBS, it is another paragraph in the lengthy bio of the Ayatollah.

Day two of the 1994 Kemper Open, June 3, was about as routine as a day on the PGA Tour can be. Mark Brooks was leading, pursued by Bobby Wadkins. Phil Mickelson, playing in his second tournament since returning from his skiing accident, was playing well and lurking just off the leader board. John Daly was fighting to make the cut. Tom Kite and Curtis Strange would miss the cut. It would be a low-key weekend for CBS. Nothing like Atlanta.

But around the CBS trailer that afternoon, there was plenty of excitement. The Ayatollah was having a birthday — his sixty-eighth — and a cake had been brought in and everyone was gathering around to watch him blow out the candles. He did just that, thanked everyone, and then tried to act gruff, ordering everyone back to work. No one was buying the gruff act. At least not today.

But Chirkinian was not all hearts and flowers. He was dealing with a storm gathering around McCord, and he wasn't happy about it.

On the last day of the Masters, McCord had made the two soon-to-be-infamous comments that had upset the Men of the Masters. The first was the crack about the greens being "bikini-waxed." The second was about the "body bags" that could be found behind the 17th green, a reference to the fact that going over 17 was not a very good idea because you had almost no chance to make par. Or in golf vernacular, you were "dead."

Chirkinian knew he was going to have trouble as soon as the Masters was over. He also knew that his long-term relationship with the tournament wasn't going to help one iota. And now he knew that this letter from Tom Watson would only give Augusta chairman Jack Stephens one more reason to go to his bosses at CBS and demand McCord's removal from the 1995 telecasts.

Watson, who had never been a fan of McCord's, had written Chirkinian an angry letter after the Masters, telling him he should be ashamed of McCord's comments and that McCord should be removed from the CBS broadcast team not someday, not soon, *now*. He called McCord "the Howard Stern of golf." Chirkinian was incensed.

"How dare Tom Watson write me a letter like that," he said. "Who does he think he is? I should be *ashamed?* I'm old enough to be his father, he has no right to talk to me that way. He is *not* the titular head of golf, and I don't need him telling me who to use or not use on my broadcasts."

Chirkinian was chagrined that the Watson letter had become public knowledge. He was convinced that it had been taken off his desk in the trailer, photocopied, and circulated. Watson was also upset that the letter had been made public. He blamed Chirkinian.

"The letter should have been between us," he said. "It was meant to be private. Frank had no right to leak it to the press. I'm still waiting for him to have the class to respond to me."

"*Respond* to him?" Chirkinian roared. "Not anytime soon."

A lot of his frustration with Watson stemmed from what he knew was going on in private at that moment. The Men of the Masters were demanding McCord's removal, and Chirkinian knew his bosses at CBS would have no choice but to accede to their demands. The Masters works with a one-year contract with the network, and if CBS didn't remove McCord, they could switch networks in a matter of minutes. Having just suffered the embarrassing loss of NFL football to Fox, CBS could not afford to risk losing one of the few major properties it had left. The Men of the Masters — and Watson — would get their way.

Chirkinian was still hoping he could do some damage control with his friends in Augusta and get McCord back on the telecasts in 1996. What he didn't know was that when the McCord dumping was announced in August, it would cause such a furor and bring about enough comments from McCord — polite but McCord-like in their irreverence — that negotiating a compromise with the Masters would become impossible.

It was time for Chirkinian to get ready for a 4 o'clock cablecast on USA Network. The way the tour structures its telecasts, the networks put on the Saturday-Sunday telecasts, and cable outlets like USA and ESPN show many of the tournaments on Thursday and Friday. Those cablecasts are produced by the network that has the weekend rights.

Chirkinian was facing a long two hours on this particular Friday. One of his leaders — Brooks — would be in the clubhouse an hour before USA went off the air. The other, Wadkins, was playing the front nine, which limited the amount of coverage he could be given to mini-cams. He paged through the computer looking for players he could focus on. When he reached the bottom, he let out a shriek. "Will you look at this Wagner kid," he said. "He shot eighty-nine yesterday and he started with a triple bogey today. I wonder what the hell he's going to end up shooting."

Jeff Wagner was a four-spotter. He had shot 69 and won a playoff the previous Monday to get into the field. He was a twenty-four-year-old who gave lessons at a driving range in Northern Virginia. Clearly, the TPC at Avenel was just too tough for him. High scores by local players, especially those given sponsor exemptions, are not un-common on Thursdays and Fridays. But the upper limit is usually around 82 or 83, and most players will break 80 one of the two days. Usually, a player good enough to four-spot is at least good enough to break 80.

There was no doubting the fact that 89 was a horrendous score. It was the highest on tour all year. Now Wagner was starting out as if he might shoot a similar number. "We gotta do something on this guy," Chirkinian said as his troops gathered.

They did. A graphic was put together, a takeoff on the David Letterman top-ten list, suggesting Jeff Wagner's next five jobs. Among them were "swing-guru to Gary McCord," a playful swipe at McCord; "Sports TV columnist for *USA Today,*" a playful swipe at Rudy Martzke; and "he's next week's New Breed!" a playful swipe at the weekly Nantz feature on younger tour players.

Later, as the two hours wound down to a very anticlimactic close, Chirkinian sent a mini-cam over to show Wagner in action to the viewing audience. There was absolutely nothing else going on, every-one even remotely near the lead was already in the clubhouse. Seeing the camera trailing him, Wagner turned and said, "What do you ex-pect? I only play one day a week. I teach the other six."

The mini-cam actually showed one of his more glorious mo-ments — a par — as he slogged his way to an 86. In the locker room, a number of players who had finished their rounds watched what was happening and were incensed. Chirkinian and company were kicking a guy when he was down. In the press tent, the reaction was similar. Here was big, powerful CBS beating up on some poor kid playing in his first tour event, who couldn't break 80. When Wagner finally fin-ished, several reporters were waiting for him. He didn't seem that upset.

"I guess it was kind of nice to make TV," he said. "Of course this isn't exactly the way I had pictured it."

Of course not. Had Chirkinian gone too far? Maybe. The Let-terman list *was* funny and anyone who found that offensive was over-reacting. Following him to the clubhouse with the mini-cam and giv-ing updates on his horrendous round might have been a bit much. No doubt if there had been real golf to put on the air, Chirkinian would have done that. He didn't, though, and many people found his treatment of Wagner cruel.

But was it? The Kemper Open was, after all, a professional golf tournament which the public bought tickets to see. By entering the tournament at any level, Wagner and any other player had to know — should know — that just as they would willingly accept the $234,000 winner's check, they had to willingly accept whatever might come should they play poorly.

Was Wagner a public figure in the same sense that Daly, Mickelson, Kite, Strange, or any of the tour players were? Of course not. But he wasn't subjected to the same scrutiny either.

The person most disturbed by the overnight Wagner uproar was Jim Nantz. This was only his fifth tournament as Summerall's replacement and, since he was the one on the 18th tower, a lot of the criticism was directed at him. He felt uncomfortable with that and wondered if perhaps he and his colleagues had gone too far in making Wagner a laughingstock. On Saturday morning, he suggested to Chirkinian that they contact Wagner and invite him to come and sit in the booth with him and Venturi. They would explain his work situation and try to cast a kinder light on his two-round total of 175 — 33 over par — which left him 42 shots behind Mark Brooks and 30 shots outside the cut.

Reluctantly, Chirkinian agreed. He hadn't wanted to humiliate the kid and he knew people were saying and writing that he had. But he also didn't want to turn his telecast into a circus. By midafternoon, that possibility loomed. In the midst of a less-than-scintillating tournament, the media had latched onto Jeff Wagner. At 3:30, half an hour before the telecast was scheduled to start, Chirkinian was in the production truck when a call came in from Alan Shipnuck, a writer/researcher for *Sports Illustrated*'s new Golf-Plus section. Shipnuck wanted to know if he could come over and take a look at a tape of the Friday cablecast.

"Now why would you want to do that, son?" Chirkinian asked.

He listened as Shipnuck explained he wanted to be fair to CBS and accurately portray exactly what had been done to Wagner. "Why do I think you're up to no good?" Chirkinian asked. He listened again. "Look, this is what we did," he said when Shipnuck was finished fending off that charge. "We always show the leader board, the guys making all the money. There is another side of golf, though, the flip side of the leader board, and we showed that. We did it one time. We weren't trying to be cruel to Jeff Wagner. In fact, we showed him on one of his best holes."

He hung up. "I have nothing against Jeff Wagner or any kid who wants to try to make it on this tour," he said. "But for crying out loud, I've got five announcers who could give this guy two shots a side! He wants to walk the same fairways as Nicklaus and Palmer and Hogan and Hagen, fine, but if he can't play at a respectable level, then don't ask *me* for sympathy."

Wagner was going to get sympathy — in buckets. As the telecast began, Nantz reported to Chirkinian that Wagner was supposed to be on his way. By 5 o'clock Chirkinian was convinced that Wagner was a no-show. "Maybe that kid from SI convinced him he shouldn't go on," he said. "Figured he'd get some kind of exclusive."

Chirkinian didn't lose his sense of humor during the telecast even with the spectre of Wagner hanging over him. When one of his cameras showed a closeup during a commercial of two guys passed out behind the 18th green, Chirkinian suggested that someone should paint a white line around them to indicate that they were "immovable obstructions," in case a ball landed near them.

At 5:14, as director Artie Kempner took the telecast into commercial, Nantz's voice came into the truck: "He's here."

No one had to ask who he was referring to.

"Did he talk to SI?" Chirkinian asked.

"Yes."

"Okay, put a headset on him."

When Wagner had a headset on, Chirkinian introduced himself. "Have you gotten a lot of phone calls on this, Jeff?" he asked.

"Yes," Wagner answered.

He was wearing a Taylor-Made cap, no doubt stuck on him by the company in honor of his upcoming appearance on national TV. "You tell the Taylor-Made people they owe you one," Chirkinian said.

"I called and left them a message to watch," Wagner said.

"You're the only one we'd let wear a cap in the booth," Venturi said.

They were coming out of commercial. Golf fans around America now had the opportunity to see Nantz, Venturi, and Wagner. The leaders, Mark Brooks and Bobby Wadkins, would have to wait.

Nantz briefed the viewers — most of whom would not have seen the Friday cablecast — on the fact that Wagner had put up a couple of high numbers, that he had been part of the show Friday, and that there was more to his story than those numbers. He went through the litany: parents divorced while he was in high school; never graduated; working six days a week as a teacher, hoping to *get some financial backing* so he could have time to work on becoming a touring pro.

Venturi chimed in and talked about how proud he was of Wagner for not withdrawing after the 89, which "a lot of guys would have done." Not a lot of guys. John Daly, yes. Maybe four or five others. But not a lot of guys, especially guys in their first tournament. Wagner nodded and said he just wanted a chance to play and all he needed was *some financial backing.*

"Anybody got a towel?" Chirkinian asked.

"Maybe Kenny and Jim can give him some of *their* money," associate producer Chuck Will suggested.

"Anybody got a hat we can pass?" Chirkinian added.

Mercifully, Kempner was calling for another commercial. "Let's keep him a few more minutes," Nantz suggested. Then, jokingly, he added, "Jeff wants to know if he can do this again next week at Westchester."

Chirkinian rolled his eyes. "Tell Jeff we're getting calls on the 800 number we've set up for him."

Wagner's eyes opened wide. "Are you serious?"

No, Chirkinian wasn't serious, although CBS did everything but flash a 1-800-PAY-JEFF phone number on the screen. Back from commercial, Nantz again mentioned that anyone who wanted to help Wagner out with *some financial backing* could find him at the Northern Virginia Golf Center in Herndon, Virginia.

"How much do you get for a lesson?" Venturi asked.

"Thirty dollars," Wagner said. "But I only get to keep ten. My boss gets the rest."

"We got to get you a new job," Venturi said. (He wasn't kidding either; he tried for several weeks afterward to find Wagner work in Florida.)

Wagner was finally dismissed. The media was waiting for him when he climbed off the tower. CBS had, for all intents and purposes, put on a fifteen-minute telethon on his behalf on a telecast that had ten times the viewership of the Friday cablecast during which he had been ridiculed. Had they made it up to him?

"We'll see," he said. "If I get some calls and get something out of it [like *financial backing,* which he did get in the form of a $10,000 contribution from a viewer that sent him to the Florida mini-tour for the winter] then maybe I'll feel different. Right now, I still feel like they humiliated me."

Of course "they" hadn't shot 89–86.

A few minutes later, as Mark Brooks walked up to the 18th green, he turned to the mini-cam following him and put in a plug for a golf course he owned in Fort Worth. The Ayatollah sighed. "What do you think, guys," he asked over his intercom to all the towers, "should we take up a collection for him too?"

It had been a long two days.

Two days before Wagner-gate began to unfold, Deane Beman cleaned out his desk at tour headquarters and headed for the practice range. He had been showing up at recent staff meetings wearing a Ben Hogan–style hat and a golf glove, either coming from the range or on his way to the range. He was more than ready for June 1 to come even though it meant that the parking space marked "Commissioner Beman" — the only reserved spot in the entire lot — would be painted over. By lunchtime on Wednesday, it read "Commissioner Finchem."

Timothy William Finchem wasn't there that day to take advantage of his new perk. He was at the TPC at Avenel holding his first press conference as commissioner and starting the process of getting to know the players. Or, to be more accurate, getting them to know him.

"I've been a behind-the-scenes guy most of the time I've been here," he said. "I think now the players need to see me and feel more comfortable with me." His goal, he said, was to shake hands with every player on all three tours — PGA, Senior, and Nike.

More important than the universal handshake, Finchem wanted to dispel the notion that he was a Beman clone. He wasn't, but that perception existed anyway. Finchem was forty-seven, as much a Democrat as Beman was a Republican. He had worked in the Jimmy Carter White House and on Democratic campaigns after Carter's defeat. He made a point of telling everyone his political days were behind him, knowing that having voted for Bill Clinton wouldn't win him many friends on tour.

Finchem had joined the tour in 1987, first as vice president for business affairs, then as deputy commissioner. He was one of the few people on the planet who was actually close to Beman. The day after Beman announced his resignation, Finchem broke down during a staff meeting talking about how much he would miss him. He was Beman's hand-picked successor and, when the search committee got around to making a final decision, no one ever emerged to seriously challenge him.

In the days after Beman's announcement at Doral, all sorts of names were floated as a replacement, ranging from Dan Quayle to Hale Irwin to Donald Trump. But once Richard Ferris withdrew his name, Finchem was the clear-cut favorite for the job. That didn't mean he thought he was a lock. He even had moments when he wasn't absolutely certain he wanted it. He already traveled too much for a man with three young children (six, four, and two) and being commissioner, especially if he did his Forrest Gump routine and crisscrossed the country to shake hands with everyone holding a golf club ("Hi, my name is Tim, Tim Finchem"), would mean even more time away from his family.

Deep down, Finchem knew he wanted the job. He had been training for it for five years and Beman had turned more and more responsibility over to him. He already ran most of the player meetings, and when the tour decided to go ahead with the start-up of the Presidents Cup (U.S. vs. the World in a non–Ryder Cup year version of the Ryder Cup), Finchem was put in charge of the project and he — not Beman — had made the formal announcement in April that the event would take place.

Frank Chirkinian was at that press conference at Hilton Head and when it was over, he told anybody who would listen, "Well, I guess it's pretty apparent who the next commissioner is going to be."

It was — and it wasn't. The search committee invited eight candidates to an airport hotel in Atlanta in April for round one of the interviewing process. Finchem came out of that session with the committee thinking he had done poorly, that he hadn't gotten his message across and made it clear to them that he was the best choice for the job. "I just didn't feel right about it," he said. "I can't tell you why, it was just a feeling."

It is very unusual for Finchem to feel that way. Growing up in Virginia he had starred on the debate team in high school, and it was that skill that earned him a scholarship to the University of Richmond. His background as a debater and as a lawyer had made him a master of the nonanswer. If you asked him how he was feeling in the morning, his reply might be something along the lines of "Well, if we're in agreement that it is morning — and I'm not saying that we are — then I will study the question of how I feel, in consultation of course with the board, without whom I would never take any action or make any key decisions because they are the backbone and heart and soul of all that goes on on tour and if we decide that this is morning, then we will make a decision — which will not be announced publicly — as to whether we feel fine, not fine, mediocre, or terrible, which are the options we have available to us, if in fact we agree that we need to seek an option, which I'm not necessarily saying that we are. I hope I've made that clear, but if I haven't I'd be glad to clarify."

Behind the lawyer/debater, though, Finchem had a sly sense of humor, a strong sense of what he needed to do as commissioner, and the ability to be more pragmatic than Beman, who always tended to take things personally.

When he flew to Dallas on the Monday before the Byron Nelson Classic for a final interview with the board, he was nervous but ready. Only two names had been sent to the full board by the search committee: Finchem and Jack Frazee, former CEO of Centel. This time, Finchem walked out of his ninety-minute interview thinking he had hit a home run. It was noon. He knew Frazee was going in after lunch. He went back to his room to wait. By 4:30, he was panicking. Had Frazee knocked their socks off? Had he not done as well as he thought he had done? He paced up and down in the room, trying to remember everything he had said. The phone rang. Could he come back downstairs? He bolted to the elevators. When he walked in, Ferris told him the vote had been unanimous. Congratulations. You're it.

Several hours later, ESPN's Sportscenter announced that the tour had a new commissioner: *Tom* Finchem. "I've spent years negotiating with those guys to give us a regular spot on the show each night," Finchem said, laughing. "They finally give us big play and that's what happens."

Commissioner-elect Tom/Tim flew back to Ponte Vedra the next morning. He and Beman walked into a regularly scheduled quarterly staff meeting that afternoon and Beman introduced Finchem as the new boss. Then he went back to the range and left Finchem in charge.

"People really don't understand Deane," Finchem said later. "He's tenacious and driven but he also really cares about people. He's a lot more flexible than people give him credit for. You tell him an idea isn't going to work, he doesn't argue. He goes on to the next thing. I don't think the public really understands that."

The public's understanding of Beman was not on Finchem's mind on the morning of June 1. He was commissioner now, the boss. "It does feel different," he admitted. "I know now when a problem comes up, I'm the one that has to deal with it and make a final decision. I can't walk in to Deane anymore and say, 'What do you think about this?' It's all on me now."

He had no way of knowing what that was going to include in the months to come.

16

OPEN HEAT

Jeff Sluman was walking onto the practice tee at Oakmont Country Club. Davis Love III was walking off.

"Hey, Slick, what do you think?" Sluman said.

"I can't wait till tomorrow," Love answered. "By then, I may be able to hit a ball on one of the greens."

Sluman laughed. "I told you. It's harder than Chinese geometry — Mandarin or Szechuan."

It was late Tuesday afternoon of U.S. Open week, June 14, and the temperature had cooled from the high 90s to the low 90s. The entire Pittsburgh area was in the midst of a record heat wave and Oakmont, the venerable old club that was hosting its seventh Open, was broiling. Combine the heat, which was expected to last all week, with a golf course that many of the players — Sluman and Love among them — thought was as hard as any they had ever played, and you had conditions about as brutal as anyone on any tour in the world would face all year.

All of which left the U.S. Golf Association — the governing body for national golf championships, pro and amateur, in the U.S. — and the Oakmont members walking around with wide grins on their faces. There is no tournament in the world that thrives on sadism like the Open. The USGA selects difficult golf courses, then lets the rough grow knee-high, cuts the greens so that they're practically white by week's end, and then sits back and giggles watching the world's greatest players thrash and crash for four days.

Some call it the world's greatest test of golf. Others call it trick golf, courses made so unfair that it is as much luck as skill that determines the winner. The Open's list of winners includes most of the great names in the game's history (Sam Snead being the most notable exception). But it also contains names like Sam Parks Jr. (a club pro who won at Oakmont in 1935), Jack Fleck, Orville Moody, and Andy North. Fleck and Moody each won one tournament — the Open. North won the Open *twice* and won only one other time during his career.

Of course Ben Hogan and Jack Nicklaus each won four Opens, and Lee Trevino launched his career when he won at Oak Hill in 1968. He came back three years later to beat Nicklaus in the famous "snake" playoff at Merion. Arnold Palmer and Tom Watson won only once, but each would call his victory — Palmer at Cherry Hills in 1960, Watson at Pebble Beach in 1982 — the most dramatic of his career.

It takes a certain kind of player to win the Open. John Daly will probably never win it because Open golf courses invariably are set up to take the driver out of your hand and force you to hit irons off the tee to make sure you find the fairway. Beyond that, winning the Open takes patience, patience, and more patience. As the players say, if you don't want to grind for four days, don't even bother showing up.

You have to accept the crazy bounces and five-foot putts that roll eight feet past. You can't moan about a bad shot because, as Curtis Strange says, "You start feeling sorry for yourself and you'll turn a bogey into double or worse in no time."

Open week is very often hot and humid, the pressure builds each day, and every mistake is magnified, especially on Sunday afternoon. In 1994, all the elements were at their most difficult. The USGA had heard whispers after the '93 tournament at Baltusrol that the rough lacked its usual bite, so it had made certain no one would make *that* comment again. The greens, always fast at an Open, were faster because the members at Oakmont take great pride in the speed of their greens. Many of them could be heard during the week saying repeatedly, "The greens are much faster when we play our member-guest."

Having hosted six Opens previously, Oakmont was full of lore and tradition and stories. Ben Hogan had beaten Sam Snead here in 1953, and Nicklaus had beaten Palmer in a playoff in 1962, a tournament that marked the arrival of the chubby twenty-two-year-old rookie as Palmer's successor on the game's throne. Eleven years later, Palmer had made his last real run at an Open, leading on the final day before Johnny Miller came out of nowhere to shoot 63 and win the tournament. The members were still grumbling about Miller's 63 and the soft greens that allowed him to fire at the flags all day. Ten years later, the tournament ended on Monday because of rain and Larry Nelson broke Tom Watson's heart with a 60-foot putt on the 17th green to beat him by one shot.

Nicklaus, Palmer, Miller, and Nelson were all in the field. Nicklaus had earned his way in by winning the Senior Open (and an automatic exemption) in '93. The other three had received exemptions from the USGA. Remarkably, Palmer's invitation had caused some controversy.

Unlike the Masters and the PGA, which declare their champions exempt for life, and the British Open, which unofficially makes its champions exempt for life, the U.S. Open gives a champion a ten-year exemption — period. Palmer had played in Open qualifying seven times after playing at Oakmont in '83 and had failed to make the field each time. Now, at sixty-four, the USGA had invited him back, to a course that was twenty miles from where he had grown up in Latrobe, and a place where he had twice almost won the Open.

It made sense to almost everyone. One exception was Frank Hannigan, the former executive director of the USGA, now a columnist for *Golf Digest* and a commentator for ABC. Hannigan is one of the great curmudgeons of all time, a wickedly funny man with a caustic sense of humor that can sting anyone, anytime. Hannigan didn't think Palmer belonged in the tournament and had said so in *Golf Digest.* He couldn't make the cut, he might embarrass himself, and that exemption might be better used on another player.

Seve Ballesteros agreed. Ballesteros hadn't won a tournament since 1992 and, at thirty-six, had become a shadow of the swashbuckling genius who had won five major titles. Although he made several putts over hill and dale during the team matches at the Ryder Cup, he had hit the ball so poorly, especially during his singles loss to Jim

Gallagher Jr., that a cruel joke had circulated through the golf world after the weekend was over.

"Did you know that there were *two* Scandinavians on the European Ryder Cup team?"

"Two?"

"Yes, Joakim Haeggman, who's Swedish, and Seve, who's Finnished."

Ouch. Ballesteros was furious when the USGA announced three sponsor exemptions — Miller, Nelson, and Palmer — in March. He was shocked and angry that he hadn't received one and couldn't understand why Palmer had gotten one when everyone knew Palmer couldn't play anymore. As if to back up his case, Ballesteros went out and won a tournament. By year's end, he had come all the way back to finish third in the European Order of Merit.

Did Ballesteros belong in the field? Probably. He had not won the Open, but the only time he had come close had been at Oakmont in 1983. And, the fact was, people still wanted to see him play. Which was the same reason Palmer belonged in the field no matter how much Frank Hannigan disagreed. He didn't belong every year, and if Ballesteros didn't qualify in 1995, he didn't belong either. But a one-shot deal, sure, why not let them both play?

The USGA finally relented and invited Ballesteros in late May. Just to make certain no one thought they had been bullied into inviting him, they also invited Ben Crenshaw. Their message was that Ballesteros and Crenshaw, although they hadn't qualified, had both played well recently — Crenshaw had won in New Orleans — and that was why they were invited.

Sure. And the greens really were faster at the Oakmont member-guest, and the traffic getting across the lone two-lane bridge that led from the Pennsylvania Turnpike to the club wasn't going to be *that* bad.

"You know the first time I played here in 1942, they hadn't built the Pennsylvania Turnpike yet," Palmer said during a joint press conference with Nicklaus on Tuesday.

Nicklaus leaned close and whispered in Palmer's ear. "Yes, Jack," Palmer said, "they *did* have cars back then."

Even Frank Hannigan giggled at that one.

*   *   *

Lee Janzen was on the range late Wednesday afternoon, his longtime teacher Rick Smith a few feet behind him as he hit balls. As Janzen drilled one shot after another, Smith shook his head and said, "The only advice I've given him all week is to make sure he stops at every red light driving home. There's nothing I can tell him to make him hit it better than this."

Twenty-four hours before he began defense of his Open title, Lee Janzen had again become the talk of the golf world. After eleven months of struggling, he had suddenly exploded back into everyone's consciousness in two weeks. First, he had shot a final-round 66 at the Kemper Open to finish fourth — his first top-twenty finish since Baltusrol — and then he had strung 69–69–64–66 together at Westchester on one of the more difficult courses on tour to beat Ernie Els and win the Buick (Westchester) Classic.

Life was good again. And now, people were wondering if Janzen couldn't do the near-impossible and win the Open back-to-back. After all, a course like Oakmont, which put a premium on driving the ball straight and making a lot of tough putts, was a Janzen type of golf course.

"I'm just happy knowing I can play again," he said. "You get to a point where you actually wonder if you're ever going to play well again."

Janzen hadn't gone through anything that Jeff Sluman, Billy Andrade, or John Cook hadn't gone through in the last year. The difference was he had gone through it as the U.S. Open champion. He couldn't shoot 73 and just head for the range. He had to talk to the media, shake hands with sponsors, and spend time with his agent. At times, he felt he was not living up to the title he had won: U.S. Open champion.

The turning point had come after the Masters. First, he forgot to commit to Hilton Head, a mistake many players periodically make. Sometimes, players show up on-site thinking they have committed to a tournament only to find out they haven't. Janzen had never done anything that careless before. To him, the mistake was symptomatic of the fact that his mind wasn't as sharp or as focused as it should be. He was distracted, perhaps by fatherhood, perhaps by being the Open champion, perhaps — most likely he thought — by the fact that he lacked confidence in his new clubs.

At Greensboro the next week, he finally decided he had to go back to playing forged-blade irons even if it made the Hogan Company unhappy. He certainly wasn't doing the company or himself any good by finishing 34–cut–cut–35–30 since Doral. He had missed more cuts (four) during the first eight weeks of 1994 than he had missed in all of 1993. He had finished in the top ten in seven of his first sixteen tournaments in 1993, none of his first ten in 1994.

"I just figured things couldn't get any worse," he said.

Things didn't turn around right away, although his twenty-second-place finish at Greensboro was his highest since he had been twentieth in the short-field Mercedes Championships in January. He finished sixtieth at the Memorial and thirtieth at Colonial but, slowly, he thought he was beginning to see the proverbial light at the end of the tunnel. Of course he had thought that in the past and it had just been another train.

The two weeks before the Open would be critical, not only because Janzen didn't want to go into his defense being asked why he hadn't had a top-twenty finish in a year, but because the two tournaments leading to Oakmont — Kemper and the Buick Classic — were played on two of his favorite golf courses, the TPC at Avenel and Westchester Country Club. If he couldn't get something going at those two places, courses that put a premium on driving the ball straight and chipping and putting, then he was in trouble.

There were signs of life on Saturday at the Kemper when he pieced together a 68 to sneak onto the bottom of the leader board. Sunday, on a humid, cloudy day that brought back memories of the last day at Baltusrol, he suddenly started making the birdies he hadn't made for months. He had four in eight holes before a bogey at the ninth slowed him down.

All of a sudden, everything was different. His caddy, David Musgrove, who had worked for Sandy Lyle during Lyle's glory years, saw a difference in the way he was walking and sounding and looking. "The jaw is starting to come out again," he said.

The jaw was locked firmly in place on the back nine. Janzen was shouting at shots while they were in the air, waving them to go in the right spot, and resolute even when he got into trouble. Still three under for the day through sixteen holes, he hit a perfect four-iron at the par-three 17th that floated just over the water to a soft landing eight feet left of the pin. He rolled in that birdie, then at 18, one of the toughest holes on the golf course, he hit a seven-iron second shot that slammed to a halt one foot right of the flag. Janzen tapped in for a birdie and a 66. "I misread the seven-iron," he said, a huge grin on his face. "I thought it would go another foot left."

He hadn't won, but he had finished tied for fourth and the feeling was back. He knew he could make birdies in bunches again and he could knock down flags with his irons. He did that for four straight days at Westchester, holding off Els on the final day with a 35-foot birdie putt at the 15th that gave him the lead for good.

The timing could not have been better. Not only was the Open coming up, but *Golf World* was running a feature on him which showed him literally disappearing off the page. When he arrived at Oakmont Tuesday morning, his buddy Rocco Mediate said he had a game for them: Nicklaus and Palmer. Standing on the first tee, Nicklaus turned to Palmer and said, "What do you think, should we take these two kids on?"

"Will they give us shots?" Palmer asked innocently.

"Give you shots?" Janzen said. "Are you kidding. Didn't you know I've disappeared from the game?"

He could joke about it . . . now.

At any major tournament the days leading up to Thursday always produce some kind of controversy. At the Masters it had been Mac O'Grady, the former player and longtime tour gadfly claiming that he knew for a fact that seven of the top thirty money winners on the PGA Tour were taking beta-blockers, a drug that slowed one's heart rate. A slower heart rate kept you calmer and made a smooth golf swing easier to execute.

Nick Price had taken beta-blockers once, under medical supervision, and he said they had hurt his golf because he couldn't get an adrenaline rush when he needed one. What's more, he hadn't slept very well at night because he didn't use up as much energy as he normally did during the day.

At the '94 Open, O'Grady wasn't around to stir anything up, so most of the talk focused on the golf course and the recurring question about whether the USGA made its courses unfair. Greg Norman stirred things up a little when he said that he didn't like a golf course that took the driver out of your hands and that was what Oakmont did.

One person who wasn't engaging in any of the pretournament rhetoric was Curtis Strange. It had now been five years since his historic back-to-back Open victories and, even though he had played some good golf in the past twelve months — eight top-ten finishes — he was almost a ghostlike figure at Oakmont. He wasn't one of the pretournament favorites, he wasn't stirring up any controversy, and he wasn't one of the Grand Old Men à la Palmer and Nicklaus.

But he was playing pretty good golf. Since the Masters, he had struggled with his game, playing well for two weeks — tenth at Houston, fourteenth at Memorial — then playing poorly for two — missed the cut at Colonial, missed the cut (by a mile) at Kemper.

He couldn't quite figure out what the problem was. Sarah's health was much better; she felt 95 percent recovered and had learned to adjust to what had happened to her by not going a thousand miles an hour, twenty-four hours a day. Almost every day she put aside two hours in the middle of the day to relax. Occasionally, Curtis would notice her slipping back into her routine of saying yes to everyone and everything and he would lecture her. She knew he was right and — most of the time — she listened.

With Sarah feeling better, there was no reason for Curtis not to be able to focus on improving his game. The problem was, he wasn't sure what he wanted to do with his golf swing. During his golden years in the 1980s, he had constantly relied on two swing thoughts: keep the left shoulder behind the ball and be certain to release the club on the follow-through. If he did those two things he would almost always hit the ball well. "Those two thoughts worked for me for about eight years," he said. "I might tinker a little, but everything revolved around those two thoughts."

For most of four years, he had been searching for something that would replace those thoughts because they didn't seem to work anymore. Each week, he tried something new. In the weeks leading to the Open, he was changing his thoughts daily, sometimes more often than that. He knew that was far from ideal, but he hadn't yet hit on anything he felt comfortable with.

He went out to practice on Monday afternoon and ran into Arnold Palmer and Paul Goydos on the back nine. Goydos felt as if he had landed on Fantasy Island. There they were, stalking the fairways of Oakmont: Palmer . . . Strange . . . Goydos.

A couple of months earlier, Goydos had been in a group at dinner that included Tom Watson. He had listened intently as Watson told stories about U.S. Opens and British Opens and Masters past, about victories and defeats and moments of glory and infamy. Walking out of the restaurant that night, Goydos shook his head and said, "Well, I've finally figured out the difference between Tom Watson and me. He dreams about winning another major; I dream about *playing* in a major."

Goydos had fulfilled his dream, although it hadn't been easy. He had birdied the thirty-sixth hole of Open qualifying to get into the tournament right on the number the day after the final round of the Kemper. On that same day, Billy Andrade had three-putted the last two holes of his afternoon round and missed qualifying by one shot. Andrade had charged a 15-foot birdie putt on 18, thinking he needed to make it to avoid a playoff. He was right, but when he missed coming back, he didn't even make the playoff.

When Goydos arrived at Oakmont, he was told that you had to sign up for tee times in order to get on the golf course for a practice round. He looked at the Monday sheet and saw Palmer's name listed, so he wrote in his name next to it. Thus the historic pairing was made: Palmer in his 130th major and Goydos in his first.

By the time he ran into Palmer and Goydos, Strange had decided it was time to clear out his mind. (Maybe he had been reading Norman's Zen book.) He was going back to basics: left shoulder behind the ball; release the club and a weak grip so he wouldn't chance losing the ball to the left too often. He played in with Palmer and Goydos and when they were done, Palmer looked at him and said, "You know, the way you're hitting the ball there's no reason you can't win here."

"Come on, Arnold, don't start."

Palmer was serious. "You know you're still not yet forty," he said. "You have a lot of good golf left in you. I had a couple of great chances to win majors when I was your age. There's no reason why you shouldn't be able to do the same thing."

Strange appreciated the pep talk. He appreciated it less when Palmer said almost the same thing to the media and picked him as one of the favorites. Fortunately for him, no one was really listening. They were more interested in hearing Palmer tell stories about his fifty-two years of playing Oakmont than in picking any winners.

He had been assigned the same wooden locker — number 108 — that he had been assigned at all his previous Oakmont Opens. Right across from the locker was his portrait. Three lockers down was Nicklaus and across from his locker, his portrait. Of course no one lingered in the locker room for too long since it was not air-conditioned. Nostalgia went only so far when the temperature got close to 100.

It was already close to 90 on Thursday when the tournament started at 7 o'clock in the morning. Unlike at regular tour events, which send players off the first tee and the 10th tee on Thursday and Friday in order to save time, all four majors insist that everyone plays the golf course from hole 1 to hole 18 each day. At the Open, that meant a first tee time of 7 A.M. and a last one of 4:20.

It also meant that when play slowed to a virtual halt in the after-noon because of the heat and the lightning-fast greens, rounds were taking more than five and a half hours. That meant play couldn't possibly be completed before dark even on two of the longest days of the year. The USGA was saved the embarrassment of being unable to complete a round for no reason other than slow play by evening thundershowers that gave them an excuse to bring the remaining golf-ers in about an hour before dark. That way they were able to list weather as the official reason why the round hadn't been completed.

"The pace of play is absurd," Palmer said after he finished his first round in five hours and thirty-five minutes on Thursday evening. He grinned wickedly. "Heck, in '62 we never took more than four and a half hours even with Jack playing as slow as he did back then."

Palmer and Nicklaus had become friends over the years, but every once in a while the little knives would come out. Nicklaus often said he would never play in the major championships after he became noncompetitive because he wouldn't want to embarrass himself. "Ar-nie can do that," he said. "I can't."

Nicklaus had been embarrassed for most of the year, but on open-ing day at the Open, he went from Olden to Golden one more time.

His morning round of 69 made him the leader until Tom Watson, playing in the afternoon, came in one shot better at 68. "I looked up at the board and figured if Nicklaus can do it at fifty-four, why can't Watson do it at forty-four?" he said. Ernie Els — at twenty-four — had also shot 69, as had Hale Irwin and a New Zealander named Frank Nobilo. John Daly, who had insisted all week there was no reason for him not to hit the driver on most holes, hit it hither and yon all afternoon and shot 81. The good news was that he didn't withdraw.

Watson and Nicklaus, who finished his round by draining a 50-foot putt at 18 to one of the loudest roars ever heard, were the story of the day. But that was only because Strange botched the 18th hole, making a double-bogey six after pushing his drive into jail.

Until then, Strange had been cruising along at three under par, playing just the kind of golf Palmer had watched him play on Monday. He felt confident and relaxed and, being a Virginia boy, the 97-degree midday heat (not to mention the sky-high humidity) didn't really bother him. "I sort of like it," he said, "because I know it'll bother some other guys."

He was two under at the turn and you could see the old look in his eyes. Nine holes on Thursday prove nothing at a major championship. If they did, Jumbo Ozaki would probably have as many major titles as Nicklaus because he always seemed to play the first nine holes at every major in 32. Ozaki was a very good player, a man who had become incredibly rich by dominating the Japanese Tour. Everything he wore was silk, and he could hit the ball as far as anyone on the American tour with the exception of Daly. But he never seemed able to go the distance when he got out of Japan. One day ABC flashed a graphic on Ozaki that said, "Has won 48 tournaments worldwide." It failed to mention that 47 of the 48 had come in Japan. Still, the graphic was right; Japan is in the world. And Ozaki was certainly quite wide.

He went out in 32 — of course — and came back in 39. Of course. Strange, after turning in 34, three-putted 11 to drop to one under and walked off the green talking to himself. But he came right back to birdie the long par-five 12th and the short par-three 13th. By now the word was out that Curtis was in red numbers and the crowd walking with his group, which also included Nick Price and Ben Crenshaw, had swelled. Price was en route to shooting 76–72 to miss the cut and was about as close to being truly angry on the golf course as he would ever get.

It was Strange the crowds wanted to see and Strange who caused ABC to send its number one foot soldier, Bob Rosburg, to join the threesome. Rosburg, the 1959 PGA champion, had been ABC's original foot soldier and had become a tour legend in that role. Rosburg had never seen a shot he didn't think was impossible. "That's dead, Jim, he has absolutely no chance" had become his trademark. Rosburg had been imitated so often that McCord had looked at a lie one day during a CBS telecast and said, "Oh boy, he's got a Rosburg here."

Hearing Rosburg's name mentioned on CBS, Chirkinian had screamed into McCord's headset, "Don't you ever say that again!" Of course everyone watching knew just what McCord was saying.

Now Rosburg was talking about Strange as he lined up his second shot at the 14th. "Curtis just hasn't been as angry the last few years as he used to be," Rosburg said. Strange's seven-iron floated right — way right. "Sonofabitch!" he yelled in frustration as if on cue. "Looks to me like Curtis is back," Rosburg said.

He was. He bogeyed 14, but then birdied 15. He was three under and leading the tournament when he reached 18. The bad drive and an ill-conceived second shot led to the double bogey and left Strange steaming. But not *that* steamed. It was still 70, no one was going to do a whole lot better than that, and he knew everyone was going to have a bad hole before the tournament was over. He hit balls in the heat for a long time in the afternoon and then took Sarah to dinner.

To her amazement, when they returned home, Curtis went right to sleep. No tossing and turning, no mental review of the round, even the double bogey. Just exhaustion and sleep. It hadn't happened more than a handful of times in eighteen years of marriage.

It rained Thursday night, which mercifully slowed the greens a little bit on Friday. Tom Watson had predicted before the tournament that there would be more rounds in the 90s than in the 60s. He had exaggerated. But there had been only five rounds in the 60s on Thursday and thirteen in the 80s. God only knew what Jeff Wagner might have shot.

The rain did nothing to cool things off and the haze and heat were still hanging over the course when Arnold Palmer hit his tee shot at 10 A.M. to begin his 115th and final round at the U.S. Open.

Palmer had shot a respectable 77 on Thursday, dousing any fears that he would come out and not be able to play the golf course at all. He had finished in typically melodramatic fashion at 18, putting his second shot into a bunker 80 yards in front of the green, then hitting a wonderful shot to about ten feet. It was almost dusk, but the grandstands around 18 were still packed, everyone having waited for Arnie to arrive.

After Rocco Mediate missed his birdie putt, he walked up to mark, since he still had four tricky feet left. Palmer looked at him and said softly, "Your call, Rocco." Mediate looked at him. Palmer repeated himself. "Your call." Then he winked. Mediate understood. Palmer had every intention of making his putt and when he did, he knew the place was going to go nuts. Mediate wasn't ready to deal with his putt yet. He told Palmer to go ahead.

Palmer shrugged, looked his putt over, and blasted it into the back of the cup. Pandemonium. Palmer took his hat off and bowed to his disciples. Mediate had a grin as wide as the Pennsylvania Turnpike (wider than some places) on his face. "He just *knew* he was going to make it," he said later.

Mediate managed to coax his putt in and Palmer put an arm around him and said, "It's bedtime."

Palmer felt good about his round. He had broken 80 and he was still nominally in the hunt for the cut. "If that putt doesn't go in, it's back in the trap I'd just hit it out of," he said, laughing. "Tomorrow, if I can have a reasonably good round, I can make the cut. That was my goal starting out." He grinned the famous grin. "After that I'll worry about winning the tournament."

Palmer, Mediate, and John Mahaffey — who had won the PGA at Oakmont in 1978 — began their second round with a large, appreciative gallery trailing them. As the day wore on, the gallery kept growing almost as if the Pied Piper was weaving his magic. Which is exactly what Palmer was doing. He knew this was an ending for him and he wanted to savor every second of it. He walked the fairways, his head on a swivel, nodding, smiling, doffing his hat over and over again. He hit some very good shots and came to the turn only two over par for the day, which put him at eight over for the tournament. The cut was looking like it would be six over. What if Arnie could somehow sneak a couple of birdies in on the back nine . . .

Stranger things have happened. But the heat just wasn't going to allow it. By the time Palmer's group reached the 10th tee at 12:35, the temperature was again close to 100. Palmer insisted the heat "wasn't that bad," but you could see it getting to him, slowly but surely, as he struggled through the last nine holes.

On the 10th green, a woman sitting by the green waved Palmer over. "Arnie, I love you," she said. Palmer winked.

"Would you like to trade hats with me?" she asked. "Yours is getting soaked."

Palmer, who wears hearing aids away from the golf course, walked closer to her and asked her to repeat the question. When she did, he peered down and looked at the hat. It had a Great White Shark logo on it. Palmer shook his head when he saw that. "No thanks," he said. "I'll keep this one."

He was starting to fade now. A bogey at 10 and a bogey at 12 ended all talk about the cut. But at 13, he nailed a gorgeous six-iron right at the flag. It stopped six feet above the hole as the army, evoking memories of the past, roared. Walking off the tee, Rocco Mediate looked at John Mahaffey and said, "How about that shot?"

Mahaffey laughed. "He's just unbelievable, isn't he? Always has been."

Mediate shook his head again. "Amazing. Just being here for this is an honor."

Mediate was in the midst of an amazing round himself. He had been out all year with back problems. He returned at Westchester and surprised himself by making the cut. He had started the Open with a 74 on Thursday but was four under par on his second round. Unfortunately, he was starting to feel pain in his back again. By the end of the round he could barely bend over to tee up his ball. He would make the cut, struggle through the third round, withdraw, and be out for six more months. But as he and Mahaffey walked onto the 13th green, they were two more members of Arnie's Army. The only difference was that they got to be inside the ropes.

In the movies, Palmer would have made the birdie putt. In real life, he three-putted, the first putt slipping four feet past, making the second one too tough. Palmer walked onto the 14th tee, shook his head, and said, "That's just terrible."

Unfortunately, it wasn't going to get better. Palmer had one more birdie chance at 14, just missing a 15-footer. After that, as the heat pounded away, he couldn't putt. He three-putted 16 for bogey and 17 for double bogey. He was frustrated because he wasn't playing better, but the army didn't care. They just wanted to be part of this, to cheer his every step.

At 2:30 in the afternoon, his face flushed from four and a half hours in the sun, he stepped onto the 18th tee, took a deep breath and a long sip of Gatorade. He made a crack about the color of the Gatorade, pulled out his driver, and hit it right down the middle.

The march began. People were screaming and waving and trying to get any view they could. This was a moment they wanted to hold onto. Palmer — as always — understood. He walked slowly, still making eye contact everywhere he could. The only moment of quiet came when he settled over his second shot. Once again, he hit the ball solidly and it bounced onto the front of the green. He had hit the last green of the last round in regulation.

Now came the last walk. Mediate and Mahaffey peeled off so that Palmer had the fairway to himself. The exhaustion and the emotion were all beginning to kick in and as the cheers got louder and louder and somehow even louder, he could feel himself choking up, tears starting to well in his eyes. On the 10th tee, a few yards left of the 18th green, the players and caddies and marshals who were there stopped what they were doing, turned around, and joined in the applause.

Palmer was so drained by the day and the moment that he could barely draw his putter back. He three-putted for bogey and 81, but it didn't matter. After he holed out, Mediate put an arm around him and said softly, "All this is because of you."

Palmer knew. He knew this was thank you for more than forty years of memories and for all the winks and smiles and waves. And it all caved in on him. When Mark Rolfing tried to talk to him for television, Palmer choked up halfway through the interview and couldn't finish.

He told the USGA people that the heat had gotten to him, that if they gave him a few minutes he would come into the media tent and talk for as long as anybody wanted him to talk. He did come in and he did start to talk. But he was still overwhelmed. He paused, trying to regain his composure. The silence in the huge interview room was deafening.

"You know I've just been so lucky," he said, the words coming very slowly. "I have had such a great life. I played okay. I won some tournaments, a few majors. To have people treat me the way they have has just been wonderful . . ."

He stopped, picked up a towel, and wiped his eyes. He took another deep breath and opened his mouth again. No words came out. He stopped and buried his head in the towel, sobbing. The only sound in the room was the whir of the air-conditioner. Palmer picked his head up. "I think, that's about all I have to say," he said. "Thank you very much."

He stood up to walk to the door. The laws of journalism say that applause is inappropriate at the end of a press conference — or at any time, in fact. But there are occasions when the laws of humanity outweigh the laws of journalism. Without any hesitation, everyone in the room jumped to their feet and applauded. The ovation was warm and heartfelt from a group that had benefitted from Palmer's presence for more than forty years. He was the star who always returned phone calls, always had that extra minute for that one last question, always came up with the quote you really needed.

Palmer stopped at the tent exit and smiled to acknowledge the applause. Then he walked back outside into the heat. Even with an escort, it took him fifteen minutes to make his way through the phalanx of people to the locker room. Naturally, he insisted on signing every autograph.

When he finally got upstairs and collapsed in front of locker number 108, there were still a few reporters left. "You know, it's incredible," he said. "In any other sport, I would have been booed for the way I played today. Instead, I get that kind of ovation. I really am lucky to have been a golfer."

The flip side of that doesn't even need saying.

*   *   *

The two stories that everyone was talking about on that second day had nothing to do with the tournament leader board. Palmer was the story of the morning and early afternoon, O. J. Simpson the story from that point on.

There was bitter irony in the fact that almost at the very moment that Palmer was walking up 18, the Los Angeles Police Department was declaring Simpson a fugitive from justice. Palmer and Simpson had been partners on Hertz commercials for years, had played golf together, and had been friends. The night before, someone had asked Palmer if he had talked to Simpson since the murders and Palmer shook his head. "I haven't, but I just can't believe he'd have any part in something like this."

Of course no one could believe it, which was why the entire country sat transfixed that night as Simpson and his friend Al Cowlings staged their slow-motion chase through Los Angeles County.

On Saturday morning, there just weren't all that many people discussing the fact that Colin Montgomerie had shot 65 on Friday to lead the U.S. Open by two shots over four players.

One of those four was John Cook, who had also shot 65 on Friday, finally putting together the great round that he had been searching for all year. Mr. Happy was actually feeling happy again. He had finished third at the Memorial Tournament, opening with a 67 in which he finally made several long putts. "I'd almost forgotten how good that feels," he said that afternoon.

He played the first forty-five holes of the Memorial without a bogey and was the leader midway through the third round. But, like the rest of the field, he ended up getting blown away by Tom Lehman, who shot four straight 67s to shatter all the tournament records and win by five shots. It was Lehman's first victory on tour and built on his performance at the Masters.

No one was surprised to see Lehman win after his two near-misses at the Masters. Robert Wrenn, who had been on tour for ten years, shook his head when he thought about Lehman's first two Masters and said, "A third and a second out of the box at that place. They ought to at least give him a green *shirt*." Lehman had plenty of green — dollars — after the Memorial.

Cook ended up losing second to Greg Norman down the stretch

but wasn't the least bit disappointed. He came back the next week with a ninth at Colonial and arrived at the Open feeling confident. He even took a slightly different approach, flying in late Tuesday because he wanted to see twelve-year-old Kristin's piano recital and eight-year-old Jason's All-Star Little League baseball game.

"It meant a lot to them to have me there, especially since I miss so much with the travel," he said. "And I figured there just wasn't that much for me to know playing extra practice rounds. The rough is high, the greens are fast, there's no room for error. I knew that before I got here."

Cook started slowly Thursday and had to work hard to get to the clubhouse in 73. But Friday, he came flying out of the box, birdieing three of the first six holes. On number one, he hit a six-iron to the green and watched the ball hit and stop. The rain had slowed the golf course down. Instead of playing bump-and-run links golf, the players could fire at the pins a little more.

He did just that all morning and the result was that he shared the low round of the day with Montgomerie and David Edwards. Nicklaus, after a fast start, shot 70. That put him three shots back of Montgomerie. Curtis Strange and Ernie Els were one shot back of Nicklaus, at 140, and Tom Watson was at 141.

The cut came at 147 — five over — as it turned out. That meant that Price was gone at 148, Nick Faldo was gone at 148, and Lee Janzen was gone at 148.

The latter two were shockers for different reasons. Faldo simply didn't miss cuts in majors. The last time had been the PGA in 1986, meaning that he had made twenty-eight straight cuts. The whole week was a struggle for him. He hated the heat and he wasn't wild about the golf course. But the problem, he knew, was with his game. He couldn't make the ball do what he wanted it to do. "If you know you can't afford to hit the ball in the rough and you hit it there anyway, something's very clearly wrong," he said. All the hours working with Leadbetter had not produced a click. And his putting was still horrendous.

In fact, Faldo would have made the cut if he had putted better. Down the stretch on Friday, he missed a 10-foot birdie putt on 15, a 4-foot par putt on 16, and an 8-foot birdie putt on 17. Not certain if the cut would be five or six, he hit an iron off the 18th tee and his second shot came up just short of the green. He missed chipping in by inches, then walked into the scorer's trailer.

"Is the cut five or six?" he asked.

"Looks like five" was the answer. Jeff Sluman, who had played with Faldo, saw all the color drain out of his face. "I think he really thought it was going to be six," Sluman said. "He was shocked."

No more shocked than Janzen, who showed up at the golf course on Thursday and didn't feel an ounce of adrenaline. Here he was beginning defense of his title, coming off a victory, and, like Morales in *A Chorus Line,* he felt nothing. He was exhausted. He sleepwalked to a 77, fought back the next day to reach five over for the tournament, then made a late bogey to miss the cut by one. He had still made the cut in only one Open. No one had an Open record like Janzen: cut–cut–win–cut.

What happened to Janzen is not uncommon. Golf is so imprecise that you can't plan a schedule that guarantees you will peak at exactly the right moment. Just as Greg Norman wished he could have bottled his game at the Players so he could take it to the Masters two weeks later, Janzen would have liked to have put some of his Westchester birdies on hold for Oakmont. He couldn't, because the game won't let you decide when you will hear the muse. It comes and goes, often for reasons you can't understand or explain.

Everyone was a bit bleary-eyed on Saturday morning, perhaps from watching the white Bronco on TV all night, perhaps from the heat. As is always the case on an Open course, players were mixing birdies with bogeys and the occasional double bogey, no one able to sustain any real momentum.

Except for Ernie Els. Paired with Strange, the young South African spent the first hour of the third round acting as if he intended to shoot 59. He birdied one and two, then rolled in a 20-foot putt for an eagle at four. A few seconds later, he knocked his second shot to three feet at number five and tapped that in for a birdie. He was five under after five holes, seven under for the tournament, and in the lead. Strange, who was going along just fine at one under for the day and three under for the tournament, was shell-shocked. "I knew he was good," he said later. "I just didn't know how good."

Els came back to earth after that, but now he was the leader and everyone had to chase him. Watson, only one under starting the day, raced out in 32 to get to five under. If it was possible, the heat was worse than it had been all week. Walking down the 10th fairway, Watson was stopped by a USGA official. There had been a mix-up in the scorecards at the turn and Watson needed to recheck his card. He paused, checked, and signed. Then he rolled a 50-foot putt to within a foot and tapped in for par.

Grant Spaeth of the USGA breathed a sigh of relief. "I figured he'd three-putt and it would be our fault," he said to Dick Stroud, another USGA official.

Watson's putter had been behaving well. But on the back nine, it began to cough. A missed four-footer for birdie at 12, then a six-footer for par that slid low at 15, and a five-footer (set up by a poor chip) that cost him another bogey at 16. That dropped him back to three under, four behind Els. Watson looked frustrated and tired. But on 18, after a huge drive, he planted a wedge four feet from the flag. This time the putt went in — barely — and he had a 68 that put him at four under. Els would finish with a 65 and have the lead at seven-under 206, followed by Nobilo and Irwin at 208, and Montgomerie (after a 73) at 209 along with Watson and Loren Roberts (who had come out of the pack with an early 64). Strange was one shot farther back after his third straight 70. John Cook, after getting to five under on the front nine, had struggled on the back. He was at 211 with several other players.

It was a classic Open leader board. The leader was a future star, who was perhaps about to announce his arrival as a current star. There were a couple of foreigners no one knew much about (Nobilo and Montgomerie), a gaggle of past Open champions in their forties (Watson, Irwin, and Strange, who was still seven months from forty), and a longtime journeyman making a bid for late stardom (Roberts).

The heat and the pressure would all come into play on Sunday. Strange was still on the range at 7 o'clock Saturday night, still hitting balls, wanting to be certain that he left no stone unturned at this stage. Sarah sat in the bleachers and waited patiently for him to finish his work, content knowing that he was content. He was four shots back of Els but felt he had a real chance to win. He had analyzed the leader board carefully. After playing with Els, he knew the kid was capable of getting on a roll and leaving everyone in his dust.

But this was the last round of the Open, and that didn't happen very often. Neither Nobilo nor Montgomerie had been through the crucible on the last day of a major either. Watson could go either way. He was a streak player. Irwin made him nervous. He had been a hot player for several months, he had *three* Open titles, and he loved tough golf courses like this one. Roberts was also inexperienced.

As for Strange, well, he had been solid for three days. But there was one difference, he thought, between what he had done and what the others had done. "They've all had a hot streak," he said. "I haven't had one yet. If I can string a few birdies together, I can be right there."

He shook his head. "I wondered if I could get in this position again," he said. "It feels good just to have a chance."

He hit one final drive into the gloaming and looked up at Sarah. "This is the way it used to be," he said. "It's nice." Then he laughed. "And the best news of all is I won't have to stay up all night watching that white Bronco drive around."

It was after 8 o'clock by the time Strange left the putting green. For a third straight night, he slept soundly.

It is often said that the toughest eighteen holes in golf are the last eighteen at a U.S. Open. The combination of the heat, the rough, the greens, and the pressure leaves everyone drained even before the last round begins. Once it starts, it only gets worse.

Watson admitted on Saturday night that he was exhausted. "Linda and I went to the movies last night and I was so tired I could barely get out of my seat," he said, smiling. "I was dragging the last few holes today. These old bones are weary." Then, more seriously, he added: "I'm forty-four, I don't know how many chances I have left."

No one ever knows how many chances he is going to have to win a major. Certainly it was reasonable to assume that Els would have dozens, but once upon a time when Jerry Pate won the Open at twenty-two and Hal Sutton won the PGA at twenty-three they were considered locks to win several. Pate had spent most of the next ten years being injured, Sutton had spent most of his next ten years getting married. He had earned the nickname "Halimony," and had just gone down the aisle for the fourth time early in the year. He had been married a lot more often than he had contended in majors subsequent to his PGA victory.

Sutton's reputation as a ladies' man was legendary. One afternoon during the summer of '94, Sonya Toms, wife of young pro David Toms, walked into the bag storage room at a tournament looking to get something out of her husband's bag. Like Sutton, Sonya Toms is from Louisiana and she is, to put it mildly, a stunning woman.

When she walked into the bag room, she ran into one of the tour's veteran caddies, a man known to everyone simply as Sampson. When Sampson spotted Sonya Toms, he introduced himself and said, "Aren't you married to David Toms?"

"Yes I am," she said.

"You're from Louisiana, aren't you?"

"Why, yes, I am."

Sampson shook his head in amazement. "How in the world," he asked, "did old Hal Sutton miss *you?*"

Given the pressure, it wasn't all that surprising that Els would hit a wild hook off the first tee. What was a bit shocking was when USGA rules official Trey Holland (a urologist from Zionsville, Indiana, in real life) completely botched the subsequent ruling, granting Els relief because there was an ABC camera crane between his ball and the green. Holland didn't realize the crane could be moved, so he let Els move his ball. On ABC, Frank Hannigan expressed amazement that Holland could so clearly blow his first call of the day.

On Sunday at the Open, everyone feels pressure. A chagrined Holland later admitted to Rosburg that he should have had the crane, rather than Els's ball, moved.

Even with Holland's help, Els still made bogey on number one. Up ahead, Strange was doing what he had hoped he would do: getting on a little hot streak. He had gotten a scare at the first green when his 15-foot birdie putt rolled four feet past the hole.

Disturbed by the low scores on Friday and Saturday — Roberts's 64 and a bevy of 65s and 66s — the USGA had decided to roll the greens an extra time on Saturday night.

The players who had gone out early on Sunday had come back to the clubhouse with warnings about the speed of the greens. Paul Goydos, who made the cut and ended his first major in a tie for forty-fourth place, told several people that the golf course was completely different than it had been the last two days.

"The greens are right on the verge of being completely gone," he said. "They're so hot and dry they're starting to look white."

A number of the contenders, most notably Tom Watson, were extremely upset about the change. "If Mother Nature changes the golf course in mid-tournament, fine, there's nothing you can do about it," Watson said later. "But if it's a man-made change, I don't think that's right."

Watson was disturbed enough that when he walked into the scorer's trailer after finishing his round, he asked Judy Bell, a USGA vice president, what had been done to the greens. When Bell didn't answer him, Watson started to repeat the question. Then he looked up and saw the ABC camera and microphone that were positioned in the trailer. He swallowed his tongue and walked out, angry and tired.

Hale Irwin, who knew all about tough U.S. Open courses after having won the tournament three times, didn't have as visceral a reaction as Watson, but he did write a letter to Reg Murphy, the president of the USGA, when the tournament was over. After thanking Murphy for all the hard work the USGA put into the event, Irwin said, "Did you really want to make the golf course *that* hard?"

"I just thought it took something away from the golf," Irwin said later.

Strange didn't really care if the greens were double-rolled or triple-rolled. As far as he was concerned, the harder the conditions were, the better it was for him. He had been through the Toughest Eighteen enough times that he figured a white-hot golf course was going to hurt others more than it hurt him.

But as he looked at the four-foot par putt at number one, he wasn't feeling quite so confident. The putt was straight downhill, and he could see that there wasn't a single blade of grass on the green that would slow the ball if it didn't hit the cup. "The odds were good if I missed, I was going to miss the one coming back," he said. "Because it might easily have gone ten feet past. I knew I had to make it because if I started the day with a damn four-putt, things probably weren't going to go my way after that."

The putt clipped the side of the hole and dropped in. Strange breathed a sigh of relief. Given that reprieve, he proceeded to birdie three of the next four holes. When his three-footer dropped at number five, he was six under par for the tournament and, since Els was one over for the day, he was tied for the lead. Strange looked at the leader board and felt a chill go through him. There was lots of golf to be played, but he had put together the hot streak he needed. The game was on.

It stayed on throughout the stifling afternoon. Els made a nervy eight-foot putt at number four to take the lead back at seven under. Montgomerie, who had seemed the most likely candidate to fade in the heat, given his florid complexion and fairly ample girth, birdied the fourth and then rolled in a 30-footer at the sixth. That got him to six under just as Strange was missing the green at the par-three eighth and making a bogey. Now it was Els at seven, Montgomerie at six, and Strange at five.

Watson was fading, perhaps because of exhaustion, or perhaps because of another balky putting Sunday. He missed the green at number one and made bogey, came back with a 35-footer at number four, but then missed another green at six and bogeyed to drop to three under. He never made a move after that.

With the crowds screaming for Watson to make a move, his playing partner, Loren Roberts, was going almost unnoticed. How unnoticed? During the first five holes, ABC managed to show every one of Watson's swings. Roberts first appeared on camera on the sixth tee. He was plugging along at even par for the day when he missed the green at eight and caught the bunker. A bogey seemed likely and that would be the end for Mr. Roberts. Except for one thing: Roberts holed the bunker shot for a birdie. Watson saw his eyes light up. "On the last day of a major, sometimes one shot will get you going," he said. "That was the one shot for Loren."

A birdie at the par-five ninth got Roberts to six under. Now everyone was on the seesaw. Els bogeyed and Montgomerie birdied. Montgomerie led by one. They swapped places again. Roberts bogeyed 10, but birdied 11. Els was seven, Montgomerie and Roberts six.

Strange knew he was running out of holes. He had made a disappointing par at the ninth. Standing on the 10th tee, he and caddy Craig Cimarillo had a long conversation about what club to hit. The 10th is one of the toughest driving holes on the course. It has a narrow land-ing area, and if you end up in the rough, there is no chance to get to the green. Strange had bogeyed the hole Friday and Saturday. Cimar-illo was convinced he needed to chance a three-wood to get the ball far enough down the fairway. Strange didn't want any part of the rough.

He won the argument — naturally — and hit a solid two-iron down the middle. But Cimarillo's concern about being too far back was justified. Strange's five-iron second shot came up short and he had to work hard to make a bogey. Now he was three back with just eight to play.

Strange didn't panic. He swished a 15-foot birdie putt at 11 and pumped his putter for emphasis. Two back. Lots of time left. He parred 12. At the par-three 13th, with 166 yards to the front, he chose a six-iron. As soon as the ball came off the club, Strange knew he had made a horrible mistake. The ball went right of the green and right of the bunker to an almost impossible spot.

"Oh God no, not now," Strange said.

It was a shot he never would have hit at his peak in the '80s and he knew it. "I didn't believe in my swing enough in that situation," he said. "Sometimes, when you haven't been in the hunt for a while, you don't trust your swing at key moments the way you need to. It was the kind of shot I've hit at times the last few years, the kind where I just want to go hide my head somewhere because I'm so embarrassed. It was just a pure flame-out right, a terrible shot."

Again, he had to work for bogey. Again, the deficit was three. Again, he came back with a birdie on the next hole. He checked the leader board as he waited for Steve Lowery to putt out. Roberts was now at seven, Els and Montgomerie at six. Strange and Cimarillo looked at one another. They both had the same thought: five was going to be the number. If Strange could play the last four holes even par, he would do no worse than a playoff. Why they both thought that at that moment, neither could explain, but they did. They knew that 15, 16, and 18 were tough holes, easy holes to bogey under pressure.

As they walked onto the 15th tee, Cimarillo said softly, "Next two holes is the deal."

Strange didn't need to be told that. They had to wait on the tee for the group in front of them, just as they had waited on 13. And, just as on 13, Strange made a swing he regretted, pushing his driver into the deep rough. He had no choice but to lay up and his wedge came up 20 feet short. The par putt was inches short. Now pars wouldn't be good enough.

He was talking to himself on the 16th tee, imploring himself to suck it up for the last three holes. He couldn't play safe now and hit the ball at the middle of the green. His three-iron started at the flag, but sailed left into the bunker. Another bogey. Cimarillo had been right. Those two holes had been the deal. He parred 17, then made a brilliant birdie at 18. A satisfying finish, though not the one he had dreamed about. He shook his fist and waved his hat to the crowd. He had played well, shooting four straight rounds of 70. That made him the first man to shoot four straight sub-par rounds in an Open at Oakmont.

He knew he wouldn't win, though. Els was six under through 16, Roberts was six under through 17. A few minutes after Strange walked off the green, Montgomerie tapped in his final putt for a 70 that put him at 279 — one shot better than Strange. That made it official. Strange couldn't win. At the USGA's request, he went to the interview room to talk about what had gone right and what had gone wrong.

He had lost the Open, for all intents and purposes, with two swings: the six-iron at 13 and the driver at 15. The bogey at 16 was the product of having to try and make birdie. He hadn't been under that kind of pressure in so long that his swing wasn't quite as solid as it needed to be.

While Strange talked, the melodrama continued on the 18th. Roberts had now become the crowd's darling because he was the last American hope. Montgomerie was in at 279. Strange was at 280, John Cook at 282. Greg Norman, who had lurked on the fringes of contention all week but never really made a move, was at 283 along with young Clark Dennis. Watson would join them there shortly.

Roberts needed a par at 18 to finish at 278 — six under. Els was two holes back, also at six under. As Roberts walked onto the 18th green, having hit his second shot just over the putting surface, the outdated "USA" chant went up in the grandstands. Foreign players were dominating the Masters and the British Open and had won two of the last four PGAs. The Open was the last bastion of American dominance. Only one foreigner — David Graham in 1981 — had won the Open since 1965. That string was in serious jeopardy. Roberts was the last hope.

His chip from behind the green rolled four feet past the cup. If he made the putt, Els would have to birdie 17 or 18 to win, or par them both to tie. Montgomerie would be eliminated. Roberts is known on tour as the Reverend One Putt, because of his silky smooth putting stroke. Knowing what was at stake, he took plenty of time looking the putt over. Maybe too much time. The stroke he put on the putt was anything but silky. After staying calm all day, he couldn't get the putter through the ball one last time. The putt was a weak push, short and right. Loud groans enveloped the green as Roberts tapped in.

"I'm not going to lie to you," Roberts said later. "I had trouble getting the putter back. I knew what the putt meant."

Now the tournament belonged to Els. He had gotten another lucky break at 17, when his drive had gone way left behind the grandstand. This time, Dr. Holland knew what he was doing when he awarded him a favorable drop because he had no choice — the ball had landed in a clearly marked-off drop area. Els got such a favorable drop that he almost made birdie. Even so, the par left him with a one-shot lead as he walked to the 18th tee. Roberts's 18th-hole bogey was on the board to the right of the tee, so Els could see that a par would win the tournament.

Only he wasn't looking.

Golfers often say that they play against the golf course, not one another. There is certainly truth to that. But not on the last day of a tournament — especially a major — not on the last nine holes and certainly not on the 18th tee of the U.S. Open. The notion of just playing your game is fine on Thursday, Friday, maybe even Saturday. But not on Sunday. And not on Sunday at 6 P.M.

Els didn't look. So he foolishly took his driver out, thinking he needed a birdie to win, and hit a wild hook left that was reminiscent of his drive at number one. With no camera cranes around, Els couldn't turn to Dr. Holland for help. He pitched onto the fairway and caught his first bad break of the day — the ball landed smack in the middle of a divot. That made it almost impossible to chip close and he didn't, leaving himself 20 feet for par. The putt stayed low all the way. No chance. Now Els had to make a four-footer for bogey just to tie Montgomerie and Roberts.

Els is young and he had made an immature mistake on the tee. But he also has the guts of a champion. Even unnerved, he rolled in a putt almost identical to the one Roberts had missed. He was at 279 with Roberts and Montgomerie. Strange and Cimarillo had been right back on the 14th green. The number was five.

It would be the first three-way U.S. Open playoff since Julius Boros had beaten Jacky Cupit and Arnold Palmer in 1963. Strange watched the wild finish as he was cleaning out his locker. Sarah was waiting outside. She had called home shortly after he finished to tell her parents that she was changing her plans. Originally, she had planned to fly home that night while Curtis went on to an outing on Long Island the next day. "I just can't leave him," she told her parents. They understood.

He had missed the playoff by one shot. Intellectually, he knew that it was silly to what-if. After all, what if he hadn't made his 12-foot par putt at 17 or the birdie at 18? Then he would have been three shots out of the playoff. Anytime you hit 280 shots in a golf tournament, there are going to be a few you want back. What if Els had looked at the scoreboard at 18? He might easily have finished at six.

But those were all ifs and buts. The bottom line was that Strange had played his heart out and needed exactly one shot back. He didn't have it. He stood up to go meet Sarah. "I really wish," he said softly, "that someone had finished at six or seven. Right now, I'm okay. But I know tonight, it's really going to hurt."

Sarah already knew that. Which is why she was staying.

The eighteen-hole playoff may be the biggest anachronism in sports today. It is a complete anticlimax and almost always produces golf that ranges from mediocre to awful. The players are drained and exhausted. They have built to an emotional peak on Sunday, then they have to come back Monday and start from the first hole again.

Every other major has abandoned the eighteen-hole playoff. The Masters and the PGA go to sudden death, the British Open has a four-hole format that may be the best tiebreaker of all. By playing four holes you eliminate the notion that one lucky shot — or one poor one — will decide the title but you still give everyone the climax they want on Sunday evening.

The USGA insists on eighteen holes, claiming it is the truest test. What is seventy-two holes? An untrue test? And so, everyone has to come back on Monday. Except a lot of fans don't — can't — and many of the volunteers who give up a week in their lives to work at the tournament also have to return to work.

Oakmont '94 was a classic eighteen-hole playoff — only worse. The winner — Els — triple-bogeyed the second hole. Montgomerie, exhausted by the heat, was never a factor, shooting an embarrassing 78. Roberts led much of the day, but couldn't hang on down the stretch.

Roberts did make a couple of gutsy putts, first at the 18th to tie Els at 74 and extend the playoff into sudden death (how come sudden death is okay after ninety holes but not seventy-two?) and then on the first sudden-death hole, the 10th. America missed that putt since ABC cut away for an update on O. J. Somehow that was appropriate, since the playoff was the same kind of endless water torture that the white Bronco chase had been.

Roberts finally put everyone out of their overheated misery by making a bogey on the 11th hole and Els was the youngest U.S. Open champion since Jerry Pate in 1976. It was a thudlike ending after four days of tension and suspense. The moral of the story is simple: golf tournaments are meant to be played in four days. Period.

17

NIKE DAZE

IT IS ABOUT FIVE HUNDRED MILES from the first tee at Oakmont Country Club to the first tee at Prestonwood Country Club in Cary, North Carolina.

In a golf sense, the distance is closer to a million miles. While the members at Oakmont were taking back their golf course from the millionaires of the PGA Tour, the members at Prestonwood were making way for 144 members of the Nike Tour, a group whose total net worth was probably slightly higher than that of Ernie Els.

In strict golf terms, this was not an exaggeration. While Els had left Oakmont with a check for $300,000 as the Open winner, the field that gathered at Prestonwood for the Nike Carolina Classic would play for a *total* purse of $200,000.

And they would play very hard for that money.

The Nike Tour, originally called the Hogan Tour, was created by the PGA Tour in 1990 to give younger players a proving ground where they could sharpen and improve their games until they were ready for, as Brian Henninger liked to call it, "the big boy tour."

The big boys are Hyatt, Marriott, and the Ritz; Nike is Budgetel and Motel Six. The big boys are The Palm and Ruth's Chris; Nike is McDonald's and Hardee's. The big boys are New York, Chicago, L.A; Nike is Raleigh, Knoxville, Shreveport.

In all, the concept had worked . . . sort of. The new tour was thriving, even though the Hogan Company had been forced to drop out after 1992 and had been replaced as title sponsor by Nike. Purses had risen on the tour from a total of $3 million in the first year to almost

$5.7 million in '94. Most tournaments the first year had been fifty-four holes, with purses ranging from $100,000 to $150,000. Now most tournaments were seventy-two holes with prize money of $200,000, and a season-ending championship with a $225,000 purse had been added.

There were glitches. The goal was to have at least thirty tournaments each year, but in 1994, sponsors had been rounded up for only twenty-eight. And while the tour had certainly become a place for younger players to hone their games — John Daly, Jeff Maggert, Tom Lehman, Mike Springer, Brian Henninger, and Paul Goydos are some of the players who came up the Hogan/Nike route — it had also become a fallback for older players who had lost their PGA Tour cards. That wasn't necessarily a bad thing, unless the older players became *too* prevalent. In 1994, the Nike top ten included players like Chris Perry, Tommy Armour III, Skip Kendall, Jim Carter, and Jerry Haas. Only Kendall was under thirty at the start of the year — and he turned thirty in September. All of them had been on tour and had lost their cards. In all, seven of the top-ten money winners were former tour players.

The goal for players on the Nike Tour is simple: get out. No one wants to be referred to as a Nike Tour veteran. The top-ten players on the Nike money list get big boy cards for the following year. The first five are totally exempt, the next five are fitted in with the Q-School graduates. Those who finish eleventh to twenty-fifth go straight to the Q-School finals. And twenty-sixth to fiftieth in Nike world gets you straight to the second stage.

In short, everyone is playing more for the escape route than for the money.

Jeff Cook certainly felt that way. He was beginning to feel like a Nike veteran, and it was not a feeling he enjoyed. He had come back from overseas to join the Hogan Tour in 1990. Three years later, he had gotten his card and had played with the big boys in 1993, finishing 164th on the money list. That put him back in Q-School, where his three-putt bogey on the 107th of the 108 holes had left him one shot away from getting his card back.

Cook had considered returning to the Asian Tour, one of many overseas proving grounds available for nontour players, after Q-

School but decided to take his medicine and go back to Nike because he thought that was still his best route back to the tour. He also decided that he needed to improve his golf swing and had gone to see David Leadbetter.

Cook's friends were surprised when they heard that Cook was working with Leadbetter. For one thing, Cook had never been very big on lessons. He was self-taught as a kid and, although he had worked at times with different people, he had never been the type to seek out a guru. The other surprise was that Leadbetter, teacher to the stars — Faldo and Price — would have time for Jeff Cook. He did, though, and Cook, for $150 a lesson, went to work with him.

At first, he thought he had found golf nirvana. Leadbetter told him he hadn't even scratched his potential and that he didn't think he would need as much work as some other players did because he seemed to understand the golf swing quite well. Cook was like a little kid with a new toy.

Only the toy proved difficult to use. The changes Leadbetter wanted weren't easy to execute, and Cook's game seemed to be going in the wrong direction. When he told Leadbetter that, the teacher told him, "You may take two steps back before you take three forward."

How soon would the steps forward come? It was hard to say. It could be a month, six months, a year. By the time the weather turned hot, Cook felt like he was out of time. He liked Leadbetter and appreciated his making time for him, but he was hitting the ball worse, rather than better. When he and Henninger roomed together in April at the Nike tournament in Shreveport, Henninger was appalled by what he saw.

"You're all messed up with all this mechanical [read, Leadbetter] stuff," Henninger told him. "You have a good golf swing. Have faith in it."

Cook wanted to have faith in Leadbetter. But by June, he was eighty-third on the Nike money list and going nowhere fast. He decided it was time to listen to Henninger and his own instincts. He would bag the Leadbetter drills and all the mechanical moves he had been trying to make. He couldn't be Nick Faldo. The next best thing was to go back to being Jeff Cook.

It worked during the first round at the Carolina Classic. The tournament did have one thing in common with the Open — brutal heat. Cook, playing early, never came close to a bogey all day and shot 66. That put him in third place, one behind the co-leaders. It also put a smile on his face for the first time in a while.

"You know, sitting and watching Brian on that last day in Atlanta was great and awful at the same time," he said that night. "I mean, I was so nervous and excited it was like I was playing that eighteenth hole with him. But it also made me realize that I *wasn't* playing that eighteenth hole. I was sitting in Greenville, South Carolina, at another Nike Tournament and I didn't want to be there. I wanted to be out there on the real tour, which is where I honestly feel I belong.

"I know I'm good enough to play out there. I had chances last year to break through and just didn't do it. That's no one's fault but my own, but I want to get back there and have a chance to prove myself — more for myself than for anybody else. I just turned thirty-three in April. The time for me is now. It has to be."

Cook is not like Henninger. He doesn't burn to be a star. He doesn't lie awake in bed at night after a bad round beating himself up. Perhaps that is because he considers himself lucky to have gotten as much out of golf as he has; perhaps it is because he has beaten cancer. Perhaps it is just different personalities. Cook would like to play well; Henninger *needs* to play well. Henninger's ultimate goal is to win consistently on tour; Cook's is to return to Indiana University as the golf coach.

Cook certainly didn't want to be back on the Nike Tour, driving his car from event to event, playing for 20 percent of the prize money he had played for the year before. He had played with Tom Watson and Tom Kite in 1993. During the first two rounds at Prestonwood his playing partners were Tad Holloway and Tom Scherrer. There are no gallery ropes on the Nike Tour because they aren't necessary. Walking the fairways at a Nike event feels a little bit like being at Q-School. It is quiet most of the time. The only sounds are of golf balls being hit, often followed by shrieks of pain or groans of disgust. The overall feeling is one of loneliness.

That feeling may explain why the Nike Tour had twice as many participants in its Bible study group most weeks than the regular tour. The need to feel as if someone was watching over you seemed to be stronger on a tour where — at least in a tangible sense — almost no one was watching.

Cook wasn't a Bible study participant. All he wanted was to play good golf. But it wasn't easy. On day two at Prestonwood, he started fast, with two birdies in five holes, and led the golf tournament. Then it all fell apart. His putter went south for several holes. He bogeyed five of the next seven holes, three-putting three times. By the time his putter came back to life, he was hitting the ball all over Prestonwood's wide fairways and needed the putter to salvage pars. A 10-foot par putt at the last hole went in, giving him a 75 that left him four shots behind the leaders, Skip Kendall and Patrick Bates.

The weekend didn't go much better. Cook shot 70 on Saturday but faded to 76 on Sunday. There isn't as much cash to spend on the Nike Tour on Sundays as there is on the regular tour, but Cook spent some. While Kendall was holding up the $36,000 first prize check, Cook was walking out the door with $1,390 to show for the week, having finished in a tie for twenty-sixth place. Sadly, that wouldn't be anywhere close to his worst week. By year's end, he would miss nine of twenty-four cuts.

He didn't throw any clubs when it was over on Sunday or pout or vow never to play the game again. But the grind was wearing on him. He wondered why golf was so hard right now. "This is typical of the way things have gone for me," he said. "If I hit the ball well, I can't putt. If I putt, I can't hit the ball." He smiled. "I guess that sounds exactly the same as every golfer who has ever played the game. I know I can play. I *know* I'm better than the eighty-third best player on the Nike Tour. I've been up there with the big boys and I still believe I've got the game to play with them. But saying it and doing it are two different things."

He climbed into his car. He was going home for a week to Indianapolis and then to the next tour stop in St. Louis. There were a lot of miles ahead.

Mike Donald missed his driving days. Of course that didn't mean he drove when he was on the Nike Tour. It just meant that when he looked back on his early days on tour, the memories made him smile.

"I remember one year I left Florida to drive to California a couple of days before New Year's," he said. "I spent New Year's Eve in the middle of a blizzard in an $18-a-night motel room in Odessa, Texas. I'll never forget sitting there watching the ball come down in Times Square with nothing but snow outside the window. But I didn't mind. I was on my way to start the year playing golf and I was psyched, excited. All that mattered was getting to the next tournament."

Donald had played a lot of golf since then and, since his famous "almost" at the U.S. Open in 1990, not very much of it had been at a level he liked. When the Q-School ended his 1993 on one more sour note, he decided to go home, throw his clubs in the back of a closet, and not even think about golf for a long time.

A long time lasted ten days.

For all his talk about walking away and not needing the life on tour anymore, Donald was, at heart, a golfer. He was no different than Curtis Strange, who often said, "You know, I tell people I'd never stay out here and struggle, but the truth is I probably would. Golf is what I eat, drink, sleep, and dream about. I can't imagine doing anything else."

Donald had never done anything else and, still eighteen months shy of his fortieth birthday, had no reason to think it was time to do something else. Still, he dreaded writing letters asking for sponsors' exemptions again the way he had done in 1992, and he knew that he wouldn't get nearly as many positive responses as he had gotten back then. "I mean, how many times can you say to a guy, 'Sure, come on back'?" Donald said. "There are young players out here who probably deserve the exemptions more than I do."

Donald knew he would get into some tournaments without asking for an exemption. As a player who had won on the PGA Tour he still had playing status as a past champion and smaller events like Hattiesburg, the B.C. Open, the Hardee's Classic, and the Buick Southern Open would probably be available to him. So would Anheuser-Busch, the tournament he had won. Anything else would come from sitting down at his little computer and writing letters. Even after that, Donald knew that if he wanted to play a full schedule, he would have to go the Nike route.

Like Henninger, he was confused about which tour to focus on: Did he play on the big tour every chance he got and just play a few

Nike events to stay sharp, or did he go the Nike route all the way and hope he could finish in the top ten and get back his playing privileges that way?

"Something has to happen this year one way or the other," he said in February. "I can't just go on in limbo, and I certainly don't want to play Nike full-time when I'm forty. I mean, sooner or later, no matter how much you want to play you have to look in the mirror and say it's time to go home."

The first five months of the year didn't provide much evidence that Donald was turning it around. He got into Pebble Beach and L.A. and missed both cuts. He got into his hometown tournament, the Honda, and made the cut — ending a string of thirteen straight misses that dated to the previous July — then shot 78 on the third day and finished tied for fifty-ninth.

He tried the Nike Tour after that and finished eighth in his first tournament, the Louisiana Open. But it was hard to stay enthusiastic walking the empty fairways and showing up each week in a locker room filled with strange faces.

About the only thing Donald seemed able to get in buckets was publicity, whether he wanted it or not. In February, he was the subject of a lengthy *New York Times* profile written by Larry Dorman, chronicling his life and times since the near-miss of 1990. That story led to several calls from people who thought he needed financial backing to get back on tour. The story said he had lost his sponsors — meaning his club, ball, and cap deals. Many readers thought that meant he was without financial backers. Donald had three offers from potential "sponsors" in a week. One guy wanted to sell 500,000 $1 shares in Mike Donald.

Donald thanked them all, explained that what he needed was a few more birdies, not a few more bucks, and went back to work. Then came a phone call from CBS *Sunday Morning.* They had read the story too and wanted to do their own piece. Donald never says no to the media; it just isn't in his nature to say no to people. This time he said no. He'd had enough, he told the producer; he was flattered by the interest, but he just didn't want to go through recounting the whole story again. The producer persisted. Politely, Donald said no, absolutely not.

The next day CBS called again. The producer understood why Donald didn't want to tell the story again, but there were a lot of people out there who still hadn't heard it. Donald gritted his teeth. No. "It's been four years," he said.

The phone rang again the next day. Donald probably should have taken his old pal Fred Couples's advice and not have answered "because there might be someone there." There was. The producer. Donald's willpower broke. Okay, he said, he would do it. He hung up and immediately regretted saying yes.

The crew followed him around during the Honda Classic. Everywhere Donald went, a camera crew trailed him. He was embarrassed. Here he was in the field on a sponsor's exemption and he had his very own network camera crew following in his wake. The piece ran on Masters Sunday. Donald was sitting in the living room with his father when the piece came on. He sat and listened for a couple of minutes, saw a shot of his mom in the gallery at Medinah, and decided he'd seen enough. He left the room.

His father told him the piece was well done, and when the producer sent him a copy of the tape, he did finally look at it. There were more calls after that, people wanting to help. Donald didn't need help — except with his game. When, he wondered, would he begin to go forward with his life again rather than constantly being asked to go backward?

He had asked for a sponsor's exemption for the Kemper Open, a tournament where he had often played well. Ben Brundred, the tournament director, was a friend, someone who had gone out of his way to help him in the past. Early in May, Brundred called to say he was sorry, but he didn't have a spot for him. Too many young players needed exemptions. Donald understood. He thanked Brundred for considering him and made plans to play the Nike event in Ohio that week.

But just before he left for the tournament, Donald got another call from Brundred. There had been some late dropouts and a spot had opened up. Did he still want to play? You bet he did. Donald changed his plans and flew to Washington Tuesday afternoon. At that moment he had played in four big tour events all year, and the $2,387 he had made at the Honda was all he had to show for it.

He shot 71 the first day at the Kemper, nothing spectacular, but for the first time in what seemed like forever, he actually made some putts. It was a day that easily could have been another in a long line of 74s. He was encouraged. The next day was a little better — 70. Not only did he make the cut, he made it with room to spare.

He started solidly on Saturday, but made a horrid double bogey at the easy par-five sixth hole, after pushing his drive into a creek. He took off his shoes and socks and rolled up his pants to try and slash the ball out. The ball never moved. Donald picked it up, dropped it — he was now lying four — hit his fifth shot just short of the green, then made a good up and down for seven. Watching all this, Mike Hulbert, his playing partner, shook his head. "Oh no," he said, "not again."

Like a lot of people on tour, Hulbert found it tough to watch Donald struggle. Only this time, it didn't happen again. Donald made a good save for par at the seventh, then birdied the ninth. He salvaged 72 out of the day and stayed in contention. The next day, he got to four under par at one point before a double bogey at 17 knocked him back to two under. He had taken a risk at 17, going for a flag that was up front, close to the water. His thinking had been that if he made one more birdie, he would finish in the top ten and that would not only give him his biggest check in three years, but would automatically get him into Westchester the next week.

The double bogey cost him about $15,000, but he still finished tied for eighteenth and made $16,380. More important than any of that was the way it felt. He was a golfer again, hitting the ball the way he wanted to hit it, feeling as if he could make putts, getting that tingle of being in contention on Sunday for the first time in a long time.

"I'm not back yet, not by any means," he said. "But this shows me I can still play the game, that I'm not just some guy who once had a good U.S. Open. It tells me that if I keep working, good things are going to happen for me eventually."

The next day, he went to Westchester to play in the qualifying tournament and four-spotted. Then he played thirty-six holes of U.S. Open qualifying the next day. He didn't qualify there, perhaps because he had played seven rounds of golf in six days after a full year of rarely playing more than two rounds in a week.

There was no doubt about one thing: Donald wanted to play golf.

On the weeks that he couldn't get in on the big tour, he played the Nike Tour. He began to make more cuts. Progress was slow, but there was progress. By summer's end, he had played twenty-four tournaments — twelve regular tour, twelve Nike. Before the year was over, he would play in at least thirty events, as many as 90 percent of the players on tour.

He would put the clubs away again in December. Probably, for at least a week.

18

TWO HANDS ON THE JUG

IN 1994, THERE WERE THREE WEEKS between the U.S. Open and the British Open. The tour stopped in Hartford (the Canon Hartford Open), Chicago (Motorola Western), and Williamsburg (Anheuser-Busch) between majors. Most players who were going to play in the British played either Hartford or Chicago and skipped Williamsburg, where the weather is usually the hottest it gets all year, not exactly perfect preparation for the weather in Scotland.

In order to try and lure players to Williamsburg, tournament organizers charter two planes on Sunday to get players to flights in New York and Boston so they can be on-site at the British on Monday. That gives them a full day to deal with jet lag and then practice on Tuesday and Wednesday.

Even with that perk, most top players skip Williamsburg and either rest or fly over early to get acclimated to the weather and the time change. Davis Love played Williamsburg in 1994, but knew he probably should not have. "The people here are just so nice, it's very hard to say no to them," he said. "And Lexie loves the theme parks."

Some players were in Williamsburg because they had no intention of making the overseas trips. For American players, the British Open is the most inconvenient tournament of the year. The trip is the longest and the most difficult; there are fewer fully exempt spots available because the tournament spreads its exemptions out among the various tours worldwide; and it comes smack in the middle of the summer at a time when a lot of players figure a break is going to be more valuable than trying to play a different game — links golf means bump-

and-run shots along the ground and dealing with wind and rain and cold and not being able to just fire at flags, because the ball doesn't stop the way it does on American greens — after a long, expensive, exhausting trip.

Curtis Strange, Hale Irwin, Fred Couples, and Scott Hoch were among the fully exempt Americans who said thanks, but no thanks, for different reasons in 1994. Billy Andrade and Jeff Sluman also passed because they would have had to go over a week early to qualify and they decided that was just too much effort. A number of other nonexempt Americans made the same decision.

Some Americans will go to the British Open every year come hell or high water. "You can't win the damn tournament if you don't enter it," Tom Kite said, clearly disgusted with some of his countrymen who no-showed.

Peter Jacobsen, nonexempt from the British for the first time in a number of years, flew over to play qualifying. "I wouldn't miss this for the world," he said. "There's no tournament like this one. This is where the whole thing began."

That was the attitude of most of the top Americans, from Arnold Palmer to Jack Nicklaus to Tom Watson to Fuzzy Zoeller to Tom Kite to younger players like Davis Love and Brad Faxon. If you were a golfer and you had a chance to play in the oldest championship of them all, you played.

"What happens with a lot of guys is they come over here dreading all the inconveniences and end up falling in love with the whole thing," Watson said. "That's what happened to me. When I first came over here, I said, 'This isn't golf,' hitting the ball on the ground and watching balls take crazy bounces all over the place. After a few years I realized I was wrong. This *is* golf. We changed the game, not them."

There is no atmosphere like that of the British Open. The crowds are more knowledgeable, they come out in droves regardless of the weather, and the history and tradition of the courses the tournament is played on is evident from the first tee to the 18th green. They love golf and golfers at the British Open in a way that is entirely different from Americans. The Brits love stars, no doubt about it, but in the end, they love the game most of all.

That's why the winner of the Open Championship is introduced simply as "the champion golfer of the year" during the awards ceremony. Nothing more needs to be said.

Of course, like any major championship, the British always produces some kind of pretournament controversy. In 1994, that controversy sprang up even before most of the players had arrived in Scotland.

On the morning of July 7, Tim Finchem called PGA Tour headquarters, the way he always did from the road, to check messages and to see if anyone on his staff needed him for any reason. He was in Jackson Hole, Wyoming, en route back from a trip to Los Angeles.

His secretary, Cathie Hurlburt, told him that one staff member had an urgent need to talk to him: John Morris, the vice president of communications. "There's some kind of story with John Daly," Hurlburt said.

Finchem groaned. Like everyone else in golf, he knew that Daly was a time bomb that could explode at any minute. He hoped whatever it was that would cause Morris to need him wasn't that big a deal. And yet he knew that Morris was about as low key as anyone who worked for him and that if this issue was a minor one, he would wait until Finchem got back to Ponte Vedra to talk to him about it.

This couldn't wait. Morris got on the phone and began reading Finchem a story that had moved on the wire that morning. It quoted from a story in a British tabloid, the *Sun.* According to the *Sun,* Daly, who was playing in the Scottish Open, had claimed a few days earlier that "plenty of guys on the PGA Tour do drugs and all sorts of crazy things." He had added, "I'm not the only one who has had substance-abuse problems out here by any means." He went on to say that he favored drug testing on tour, especially since "I know I'm one of the people who would test clean."

There was more, but Finchem had heard enough. Very few things shake him, but he knew as soon as Morris began reading that he — and the tour — had a problem. Maybe this was another case of a British tabloid turning an innocuous quote into a headline. Maybe someone had put words in Daly's mouth. That was the best-case scenario. The worst-case scenario was simple: Daly had been quoted accurately. In that case, Finchem had the first crisis of his term as commissioner on his hands.

Before he passed judgment on that, he needed more information. He asked Morris to track down a copy of the *Sun* story and gather any other clips or stories that came across the wire. He also told him to contact Marty Caffey and Wes Seeley, the on-site media officials at the Anheuser-Busch Classic, which was starting that day in Williamsburg, and have them monitor player response to the story once it started making the rounds. He knew there was going to be a lot of angry reaction to Daly's comments. He thought briefly about going to Williamsburg, then decided against it. He didn't want to make the story any bigger than it was going to be.

By that afternoon, he knew he was dealing with the worst-case scenario. Not only was the story accurate, the quotes were on tape. Finchem asked Bill Calfee and Sid Wilson, his player relations liaisons, to contact Daly or his people and tell them Finchem wanted to meet with him as soon as he arrived at Turnberry the next week for the British Open. He also told Morris to tell the media he would have no comment on the matter until he met with Daly.

Finchem's instinct about the players being angry was (surprise) correct. On Saturday afternoon, during ESPN's telecast of the third round of the Anheuser-Busch, Curtis Strange came up to the booth to sit in with Jim Kelly and Gary Koch. Strange had known all week that he was going to spend some time doing TV. Since he lived about a mile from the clubhouse at the tournament site, Kingsmill Plantation, and had a contract with the development, he was the unofficial host of the tournament.

Strange was furious when he heard what Daly had said. But he didn't want to go on TV and make some half-cocked remark that wouldn't be reflective of how all the players felt. So, before he played Saturday morning, he went up and down the practice tee, asking other players what they thought. Their reaction was unanimous: if he really said that, he's got some serious explaining to do.

Of all the major sports, golf is the one least likely to have a drug problem for several reasons. Like tennis, it is an individual sport, meaning there is almost no way to cover up a bad performance or claim an injury and still make a living. In fact, the notion that you have to play to get paid is even stronger in golf because there are no appearance fees on the U.S. tour that can guarantee a drug-troubled star income, and you have to play well for at least thirty-six holes every week to make any money at all.

Beyond that, golfers are older, as a group, than other athletes. Most are married and have children and many of them bring their families on the road with them, especially during the summer months. What's more, golf is the *only* sport in the world that asks the athletes to report to work at 7 o'clock in the morning at least once a week, sometimes as many as three days a week. It is tough to be a regular partyer and a regular winner in golf.

Are there golfers who have tried drugs, some who have used them at various times? Of course. Are there some golfers who drink too much? Of course. Daly was one example of the latter. Have there been players who have experimented with performance-enhancing drugs (like beta-blockers) over the years? Certainly. Still, it is not going out on a limb to say that fewer golfers use drugs than most segments of society. They simply can't afford to.

But as soon as Daly raised the specter of drug use, anyone who said that drugs weren't a problem on tour was going to be judged by many as either covering up or being an apologist. Because Daly was such a big name and, ironically, because he had experience with substance abuse, his words would carry weight with some people. That's what upset the players. They knew that some people were going to believe Daly no matter what. He had given the tour a black eye, and putting makeup on it wasn't going to make the swelling go down quickly.

By the time Strange joined Kelly and Koch, he knew what he wanted to say. Kelly pulled no punches, raising the Daly issue right away. "Hi, Jim, nice to see you too," Strange said, laughing. Then he answered the question: "I've talked to a lot of the guys about this today," he said, "and I think they all feel about the same way I do, which is that they wish John Daly would crawl back under that rock he came out from." He paused. "What's really disturbing about this is that by making comments like this, John is capable of tearing down in a few minutes what Jack Nicklaus and Arnold Palmer have worked thirty-five years to build, and that's the image people have of the PGA Tour. I don't think that's fair."

It was the line about crawling out from under a rock that received the widest play in the media during the days and weeks that followed. But the important point was the second one: players like Palmer and Nicklaus and Tom Watson (and dozens of others) had spent years building the image of golfers as gentlemen and sportsmen and gracious winners and losers.

It may be corny to think like that, but part of golf's magic is the notion that the players respect one another. In 1991, Watson and Nicklaus were paired together for the second round at the Masters. Watson shot 68 that day to lead the tournament. As he and Nicklaus walked up the 18th fairway, the huge gallery was standing and clapping for both men. Always a brisk walker, Watson paused as he got near the green to wait for Nicklaus.

Nicklaus stopped. "You go first," he said.

"We'll go together."

"You're the one leading the golf tournament."

"You're Jack Nicklaus."

They actually stood there for a moment, laughing, each trying to push the other forward. Finally, they walked onto the green together, and if you didn't get chills you were in the wrong place.

That was the kind of feeling golfers had for one another and the kind of scene golf fans thought made the game special. Now John Daly had said they were all on drugs. Except for him of course.

Davis Love, one of the least confrontational people on the tour, shook his head when he thought about what Daly might face when he reached Turnberry the next week. "I know a lot of guys have a lot of questions," he said, "and he better be ready with some answers."

It was Greg Norman who asked the first question. "What the hell could you have been thinking?"

He was standing on the putting green behind the new Japanese-built clubhouse at Turnberry. It was Monday afternoon and players were just starting to trickle in to begin preparing for the British Open. Norman had been in Europe for almost a week and had read all the stories about Daly's comments. When he walked onto the putting green, there was Daly. Norman walked over to Daly and asked the question.

Daly looked up from what he was doing, surprised, no doubt, by the rancor in Norman's voice. "What do you mean?" he asked.

"I mean, how could you say something like that, how could you make a blanket accusation like that? What in the world were you thinking about?"

Daly's round features clouded over. "Look, I'm sick and tired of everyone making me the bad guy on tour. I'm tired of people acting as if I'm the only one who has ever done anything wrong. So don't give me a hard time, I don't want to hear it."

It might have gotten more heated, but Daly turned around and left as soon as he was finished. Norman was tempted to follow him into the locker room but thought better of it. "It wasn't worth wasting my time," he said later. "And I didn't want to go in there and do something I might regret.

"I was livid with the guy, absolutely livid. How dare he say that any of us are on drugs. I'm not the one who beat up my wife; I'm not the one who is an alcoholic; I'm not the one who tears up rooms. It was just inexcusable."

Norman was especially sensitive to the drug issue because there had been wild rumors during his slump that he had a drug problem. One afternoon, when he picked up his then five-year-old son Gregory at school, the boy was crying when he got into the car. He had heard from other kids at school that his father was on drugs.

"Obviously, they got it from their parents," Norman said. "That's the part of being famous that's hard. If someone says something about you, okay, that's tough and you don't like it, but you develop a shell after a while. But when your kids start getting it, that's just not fair.

"People who don't know you read something in the paper, they believe it. The next thing you know it's become the gospel truth."

The story about the Norman-Daly confrontation spread through the locker room quickly. The line that kept being repeated was "I'm tired of everyone making me the bad guy on tour." In truth, no one had been given more chances to be the *good* guy than Daly.

"If I had done the things he's done, I'd have been ostracized so fast it would have been ridiculous," Norman said. "Almost anyone would have been. Then he goes around acting like people are picking on him."

That was how Norman began his defense of golf's oldest title.

There is no golf tournament in the world like the Open Championship, as it is called everywhere but in the United States. The Men of the Masters love to talk about all their traditions, but the Open was sixty-five years old — older than the Masters is *now* — when the first Masters was played in 1935. The Open is played on links golf courses, so-called because they are slices of land that link the land to the sea — the kind where the game was first played. And, while a lot of Americans like to point out that a links course without wind and rain will often yield scores that remind people of Palm Springs, the simple fact is that the weather is as much a part of a links golf course as the greens, the flags, and the cups.

Then there are the fans. As Tom Watson, who is as beloved in Scotland as anyone since Old Tom Morris (who won the championship in 1861, 1862, 1864, and 1867), points out, golf in the British Isles is a lot like baseball is in the U.S. Even those who don't play the game understand the game. They know that a shot from 140 yards one day that lands 20 feet from the flag is a mediocre shot; a shot from the same place to the same place the next day can be a brilliant one.

They are partisan and they will whoop it up with the best of them when one of their own is in contention, but they appreciate great play from anyone. You will never hear anything resembling a "USA" chant at an Open Championship.

Turnberry had been part of the seven-course Open rota only since 1977. It had replaced Carnoustie, generally considered the most difficult of the Scottish courses, for the simple reason that the tournament had become too big for Carnoustie. Getting several thousand people in and out of the little town each day was virtually impossible although new roads and hotels were being built for a planned return there in 1999.

Of course getting to Turnberry wasn't exactly easy. There were two roads that led to the golf course, both of the two-lane variety, and if you weren't fortunate enough to be paying £215 a night (about

$340) for a room in the Turnberry Hotel, heavy traffic was going to be part of your day throughout Open week.

There are four Scottish courses on the Open rota: St. Andrews is all about tradition and the birth of the game; Muirfield is the most elegant of the courses and probably the most classic test of golf; Royal Troon (which is about twenty miles from Turnberry) is tradition and has the Postage Stamp, the tiny par-three that is the second most famous hole (the Road Hole at St. Andrews being number one) in Scotland.

And then there is Turnberry, which is pure aesthetics. A Japanese corporation bought the golf course and the hotel several years ago and has poured several million dollars into redesigning the hotel and into building a new clubhouse. The golf course itself goes out toward the water for eight holes, hugs the shoreline for three, then works its way back inland. From the fourth tee, Ailsa Craig, the famous bird sanctuary that looks like a giant rock jutting out of the Firth of Clyde, seems so close on a clear day you would swear you could reach out and touch it.

The ninth tee is on a tiny promontory of land completely surrounded by water, much like the 18th tee at Pebble Beach. The famous yellow-and-white lighthouse that is Turnberry's symbol is straight ahead and slightly to your left from the tee with the fairway to the right. Hook your tee shot and the rocks in front of the lighthouse or the beach will be the landing area for your ball.

The 9th, 10th, and 11th all run along the water in much the same way eight, nine, and ten hug the water at Pebble Beach. At Pebble, the water is on your right, at Turnberry your left. Turnberry turns inland at 12 and as you get closer to the clubhouse, the huge luxury hotel looms above you.

The two British Opens that had been played at Turnberry had produced great drama. In 1977, Nicklaus and Watson staged their historic duel over the last thirty-six holes, Watson's 65–65 edging Nicklaus's 65–66. It was that tournament that marked Watson for golfing greatness and made him forever a part of Scottish lore.

The weather that year was shockingly mild, warm, and dry, especially on the weekend. Nine years later, on a day when the famous winds known as the Turnberry Giant swept in from the Firth of Clyde,

Norman shot a stupefying 63 on the second day and took control of the tournament en route to his first victory in a major.

In 1994, the Giant made an appearance on the weekend prior to the tournament and the weather stayed wet, drab, and windy through Tuesday. That sort of weather was probably the perfect setting for Finchem's meeting with Daly. By now, Daly knew he was not the most popular guy in the locker room. No one else had confronted him the way Norman had, but the whispers were around.

In truth, Daly had sensed trouble even before his confrontation with Norman. On Saturday, before playing his last round at the Scottish Open, he had called Peter Jacobsen and asked him to come to his post-round press conference that afternoon. He had already heard that Finchem wanted to meet with him and he knew he was making headlines all over Great Britain. It was ironic that Daly would call Jacobsen looking for support, since it was at Jacobsen's charity tournament the year before that he had launched his shot over the heads of several thousand fans while Jacobsen watched in horror.

"He was hurting when he called," said Jacobsen, one of the most extroverted players on tour. "I could tell he was looking for support and I was one of the few Americans over for the Scottish. I know John's not a bad guy, and I like to think I'm not the kind of person who carries a grudge. So I went."

Daly didn't deny what he had said during that press conference — the fact that the interview was on tape would have made it difficult — but he did start to backpedal a little, saying he wasn't trying to get anyone in trouble and that he was just attempting to say he wasn't the first or last guy to have a drug or alcohol problem on the tour.

Daly said essentially the same thing to Finchem during their ninety-minute meeting in the Turnberry clubhouse. He was almost apologetic, knowing full well that Finchem could easily suspend him again. Finchem didn't want to suspend Daly. He knew what his presence meant to sponsors and to the tour in general. By the next day, it was apparent that he had counseled Daly to fall back on the old "I was quoted out of context" cop-out when the subject came up and to say he was sorry he had said the things he had said and — most important — that he had no evidence of drug use on the PGA Tour.

Finchem was prepared to listen if Daly had evidence that there was drug use on tour, but he suspected he didn't. He had already started an informal investigation, asking anyone and everyone connected with the tour if they thought there was a drug problem or even the perception of a drug problem. If so, he might consider drug testing. When he was finished talking to people, Finchem was convinced that there was no need to drug test or even send out a memo to the players — which he had considered — on the subject of drugs.

His official comment on the meeting with Daly was no comment. He would leave the talking to Daly — and hope Daly got his lines right.

Daly followed Finchem's "advice" (read, instructions) perfectly. On Thursday, he did several lengthy interviews with television and then with the print media. He recited his lines and, for good measure, he added something that Jacobsen had brought up to him. "Anytime anyone asks you about *anything,* you should give them the same answer," he told Daly. "Tell them you don't have time to think about anything except playing good golf and staying sober."

Sure enough, Daly finished all his interviews with a smile, a shake of the head, and the Jacobsen mantra: "I've got enough to worry about just trying to stay sober," he said. "I don't need to worry about anybody else."

He was letter-perfect except for one thing: every time he tried to say "out of context," he said "out of content." Oh well, practice would probably make perfect.

The weather broke Wednesday, the dark clouds replaced by blue skies, the chilling winds gone, their place taken by comfortable breezes and temperatures climbing into the 70s.

Turnberry had the feel of a schoolyard on the first warm day of spring, everyone excited and rejuvenated by the gorgeous weather.

The story of the day was the two old men, Tom Watson and Jack Nicklaus, taking on the world's top two players, Nick Price and Greg Norman, in a friendly little better-ball match that drew a crowd of several thousand. Watson and Nicklaus both shot 65 and they won easily, four up with three holes to play, and walked off smiling, each £100 richer. What's more, everyone in the media had a perfect story for the last practice day: Watson and Nicklaus, reunited at Turnberry — this time as partners — both tearing up the course once again in beautiful weather. It had been seventeen years since their magical matchup, but you never would have known it as they took turns making birdies.

Norman, who had been working as an assistant pro for $28 a week in 1977, and Price, who had been in the Rhodesian air force at the time, watched in amazement as the fifty-four-year-old and the forty-four-year-old gave them a golf lesson. "I felt like I'd jumped into a time machine and it was 1977 again," Price said, laughing.

Watson and Nicklaus were not, however, the biggest winners of the day. The foursome of Davis Love III, Ben Crenshaw, Corey Pavin, and Brad Faxon made a $1,000 no-bogeys bet on the first tee. Anyone who could play all eighteen holes without a bogey would collect $1,000 from the others. Price remembered a similar bet he had been involved in the year before. He had been the last member of the foursome still alive on the 15th hole, and his playing partners did everything but kick his ball when he had a five-foot par putt left on that green.

"I missed it," he said. "No doubt the toughest gallery I've ever played in front of."

It was Faxon who had the last chance to collect the money after Love went out on the 13th hole. He ignored all the hooting and blathering during his backswing and kept on making pars. At 16, he offered to let them all off the hook for $750 if they called the bet off right then.

No. Fine, Faxon said. At 18, with his second shot heading right for the flag, he yelled out, "The price is $990 now!" A few seconds later, it was $1,000.

"The big question now," he said, "is whether or not I ever collect." Crenshaw paid before the week was over; Pavin paid two weeks later. Love was the lone holdout. "I think I want double or nothing," he said.

Of course, practice rounds mean nothing. Or do they? "I'm playing so much better now than I was at the [U.S.] Open, it isn't even funny," Nicklaus said Wednesday night. "But you never know what's going to happen when you start playing for real."

*   *   *

Tom Watson was up at 5 A.M. on Thursday. His tee time was 7:35 and he wanted to have plenty of time to shower, dress, have breakfast, and get to the range to get loose. The previous afternoon, on the practice tee, Davis Love and Phil Mickelson had both expressed amazement that a five-time British Open champion would get stuck with such an early tee time.

Watson shrugged. "You never know, it might turn out to be an advantage," he said. "The best weather might be in the morning."

The morning weather was favorable: overcast, but with no rain or wind that was a factor, and a long way from resembling the Giant. But the early wake-up was difficult for Watson. He didn't sleep very well, worrying about having to get up and, even with his meticulous preparation, he was still feeling cobwebs on the first tee. He tried to play a conservative one-iron shot, just to get the ball on the fairway, and yanked it way right.

He made par from there, but the front nine — which was playing downwind — was a struggle. He was even par at the turn and concerned that he might have a tough time coming in against the wind. By now, though, he was awake and warming to the challenge. He had spent several days in Ireland with Lee Trevino before coming to Scotland and had arrived feeling relaxed and confident.

Coming to Scotland was always energizing for Watson. He had been frustrated after Oakmont, feeling he had let a golden opportunity to win another major slip away. Three times he had been in position to win majors at Oakmont — leading on the back nine on Sunday at the PGA in 1978 and the Open in 1983, only to lose, then coming up short on Sunday at the Open in '94. He kept insisting that he considered Oakmont "a friend," the problem being that Oakmont was a friend to Watson the way Iago was a friend to Othello.

Watson played fairly well at the Western Open two weeks later, finishing tied for seventeenth, but he was not in a good mood most of that week. Davis Love and Andrew Magee, his playing partners the first two days, both wondered if something was bothering him. Watson is never very chatty on the golf course, but he was downright snappish a good deal of the time, even though he played well — shooting 68–69.

Maybe the pressure of playing so much good golf without a win was kicking in. Before the tournament, Watson had noted that his first win on tour had come twenty years earlier at the Western immediately following a final-round collapse at the Open. Perhaps he was just pushing too hard to make history repeat itself.

The trip to Ireland that he and his wife, Linda, had made with Lee Trevino and his wife, Claudia, was a superb tonic. Trevino always made him laugh and he had given him a putting lesson, telling him to move his hands forward on the putter. When the putts started dropping in practice on Wednesday, Watson began to think something good might happen.

By the end of his opening round at Turnberry on Thursday, he felt the same way. He made two birdies on the back nine, even with the wind freshening and in his face. That put him at 68, a solid first-round score, especially on a morning when you started out so sleepy you wondered exactly where the first green was. As it turned out, Watson had been exactly right about the weather. The morning players got the best of it by far. By 2 o'clock the course was windy and rainy and, as the afternoon wore on, the rain kept getting harder and harder.

When Davis Love teed it up at 1:20, the rain was just starting, but he had a feeling it was going to get worse. He had warned Robin to bring a raincoat with her even though it was still dry outside when they left their hotel room. "It'll rain," he told her. "It always rains at the British Open."

Love desperately wanted to play well, regardless of the weather. He had played better at the U.S. Open than at the Masters, finishing tied for twenty-eighth, but he hadn't broken par all week and was never in any kind of contention. He finished the tournament with a double bogey on the 18th hole on Sunday that left him so disgusted that he uncharacteristically flipped his putter at his bag as he walked off the green.

He had not played well since the Masters and he knew it. He hadn't been in the top ten, in fact, except for Atlanta, where he had been in contention briefly on Sunday before slipping to a tie for eleventh; his record since the Masters was cut–cut–T(tie)11–T45–T42–T38–T28–cut–T38. He had now missed four cuts in 1994, one more than he had missed in all of 1993.

He was struggling with his irons, especially when he hit long irons off the tee, and he felt as if he hadn't made a putt since college. At the Western, he had missed the cut by one shot after forgetting to move his mark back on a green. He had moved it to get out of Watson's line, then forgot to move it back. Or, at least he thought he hadn't moved it back. The notion that he hadn't occurred to him two holes later. He asked Watson and Magee if they had seen him move it back and they couldn't remember. His caddy, Frank Williams, had been raking a trap, so he didn't know either. Since he wasn't sure, Love had to assume that he had forgotten, so he called a penalty shot on himself. That ended up costing him the cut.

Missing the cut wasn't nearly as upsetting as the idea that he wasn't all there mentally. He went home and worked with his friend Jack Lumpkin for a couple of days on both his swing and his putting stroke. He was hitting the ball much better by the time he arrived in Scotland and wanted very much to get off to a good start. He was tired of playing himself out of majors before they had even really begun.

The beginning was not encouraging. He hit his second shot at number one almost up against a fence and had to make a tricky four-foot putt for bogey. The whole front nine was a scramble — he hit only four greens — but he had a chance to get to the turn still one over when he lined up a three-foot par putt at nine.

He missed. Love looked sick. The rain was pelting down by now and he was already seven shots behind the leader, Greg Turner of New Zealand, who was on his way to a 65. But Love didn't die. He finally made a birdie at number 11, and he kept getting out of trouble all the way to the clubhouse. At 14, he made a miraculous recovery from a buried bunker lie, making a 10-foot, curling downhill putt for par. He bogeyed 16, but came right back with a birdie at 17. When he made one more tough par out of the left rough at 18, he had shot 71 and was thrilled to be just one over par after the way he had started.

"Normally, that round is 75, especially at a major," he said. "I struggled, but now I feel good because if I can get some decent weather tomorrow I can play myself into position for the weekend."

What pleased Love was that he had done something he normally had trouble doing: grinding out a respectable round on a day when he didn't bring his best swing to the golf course. Almost no one shows up for four straight days at a major with his A game. Often, the key to contending is being able to save a lot of pars on that day when you aren't going to make a lot of birdies. Love had done that.

So had Norman, who had also drawn an afternoon tee time. When he arrived at the clubhouse forty-five minutes after Love, the wind was howling and he was delighted with 71. "The job today was to stay in contention," he said. "I did it and I'm a happy camper."

Which made him exactly the opposite of Nick Faldo. The three-time Open champion teed off ten minutes before Norman, in the 1:55 group, along with U.S. Open champion Ernie Els and American Jim McGovern.

Since his disheartening experience at Oakmont, Faldo had been searching for his swing and his putting stroke. He had arrived home from Oakmont on Saturday evening and decided his first job the next morning would be to look at tapes of his swing circa 1990 and 1992, when he was winning majors. Something was missing. Maybe he could find it on tape.

He couldn't sleep. Ideas kept running through his head about his swing, about putting, about how to attack a golf course. He would get up, make a note, then try to go back to sleep. By 3 A.M. he knew it was no use. He got out of bed, walked upstairs to his game room, which has a snooker table and cabinets containing trophies and golf clubs that he had used in winning majors.

He sat down with the gray leather notebook that he had received as a gift on the Concorde flight home and began writing everything down. Pages and pages of notes. "Every thought I'd ever had on the golf course that worked," he said. "Some I looked at and said, 'No, this isn't right,' and crossed them out. Others, I said, 'Right, we'll try this one.' "

By early morning he was downstairs watching tapes with his five-year-old son Matthew. The BBC had done a special on his landmark 1990 year when he had won the Masters and the Open Championship, so he looked at that. Then he looked at tapes from 1992, when he had won six times. He pulled out the putter he had used at the Open in 1990, then he dragged a dozen other putters out and headed for the putting green behind his house.

First, he had contests among the putters, lining up an identical putt from 12 to 15 feet and trying to put the same stroke on each putt to see which felt most comfortable. Then, referring to his notebook, he began comparing strokes — one more inside, another outside, a different one a bit shorter. More contests. He decided to go back to the 1990 putter and headed for the range to work through all the notes he had made on his swing.

"It was almost square-one stuff," he said. "The great thing about golf is that there are times when the game tells you that you need to go back and start over, look for something new — or something old, because what you're doing just isn't working.

"Oakmont was quite unnerving. Not to be able to hit the ball where I wanted to *at all* really threw me. But when I got home and started all my experimenting I was quite excited. In a way, it was fun to be working that way again."

He went to the Irish Open the next week, a tournament he had won three years in a row. He didn't win, but he did contend and he felt much better about what he was doing. Progress. Finally. He went home for a couple of days and then he and Leadbetter went to Turnberry for a couple of early practice rounds. Every shot was on a string. The putting was good. He could feel it coming back. The Click wasn't that far away. Leadbetter, who worked as a guest columnist for one of the London papers during Open week, wrote about Faldo's newfound confidence and predicted a strong championship for him.

Faldo flew home to London for the weekend, since he and Norman were scheduled to tape their Shell's Wonderful World of Golf match at Sunningdale on Sunday. He knew the match was supposed to be fun, nothing too serious, but when the ball began spraying on him again, he fell into a funk. Norman, who had brought his two children with him, spent most of the day talking to them since Faldo said almost nothing for 18 holes. The final margin was only one shot, but that was because Norman bogeyed the last two holes with a four-shot lead and Faldo finally made a birdie.

"It was awful," Faldo said. "I just couldn't understand what was going on. When Led and I were at Turnberry, it was all there. Then I get out there with Greg and I can't do a thing. I was totally and completely aggravated."

When he got back to Turnberry the next day, he and Leadbetter went straight to the practice tee. Faldo was still beside himself. What was going on here? How could he be hitting the ball exactly the way he wanted to on Friday and feel completely helpless on Sunday? Why couldn't he find the swing he had in 1992 and hold onto it?

He knew all the answers, that no one can ever hold onto the swing he wants forever or, sometimes, for forty-eight hours. But he was venting. The Open was *his* tournament and he didn't want a repeat of the Masters or Oakmont.

By the time he reached the 17th tee on Thursday afternoon, Faldo was feeling neither joy nor despair. He was two over par, but, like Love and Norman, he knew that wasn't an awful score — especially if he could birdie the relatively easy 17th and get in with the same 71 that they had produced.

It was shortly after 6 o'clock and the mist and rain had left the golf course gloomy and dark. Faldo's tee shot drifted right, putting him in a spot, he suspected, where getting to the green in two would be almost impossible. That was annoying.

He marched briskly to his ball. A few chilled fans and a lone marshal were standing a few yards away. He looked at the marshal and asked, "This the first one?" He was certain the marshal nodded yes. The lie wasn't very good, so he took out an iron and slashed it down the fairway, well short of the green.

McGovern had also pushed his drive. But he couldn't find his ball. He began walking in circles, searching for it. Terror suddenly gripped Faldo. "As soon as I saw Jim looking round, I knew," he said.

McGovern finally walked to a ball about 20 yards beyond where Faldo was. He looked down at the ball, then looked at Faldo, and pointed back down at the ball. The distinctive "Faldo" that is printed on all of Faldo's balls was on that ball. Faldo had hit McGovern's ball.

It was as if someone had dropped a piano on top of him. He felt his knees buckle and he stood there wondering just how in the hell this could be happening. Wait, he must be dreaming. If he waited a few seconds, he would wake up in bed in a cold sweat, then let out a sigh of relief because it had just been a dreary, terrifying nightmare.

He waited. Nothing happened. He was still standing, soaking wet, on a hill on the 17th hole at Turnberry and McGovern was quietly coming back to the spot from which Faldo had hit his ball. There was nothing to do but walk up to his own ball and hit it. The two-shot penalty meant he would be hitting four. By the time he had slapped it out of the rough, then missed the green, chipped on, and two-putted, he had made an eight. On a hole where four was the norm, he had made eight.

Instead of getting back to one over par, he was now five over, and the 18th was playing dead into the wind. In a daze, he somehow made par at the 18th, getting up and down from the high grass left of the green. "The funny thing is, making that par at 18 actually gave me a tiny ray of hope," he said. "For some reason, I thought at five I could still come back and make the cut. At six, I might have just fallen apart completely."

Word of Faldo's disaster had spread around the grounds like wildfire, especially in the media tent. If you had ranked the players in the tournament from one to 156 — one being the most likely to hit the wrong ball, 156 the least likely — Faldo probably would have been 156 — 155 at the highest.

He was so meticulous and deliberate and careful about everything that the notion that he would walk into the rough during the first round of the Open Championship in poor visibility and slash away at a ball without double-checking to make sure it was his was unthinkable.

And yet it had happened. If someone had walked into the press tent and announced that Princess Diana had been a late entry into the field and had just played the front nine in 29, the shock waves would have been far more muted. The next shock came a few minutes after Faldo had signed his card when he showed up in the interview room to answer questions about what had happened.

Earlier that day, Colin Montgomerie had refused to come to the interview room after shooting a 72, then stalked away from a small group of reporters standing near the 18th green when someone asked a question he didn't like. Imagine how Daly would have reacted to a request to speak to the media under similar circumstances. But Faldo came.

He explained what happened, answered several questions — all of them really the same question: How *could* you? — and summed it up succinctly by saying, "It wasn't very clever, was it?"

He had come in because he knew the tabloids were going to have a field day with him and if he stormed off it would only be worse. "Damage control," he said later, forcing a smile. The tabloids can't be controlled no matter what you say or do. The next day, the headline writers were hard at work: "Faldope," read one; "Fooldo," read another. The stories that went with them basically accused Faldo of the greatest gaffe in the country's history since Neville Chamberlain declared "peace in our time" after negotiating with Hitler in 1939. At least then Chamberlain didn't hit the wrong ball.

"You always have to be meticulous," Norman said later that evening. "That sort of thing is why golf is a four-letter word." He paused, then couldn't help a grin. "I'll bet," he said, "there were some four-letter words flying after that incident."

It had been a long first day at the Open Championship.

Faldo, Norman, and Love all got the weather they had hoped for the next morning. It was chilly and breezy, but nothing like Thursday afternoon.

Faldo had gone out to the practice tee Thursday evening and hit balls in the rain for thirty minutes for no other purpose than to release some of his anger. "It was a scream at myself that I needed," he said.

He was out early and played like the Faldo of old, shooting a 66 that not only got him comfortably inside the cut (he was at 141, the cut was 143) but put him in position to make a move Saturday if he could go low again.

Love and Norman each shot 67, just the kind of round Norman expected; just the kind Love had never been able to come up with in a major. They were both at 138, very much within striking distance of the leader.

Whose name was Tom Watson.

This was a day for Watson to savor, one of those afternoons when all the memories of Opens past came flooding back to him as he produced the kind of shotmaking that had made him, well, Tom Watson. Wide awake on the first tee at 12:05, he came out firing, using a driver on a hole where most players went with a one-iron. He hit his driver to within easy wedge distance of the green, pitched to 15 feet, and made the birdie. He was off and running after that.

At the par-five seventh, with the wind in the players' faces, the green seemed unreachable. Watson pulled out a driver on the fairway and crushed it 240 yards onto the green. He had hit almost an identical shot with a driver on the same hole seventeen years earlier. He two-putted for birdie. Then, at the tough par-four eighth, he slammed a three-iron through the wind to within eight feet and swished that putt for another birdie.

"Those were my two favorite shots of the day," he said later, "the driver at seven and the three-iron at eight. They were fun."

The whole day was fun. Watson birdied 10 with a 12-foot putt and was tied for the lead. As he walked off the green, a huge grin crossed his face. "I've got those bookies quivering now," he said.

The London bookies had sent Watson off at 50-to-1 odds on Thursday morning. Hearing those odds on Wednesday evening, Nick Price had said, "If I were making a bet, that's the one I'd take."

Watson's only bad moment all day came — naturally — on a short putt. He missed a two-footer for par at the 13th, but then made a superb save at the 14th for par, and just missed an eagle at 17 before tapping in for birdie. That sent him to the 18th tee leading the tournament at seven under.

At each hole on the back nine, the ovation grew louder. The screams of "Come on, Toom!" were everywhere, and Watson, wearing his Scottish-tweed hat instead of the white Ram baseball visor he normally wears, loved every second of it. He was feeding off their energy and their joy, the chills running through him each time he walked onto a green and heard the shouts and applause all around him.

As he and Bruce Edwards, his longtime caddy, walked up the 17th fairway, Edwards turned to him and said, "I swear, Tom, if it was you and Faldo down the stretch on Sunday afternoon, I think all these people would be pulling for you."

Watson didn't answer, but the idea clearly warmed him. On the 18th tee, he was almost like a little kid after his first bicycle ride. He blasted a one-iron around the corner of the dogleg and said, "That's solid." He handed the club back to Edwards and said, "I'll bet I've got 178 yards to the flag." He was close — 187. He made par from there for a 65 and the kind of 18th green ovation normally reserved for the winner.

"Not bad for a has-been," he said, an ear-to-ear grin on his face when it was over. He sobered for a moment. "I'm not a has-been. I still think I can win."

Which had a lot of bookies scared to death.

Friday was Watson's day, but a lot of players were bunched tightly behind him. Jesper Parnevik, the young Swede who was playing the American tour, was one shot back and so was Brad Faxon, who had played a bogeyless round when it really mattered and had matched Watson's 65. One shot back of them, alone in fourth place, was Nick Price.

No one left the golf course more frustrated that day than Price, even though he shot 66. He had come to 18 five under for the day and had hit an eight-iron second shot that came up short of the green. From there he made an aggravating bogey. Playing late in the day, he hadn't taken into account the dropping temperature and had under-clubbed. He should have hit a seven-iron. Still, he was only two shots back and felt as if he hadn't played his best golf yet.

Price was one of the few players not staying in the Turnberry Hotel. He had rented a house a few miles from Turnberry, knowing that meant he had to monitor traffic closely each day, but it was worth it to him because he liked to have room to spread out and relax, especially at a major.

He was wound tight and he knew it. As brilliantly as he had played in 1993, he hadn't really been in contention at a major and he had been awful at Augusta (T-35) and the U.S. Open (cut). This tournament was the one he most wanted to win. He had given it away to Watson in 1982 and had it taken away by Ballesteros in 1988. He knew that thirty-seven wasn't anywhere near the end of a player's career (look what Watson was doing at forty-four) but he also knew you only get so many shots at majors.

Price burned to be more than just a good player or even a very good one. He wanted to be one of the great players, and he knew that he could win the Western Open for a hundred straight years and not be considered a great player. He knew that a bogey at 18 on Friday might be what kept you up all night Sunday. But he also knew that the opening thirty-six holes was merely the prelude for a golf tournament, the lounge act before Sinatra. He went to sleep Friday telling himself that his golf had improved every day since he had arrived on Monday. He had to keep improving for two more days. If he could do that, he would take his chances come Sunday evening.

When the players woke up Saturday morning, they knew right away that they would be dealing with an entirely different golf course than the one they had played the first two days. Scottish summer — which sometimes lasts as long as a week — had arrived. The sun was out, there was almost no breeze, and the temperature would approach 80 by midafternoon.

A links course without weather is a lone Christian facing ten lions. It is helpless.

You can shoot 62 today, Nick Faldo thought as he warmed up. Scores would be low, and he felt that if he could put up a number early in the day, he might be in contention by nightfall.

One of the Brits did make a move early that day, but it wasn't Faldo. Montgomerie, the high-strung Mrs. Doubtfire look-alike, shot 65. This time he agreed to come to the interview room. But when someone asked him if he'd had a good night's sleep, he shot them a look and said, "Stick to golf please."

Faldo tried mightily all day to take advantage of the balmy conditions. He kept firing at flags, getting close, and missing putts. Nothing would go in. He ended up shooting an exasperating 70, meaning he lost ground. He had started the day eight shots behind Watson. He ended it trailing the leaders by 10. Any chance of a miraculous rally after Thursday's calamity was gone.

If Faldo was upset, Davis Love was speechless. He had started the day convinced he was finally going to get over his majors bugaboo. With the unfamiliar luxury of a late weekend tee time at a major (1:55) he slept in, wandered over to the course at around noon, and bought himself a baked potato at one of the concession tents as his breakfast/lunch.

Just like Watson the day before, he came out swinging, hitting a driver on the first hole. Els, his playing partner, hit the more standard one-iron, and Love was 60 yards past him. He hit a gorgeous wedge to eight feet. Perfect, he thought. Come out of the box flying and race up the leader board. But his putt veered left as soon as it came off the club. Two holes later, he hit another fabulous approach. This one was closer, about six feet. The putt wasn't. Another pull. Another par that should have been a birdie. At the fourth his seven-iron off the tee spun to four feet. This time he made the putt. Okay, *now* he could make a move.

Only he couldn't. Love hit the ball superbly all day. He missed two greens the entire afternoon. At one of them, the ninth, he was just off the green and chipped in for birdie. That made up for a lot and put him at four under. He sneaked a look at the leader board. There were a lot of red numbers. Everyone, it seemed, was under par. He would need to at least match the 33 he had just shot coming in.

He finally made a putt at the 13th, a trickling 15-footer. He was so happy that he threw his arms into the air as if to say "finally." The putt put him at five under. It also put him on a major leader board later in the tournament than at any time in his life. If he could make one more putt somewhere and birdie the easy 17th, he could be right there . . .

But he missed his second green at 14 and this time it cost him a bogey. He was off the leader board as quickly as he had been on it. When his shot from the back bunker there slid 15 feet past the hole, he pounded his wedge in disgust. He was even angrier when a poor chip from just in front of the green at 17 cost him his birdie. Els, who had been all over the lot throughout the day, eagled the hole. When they both parred 18, Love, who had played near-perfect golf tee to green, walked off with a 68; Els, who had looked capable of shooting 75, had somehow managed 69.

A 68 on the third day of most majors will move you past a lot of people. Not on this day. Of the eighty players in the field, forty-three shot in the 60s. Love's 68 left him right where he started — five shots from the lead. With thirty-six holes to play, that is not a daunting margin. With eighteen left, it is, especially when there are eight players ahead of you — seven of them by three shots or more.

What galled Love was the fact that he easily could have shot 65 —

or better — if he had putted decently. That evening, he found Tom Kite on the putting green and asked for a putting lesson. Like a lot of Love's friends, Kite was convinced that Love's problem was his routine. Working with psychologist Bob Rotella, Love had developed a routine where he picked a target, got over his putt, and stroked it. Rotella didn't want him to think about mechanics. He wanted him to think only about getting the ball where he needed it to go. And he didn't want him standing over the ball thinking too much.

There is a difference between standing over a ball and taking the putter back so fast that you are still moving when you hit the putt. Kite — and others, including Love's caddy, Frank Williams — were convinced that he was moving when he was putting. It is impossible to move and putt well. Kite, who was tied with Love at four under for the tournament, worked with him that evening on doing his routine, but getting still before he putted. Kite had also worked with Rotella and respected him, but he thought Love was going too far in this area. "This is the one thing I disagree with Doc on," he said. "I just don't think you can putt well if you're moving all the time."

Love left the green that night with mixed emotions: he thought Kite had shown him something that would work but he was afraid it might be too late.

Greg Norman didn't take a putting lesson that night. He left the golf course quickly and quietly. He knew his chances of defending his title had drowned earlier in the afternoon at the 16th hole.

All week, Norman hadn't felt quite right over the ball and neither he nor his teacher, Butch Harmon, were sure what the problem was. Friday afternoon, they figured it out. He had gotten too square in his swing, a little too upright. A slight adjustment and, boom, the ball was soaring again. The timing couldn't have been more perfect. Five shots back, Norman could make his move on Saturday.

He did, with a birdie at number one and a birdie at number two. Watson hadn't even teed off yet, and Norman was already within three shots of him. "He's going low today," Harmon said walking down the third hole. "Way low."

If golf was merely about ball striking, Norman and Love probably would have led the tournament that night. Norman kept hitting the ball close and — like Love — kept missing makable birdie putts. Even so, he was still five under for the tournament when he reached 16 and still in contention.

His drive was in the right rough, but not in any serious trouble. Thinking the ball would fly out of the rough, Norman took a nine-iron and put an easy swing on the ball. The moment it left the club, he knew it was in trouble. The lie had been fluffier than he thought. The ball took off in a lazy arc and Norman knew it was headed straight for the burn that runs in front of the green. "Just stay dry," he pleaded.

No such luck. The ball spun into the burn. A chip and two putts later, Norman had a double-bogey six. He was back to three under. Grinding his teeth, he walked onto the 17th tee knowing he had to make *at least* a birdie, perhaps an eagle. If he could get back to five under by the end of the day, there might still be a chance.

He couldn't. Playing for a right-to-left wind, he aimed straight for the right fairway bunker off the tee — and hit the ball right into the bunker. From there, he had no chance to get home in two. A par. "Which was like a bogey," he said. "Just like that, I'd lost three shots to the field — two at sixteen, one at seventeen. I knew I was a dead man."

When he signed his card and looked at the scores, it confirmed his thinking. He was at three under. By dusk, that would put him behind nineteen players with one round left. That was too many. When an interviewer from the BBC mentioned that he might make one of his famous charges on Sunday, Norman shook his head.

"No, not this time," he said. "Too many strokes and too many guys."

Watching the interview, his agent, Frank Williams, almost gagged when he heard his boss/client say he couldn't charge on Sunday. "Don't you ever say that on television," he told Norman. "Never say you *can't* win."

"But Frank, I can't," Norman said. "Let's get out of here." He was tired. It had been a long, difficult week.

The leaders that night were Fuzzy Zoeller and Brad Faxon. Zoeller, whistling all the way, had shot a brilliant 64 to get to nine under, and Faxon, without a bogey (of course), had shot 67 to match him. Watson, who had missed two short putts on the back nine ("hiccups," he called them) and then birdied 17 and 18, was one shot back along with Jesper Parnevik, Ronan Rafferty, and Nick Price.

Price would have been tied with Zoeller and Faxon, but he bogeyed 18 *again,* this time going *over* the green with a seven-iron.

"I'm going to get it right one of these days," he said, forcing a smile. Once again, he had mixed emotions. He knew he was in excellent position. He also knew it could have been better. That night at dinner, Leadbetter said to him, "Well, Nick, you hit an eight-iron short at eighteen on Friday and a seven-iron long today. Maybe you should carry a seven-and-a-half-iron tomorrow."

Price laughed, but he couldn't help but think about what 18 would be like the next day. The only thing he knew was that there was absolutely no more room for error.

Watson had hoped against hope that the Turnberry Giant would show up on Sunday. A golf course where pars were at a premium would suit him a lot better than the Turnberry that the players had destroyed on Saturday. Looking at the scores Saturday evening, Dave Marr, the 1965 PGA champion who worked for the BBC, shook his head and said, "Is this Turnberry or Tucson?"

Turnberry looked a lot like Tucson again on Sunday. More mild weather. The general thinking was that a score in the mid-60s would be needed to win.

Long before the leaders teed off, a number of mini-dramas were unfolding. The one that unfolded — unraveled might be a better word — the fastest was that of John Daly. He had started the tournament well, shooting 68 on Thursday and had actually gotten to five under par through nine holes on Friday.

But he hooked his tee shot onto the beach at the 10th and, even with thousands of fans helping, no one could find the ball. He made a triple-bogey 7 there, then made a double bogey at the 11th. He was even par for the tournament after thirty-six holes but could do no better than 72 against the defenseless golf course on Saturday. That seemed to kill his interest and he practically ran around the course on Sunday, shooting an embarrassing 80 that included an 8–6–5 finish. He was in his car and gone within minutes of signing his card. He was the only player in the field who failed to break 80 on either Saturday or Sunday, and he finished eightieth among the eighty players who made the cut.

No doubt he shot that 80 because so many people were picking on him.

Davis Love didn't do all that much better on the final day, but it wasn't because of lack of effort. Still harboring some hope that his putting lesson with Kite might turn him around on the greens and allow him to produce a very low number, he hit two beautiful shots at number one for the second straight day to within eight feet and, for the second straight day, missed the putt.

All color seemed to drain from his face. His expression said, "Here we go again," and he was right. Only this time, knowing the golf tournament was lost, his concentration suffered. He finished an awful day with a 74 that dropped him from a tie for ninth all the way back to a tie for thirty-eighth.

Nick Faldo passed Love going in the opposite direction. He finally got his putter going on the back nine of the last day, and when he made a fine up and down from the gorse at 18, he had shot a 64. It was a satisfying round for Faldo, not because it moved him into a tie for seventh place, but because it meant that he hadn't let the wrong-ball incident destroy him. He had played the last three rounds in 10 under par and if there was ever an example of the difference between a champion and a spoiled brat, all one had to do was compare Faldo and Daly on the final day.

Daly, it should be remembered, started the round only one shot behind Faldo. He never even bothered to try. Faldo, who had as much chance to win as Daly — zero — worked hard on every shot. He beat Daly by 16 shots on the final day — 16! And yet the fans still screeched for Daly as if he were some sort of folk hero. Faldo received warm applause when he made his final putt at 18, but nothing that even bordered on raucous or wild.

And, just as he walked off the green, a huge roar went up from the first tee. Watson had just been introduced. Bruce Edwards had been right on Friday. To the Scots, Faldo, the reserved Englishman, was someone to be respected. Watson, the American with the warm, gap-toothed grin, was a hero.

Faldo could handle that. What hurt him most was to be driving away from the golf course on Sunday just as the leaders were teeing off. He was proud of what he had done the last three days. But he didn't play the game to accumulate moral victories.

With all the talk about low numbers being inevitable again, none of the leaders made any kind of move on the front nine. Zoeller birdied the second hole to briefly go to 10 under, but he bogeyed the fifth to give that back. Faxon, who hadn't made a bogey in forty-one holes, bogeyed the first. It was a bad omen. On this day, in serious contention on a Sunday at a major for the first time, he would fail to make a birdie.

Watson and Parnevik were paired together for the second straight day. It was tough to take Parnevik as seriously as his golf game merited. He had gotten into the habit of wearing his white Titleist cap with the brim turned up because he liked to get sun on his face. Disturbed because the up-turned brim hid its logo, Titleist had made him a special cap with the brand name under the brim. It looked goofy. Parnevik, the son of a Swedish comedian who was known as the David Letterman of Sweden, didn't seem to mind.

"If he wins, those things will be all the rage in Sweden on Monday," Watson joked Saturday night.

Watson had changed his headgear for Sunday, going back to his standard Ram visor — no doubt at the company's insistence — and eschewing the tweed cap that looked so perfect on him walking a links course. Both players matched pars for the first six holes, Parnevik having to scramble several times while Watson kept hitting greens and two-putting.

The seventh was dead into the wind, making it virtually unreachable in two. Watson laid up 50 yards short, then hit a stunning chip to two feet. The screams were even louder than on Friday. A huge smile on his face, he tapped in for birdie. Zoeller's bogey had just been posted on the board. He and Watson were tied for the lead. Eleven holes were left, and Watson had saved his best golf all week for the back nine.

The previous evening, leaving the golf course, Bruce Edwards, mindful of Watson's shaky Sundays all year, had said to him, "I just have a feeling tomorrow's going to be your best Sunday of the year."

Watson was feeling that way too as he walked to the eighth tee. He was full of adrenaline. The shaky starts that had hurt him on Sunday in recent majors hadn't happened. He was tied for the lead in his favorite golf tournament on a course that had produced what might be his fondest memory in golf.

He had driven the ball superbly all week, and he stepped onto the eighth tee wanting to be sure not to lose the ball to the right. He overcompensated. The ball hooked into the rough, near the gallery ropes. Hands on knees, he stared at the lie, trying to figure out just how fast and hard the ball would come out.

The answer was faster and harder than he thought. He hit a five-iron right at the flag, and the crowd went crazy until it saw that the ball had come out hot. It went through the green into the thick rough behind it. With very little green to work with, Watson's chip raced 20 feet past the pin.

Even then, he still thought he could save par. It would be an old-fashioned Watson par if he could make it and as much of a momentum builder at this point as the birdie at seven had been. For a split second, it looked as if he had made it. Watson bent at the knees, hoping, but the ball slid just past the cup. Too far past. Four feet. Watson stared at the ball and you could almost read his mind: Oh no, not again.

Yes, again. The bogey putt spun inches to the right. Watson tapped the ball in, reached down for it, and said, "Dammit, Tom!" Stunned and angry, he flipped his putter at Edwards harder than he had intended and Edwards had to throw up his hands to catch it at the last second.

They marched to the ninth tee. Standing on what may be the most beautiful spot in all of golf, Watson stared out at the water, arms folded, seeing nothing. He was now at seven under, trailing four players, tied with two others. After Parnevik, who was still at eight under, had teed off, Watson crushed his tee shot right at the directional flag in the middle of the fairway.

"Good one, Tom," Edwards said. "Come on, let's go."

Watson wasn't ready yet. He had to regain his composure. He stopped for a long drink of water while everyone else headed up the fairway. As he walked through the narrow path from the tee to the fairway, the fans were imploring him to come back. For the first time all week, he did not look up at them as he went past.

His drive had looked good, but wasn't. The directional flag was actually deceiving. You had to aim left of it to hit the fairway. If your ball went directly over it, you were headed for the right rough. That was where Watson was. As he walked over the crest of the hill, he asked an official where his ball was. When the man pointed to the rough, Watson's shoulders sagged a little more.

He had no chance to get to the green from where he was, and he hacked the ball left, to another tough lie. He knew he couldn't afford another bogey so, even though it was an almost impossible shot, he tried to land the ball just short of the green and hope it would trickle downhill to the pin.

Instead of trickling, it kicked straight right. He was still on the fringe. The next chip was better, but not good enough. Four feet. Again. It was almost too painful to watch. The same nervous stroke, the same horrid result.

Two holes, two double bogeys. Just like that, it was over. Three and a half days of joyriding had become the Nightmare on Elm Street in two holes. Watson never made another birdie. The cheers were as loud as ever when he walked onto 18 — someone in the crowd even yelled, "Next year, Toom!" — but they were hollow now. He missed one last short putt at 18 and finished tied for eleventh — one shot behind, among others, Nick Faldo.

He had shot 74 in the final round at Pebble Beach, 74 on the last day at Augusta, 74 on Sunday at Oakmont, and 74 at the finish at Turnberry.

He walked off the green in a state of shock, forcing the smile he had forced in defeat in the past. "Thirty-eight putts," he said softly. "You can't win with thirty-eight putts."

He patiently answered all the questions. "This hurts," he said. "I'm having some problems with my putting, but I'll figure it out, I won't give up."

Someone asked him what he would take away from the week. For a split second, Watson's eyes clouded. "Nothing," he said, finally. "Nothing."

But a moment later when they asked him if he still thought he would win again, he squared his shoulders one last time. "You bet," he said.

Why?

The jaw shot straight out. "Because," he said, "I believe it."

He left then, slowly walking up the 112 steps from the golf course entrance to the hotel entrance. They were the same 112 steps he had walked after his greatest victory in 1977. Then he had flown. Now he felt each step. He was exhausted, battered, and bloodied. But he would get up again, even if it meant getting up to be battered again.

Tom Watson was not the British Open champion, but he was something that any golfer should feel proud to be. He was Theodore Roosevelt's Man in the Arena. The same Man in the Arena who was taped to the mirror in his bathroom. Battered and bloodied. But never beaten.

By late afternoon, most of the contenders had dropped back, not as melodramatically as Watson, but just as thoroughly. Two men were left with a chance. One was Parnevik, who, after Watson's collapse, had put on the first real charge of the day, birdieing three straight holes, bogeying one, then birdieing two more. That got him to 12 under par with one hole to play.

It also seemed to put him in control of the tournament. The only player even within hailing distance of him was Price, and he was struggling. He had started slowly like everyone else, making three-putt bogeys on two and five, the second one from 25 feet.

Seeing that his boss was as angry as he ever got, Squeeky Medlen, Price's caddy, said softly as they walked off the sixth tee, "That just stoked the fire, Nick. Let's go."

Slowly, they went. Price finally got a birdie at the seventh and hung in. But when he got to the 13th and found himself trailing Parnevik by three, he began to wonder if this wasn't going to be another opportunity lost.

"I was too careful the first five or six holes," he said. "I was trying not to put a foot wrong, and that's not the way to play. I had to just *play*."

He did, but Parnevik had gotten so hot it appeared it might be too little, too late. The Nick Price of the 1980s might have looked at Parnevik's number on the board and thought, oh well, too good, well played, let's see if we can't get second. But the Nick Price of the 1990s never thinks a tournament is over. He always thinks there may just be a way to pull it out.

He had to save par from behind the green at 13. Then at 14, he caught a flyer in the rough and hit his second shot way over the green. A bogey would finish him, he knew that. He got lucky that he was so far over the green that he was in a trampled-down area and had a decent lie. He hit a running seven-iron that skidded to a halt three feet past the pin. Relieved, he tapped in for par. He was still nine under, Parnevik, 11. He hit a good five-iron at the par-three 15th, but his 18-foot putt spun past. Walking up 16, Price heard a roar and knew Parnevik had birdied 17. Somehow, he had to make a birdie.

He did, knocking a sand wedge to 12 feet and making the putt. Parnevik was at 12 under, he was at 10. The 17th was eminently reachable in two. If he could birdie it and birdie 18 . . . there was still a chance.

Up ahead, Parnevik was doing his Ernie Els imitation. He had decided not to look at any leader boards and had ordered his caddy not to tell him anything. Hearing various shouts and cheers behind him, he somehow figured that he was either behind or tied as he stood on the 18th tee. In truth, since Price was still on 16 at that moment, he was leading by three.

He hit his tee shot to the right side of the fairway. If he had known he was leading, he would have played a four-iron to the middle of the green. But thinking he needed a birdie, he aimed a five-iron right at the flag, which was tucked front and left in an almost impossible spot to get close.

The shot sailed left into the gorse, a terrible spot. Parnevik flopped a good wedge shot out to within 10 feet, but missed the putt. He tapped in for bogey, a round of 67 and a total of 11 under. When someone told him that he had been leading by three, all the color drained out of his face.

The three-shot lead was down to one after the bogey and Price's birdie at 16. Price had crushed his drive at 17 and had a four-iron left to the green. He knocked it on, 50 feet past the flag. A two-putt birdie would tie him with Parnevik. A playoff suddenly loomed. As they walked onto the green, Medlen had a thought.

"You know, we haven't made a long one all week," he said.

Price glanced at the huge yellow scoreboard. Parnevik's bogey wasn't up yet. He thought he needed to make the eagle putt to tie. "I put every drop of blood I had into making that putt," he said.

The putt had very little break in it, only about eight inches, so speed was the key. As soon as Price saw it go over the crest of the little hill on the green, he could see that it was headed straight for the hole. "I wondered if it would hang on," he said.

About eight feet away, the ball took a tiny hop to the right — Price saw later watching it on tape that it had hit a spike mark — and for a split second he thought it might slip past the cup on the right side. But at the last possible second, it hit the corner of the cup, spun around the edge briefly, and dropped.

Standing in the fairway waiting to play his second shot, Brad Faxon saw Price jump what looked to him like 20 feet straight into the air. "I was waiting for Squeeky to catch him, but then I saw him up in the air too," he said.

Faxon knew what had happened. The roar told everyone else. The putt was exactly 17 paces — 51 feet — long. By nightfall it would be described in various places around the world as between 70 and 80 feet long. In any event, it was the shot of the year.

When he came back to earth, Price looked at the leader board again. He was much too experienced *not* to look. He saw Parnevik's bogey. After seventy-one holes, for the first time all week, he had the lead. Now all he had to do was par the hole he had bogeyed the last two days. Where the hell was that seven-and-a-half-iron Leadbetter had talked about?

Price has had high blood pressure all his life. Now he took a few deep breaths to stay calm as he stood on the 18th tee. All he wanted to do was hit a three-iron around the corner and hope he ended up in a good spot to get to the middle of the green. He hit the shot solidly, but thought it might be a little farther left than he wanted it.

"It's fine," Medlen said as they walked off the tee. "The only thing

I care about is that we're not between clubs again."

Price was thinking the same thing. When they got to the ball, the lie was fine. Medlen checked the yardage — 165! A seven-iron! No more, no less, exactly a seven-iron. "My favorite club, my favorite shot," Price said. "If I couldn't put that shot on the green, I'd quit golf."

He took his time and the ball sailed directly at the center of the green — right where Parnevik should have aimed. When it landed, the crowd was screaming. Short of Watson, they could think of no one they would rather see win than Price.

As he began his walk to the green, Price felt chills racing through him. He had waited all his life to make this walk — to the 18th green at the Open championship, needing two putts to win. He started to say something to Medlen, but when he turned his head, he wasn't there. Thinking that Price deserved this moment to himself, Medlen had dropped behind him.

No way. Price turned to Medlen and waved him up. Medlen hesitated. "Come on, Squeek," Price said, "let's enjoy this together. Who knows if we'll ever get to do it again."

And so they walked onto the green together, both of them tingling. There were still 30 feet to negotiate, though, and Price suddenly flashed back to the three-putt at the fifth. "I didn't want to stand there taking all the bows and then make a fool of myself by three-putting," he said.

He didn't. He carefully lagged to three feet, looked the putt over, and tapped it in. He was in Medlen's arms, the two of them pounding one another for joy. Sue Price didn't really want to go out onto the green, she felt it was Nick's moment not hers, but her parents and their friends were pushing her and she finally went out there and Nick practically crushed her with his bear hug.

A few minutes later, at 6:18 P.M. on a sparkling summer evening, Charles Jack, the captain of Turnberry, introduced "the champion golfer of the year," and handed him the coveted claret jug. Price grabbed it in his huge hands and kissed it with all his might. "In 1982, I had my left hand on this trophy," he said. "In 1988, I had my right hand on it. Now, at last, I've got both hands on it."

They cheered and cheered and cheered, and Price smiled and

smiled and smiled. He had read a magazine article a few weeks earlier previewing the tournament that had mentioned that he had twice had one hand on the trophy. When he finished reading the story, he had made a vow: "Someday, I'm going to get both my hands on that damn thing."

19

WELCOME BACK, ZINGER

THE BRITISH OPEN is the only tournament from which almost no one leaves on Sunday night. Unless you have a private plane, there's no way to get out of the remote places where the tournament is held, especially if you have to fly overseas to get home.

Greg Norman's private plane left Prestwick Airport less than an hour after Price put both his hands on the claret jug. His former plane, which now belonged to Price, was parked directly across from his new plane, so Norman wrote Price a note and taped it to the door of the plane before departing.

"Two years in a row this plane has carried the claret jug home," he wrote. "Congratulations. Well played."

Norman had listened to the final few holes of the tournament on BBC radio during the forty-five-minute drive from Turnberry to Prestwick, and it had given him a boost. He had left the golf course feeling hollow, disappointed that he had been close to contention without ever really being in the hunt. His parents had been with him for the week since they were coming to Florida for a visit and he had wanted them to see him win a major championship — or at least have a chance to win one.

Norman made about $33,000 (£19,333) for finishing tied for eleventh, meaning he probably broke even for the week if you figure the cost of flying his twelve-seat G-3 jet back and forth across the Atlantic and the cost of four rooms for seven nights at the Turnberry Hotel (one for him, one for his children, one for his parents, and one for his pilots) into the equation.

The expense of playing in the British Open had been an issue all week, since a number of top Americans, including Curtis Strange, Fred Couples, and Hale Irwin, had stayed home. Strange skipped the British Open about as often as he played it, and although he had entered the tournament in 1994, he had never intended to play — unless he won the U.S. Open. Strange had enjoyed himself when he had played in the tournament in the past, but he didn't think he had a good chance to win and thought the effort and expense were too much if he didn't honestly think he could win. There was another reason he didn't play: "Because everyone says I have to," he said.

He might not be as angry as he once was, but he was still just as stubborn.

Price and his friends celebrated his victory with a raucous party at the Turnberry Hotel, the claret jug serving as a champagne holder for most of the night. Late in the evening, Davis and Robin Love and Brad and Bonnie Faxon happened upon the party and were invited to join in. They did, taking their sips from the jug along with everyone else.

"It's amazing how much colder and fresher champagne tastes when you drink it out of this jug," Jeff Medlen said.

"You're right, Squeek," Price said.

"Funny thing," Davis Love said, "to me it tasted tinny."

It is all a matter of perspective.

Naturally, the Price party ran over into the wee hours. Earlier, Tom and Linda Watson had eaten dinner with Jack and Barbara Nicklaus. As soon as he finished his work for ABC, Nicklaus had gone back to the hotel and called Watson.

"Let's get some dinner," he said.

Watson sounded awful. "I don't think so, Jack," he said. "I think we'll just order room service."

"I understand how you feel," said Nicklaus, one of the few people on earth who really could understand how Watson felt. "But I think you need a good dinner with some good wine."

"I appreciate it," Watson said. "But I don't think I'm up to it."

Nicklaus knew not to push too hard. Five minutes later, the phone rang. It was Watson. "What time?" he asked. Apparently Linda Watson had disagreed with the idea of spending the night wallowing. The Watsons and the Nicklauses had a sumptuous meal that included two bottles of wine. At about 11 o'clock, with the Scottish sun just disappearing over the western horizon, the two couples decided to adjourn for an alternate-shot golf match on the par-three course that spreads out across the vast front lawn of the hotel. Watson had a cigar stuck in his mouth and a huge grin on his face. Nicklaus had been right to call him. Linda Watson chipped a ball to about four feet. Tom's turn to putt.

"Oh no, Linda, look what you've done now," Nicklaus said. "You've left him a four-footer."

Watson glared at Nicklaus, stalked up to the putt, and rammed it into the hole. "You see," Nicklaus said, smiling. "You *can* make those putts."

They all dissolved in laughter. Watson would feel the pain again the next day, but at least for one night, he was laughing. A few hours earlier he would have thought that impossible.

The next morning, although he wasn't in the greatest condition of his life, Price (after pulling Norman's note off the plane) flew to Nottingham to see his mother. He walked into the dining room carrying the now-empty claret jug and put it on the table. Wendy Price's eyes went wide. "I'll be right back," Price said. "You just sit here and enjoy it for a while."

He left her sitting there, eyes glistening with pride. Price, who hadn't cried the day before in the midst of his stunning victory, felt his eyes misting too. He had dreamed often of handing his mother the claret jug. Now he was living his dream.

On the other side of the ocean, real life went on. The PGA Tour always held an event opposite the British Open for those who didn't qualify for the tournament and those who didn't choose to go. Once, the tournament had been held in Chattanooga. Now Chattanooga was gone, replaced by the tournament that had in the past been held the same week as the Masters: the Deposit Guaranty Classic, which had been moved from Hattiesburg, Mississippi, to Jackson.

The prize money — $700,000 — was the smallest on tour all year, but the event carried the same two-year exemption as any other for the winner and the same ticket to the Masters, the World Series of Golf, and the Tournament of Champions.

And the winner of all those extras, in addition to the $126,000 first prize, was Brian Henninger. His first PGA Tour victory didn't turn out exactly the way Henninger had envisioned it. He won the tournament on a soggy Sunday morning by winning a playoff from Mike Sullivan after tournament officials had determined that the golf course, drenched from three days of on-again, off-again downpours, was not going to be playable that day. Henninger and Sullivan had been tied for the lead after thirty-six holes, so they were brought back to the course to play off.

The only hole that was even close to playable was the 18th. Henninger and Sullivan were told they would keep playing the hole until someone won. As it was, eighteen was soggy and drenched. Henninger got it over with quickly, rolling in an 18-foot birdie putt. There was no gallery, no television, no one screaming for John Daly. But it was a win.

Henninger told the media that he was thrilled and proud to be the Deposit Guaranty champion, but he wouldn't feel as if he had really won on tour until he won a seventy-two-hole tournament. A number of players read those comments that week and were impressed. Billy Andrade made a point of telling Henninger when he saw him the next week that what he said had merit, but he should never feel as if he hadn't earned the victory. "You can only do what they give you the chance to do," he said.

When he finished with the media, Henninger called Cathy at home. His mother answered the phone since she and Brian's father were visiting. Thinking that Brian was about to go out and play his final round, she chattered on about how cute the baby was and how much fun they were having. Finally, Brian broke in.

"Mom, I won the golf tournament," he said.

"You what? But how?"

He explained what had happened. Everyone was thrilled . . . sort of. "I love the idea that I'm in the Masters and that I have a two-year exemption," he said. "But my goal is still to go out and win a seventy-two-hole tournament."

At least now he knew he would be able to play anywhere he wanted to through 1996 in search of that goal.

There are three weeks between the British Open and the PGA, just as there are three weeks between the U.S. Open and the British Open.

Because of the travel to and from Europe, the two tournaments that suffer the most in terms of getting name players in their fields are the one just before the British — the Anheuser-Busch — and the one immediately after it — the New England Classic.

For the past several years, the New England, played in the twenty-eighth week of the season, has been the first nontelevised tournament of the year (not counting the Deposit Guaranty, which goes up against the British). With the economy in the Northeast struggling, Ted Mingolla, the man who invented the tournament and runs it, has been unable to come up with a title sponsor who will make the TV buy necessary to get on a network or ESPN.

Even so, the New England is an event most players respect and try to play. Mingolla's golf course, Pleasant Valley Country Club, is in Sutton, Massachusetts, about ten miles outside Worcester. It is a pretty, tree-lined course with lots of variety in its holes and a small clubhouse that looks like an elementary school from the outside.

One player who had always come to the New England was Paul Azinger. When Azinger was still a struggling young player, Mingolla had given him a sponsor's exemption into the tournament, and Azinger never forgot. Regardless of the date, Azinger always showed up at the New England. In 1993, he had won the tournament.

And, in 1994, he had hoped to make the New England his first tournament back on tour after his chemotherapy and radiation treatments were over. That would have worked perfectly: defend at the New England, perhaps get one more tournament under his belt before the PGA, and then hope to play at least respectably when he defended his PGA title.

Life is never that simple. Azinger had made his first post-chemo public appearance on May 16 at the PGA's pretournament media day in Tulsa at Southern Hills, the site of the 1994 tournament. He had talked on the phone to a couple of reporters during the process but had, for the most part, stayed away from the public eye. He had decided early on that he didn't want to fight a public fight, that he would talk about the whole thing once it was over. His last chemo treatment had been on May 3. A CAT scan on his shoulder the next week showed no signs of cancer.

Staying home and not seeing his buddies and not playing golf and not exchanging barbs with the media had been both a blessing and a curse to Azinger. He missed the people, but not the attention. He missed the competition, but not the tour life. He missed the game, but not the time away from his family. He loved being at home, spending time with Toni and Sarah Jean and Josie Lynn. He hated knowing how worried they were about him.

When the family flew home from Los Angeles in December after the first round of chemo treatments, Paul and Toni sat the girls down on their bed one night and tried to explain to them what was going on. Daddy was sick, they said, and he was taking some medicine that would make him feel bad for a while but was going to make him better. His hair was going to fall out, but that was okay too, because it would come back in a few months when he was all better. Most important, he *would* get better.

They never mentioned the word cancer. Which was a mistake.

"The first day Sarah Jean went back to school after Christmas break she came home crying," Azinger said. "All the kids had come up to her and said, 'Oh, we're so sorry about your dad, he's got cancer, isn't that awful?' She was terrified. She asked me if I had cancer and what was it and was I going to die. It hadn't occurred·to us that second-graders would know about cancer, but they did."

Azinger had to explain to Sarah Jean that cancer was scary, but it was curable and that his kind was especially curable. That calmed her, but even after his chemo was over and his hair began to come back she continued to be frightened of cancer. "We all fear cancer," Azinger said. "It's just that, in my family, we fear it a little bit more now."

The next five months fell quickly into a pattern: a flight to Los Angeles, chemo treatments, a week of misery, then three weeks of feeling better just in time to go back for another chemo treatment. His mood swings were predictable, but by the time April rolled around, he was beginning to see the end and he realized that all the talk about getting better hadn't just been talk. He was getting better.

When he walked into the packed ballroom in the Southern Hills clubhouse, he looked different than the Azinger everyone remembered. He was a little thinner and he was bald. That didn't bother him, he had gotten used to that. What had bothered him was having his eyebrows fall out in the fifth month. He had never dreamed he would look forward to shaving again, but he couldn't wait to get his hands on a razor.

With close to two hundred reporters in the room and another sixty from around the world hooked up by phone, Azinger gave a painstakingly detailed account of what he had been through, including a re-creation of what he had sounded like dry-heaving for nine hours after the first round of chemo. Several times he had to stop because he began to choke up, talking about his family or about the outpouring of affection he had received from thousands and thousands of people. He talked about his Christianity and how he felt closer to God now than he had before.

"Some people might say, 'Why me, God, why me?' he said. "I just ran to God and he helped me through it."

It was a long day in Tulsa. After his mass interview, Azinger did a dozen TV interviews and then another dozen brief one-on-one interviews with print reporters. From there, he flew home for a day and then on to the Memorial Tournament, where he was the defending champion. He spoke briefly at the pretournament awards ceremony and then took part in the junior clinic later that day.

He was tired by the time he flew home that night, but he felt good. Tulsa and the Memorial represented his reentry into the world that had been his life for twelve years. He was glad to see all the players again. He was even glad to see the media. And everyone was glad to see him.

His treatment wasn't over yet. He had to fly back to Los Angeles for five weeks of radiation treatment. Dave Stockton, who had been Azinger's Ryder Cup captain in 1991, insisted that he and the family use his house — he was away playing in senior tour events most of that time — so they stayed there. The privacy was nice, but the girls missed their friends and the days were long, since he received his treatment first thing in the morning and was finished after that.

Shortly after arriving in Los Angeles, he began to swing a golf club and hit some shots. A couple of days into the regimen, his shoulder began to hurt. It scared him. He called Dr. Jobe. "You're going too fast," Jobe said. "Nothing's wrong. But stop. Don't push yourself."

He stopped. Four weeks into the radiation treatments, he had some fatty tissue removed from behind his chest. He had noticed it well before the cancer diagnosis and had pointed it out to Jobe, who had been convinced it was just fatty tissue. His oncologist, Loren Feldman, decided it should be removed, just to be certain.

It was removed and it proved to be just what everyone thought it was: fatty tissue. Nothing more. But somehow word got out on tour that Azinger had undergone more surgery and the cancer might be back. At the Western Open, Davis Love asked Larry Moody, the man who ran the Bible study group on tour, point-blank what was going on. "Honestly, Davis, it was just fatty tissue," Moody said.

"You can understand," Love said, "why everyone's worried."

Moody understood. So did Azinger. Jobe and Feldman had both told him after the surgery that it would be four weeks before he could start taking full swings with a golf club. That meant he couldn't possibly play New England. He called Mingolla and told him what was going on. Mingolla understood but wanted to know if there was any way Azinger might come up for a day. Absolutely, Azinger said.

And so he was there on Pro-Am day, riding around in a cart for a while to see some players, notably his buddy Payne Stewart, who was suffering through a horrible year. He met with the media and updated them on his progress. Now, he said, he hoped to play in the Buick Open, which was the week before the PGA. He didn't want the PGA to be his first week back, not only because it would mean he would have no warm-up at all for the tournament, but because it meant that week would be even more of a zoo for him than it was already going to be.

Everywhere Azinger went, someone stopped him to tell him how much they had been thinking about him or how glad they were to see him back. As he walked into the lunchroom, Tim Simpson, a veteran player who had never been close to Azinger, hugged him and told him he had been praying for him and thinking about him a lot.

"That's why I have to play the Buick," Azinger said. "You see, every guy out here is going to feel he has to say something to me. They feel a need to say something. I understand that. The funny thing is, there are going to be people out here who didn't much like me before this happened, who are going to like me now. The rest of my life, whenever I walk around a golf course, there are going to be people who are going to come up and talk to me about cancer; how they had it or someone in their family had it, or a good friend had it. Everyone's been touched by cancer in some way, and I'm out here in public having been touched by it.

"I understand that. And I think I have a responsibility to use that public forum to help raise money to fight the thing and to help out anyone I can who is fighting it. I know what it's like. Other guys don't. It would be brutally insensitive of me to just walk away from it and I don't intend to.

"But there's a part of me that just wants to come back out here and *play*. Compete. I haven't sat around missing golf for the last few months, I've been too busy trying to get healthy. But today, out there with Payne, I wanted to say to him, 'Okay pards, let's just drop a couple balls in the bunker and see who can get closest to the pin for five bucks.'

"I want to compete. I don't want to walk around saying, 'Oh well, I made a bogey, but at least I have my health.' I don't expect to come back and be where I was as a player, but I want to get back to the level I was at sometime. The sooner the better."

Tulsa and the Memorial had been the first step, New England was the next one. The big step, though, was the Buick Open in Grand Blanc, Michigan, about an hour north of Detroit. Azinger had been practicing at home for two weeks and had been given clearance to play. The national media showed up again, first for his initial practice round on Tuesday, then when he did it for real on Friday.

He had to wait until Friday because torrential rains early Thursday wiped out the first round. Instead of teeing it up at 12:50 as scheduled, Azinger spent the afternoon at the movies, going to see both *A Clear and Present Danger* and *Speed*. He hated waiting an extra day because he wanted to get the anticipation behind him and start playing again.

Friday was a perfect day, cool and gorgeous, and Azinger's every move was documented by TV cameras, still-photographers, and reporters. When his playing partners, Ben Crenshaw and Corey Pavin, walked onto the 10th tee (they were playing the back nine first) Crenshaw looked at Pavin and said, "Gee, Corey, it's real nice of all these people to come out here and watch us tee off."

Randy Hutton, a local product analyst, was doing the player intro-ductions on the 10th tee, something he had done at the tournament for ten years. He knew this was different. "It's a once-in-a-lifetime thing," he said. Hutton introduced Pavin first: "From Orlando, Florida, please welcome Corey Pavin!"

Pavin smiled at the applause and launched a bullet down the middle.

Azinger's turn. Hutton again: "From Bradenton, Florida, please welcome back to the game, Paul Azinger!"

It was the four extra words, "back to the game," that got Azinger. He had joked beforehand about getting on the first tee and being so emotional that he couldn't draw the club back. Now, he stood behind the tee as the applause and cheers washed over him, taking several extra practice swings, his eyes looking straight at the ground. He didn't want to look up, because if he did, people would see they were glistening with tears.

"Corey told me later I should have just said my eyes were sweat-ing," he said.

Pavin's eyes were sweating and so were Crenshaw's.

Finally, Azinger took a deep breath, gathered as much composure as he could, and somehow hit the ball solidly down the right side of the fairway. The shouts could be heard in every corner of the golf world.

Zinger was back. He shot 76 that afternoon, but came back with 70 the next day. He missed the cut, but that hardly mattered. He had hit some good shots and some bad shots. He had gotten angry at himself for missing putts. He had competed. The warm feeling he had every time the crowd cheered him one more time was just a bonus.

"My victory was getting up on that first tee and hitting the ball," he said. "The whole thing is over. I'm a golfer again. I'm back in my element."

When he got back to his locker that first evening, exhausted from the walk and the work, the exhilaration of the whole day, and the post-round media circus that he had known would be part of the deal, he collapsed on a bench. Several players came by to ask him how it went. He recounted a couple of missed putts and his concern on the first tee that he was shaking so much that he might heel one into the crowd and kill someone. "That would have been some comeback, huh?" he said, laughing.

He started to open his locker and found two notes taped to it. Each was from someone who had a friend fighting cancer. Could he possibly call, even if it was just for a minute?

Azinger pulled the notes off his locker. "There are some things I have to do now that I'm back," he said, "and some things I don't have to do. These are the ones I *want* to do."

He made the calls that night. There would be many more to come. That was fine with Azinger. "I tell them all that cancer is beatable," he said. "I tell them to go out there and beat cancer's butt."

He smiled. He didn't say, "I did." He didn't have to.

The three tournament winners between the British Open and the PGA were Kenny Perry, a veteran having the year of his life, who won at New England; Dicky Pride, a rookie who came from nowhere on the money list to win at Memphis in a playoff; and Fred Couples, who finally had put his back miseries behind him.

Couples hadn't been on tour for long stretches in 1994, and his 65–68 finish during the thirty-six-hole Sunday windup, which was brought about by the Thursday rainout at Buick, was one of the more heartening stories for American golf in a year when there were a lot more Americans out with injuries and illness (Couples's back, Mickelson's leg, Azinger's cancer) than competing for major titles.

Couples played superbly on the last day at the Buick in spite of a bizarre incident that occurred on the range shortly before he teed off for his morning round.

While he was warming up, a man in his thirties who was standing behind the ropes several yards away from Couples, began yelling at him to please come over and sign his hat and shirt and talk to him. He was yelling so insistently that Couples finally turned around and said, "I can't right now, I'm trying to get ready to play."

The man persisted. When Couples left the range to head for the first tee, the man followed him, insisting that he had to talk to Couples, that he *had* to have him sign his hat and that this was very, very important. Security people were called in so that Couples could get to the tee unimpeded.

When the man was taken to tournament officials, he explained to them that he had had "a vision" the previous night about Couples and that it was vital that he talk to him if only for a minute. If he didn't, the vision would be gone and his life would be ruined. He had even gone so far as to write a four-page letter to him, explaining the vision and why it was important that they talk.

Couples couldn't talk now, he had thirty-six holes of golf to play. Fine, the man said, would you at least give him this letter and I'll go watch him play and not bother him. He had made no threats, so the officials took the letter from him and let him leave. PGA Tour officials were called in. The local police department sent an undercover officer to trail the man in case he should make any kind of move on Couples. Extra security was also assigned to his group.

The next question was how much to tell Couples. Since 1977, when Hubert Green was subjected to a death threat during the final round of the U.S. Open, each player on tour has filled out a form at the start of each year in which he is asked how much — if anything — he wants to be told if any kind of threat or bizarre request (like this one) involving him is made during a round of golf. On his form, Couples had asked to be told nothing. Some players ask to be told everything and anything; others take a middle ground and ask to be told only if tournament officials think the matter is serious. Like any group of visible athletes, professional golfers are subjected to occasional threats or crank phone calls. Usually they involve well-known players like Couples or Greg Norman or John Daly.

Fortunately for everyone involved, this incident blew over early in the day. The "vision man," as officials called him, followed Couples for a number of holes and then left. Noticing the extra security, he told an official, "I didn't mean to cause any trouble," before departing. The letter itself was rambling, confusing, and full of misspellings. It invited Couples to a party that day so that the "vision man" and a number of his friends could explain to Couples what he could do for society. The man signed his name and gave his phone number and the address of the party. He also asked Couples to bring Azinger along with him.

Couples didn't show. Instead, leading Corey Pavin by one shot on the final hole of the day, he carved his second shot at the 18th to within two feet of the flag for a birdie that clinched his first victory on tour since the 1993 Honda Classic.

Couples was back. Azinger was back. Phil Mickelson was back. Pavin, who had gone through a midyear slump, was playing well again. Curtis Strange tied for third at the Buick.

Things suddenly looked a lot better for American golf. The PGA was next. Nick Price and Greg Norman were waiting.

20

THE NEW KING

ALL YEAR LONG, everyone on tour had been talking about how hot it was going to be in Tulsa in August. Mike Carrick, the president of the caddies association, had written a letter to the PGA of America pleading with it to suspend its "no shorts" rule for caddies during the PGA championship. The request — naturally — was turned down. Nick Faldo had brought a dozen of the thinnest white shirts he could find and specially made extra thin, extra light pants.

Nick Price had planned to play at both Memphis and the Buick to prepare for the PGA. But after finishing fourth at Memphis, he changed his mind. He was still exhausted from the British Open and the post-tournament exhilaration; knowing how hot it would be at Southern Hills, he decided a week off was better preparation than another week grinding away on the road. "I'm fried," he told the Buick people. "Please forgive me, but I just have to be rested for next week."

He arrived in Tulsa on Monday afternoon, went to the house that he was renting about a mile from the golf course, and went straight from there to the club to hit some balls. He and Jeff Medlen found a quiet spot on the back end of the range and began to work. After about thirty minutes, Price looked at Medlen and said, "I feel so good and so relaxed, it's unbelievable."

If the other 155 players preparing for the fourth major had heard that, they might have decided not to bother killing themselves in the heat. These days, Nick Price feeling good usually meant that everyone else was going to go home Sunday night feeling bad.

*   *   *

For many years, the PGA Tournament has been the wayward stepchild among the four majors. Timing has a lot to do with it. There just aren't very many places you can take a golf tournament in the United States in mid-August without running into brutal heat. Perhaps if a permanent home was established in Michigan or Minnesota, you might have a fighting chance, but the PGA of America likes to move the tournament around to great golf courses the same way the USGA moves the Open around.

There is also the question of who plays in the PGA. Once upon a time the PGA was *the* governing body of professional golf in the United States. But as the tour grew, the pros began to feel the need for an organization set up strictly to deal with their needs, not the needs of club pros. After all, the two jobs could hardly be more different. A club pro spends twelve to fourteen hours a day servicing other people's golf games. A touring pro spends his days being serviced so that he can work on his golf game.

In 1968, the touring pros broke off from the PGA and established the PGA Tour. People still confuse the two entities, referring to the PGA Tour simply as the PGA. If you want to upset someone who works for the tour, just ask him what it's like working for the PGA. Then duck.

The PGA Tour and the PGA of America have co-existed peacefully, if at times uncomfortably, since the split. There is a PGA member on the PGA Tour policy board, and almost all tour players are members of the PGA, partly as a courtesy, partly because you must be a PGA member to play on the Ryder Cup team and also because it allows them to have insurance coverage should they be involved in an accident (like hitting a spectator) during a tournament.

The PGA's two big events are the PGA Tournament and the Ryder Cup. It always galled tour commissioner Deane Beman that the PGA made the money it did on the Ryder Cup when it was dependent on tour members to make up the team. The players don't mind that as much as they mind the fact that until 1995, the PGA Tournament still reserved forty spots in its field for club pros.

"How can you call it a major tournament with that field?" Peter Jacobsen asked the week before the 1994 tournament. Jacobsen, who has twice finished third in the PGA, was upset because he was seven spots out of making the field. It upset him, just as it annually upset players who didn't get in, that he wasn't going to be playing while forty club pros, none of whom could begin to compete with him on a regular basis, would be playing.

Jacobsen was right. He was also wrong. By letting club pros into the field, the PGA sacrificed depth. The tournament did not have the 156 best professionals in the world; it had the 116 best and forty club pros, and that meant that some good, deserving players — like Jacobsen, among others — got left out of the field. For 1995, the PGA of America relented and dropped the number of club pros to twenty.

Major championships are built on tradition. It is Masters tradition that several amateurs be invited to play and that all past champions hold lifetime exemptions. With a field of fewer than ninety players, a number of them amateurs and older champions who have no chance to seriously compete, it has the weakest field of the four majors. Both the U.S. Open and the British Open save a large chunk of their spots for players who get into the tournament through open qualifying — anyone with a two-handicap or better, amateur or professional, can enter the qualifying field just by paying the entry fee. The U.S. Open had close to 5,000 players seeking about a hundred slots in 1994. That means someone like Billy Andrade, fortieth on the U.S. money list in 1993, didn't get into either tournament in 1994. Qualifying is a crap shoot and, without fail, some deserving players don't survive. And the PGA, which is an organization for club pros, run by club pros, allows a group of them to compete in its championship each year.

Each major has a different tradition that in some way waters down its field. But those traditions are also part of their charm.

The PGA had bottomed out, really, at Shoal Creek in 1990. That was the year that Hall Thompson, the founder and president of the Birmingham, Alabama, club, which was hosting the tournament for the second time in six years, said publicly that the club would not accept black members. "That's just not done in Birmingham," Thompson had told an interviewer when asked what might happen if a black was proposed for membership in his club. A firestorm followed, and there was talk that the tournament might be moved to another site. Shoal Creek finally agreed to admit a black member (talk about blatant tokenism), and the PGA Tour, PGA of America, and USGA all established guidelines for clubs hosting events that required minority membership.

It was not exactly a feather in the cap of the white males who run golf that they finally got around to making this demand in the wake of a public humiliation. They also made no requirement of clubs (like Augusta National) in terms of female membership. And some clubs chose to give up tournaments rather than follow the new guidelines. Among them were Cypress Point, part of the three-course AT&T Pro-Am rota, and Butler National, the longtime home of the Western Open.

There was very little talk about golf during the PGA at Shoal Creek, and no one really noticed or cared very much about Wayne Grady's victory. Since then, though, the PGA's luck had changed, starting with John Daly's startling, Cinderella victory at Crooked Stick in Indianapolis in 1991. By the time Daly's last putt went into the hole on Sunday afternoon, everyone in the country seemed to know the story of the Bunyanesque character who had gotten into the field as the ninth alternate and could hit the ball nine miles.

Daly's emergence as a folk hero, even with all his ensuing problems, did nothing to diminish the effect his victory had on a tournament that desperately needed a charisma boost. Nick Price's victory a year later wasn't as dramatic, but it was certainly popular and the shootout at Inverness in 1993 that had ended with Paul Azinger beating Greg Norman in a playoff that Nick Faldo just missed gave the tournament another boost.

Now, Azinger's dramatic comeback as the defending champion gave the PGA a story line even before it began. Azinger had been right about the importance of playing in the Buick. He flew into Tulsa late Saturday afternoon and went out to play nine holes before sundown. He and his caddy, Mark Jiminez, had almost the entire golf course to themselves and Azinger reveled in the privacy.

By the time Monday came around and he had to start dealing with all the tugs on his time, he felt settled in and relaxed, ready to play a golf tournament rather than experience the kind of catharsis that the Buick had been. He knew he was a long way from playing well and there was some stiffness in his shoulder — understandable after all it had been through — but at least he was beginning to feel like a golfer again rather than a martyr or a victim.

The person feeling most like a victim during the practice days was, of all people, Jack Nicklaus. The subject causing Nicklaus difficulty (this was, after all, the tournament that had given golf Shoal Creek) was race — specifically, comments Nicklaus had made a month earlier when asked the nagging question about the lack of black players on the PGA Tour.

In 1994, there were two blacks on tour: Vijay Singh, who was from Fiji, and Jim Thorpe, who was from Buffalo. At forty-five, Thorpe was the last in a line of very good black players who had started playing the tour in the 1960s. Men like Charlie Sifford, Pete Brown, Lee Elder, Jim Dent, Calvin Peete, and Thorpe had played the tour successfully. Elder had become the first black to play in the Masters in 1975, and Peete had followed him there and had won a total of twelve tournaments, including the Players and the Tournament of Champions. Both Elder and Peete had played on the Ryder Cup team.

But no one had come along to replace them as they grew older. There were dozens of theories on why this had occurred: the death of caddy programs around the country; lack of role models; lack of access to most country clubs; and the fact that a majority of the black population lived in cities and were nowhere near 99 percent of the existing golf facilities.

There wasn't a single black player on either the PGA Tour or the Nike Tour between the ages of twenty and forty. Already, Tiger Woods, the eighteen-year-old who would become the youngest player to win the U.S. Amateur later in August, was being burdened by huge expectations. He was the Great Black Hope.

The tour was aware of all this and was taking steps to change things. Several years earlier, Finchem had told the policy board that he believed lack of minority participation was a tremendous problem for the sport and needed to be addressed. Since then, the tour had started a minority internship program that had brought several bright young people into the game — although not as players. The tour also ran junior clinics at most tour stops and brought minority youngsters to the clinics. Earlier in the year, looking for role models anyplace he could find them, Finchem had persuaded Michael Jordan to host the tour-produced weekly TV show *Inside the PGA Tour.* Jordan, Charles Barkley, and other black athletes who played golf for fun were offered spots in Pro-Ams on tour anytime they wanted them.

That was a start, but it certainly wasn't a solution. Thorpe had summed the whole thing up best when he told a story about convincing a golf club maker to give him three hundred sets of clubs to give away to minority youngsters in the Buffalo area. A year later, he had found takers for only thirty of the three hundred sets. Black kids wanted to play basketball, football, baseball. Even tennis had the memory of Arthur Ashe and excellent female players like Lori McNeil and Zina Garrison to use as role models. Golf had Jim Thorpe, a twenty-seven-year gap, and Tiger Woods.

Nicklaus had gone to Vancouver, B.C., to spend a day at the site of a new golf course he was designing. During what is normally a routine press conference, he was asked by one of the local reporters about the dearth of black players in golf. Nicklaus answered that he thought it had a lot to do with environment, that most black kids grow up in a city environment, that they are routinely introduced to baskeball and football and — less so now than in the past — baseball, but not introduced to golf. White kids, most of whom grow up in the suburbs, were introduced to golf and tennis in addition to the traditional team sports.

At some point, Nicklaus said something about black muscles and white muscles. He believes that what he said was, "Black kids and white kids grow up using different muscles because of their different environments." He was quoted as saying "Black kids and white kids have different muscles and as a result develop differently."

Those quotes are very different. The interview is not on tape, so neither Nicklaus nor the reporter can prove definitively who is right and who is wrong. "If I said what I was quoted as saying, then I would have to say I was wrong," he said. "But I honestly don't think that's what I said, and it certainly wasn't what I intended to say. The guy asked me the question about twenty different ways, so I can't *swear* to you that I didn't misspeak, but I'm pretty sure I didn't."

Regardless, the story began to spread — slowly at first, then building momentum. Once it got picked up in the national media, the good ship Nicklaus began taking on water fast.

In his early years on tour, Nicklaus had developed a thick skin while playing the role of black hat to Palmer's white hat. He was called cruel names because of his weight and made fun of because he was so deliberate over every single shot. As he lost weight and gained stature, he graduated from bad guy to popular star to icon. His victory at the 1986 Masters had sealed that status, the Augusta throngs going about as berserk as Augusta throngs are allowed to go.

He would never be as popular as Palmer with the fans, the media, or the other players. But he had come a long way. Even players who looked at him as aloof and arrogant were awed by what he had achieved. After all, if you added up all the majors won by Ballesteros, Faldo, Norman, Price, and Strange they didn't equal Nicklaus. Palmer and Watson combined fell short of Nicklaus. You simply couldn't touch his record. And, for the most part, the media liked him. He might get snappish occasionally, but he was always honest and almost never ducked a question.

Now, though, he was under attack. And, it was for a crime he didn't believe he had committed. "Regardless of who or what you believe about that press conference, check my record," he said. "I am not the person they're saying I am."

In fact, when he had built his golf club at Muirfield Village outside Columbus, Nicklaus had made certain to include blacks, Jews, and women in the membership from the very beginning. He and Chi-Chi Rodriguez had done fund-raising work for minority programs that had raised several million dollars in recent years.

The case could be made that Nicklaus — like almost all the great players of the last thirty years — had not used his platform as a public figure often enough to protest racist and sexist practices in country clubs and golf organizations throughout the country. Watson, whose wife and children are Jewish, was an exception. He had resigned from Kansas City Country Club when the club refused membership to tax genius Henry Block, who is Jewish. Sexist practices are still routinely accepted in golf. At the PGA champions dinner in 1994, the men still sat in one room, the women in another. No one complained.

"We can all do more, I don't question that," Nicklaus said. "But when I turned pro, there were quite a few good black players on tour. The first round of golf I played as a professional one of my playing partners was Charlie Sifford. I was a twenty-one-year-old kid and,

from what I could see, Charlie Sifford had the same access to tournaments that I did."

Could Nicklaus be more outspoken? Yes. Was he a racist? No. Was
he anywhere close to being the least sensitive player in the locker
room on the subject of race? Not even in the ballpark. Had he probably oversimplified the problem in the Vancouver press conference,
regardless of how the words came out of his mouth? Yes. Did he
deserve to be crucified? No.

Nonetheless, he was feeling like a martyr by the time he arrived
in Tulsa. The flight from Palm Beach was spent discussing strategy
for dealing with the inevitable questions that were going to come up,
especially at a tournament that had been touched by racial controversy
in the past.

The final decision was, basically, to punt. Nicklaus would not accept an invitation to come into the media tent for a pretournament
interview, and if (when) he was asked about the subject in the locker
room, his answer would be no comment. A brief statement was
drafted, and Andy O'Brien, whose father, Larry, had been Nicklaus's
right-hand man forever, was authorized to hand it out to anyone who
asked about the controversy.

The statement said: "I have never knowingly or willingly made a
statement or action that is racist. God created all of us equally. We
are then influenced by our environment. That is all I have said. If
confusion regarding my feelings has caused any offense, I hope my
clarification here will remind everyone of my personal convictions,
which are as strong today as they have been throughout my life."

Nicklaus hoped that would calm the waters. To some extent, it did,
although he was criticized in some quarters for refusing to answer
questions. It was the climax of a frustrating year for Nicklaus. It had
started with high hopes when he won the senior division of the Mercedes (aka Tournament of Champions) Championships but then went
straight downhill. The only cut he had made on the regular tour had
been at the U.S. Open. Even there, after his stirring 69–70 start left
him three shots out of the lead, he had faded into the pack with a 77
on Saturday. And now this.

He played in a daze Thursday, hitting shots that would have embarrassed him as a twelve-year-old. Jeff Sluman, one of his playing part-

ners that day, had never seen Nicklaus so lifeless, so totally lacking in energy or fire. "I just can't stop thinking about all the things people are saying about me," Nicklaus said to Sluman. "It's devastating."

Nicklaus felt so awful during the round that he actually considered signing his card at the end of the day and withdrawing. The only time he had ever withdrawn from a tournament was with an injury. He was injured now — wounded was more like it — but not in a manner that made withdrawing excusable.

When he walked onto the 18th green, they gave him a long, warm ovation. The heat wasn't as bad as had been expected, but that meant that it was "only" 93 degrees and muggy. It had been a long day. Nicklaus waved a tired hand in thanks. His ball was just over the green and he had hit 77 shots. He needed to get up and down to break 80. He took his time, chipped the ball to four feet, and then, after a long look, drained the putt. Even in an embarrassing round of 79, he had found something to play for on the 18th hole. "I just didn't want that snowman [8] on my card," he said later.

He didn't withdraw. He knew that was wrong, and he came back the next day and shot a respectable 71, missing the cut by six shots. His wife, Barbara, couldn't ever remember seeing him so down, so beaten up by an experience. "He just can't let go of it," she said. "He's never been through anything like this before."

Through it all, the bashings and the 79, Nicklaus didn't lose his sense of humor. He and Barbara were renting a house on the Southern Hills property, and Barbara had promised the people who owned the house that they could bring their neighbors over to meet Jack and have their pictures taken with them on Thursday evening.

When he came out of the house to greet them all, someone said, "Mr. Nicklaus, we hope you come back real soon, no matter how tough a day you had today."

"That's nice of you," Nicklaus said. "You just tell me who here can beat 79 so I'll know who to get shots from."

He would be fifty-five in January and 1994 had been a disaster for him. He had always said he wouldn't keep playing if he didn't think he could compete. "And that's still true," he said. "But I don't think I'm there yet. I think I need to be in better shape than I am, especially below the waist. I'm going to work on the same conditioning program

Greg Norman's been on. If that doesn't work, well, then I have to think about quitting."

He wouldn't ever just play the senior tour, where he was still competitive, because, he said, to him golf was still about winning major championships. That was still his goal. At fifty-five.

"I've been told before that I'm crazy to think I can win another major," he said. "The first time was at the start of 1980 when I turned forty."

That was the year he won his fourth U.S. Open and his fifth PGA. It was also six years before he won his sixth Masters.

In all likelihood, Nicklaus won't win another major. But if you know anything about golf, you know that you never say never where (choose a title) the Golden Bear/the Great Man/Carnac/Jack William Nicklaus is concerned.

The pretournament stories were Nicklaus, the heat, Nick Price's quest for back-to-back major titles, and whether or not Greg Norman, who had done everything else you could do, would win a major title in 1994.

And the pending American shutout. Never, not once, not a single time (is that enough redundancy?) had a year passed since the first Masters was played in 1935 without an American winning at least one of the four majors. In fact, never before had a year reached the PGA without an American winning at least one title. But with José María Olazabal, Ernie Els, and Nick Price holding the keys to majors one, two, and three, and with Price the clear favorite in number four, the question again came up: What has happened to American golf?

"We are definitely in a cycle where most of the world's best players are foreigners," Tom Watson said. "I still think we have the most depth, but they have the stars."

There was also no doubting the fact that the prolonged absences of Azinger, Mickelson, and Couples — arguably the three best American players in the game — during much of 1994 had made a difference. But, even before their absence, foreign players had dominated the Masters (one U.S. victory since 1987) and the British Open (one U.S. victory since 1983). The U.S. Open had stayed in American hands until this year, and the PGA had been a mixed bag in the 1990s with two American champions and two foreign champions.

To the media, this was a big story. To the players, it wasn't that big a deal. After all, the theory that players on the European Tour were tougher under pressure than PGA Tour players didn't hold up when you considered the fact that Price and Norman had played on the PGA Tour most of their careers. And Nick Faldo and Seve Ballesteros had come to prominence during periods when they were playing the U.S. Tour frequently.

"It's all cyclical," Curtis Strange said. "And you know what, it really doesn't matter. When I go out to play, if it isn't Ryder Cup, I'm not playing for the U.S. and I'm not playing country against country, I'm playing for me." He flashed a grin. "If it's Nick Price against John Daly coming down the stretch on Sunday, who do you think I'm going to be pulling for? Who do you think most of the guys in the locker room will be pulling for?"

Everyone knew the answer was Price, in part because of his popularity, in part because Daly was still in the doghouse for his "everyone's on drugs" comments.

Things had almost gotten ugly at Memphis during the Tuesday shootout in which both Daly and Strange were participants. After checking with Daly, the master of ceremonies, Jack Sheehan, made a big show of placing a large rock on the tee just before he introduced Daly, saying, "And now, climbing out from under his rock . . ."

Strange, who had not been consulted, was not amused. He turned to several tour officials on the tee and asked, "You guys know anything about this?" Absolutely not, they said. After he had hit his own tee shot and the group started down the first fairway, Strange went after Sheehan.

"What was that supposed to be?" he demanded.

"Well, John and his guys thought it would be kind of funny . . ." Sheehan said.

"John and his guys? What about me? Do you think I thought it was funny?"

What bothered Strange was the notion that his comments about Daly might become a subject for schtick rather than debate. Most players he had run into since then had complimented him for what he had said. Daly had not said a word to him, which was fine with Strange.

"I don't need to talk to him," he said. "If he wants to apologize to everyone for what he did, that's fine. But until then, I really don't see why anyone would want to talk to the guy. If he doesn't like me, that's fine too. He won't be the first."

Like a lot of players, Strange was hoping the PGA would provide a fitting climax to his year. He had played well — better than any year since 1989 — but was hoping for one more big splash. The same was true of Tom Kite, who had a second, a third, and seven top-ten finishes in all, but hadn't won. Since breaking out of his slump at the Memorial, John Cook had five top-ten finishes in six tournaments. And then there was Norman. He had finished in the top ten nine times in thirteen tournaments and in the top twenty in twelve of thirteen. He had not missed a cut since the 1993 U.S. Open.

That was the kind of consistency that only a few players in history had ever produced. But his record in the majors in 1994 was T-18 at the Masters, T-6 at the U.S. Open, and T-11 at the British. Only Watson, among nonwinners, had a better record for the year. But for Norman, it was disappointing.

"If I win here, I've had a great year," he said after his practice round on Tuesday. "I wanted to make changes in my life, on and off the golf course, and I've done it. I've set up a new business, which has been great for me. I've worked very hard to be consistent week in and week out, and I've done that. I've tried to make a point of spending more time with my kids now that they're a little older, and I've done that. But the year's not over yet."

The last sentence was code for "I haven't won a major, and if I don't win here, my pal Nick Price is going to finish the year as the unquestioned number one player in the world."

If Norman couldn't be number one, his first choice to hold the title would be Price. Their friendship was genuine, not just a public relations ploy. But Norman didn't like playing second fiddle to anybody and, right now, Price had leapfrogged past him. In 1993, even though Price had won the player-of-the-year award, there was considerable doubt as to who was number one since Norman, not Price, had won a major and Norman was still ahead of Price in the Sony Rankings which ranked players worldwide based on performance around the globe.

Of course the Sony Rankings had to be taken with a large grain of salt. They were run by IMG, which was able to skew the rankings by putting extra emphasis on tournaments it managed and by inviting players it represented to those tournaments. But, since they were the only international rankings available, people did pay some attention to them.

Even now, as the PGA began, Norman was still ranked ahead of Price on the Sony Rankings — which only proved how fallible they were. Price had won nine tournaments worldwide in eighteen months; Norman, four. "Right now Nicky's number one, no matter what any ranking says," Norman said. "It's up to me to change that."

That was going to be a daunting task. Price had started the year unsure about a number of things, most notably his ability to match his performance of the year before. He knew that doing it once didn't make you a great player, and he also knew that not winning a major meant there was a large asterisk next to his player-of-the-year title.

When he won the Honda in only his second tournament of the year, that did two things: built his confidence, which was good, and redoubled the attention and demands coming his way, which was bad.

Price had watched with interest when Norman decided to break away from IMG and form his own company. Price had been with IMG throughout his pro career and had, for the most part, been happy with its work. Now, though, he needed more attention than he had received from IMG in the past, and its structure simply wasn't set up for that.

"I'm the type person that if someone calls me about a business deal or with a request of some kind I like to deal with it promptly," he said. "At IMG, if I tell someone to call, it may be two days before they have a chance to call back. That's not because they're irresponsible, it's because they're so big and they have so many clients. I was uncomfortable with that structure and that's why I started thinking about leaving." That and the fact that he was making so much money it would cost *less* to hire his own staff than pay IMG's 20 to 25 percent commission on business deals.

March and April crystallized his decision. At the Players, he was so snowed by requests and demands that he spent a total of ninety minutes on the practice tee before he played his first round. "That was disgusting," he said. He missed the cut there, finished a disappointing thirty-fifth at the Masters, and then missed back-to-back cuts at Houston and Atlanta, the latter by one shot, when he and Medlen miscalculated the number and thought they needed birdie at the 18th. Price went for the green when he didn't have to, knocked the ball in the water, made bogey, missed the cut by one, and went home furious.

He wasn't so far off his game that he wondered what was going on, but he was just far enough off that he was convinced that lack of practice time and concentration were killing him. He had missed only one cut in 1993; now, in April, he had missed three in 1994.

Several months earlier, John Brendecamp, a close friend from Zimbabwe, had told him he was planning to start a sports-marketing firm in London. Price had known Brendecamp, who had made millions in the tobacco business, for twenty-six years. When he decided he needed more attention than he was getting from IMG, he called Brendecamp. By the time he played in the Byron Nelson, the week after Atlanta, the decision had been made: he would leave IMG (he had a clause in his contract allowing him to leave if he gave thirty days' notice) and put his business in the hands of a new company. Two people would be hired to move to Florida and take over the day-to-day handling of any and all requests he received.

Perhaps it was coincidence, but two weeks after making his decision — in his next tournament — Price won the Colonial.

He played a practice round there with Norman, who noticed that he was holding his left shoulder a little higher when he putted than he had been the year before during his hot streak. Price made an effort to drop the shoulder a little and — bingo! — putts started dropping again.

When Price putts well, he is difficult to beat. Throughout his career he had always been a great striker of the ball but never a consistent putter. The Nick Price of the mid- to late 1980s was not that different than the Davis Love of the mid-1990s. If the putts are dropping, watch out.

Both his ball striking and his putting were way off at the U.S. Open and that was a letdown. Price couldn't help but wonder a little bit if he was going to be one of those players who was great week in and week out on tour but couldn't turn it up the extra notch at the majors. Fortunately he had the 1992 PGA win so he didn't have to deal with the best-player-never-to-have-won-a-major label.

He bounced back after the Open to defend his title at the Western Open before his breakthrough week at Turnberry. The last of his doubts was finally put to rest there. Now, with his new business setup in place, with winning the British Open no longer an unfulfilled obsession, with a new mallet-headed putter he felt comfortable with, and with a much-needed rest week behind him, Price knew he was ready to make a run at a second major. No one had won two majors in the same year since Watson had won the U.S. and British Opens in 1982.

By the end of the day Thursday, it was apparent that Price was going to have a shot to match Watson. His 67 put him in a tie for the lead with Colin Montgomerie. No one had done much to damage Southern Hills, a golf course all the players had great respect for. There were no tricks to Southern Hills, just a lot of different-looking holes that forced you to use every club in your bag. The heat was oppressive, but not as overwhelming as it had been at Oakmont. Every time it seemed ready to become completely impossible, a breeze would come whispering through the trees, giving just enough relief to make the conditions bearable.

Paul Azinger's dream of making a miracle comeback died quickly when he shot 40 on the front nine Thursday morning. He had to work to shoot 35 on the back nine for a respectable 75. He improved the next day with a 73, but that wasn't enough, the cut coming at 145. As with any golfer coming back from a long layoff, Azinger struggled around the greens. He didn't make very many putts, and he couldn't get the ball close to the hole the way he did when he was sharp.

"I missed the game more than I thought I did," he said. "I missed hitting wedges knee-high to a grasshopper that ended up three feet from the hole, I missed that feeling when you hit a seven-iron so pure you can't even hear the ball. I haven't had that feeling much yet, but I know it's going to come back. I can wait. I know now the worst is over, I know in my heart the cancer's gone. It's been an unbelievable experience — good and bad — but the important thing is that it's over."

It was the golf tournament that was over on Friday. At least in realistic terms. Having shot 67 on Thursday to tie for the lead, Price grabbed the tournament by the throat with a five-under-par 65. The 31 he shot on the back nine was a clinic of shotmaking and putting. He didn't miss a single green, and he was so dialed in on the greens that every putt seemed to hit the back of the hole. On the 13th, a butterfly landed on his ball just as he drew the putter back for a 15-foot birdie try. Price didn't flinch. He followed through and the putt rolled straight into the cup.

"It was too late to stop," he said with a huge smile, walking off the green. "I was committed."

He was committed to leaving the entire field in his wake. By the time Price was finished, he had a five-shot lead — unheard of after two rounds in a major championship.

Price had never felt more comfortable during a tournament week. He knew his swing was good and he was making his putts. His business questions had been answered. Each day, he went to the press room, talked about how dangerous everyone lurking behind him was, hit balls for an hour in the heat, and went back to his rented house to soak in the backyard swimming pool.

"I don't even want to think about what may happen on the weekend," he said on Friday evening in mid-soak. "In a sense, I've put pressure on myself now because if I don't win with this lead I'll have to wonder what I did wrong. But I'm mature enough now to know that no lead is safe."

He smiled. "If I do win, though, I know I'm ready for whatever comes with that victory. I'm prepared. Because right now, I'm already thinking that next year I'll be better organized at the start of this year than I was last year and I can *really* get after things."

As is always the case at any tournament, especially a major, there were story lines that had nothing to do with who was going to win. Bruce Fleisher shot the same 75 as Azinger on Thursday, and it looked as if he would be slamming his trunk on Friday one more time. Since he had knocked himself out of the Players with his final-hole bogey, Fleisher had fallen into a horrendous slump, missing ten of twelve cuts. The biggest paycheck he had cashed since early March had been $4,569 for finishing twenty-sixth in the rain-shortened Deposit Guaranty. His earnings for the year entering the PGA were $73,672. The possibility of a return to Q-School — at the age of forty-six — was becoming more and more real with each passing week.

"I think about it all the time," he said. "You can't help but think about it. I dread the idea of going back but I have to face facts. It may happen."

Fleisher actually walked away from his Thursday 75 feeling pretty good about the round. He had started out very nervous, knowing this was a week when he had a chance to make up some serious ground because of the size of the purse. He was spraying the ball all over the place before settling down on the back nine. "I could have shot eighty-five," he said, "but I got out with seventy-five. That left me feeling better than I had in a while."

It is funny how different a scrambling 75 can be from a bunch-of-missed-putts 75. Fleisher shot a 75 that gave him a confidence boost. It showed the next day when he shot 68, his lowest score since the first round of the Honda Classic (thirty-four rounds earlier) and made the cut by two shots. That put him in a position where a good weekend could make up for a lot of lost weeks.

For eleven holes Saturday, Fleisher did exactly what he had to do. He kept grinding out pars, no easy task at Southern Hills, and he birdied the 11th, hitting an eight-iron to seven feet after having to back off several times because a workman was pounding a hammer on the side of a house several yards away from the tee. When no one could get the workman's attention, Fleisher shrugged and hit his shot anyway. Walking off the tee, he turned around and jokingly shouted, "You just keep pounding like that all day if you want to."

The birdie put him one under for the day and only two over for the tournament. He was close to getting into contention for a good-sized check. But at the 12th he pulled a five-iron second shot way left of the green and missed a five-foot par putt. Okay, still even par for the day. Then, at 14, his 15-foot birdie putt looked dead center but rimmed out. A marshal standing a few feet away said, "I don't believe that!"

"Neither do I," Fleisher said.

He looked tired, worn out by the heat and the pressure. At 16 and

17 he missed the fairway badly with his driver, producing bogeys. He scrambled out a par from a bunker at 18. That left him with 72, not awful, but not good enough to move up in the standings on a day when it looked like he might shoot another 68 and pass a lot of people.

"There are times when you want to hide when it gets going bad," he said. "Today was typical. I get to a point where I start to feel confident and then one bad shot [the five-iron at the 12th] throws me off and I can't get it back. I don't know why that happens — if I did, it wouldn't happen. But it does, week after week.

"I've still got time left, but I know the clock is ticking. I ain't done yet though. I've still got some game left in me."

On Sunday, Fleisher shot 75 and finished tied for sixty-first. He made $2,800 for his efforts. He knew he needed to make a lot more than that. Soon.

Jeff Sluman had no Q-School worries. He had already made $166,000 for the year coming into the PGA, and even if he hadn't, he was exempt through 1998 because of his victory in this tournament in 1988.

This was an especially nostalgic week for Sluman. The tournament had originally been scheduled to be played at Oak Tree, the same course where he had won the title six years earlier, but financial problems there had forced the club to give up the host role. That was why everyone was at Southern Hills.

It was still Oklahoma and it was still the PGA, and even though he had missed the cut at Memphis, Sluman arrived feeling confident. All year long he had been improving slowly but surely. It hadn't been easy by any means. At the Masters, he had put in an exhausting week working with his teacher, Craig Harmon, and had been convinced on Sunday that they had turned a corner. He had gone from being virtually unable to drive the ball in the fairway on Thursday to feeling confident over almost every shot on Sunday.

He shot 73 that day, but felt as if he had hit the ball much better than that. He certainly hit it better at one hole — the 17th. There, he hit a perfect drive down the right side and walked over the crest of the hill expecting to see his ball all the way at the bottom, leaving him a short iron to the green. Instead, the ball was just over the hill, a good 50 yards shy of where he had thought it would finish.

One of the observers — men assigned by the tournament to observe play (in other words, watch with an ideal view) — was standing nearby. "Did you see what happened to this ball?" Sluman asked.

"It hit something," the observer said.

"Hit something?" Sluman was baffled. There was nothing around for the ball to hit except grass. "What could it have hit?"

The observer looked a little embarrassed. "Well, you see, I'd set up my chair here and it bounced and hit the chair leg and stopped."

Sluman felt himself reddening. The observer was supposed to be hugging the ropes, not lolling around near the fairway. As politely as he could manage, he explained that to him.

"Yes, yes," the observer said. "I understand."

"Apparently not," Sluman said, walking away, still angry.

He was left with an almost impossible downhill lie a long way from the green. He chopped the ball close to the green, but his pitch rolled too far and he made an aggravating bogey.

When his birdie putt on 18 hung on the lip and didn't drop, Sluman was uncharacteristically furious. He was convinced that the extra shot would cost him a spot in the top twenty-four — significant since the top twenty-four finishers at the Masters receive automatic invitations to the following year's tournament.

His thinking proved correct. He finished tied for twenty-fifth, one shot away from a five-way tie for twentieth. "I should have told him what I really thought," he said after signing his card. "Come to think of it, no I shouldn't have. Then I wouldn't have been back here again no matter what."

He took care of any questions about the 1995 Masters at the U.S. Open when he finished tied for ninth, since the top sixteen at the Open qualify for the Masters. More important, he played golf the way he had played it before 1993. He jumped into contention with a 69 on Friday that left him five shots behind the leaders and was still only five shots behind on Saturday when he ran out of gas in the heat and bogeyed 17 and 18. That was upsetting, and not making any birdie putts the next day was disappointing, but he hit the ball consistently well for four days.

"I never had to worry about it going sideways," he said. "I feel as if someone has passed a hand over me and said, 'You're cured, you can hit the ball well again.' "

It hadn't been magic though, it had been hours and hours on the range. Sluman has built his life on patience. He was patient when he stayed short all those years because of the medication he was taking. He was patient as he bounced from one college to another because no one believed he could play golf on the college level. And he was patient when nothing happened for him his first three years on tour.

Now he was being patient again, knowing he had the game to compete with the big boys but that getting back to that level consistently wouldn't happen overnight.

That patience was evident again at the Western (most notably when the program for the Pro-Am in his adopted hometown listed him as "Jim" Sluman) when he found himself one shot out of the lead on the back nine on Sunday only to have his swing fall apart down the stretch. He still finished tied for sixth (his best finish since a fifth at Hartford in 1992), but it was a letdown because he had been in position to win for the first time in what seemed like forever. Even so, he knew he was headed in the right direction, and he wasn't going to let a couple of bad shots late on Sunday knock him down.

He came to the PGA believing that a tough golf course in a major championship was perfect for him. And, just as at the Open, he was in contention (for second, since only one person was really in contention for first) through most of the tournament. He shot 70 the first day, struggled a little on the second with a 72, then roared back to shoot 66 on Saturday. That put him at 208, only three shots behind Jay Haas, who was alone in second place — three shots behind Price.

His tee time on Sunday was 1:40 P.M. He and Ben Crenshaw had only three groups behind them when they teed off. This was where Sluman wanted to be, where he felt he belonged, playing late on Sunday at a major championship. The day turned out to be a disappointment, he shot 75 to drop back to a tie for twenty-fifth, but Sluman knew the struggles of 1993 and early 1994 were behind him. He was a contender again. He would win again and he would be a factor on tour in the future. Like everyone who goes through a slump, he had wondered if that would happen. Now he knew.

"And someday," he said, "I'm going to figure out a way to do something about Rwanda and Haiti. "I love this life and what I'm doing, but I wish I was doing more."

Someday, he probably will. Some golfers are obsessed with their games. Sluman knows there are more important things to worry about.

Tom Watson wasn't obsessing about his game after the British Open, but he did have trouble bouncing back from what had happened to him there on Sunday.

"It really hurt," he said. "A lot. As badly as anything I can remember in my career. I guess I just got to the point where I was sick and tired of being hurt like that. I started feeling sorry for myself. I can't stand feeling that way."

He went home, took in a few Kansas City Royals games (while there were still games to take in), and played in an exhibition in Canada. He missed short putts on the first two holes at Southern Hills on Thursday, but somehow bounced back to shoot 69. He was still in contention in the B-Flight (non–Nick Price) going into Sunday at 208, but a 71 — with 34 putts — knocked him down to a tie for ninth place. Still, it wasn't a 74 and it meant he had finished 13th–6th–11th–9th in the four majors in 1994. It could have been a whole lot better, but for someone who had already been a Ryder Cup captain, someone who would be forty-five in September, it was pretty good golf.

And, when the PGA was over, Watson conceded he needed to do some thinking over the winter about his putting. He had hit the ball superbly for two years and didn't have a win to show for it. "I didn't putt very well here either," he said, sitting in front of his locker. "Yesterday, I shot sixty-seven with thirty-two putts. What could I shoot in some of these rounds if I got back to just being an average putter?"

He would go home and experiment with cross-handed putting and even with a long putter. He wasn't willing to say he would show up on tour in January with a cross-handed stroke or a long putter (he didn't), but he wasn't ruling it out. Not anymore. Not when he knew what his putter had cost him in 1994.

*   *   *

Price tried to give the masses hope during the third round Saturday. He had his one mortal day of the week, missing greens all over the place and rarely putting himself in position to make birdie. For a while, it seemed as if every time you looked up, Price was in another bunker.

Even though he had told himself on Friday night not to change his game plan at all, he couldn't help himself. With a five-shot lead, he couldn't help but play conservatively and that isn't his game. His lead actually shrank briefly to one shot when Jay Haas made a run, but just as he did, Haas made a triple bogey (his second of the tournament) to drop back. Price, having gotten up and down from six different bunkers, finally split the fairway with a driver at the 17th and threw his arms up in mock celebration since it seemed as if it had been days since he had found a fairway. He made a birdie on that hole, and when the day was over, after all the trials and tribulations and trips to the beach, he had shot an even-par 70.

This was the round that in the past would have ruined Price's chances. This was the day he would have shot 75 and lost his lead and not been able to rebound on Sunday. Now he kept things under control, got to the house in 70, and still had a three-shot margin on Haas, four on the Gritty Little Bruin and Phil Mickelson, and five on John Cook and Greg Norman.

Price readily admitted that it was Norman who most concerned him going into Sunday. "He's the guy who has the best chance to go out there and really go low, put up a sixty-three or a sixty-four," he said. "I'll be watching him all day."

He was on the practice green when Norman started out as if he was going to make Price look like a seer. He birdied the first two holes, and at the third, a hole where almost everyone hit an iron off the tee, he took out a driver and smashed the ball straight down the middle. Norman was pumped. He had started five shots back, only one less than he had been at the British going into the last round, but instead of having nineteen players ahead of him, he had only four. And he honestly believed the only one he really had to worry about if he could piece together one of his charges was Price.

In the CBS truck, Chirkinian and crew were doing everything but shouting at Norman to make his move because they knew that a Price blowaway would have people clicking the tournament off all over America. Norman missed a 12-foot birdie putt at the third; Price parred the first. Norman missed a 6-foot birdie chance at four; Price parred number two.

Norman was stalled, but there was still plenty of time left. A three-stroke margin with fourteen holes left for the challenger and sixteen left for the leader meant there was all sorts of time for things to happen.

Norman and Cook walked up the hill from the fourth green to the fifth tee, the huge gallery urging them on. Cook was one under for the day and four shots back, so he too had a chance. The fifth is a par-five, 614 yards long, unreachable in two. But two good shots will put you in a strong position to make birdie.

Norman, in a white shirt, black pants, and his trademark black GWS hat, stood over his drive even longer than usual. He had heard a number of "You-da-mans" the first few holes, something he had become oblivious to. Now, though, he heard one more. Only this one came on his downswing.

Norman flinched just a tiny bit and his ball flew just a tiny bit off line into the right rough. Furious — and rightfully so — he stood for several seconds glaring at the fool who had yelled.

"What in the world is your problem?" Cook said to the young man, almost as upset as Norman.

As the two players walked down the fairway, Norman was still clearly upset with what had happened. There was no margin for error, not when you were chasing Nick Price, and now, through no fault of his own, he faced a fairly difficult second shot.

He needed to regain his composure quickly. Only he couldn't. Still clearly fuming, he pushed his second shot and it clipped a tree and came to rest in a grove of trees. He had no shot to the green and no choice but to pitch out onto the fairway. His fourth shot, which should have been his third, ended up 18 feet right of the cup. The putt was dead center, only it came up two rolls short.

Bogey. Cook had made his birdie to get to five under. Norman was now back to four. And, as the two men walked off the green, the scoreboard showed that Price had just birdied the third. Norman was five back again. Only now, he had only thirteen holes to play. The charge, as it turned out, was over.

As he walked off the sixth tee, Tony Navarro could see his shoulders sagging. "That was a good swing, Greg," he said to his boss, referring to the tee shot he had just hit.

"I haven't really made a bad swing yet, have I?" Norman said. "I still can't believe that three-iron clipped that tree. Can you?"

Unbelievable or not, it had happened and it had quashed any momentum Norman might have gathered. He never did get to six under; the only pursuer who did was Mickelson. Just as he did, Price birdied the fifth, so even then his margin was still four shots.

It was never less than four shots the rest of the day. CBS had a runaway on its hands. Norman's quick start had, as it turned out, helped Price. It had gotten him focused right from the start and reminded him that he needed to play aggressively. He did just that, shooting 32 on the outward nine. By the time he made the turn, his margin on the field was six shots. When Norman and Cook walked onto the 10th green and saw that Price had reached 11 under, they looked at each other with the same thought: we're all playing for second.

Norman couldn't help but feel saddened to have played as well as he had all year long and still come up empty in the majors. He and Cook ended up tied for fourth with Faldo, one shot behind Mickelson and two behind Pavin. All the contenders played well. For Pavin and Mickelson, their finishes were their best ever in a major. Cook felt good to have played as well as he had both in the PGA and for three straight months. His confidence was back. But, like everyone else, he knew that Price was playing a different game than the rest of them.

"There was one tournament between three under and six under and then there was Nick," Cook said standing behind the 18th. "We should have stuck an extra club in his bag. Then we might have had a chance." He shook his head. "No, come to think of it, that wouldn't have helped either. The most it could cost him is four [penalty] shots."

Cook was right. Price's final margin was six, and it could have been more. He even admitted that he knew it was over before it was actually over. "When I made the birdie at sixteen, I turned to Squeek and said, 'You know I can double-bogey the last two holes and still win,' " he said. "I felt pretty good about my chances at that point."

As if to prove that he was human, he did bogey the 18th, but all that did was keep him from equaling the largest margin of victory in the tournament's history. He hugged Medlen and Sue just as he had done at the British Open, but the feeling was entirely different. There was no catharsis, no dramatic moment that moved him from contender to champion. He was the boss for all four days, never seriously challenged and, any false modesty aside, the clear-cut king of the game of golf. He had now won three of the last nine major championships and had done what the great players do: proven that when he is at his best no one in the world can keep up with him. As Price held the Wannamaker Trophy in his arms for the second time in three years, Leadbetter turned to Medlen and said, "You know, he's not quite in a zone yet, but he's getting close."

Medlen shook his head. "If this isn't a zone, the next place he's going is Deep Space Nine."

Having erased the one doubt that nagged him at the end of 1993 — his record in the majors — could Price now rest on his laurels?

"I certainly hope not," he said. "I want to reach a point where I'm thought of as a truly great player. I think one way to do that is to win all four majors. Only four players [Nicklaus, Sarazen, Player, and Hogan] have done that. I know it will be very hard for me to win Augusta and the U.S. Open, but that's what I really want to do. I think I'll be hungrier now than I've ever been."

Price had done the hardest thing there is to do in the game of golf: he had *controlled* the game rather than having it control him.

"Out here, you're always trying to get control of something that's uncontrollable," he said. "On the front nine today, from the first tee on, I felt like I was in control. That's such an unbelievable feeling."

He was relaxed now, unwinding, enjoying what he had done. "You know, I have this memory of being on the range at Bay Hill last year," he said. "I was working, working, working, and I look over and there's Arnold with three different sets of irons, looking for the right ones. He was just having the time of his life.

"The key to success in this game is finding a way to enjoy it no matter how you're playing. Arnold's done that better than anyone. He's sixty-four and he still loves it every single day.

"I know I'm not going to play this way forever, maybe I won't even play this way next year, next month, or next week. But I've played the game long enough now that I think I've learned to enjoy it whether I'm first or twentieth."

He laughed. "Of course, I enjoy first a lot more. But if you can still love golf on the days when it controls you, then you've got it made. Because there are going to be a lot more days like that than days like this."

Every one of them knows that. They all know the game will knock them down over and over again no matter how many championships they win. The best of them — from Palmer at sixty-four to Tiger Woods at eighteen — figure out somewhere along the line that all the aggravation, all the anguish, all the lonely hours, all the blood, sweat, and tears, is, somehow, all worth it in the end even though the game will always own you rather than you owning it.

No game is more imprecise, more elusive. The greatest players alive wake up most mornings having no idea whether the day will produce a 65 or a 75. If they have a gut feeling, it will be wrong nine times out of ten.

Jeff Sluman, who has known the highest of the highs and, far more often, the lowest of the lows, offers the most eloquent description there is of life as a professional golfer.

"I hate this game," he says. "And I can't wait till tomorrow to play it again."

EPILOGUE

THE PGA IS THE LAST TOURNAMENT for which all the big names turn out, although the next two weeks provide most of them with lucrative warm-down events: the International and the World Series of Golf. The World Series is supposed to be a major event, an invitation-only tournament for those who have won tournaments around the world (thus the name) but its importance has been watered down by two nearly identical tournaments: the Tour Championship in October and the Tournament of Champions in January. The money at the World Series is huge and the big names all play, but the intensity level is no different than at a regular tour event.

Once the World Series is over, most of the stars go home, picking and choosing an event or two to play in during the last two months of the schedule. The PGA Tour in September is a stage where the spotlight has been turned off. The purses are smaller — from Milwaukee to Texas the seven events average just under $1 million in purses as compared with a little more than $1.2 million per week from January through August.

Network TV, not wanting to compete with pro and college football, goes home for the winter. ABC televises two days of the Greater Milwaukee Open and the final day of the Tour Championship. Other than that, it is ESPN or no television at all. Four of the six tour events not on television at all take place in September and October.

For most people, unless the Ryder Cup is being played, golf goes away in the fall. They may read a paragraph or two in their local newspaper telling them who won in Milwaukee or in Coal Valley,

Illinois, or in Endicott, New York, but that is about it. They will pay more attention in November and December when the made-for-TV events start popping up because that is when the Shark and Freddie and Nicky and Els and the other glamour names are likely to start showing up again.

But even if the public is largely unaware of it, there is very important golf being played in conjunction with the turning of the leaves. Desperate golf. In many cases it is golf played by men fighting for their professional lives. Each week the faces look a little more tense, the Thursday and Friday threesomes become a little more quiet. The saddest sight of all is that of the longtime tour player walking up to a tour official and saying very softly, "Have you got a Q-School application handy?"

The battles are waged at many different levels in the fall. At the very top of the money list, a couple of players may be fighting for the money title, the Vardon Trophy, or the player-of-the-year award. They tend to focus on the Tour Championship, which is played the last week in October with thirty players splitting up $3 million.

In 1994, Nick Price had locked up player of the year the moment his last putt dropped at the PGA, but if anyone had any doubts, he erased them in September by making the Canadian Open his sixth title of the year. Even so, Greg Norman still led the Vardon Trophy race and had an outside chance of catching him for the money title going into that last week at the Olympic Club in San Francisco, the site of the 1994 Tour Championship.

Farther down the list, a number of players scrambled to try to make the top thirty on the money list. For someone who had not won a tournament, making the top thirty was doubly important. Not only did it put you into the Tour Championship — where *last* place was worth $48,000 — it put you into the 1995 Masters. That was why Davis Love III was so disappointed when he missed the cut in Las Vegas — a tournament he had won a year earlier — and dropped from twenty-ninth on the money list to thirty-third. Vegas was the last full-field week of the year and everyone knew that the number thirty-one player on the money list would get into the Tour Championship since José María Olazabal, number four on the list, was not a PGA Tour member and therefore would not play.

If Love had been able to get in, even at number thirty-one, he would have needed to pass only one player to make the top thirty. As it turned out, he finished $766 behind Mark Brooks, who was thirty-first with winnings of $474,831. What made it all even more painful was the memory of the one-shot penalty he had called on himself at the Western Open. Without that penalty, he would have made the cut there and a minimum of $2,000. That money would have been enough to get him by Brooks and Craig Stadler, who was thirty-second. Thus, Love ended the year knowing he needed a victory in the first three months of the new year if he wanted to play in the '95 Masters.

"It's been a long year," he said. "I've got to go home, figure some things out, and get off to a good start next year."

One thing he would go home and figure out was what golf clubs he wanted to play with. He was now convinced that he had to make the move to blades, even though he had three years left on his contract to play Tommy Armour investment casts.

Love's 1994 ended — for all intents and purposes — at the Masters. Going into that tournament, he had played eight times and made eight cuts. He had a second, two fourths, and a sixth, and had made more than $334,000. After missing the cut at the Masters and being as upset as he had ever been about a golf tournament, he never finished in the top ten again; he missed seven of his last twenty cuts (more than in 1992 and 1993 *combined*), and he lost confidence in his putter and his long irons.

The only saving grace of the last few months was his play in the inaugural Presidents Cup and in the World Cup. He won four matches and tied another and was the anchor in the United States victory over the International Team in September. In November he and Couples won the World Cup for the U.S. for a third straight year. Even so, it was the first time in five years that he did not win a tournament. Two years after winning almost $1.2 million and finishing second on the money list, Love wasn't anywhere close to being the kind of golfer he wanted to be or had the potential to become.

Of course there are struggles and there are struggles. In his worst year, Love still won almost $500,000 in official money. Well below him on the money list was where the real heartaches came. The magic number for keeping your playing privileges for 1995 turned out to be

$137,587. That was how much money Curt Byrum made to finish 128th on the money list. (Since three European Tour players were in the top 125, the cutoff number dropped by three places.)

Of the 125 who kept their cards, eighteen had come out of the Q-School in 1993 — an increase from the twelve who had survived from the 1992 school. Two — Mike Heinen and Dicky Pride — won tournaments. Heinen made the most money of those eighteen, earning $390,963 to finish fortieth on the money list. Glen Day — who acquired the nickname "All," as in Glen (all) Day, because of his (ahem) rather deliberate pace of play — was forty-fifth with $357,236.

Paul Goydos finished seventy-fifth on the list, making $241,107, nearly tripling what he had earned in his rookie year. He ended up with three top tens — including a seventh at the B.C. Open in September, his highest finish ever — and was in the top twenty-five nine times. He tired down the stretch, missing six of his last ten cuts after making eighteen of his first twenty-one. But he came away from the year feeling good about himself and about his golf.

"I think what I learned this year is that I'm good enough to play on tour for a while," he said. "Before this year, I really didn't know. I can still get better, a lot better, but I feel now as if I'm a pretty good player. I'll never be a great player, but I can do okay."

Goydos calling himself okay is akin to most people calling themselves the greatest. It had been a good year.

For his pal Brian Henninger, it was a fantastic year. He started out in no-man's-land, having missed the top 125 by two spots and at Q-School by two strokes. That put him in the 126-to-150 category, meaning that he was in on the big tour some weeks, stuck on the Nike Tour on others.

By the end of the year he had made $294,075 to finish sixty-third on the money list. More important, his victory at Deposit Guaranty, rain-shortened or not, made him exempt through 1996 and got him into the 1995 Masters. Even a mediocre fall — he didn't finish higher than twenty-sixth after his victory — couldn't dampen his excitement about the year. Like Goydos, he had arrived. There was no reason to think he wouldn't be on tour for years to come.

Of course he and Goydos, although friends, were quite different when it came to celebrating their success. All year Goydos had hoped that he would make enough money to get invited to Kapalua, the vacation/tournament played on Maui the week after the Tour Championship. He thought it would be a wonderful way to cap the year and give Wendy a much-deserved vacation. He was thrilled when he made the field.

Henninger also made the field. But he didn't go. "Elk-hunting season starts that week," he said.

Of course. So, instead of playing golf and snorkeling for a week on Maui, he headed off into the snow in Oregon with his brother to hunt elk. Who says golfers are faceless clones?

Billy Andrade and Jeff Sluman had gone on vacation before the season ended, taking their wives to Bermuda in late September along with Davis and Robin Love and Billy Ray and Cindy Brown.

Sluman's mood that week would have been euphoric if golf had been the only thing on his mind. On the Sunday prior to the start of the trip, he had finished second in the B.C. Open, his best finish since the 1992 U.S. Open. Even though he shot 72 on the last day and lost by four shots when Mike Sullivan shot a remarkable 66, Sluman had to feel that the week (he led the first three days after starting with a 64) was proof that all the hard work was paying off.

But Sluman's mind wasn't really focused on golf. Five weeks earlier, on the day before the start of the Buick Open, he had gotten a phone call from Rochester: his mother had a spot on her lung. Being the husband of an oncologist, Sluman knew exactly what that meant. He withdrew from the tournament and flew home right away. His parents pushed him out the door to play the PGA the next week. His mom insisted she felt fine.

For a while she did feel fine. The week of the B.C. was especially gratifying since Rochester is only about 100 miles from the tournament site in Endicott, N.Y., and it looked for a while as if Jeff might be able to give her a victory. He didn't, but he came close enough to know that "I put a smile on her face."

Sluman finished the season with another top ten — seventh at the Buick Southern — giving him four top tens since the U.S. Open. He even thought he had a chance to sneak into the Tour Championship if he played well in Texas and Las Vegas. "I hit the ball well both weeks," he said. "But I putted like Bozo the Clown." He ended up fifty-ninth on the money list with $301,178 up thirty-four spots (and $114,000) from 1993. Not as good as he wanted, but a noticeable improvement.

"All I know is, a year ago I wondered if I would ever hit another fairway," he said. "Now, I honestly think I'm going to win out here again and I know I've got my swing back where it should be. All of that makes me feel a whole lot better about the game."

Sadly, the news off the golf course wasn't nearly as good. On December 9, after the family had spent Thanksgiving together, Sluman's mother died. It was, to say the least, a tragic loss for Sluman but as 1995 began, he was trying to move ahead the way he knew his mom would have wanted.

"I miss her every day," he said. "And I don't expect that to change or want it to. But I do feel like she's still alive in the sense that I can still hear her voice and remember her smile and all the things that made her happy. As long as I feel that way, she'll always be with me."

Sluman hadn't told very many players about his mother's condition but Linda had told Billy Andrade. When Andrade heard the news, he jumped on a plane and flew to Rochester for the funeral. When Sluman greeted him, they collapsed into each other's arms and Sluman said, "It was great of you to come."

"I had to come, Jeff," Andrade said. "Your mom did my wash."

It was exactly the right thing to say. Sluman remembered his mom doing Andrade's wash during the B.C. Open and the memory made him laugh.

Andrade had also ended the golfing year on an up note, thanks to a third-place finish in Vegas. He had played indifferently most of the fall, unable to get his game back to the level he had reached when he almost won at Doral. But after spending some extra time working with his teacher, Rick Smith, he put together five straight rounds in the 60s at Vegas and was briefly tied for the lead on Sunday afternoon.

He couldn't quite keep up with the birdie barrage put on by winner Bruce Lietzke and runner-up Robert Gamez, but finishing 24 under par, even on a relatively easy course, was an encouraging way to finish the year. He won $342,208 to finish forty-eighth on the money list — eight spots lower than he had finished in 1993. Still, he felt as if he wasn't that far off.

"Money is great," he said. "But winning is what it's about out here. I just have to keep working and keep believing in myself."

One reason Andrade would like to have won was that a victory in Vegas would have put him in the Tour Championship and the Masters. He had missed playing in the Masters in 1994 and had been in the Tour Championship only once — in his double-win year of 1991 — and he felt as if that was an elite group he should belong to at the end of each year.

Paul Azinger had been in every Tour Championship since the event had been created in 1987. As late as August, when he made his triumphant return to the tour, he held out hope that he might get hot in the fall and still sneak into the event. Not surprisingly it didn't turn out that way. His shoulder was sore — from lack of work, nothing more serious — after the Buick Open and the PGA, and his instinct was to just sit out the rest of the year and start all over again in 1995.

But his shoulder started to feel better in mid-September and he changed his mind, entering both the Southern Open and the Walt Disney World Classic. He actually played pretty well in both events, tieing for nineteenth at the Southern and for thirty-third at Disney. Encouraged, he entered both Texas and Vegas, still hoping a couple of high finishes might keep his Tour Championship streak intact.

He never got to the starting line in either tournament. This time it was his back that flared up. Again, he decided not to push it. His year really was over. In all, he made $13,422, exactly $1,445,036 less than he had won in 1993. And yet, without question, no one was more of a champion on tour in 1994 than Paul Azinger.

Curtis Strange had won the Tour Championship in 1988, becoming the first man to make more than $1 million in a single season as a result of that victory. He qualified for the event again the next year, but hadn't been close since then.

In 1994, he had a chance. And if it had been a priority, he might have qualified. He had made a little more than $368,000 going into the fall and was thirty-first on the money list. But he played in only three more tournaments — skipping his usual trip to Disney when he was invited to play at St. Andrews in the Dunhill Cup — and ended up forty-first.

Strange took some heat in the media for accepting the invitation to Dunhill after skipping the British Open. Dunhill is a team event, three-man teams representing their countries with every player given a guarantee just for playing. Many saw Strange's decision to play in the IMG-run event (he is an IMG client) as a cop-out after not playing the British.

Strange saw it differently. For one thing, he planned to play in the 1995 British Open — which is at St. Andrews. For another, he was able to take his oldest son with him and show him Scotland in an atmosphere far more relaxed than a British Open week. What's more, if money was all Strange cared about, he would have played Disney and a couple of other events to try and lock up a spot in the Tour Championship, which carries a $48,000 guarantee *and* the possibility of winning $540,000 at week's end.

In all, Strange had to feel happy with 1994. It was his best year since 1989, and he had a real live chance to win the U.S. Open. Most important, Sarah felt almost entirely recovered from her bout with Chronic Fatigue Syndrome and the two of them were closer than they had ever been.

"We both learned a lot of things about each other this year," Sarah Strange said. "And almost all of them were good."

John Cook hadn't been through anything quite as traumatic as Strange, but he had dealt with the worst slump of his career and had finally come to grips with his relationship with his father. He had a superb summer, finishing in the top ten six times in seven tournaments. That included a fifth at the U.S. Open and a tie for fourth at the PGA.

He didn't play well in the fall and, like Strange, fell short of making the Tour Championship, ending up thirty-seventh on the money list at $429,725. The summer had sapped him, but for the right reasons. He had played a lot of high-pressure, high-stakes golf and had acquitted himself well.

"I'm really getting to the point where, a couple of years from now, I may want to cut back on my schedule," he said. "Maybe play only fifteen times a year. Early in the year, I was beginning to think the game might cut me before I was ready to cut it. At least now I know I can still compete out here for a few more years. It's a relief."

Tom Watson turned forty-five on September 4, and having earned $380,378 in just fifteen tournaments, he had no doubts about his ability to continue to compete and play well on the tour. He felt good enough about his game that he briefly considered changing what had become his fall ritual — going home to be with his kids when they returned to school — because if he had changed plans, he probably would have qualified for the Tour Championship for the first time since 1987, when he had won the inaugural version of the event.

In the end, though, he decided to stick to his original plan. His last tournament of the year was the International. Resting in the fall had worked well for him the previous year, so why not rest again? At forty-five, the last thing in the world he wanted to do was overplay.

The question for Watson as 1994 ended was exactly the same as it had been when 1994 began: could he find a putting stroke that would get the ball in the hole on Sunday afternoon? Clearly, that was the only thing keeping him from breaking his seven-year victory drought. Just as clearly, he wanted to win badly enough that he might show up on tour in 1995 putting cross-handed, one-handed, left-handed, or — believe it or not — with a long putter. Watson is extremely traditional, extremely proud, and *extremely* stubborn. But the near-misses in 1994, most notably that last torturous day at Turnberry, made him think about taking the plunge.

"I watch him hit the ball and then I watch him putt and I just don't get it," Nick Price said. "If you aren't getting the ball in the hole, you *have* to try something else. He's just hitting the ball too well not to win out here. It's gotten to the point of being painful to watch at times. I wish he would try something different."

In the end, he didn't. Tom Watson is *very* stubborn.

For Janzen, 1994 was a strange odyssey. It started terribly, came together with a brilliant two-week rush, and then faded into mediocrity again almost as quickly.

After a fourth at the Kemper and a win at Westchester in back-to-back weeks, Janzen played twelve more times before the year was over and failed to finish higher than thirteenth. Although he insisted the hernia operation he had in July didn't affect his play — he missed Memphis and then missed the cut his first week back at the Buick Open — it seems likely that it was just enough of a problem to keep him from getting back to where he had been during his two-week hot streak.

He finished the year thirty-fifth on the money list with $460,331, not exactly a terrible year, but enough of a drop that some golf writers were already labeling him a one-major wonder who would never be heard from in an important tournament again. Other players didn't buy that theory. The consensus remains that Janzen, who turned thirty during the World Series of Golf, will show up on some important leader boards in the near future.

The same could probably be said of Nick Faldo, Tom Kite, and Greg Norman. All three flirted with contention at the majors during 1994, but none was ever right *there* at the finish. Each had a fourth-place finish (Kite at the Masters, Norman and Faldo tieing at the PGA), and Kite had three top tens, Faldo and Norman two.

Norman won the Vardon Trophy for the lowest scoring average on the PGA Tour, finished second on the money list, and didn't miss a cut all season. He had eleven top-ten finishes in sixteen tournaments, an extraordinary run of consistent golf, and for the second straight year, won well over $1 million. Kite was no slouch either with more than $700,000 in earnings and eight top-ten finishes.

Faldo won a tournament in Europe and made a firm decision (as did Ernie Els) to play on the PGA Tour in 1995, being convinced that the best way to prepare for the majors is to play against the best competition as often as possible.

All three men conceded that they could hear little clocks ticking in their heads. Kite turned forty-five in December, Norman turned forty in January, and Faldo would be thirty-eight in July. That didn't mean any of them was being fitted for a walker, but it did mean that time *was* a factor.

"If you had the same sense that the clock is ticking when you were twenty-four that you have at forty-four, you would probably have been a lot more intense down the stretch in big tournaments back then," Kite said. "But that's impossible to do. When you're young, you think you'll play forever. You think you're bulletproof."

Norman claimed he couldn't wait to turn forty because he remains convinced he will play his best golf in his forties. Given his conditioning and the success so many others have had recently in their forties, there is no reason to doubt him.

But can he beat Nick Price? Can anyone? That was the game's most-asked question as 1995 began. No one dominates in golf the way a top player can dominate in tennis. But Price went into the 1995 Masters having won back-to-back major titles to close out 1994, a record total of $1,499,057 in official earnings for the year, and with a hunger that seems to grow, rather than dissipate, with each new accomplishment. He says he wants to become the fifth player to have won all four major titles, and right now he would seem to be the player on tour with the best chance to do that, even though Watson only needs to win a PGA to join the elite group.

One outgrowth of the Norman-Price versus Watson-Nicklaus Wednesday matches at the British Open and the PGA was a proposal for yet another made-for-TV event. This time, Price and Norman wanted to take on all challengers in match play, probably in some kind of thirty-six-hole format, with a corporate sponsor putting up big bucks for each match.

The germ of the idea actually began when Price and Norman sat in the clubhouse at Southern Hills having lunch after they had beaten Watson and Nicklaus in the rematch of their Turnberry duel. "We should do this all the time," Price said to Norman. "This is great for getting you sharp, getting you ready to play."

Price was thinking as a golfer when he made the comment. Norman, always thinking as a businessman, took the concept to the next step: one where there was money to be made.

One group that Norman contacted about the proposed matches was the Fox Television Network, which is owned by Australian media-magnate Rupert Murdoch. Before Norman and Fox were finished, the match-play concept had been scrapped.

In its place was a proposed eight-tournament, $25 million "World Tour." The idea was to take the top thirty players in the world, throw in ten sponsor exemptions — to get names like John Daly into the mix — and develop a tour that would compete with — and no doubt damage — the PGA Tour.

Fox wanted in because it had decided, after purchasing the rights to the National Football League and the National Hockey League, that acquiring sports properties was the best way to build the network. Norman clearly wanted to be more than just the second-best player in the world; he wanted to be a mover-and-shaker, not just a golfer. This was his way of making that move.

The new tour clearly had the potential to make the very rich in golf even richer. It also had the potential to severely damage the fabric of the PGA Tour, since it is built on the notion that the stars will play at least fifteen tournaments — and usually between twenty and twenty-five — a year and that the weekly tournaments truly mean something to them as well as to the journeymen, who sometimes rise up and beat them.

There would be no one like Brian Henninger or Paul Goydos on the World Tour. There would be no rookies like Dicky Pride or Mike Heinen who would come from nowhere to win. The money — $3 million a tournament with $600,000 to the winner and $30,000 for last place — would become like Monopoly money. There would be no grinding to make the cut because there would be no cuts. Each player would be given $50,000 annually in travel expenses in addition to the guarantee of thirty grand a week just for showing up.

If all of this sounds familiar, it should. In the 1970s, professional tennis became a battleground with two separate tours competing for players. The money went higher and higher, and by the time the dust had cleared there were so many tournaments in so many places that almost no one following the sport could understand what tournaments mattered and what tournaments didn't matter.

Top players didn't even try very hard very often, and appearance fees skyrocketed so high (stars now routinely get $250,000 just to show up for some tournaments) that most tennis tournaments nowadays are nothing but glorified exhibitions for the big names. Golf has avoided that by maintaining the integrity of the week-to-week events with everyone playing toward a goal, whether it is winning player of the year, finishing in the top thirty, or keeping one's playing privileges by making the top 125. The tour certainly needs its stars, and if they go off to play elsewhere eight weeks a year and either cut their schedules on the PGA Tour drastically (which would be against the current fifteen-tournament-minimum rule) or play in fifteen but only half-heartedly, *or* are banned from the tour if they sign up for the World Tour, the entire sport will take a major hit.

Golf does not need a so-called World Tour. It already has one in the four majors, a half dozen PGA Tour events that draw most of the world's top players, the Ryder and Presidents Cups, and a small handful of important overseas events. Already, most of the world's top players get together a dozen times a year. And when they do, the pretenders to their throne get a shot at beating them. The Fox/Norman tour would be elitist and would lack story lines like Mike Donald almost winning the U.S. Open or Tom Lehman coming from mini-tour exile to almost win the Masters.

The World Tour is strictly about making the rich richer and Greg Norman's ego bigger. Finchem reacted quickly to the mid-November announcement, saying it was against the rules for PGA Tour players to take part in such a tour and, in his opinion, would hurt the game. By January 1, not a single player had signed up for the World Golf Tour and the idea, if not totally dead for 1995, was on life-support. Start-up was delayed until November 1995 at the earliest.

While Norman and friends wondered where their next few million would be coming from, Bruce Fleisher, Mike Donald, and Jeff Cook ended the season wondering where they would be playing in 1995.

Fleisher had hoped that making the cut at the PGA would provide a springboard to the strong fall he needed to keep his card. It didn't work out that way. Fleisher made only two cuts in his last nine tournaments and was twenty-ninth the two weeks he did play on the weekend.

He kept slogging along, even with a bad shoulder, week after week, hoping he would catch fire someplace. Instead, he played himself into such a state of exhaustion that he had to withdraw from the Texas Open with two weeks left on the schedule. He turned forty-six that Sunday and tried to come back for one last try at Las Vegas. But with his shoulder killing him, he shot 72–74 the first two rounds and withdrew, knowing he had no chance to make the 54-hole cut.

That left him with winnings of $88,680 for the year, only $22,800 of it coming after the disastrous bogey that cost him the cut at the Players. He had been eight-for-eight making cuts going into that week. He was just five-for-twenty-one the rest of the year. Since he finished 163nd on the money list, he had to go all the way back to the second stage of Q-School. That was a long road back — four rounds at the second stage, then six more at the finals — to the big tour. But he survived, finishing seventh at the Q-School finals. He was back on tour for 1995 and one year closer to the promised land of the seniors.

Jeff Cook also found himself playing the second stage of the Q-School. But for him, that was a victory, since it had looked for much of the year as if he would be all the way back to the first stage. He struggled through most of the summer, unsure whether to abandon what David Leadbetter had shown him during the winter or stick with it, hoping for a turnaround. By the fall, he had given up on Leadbetter and was trying to find some consistency with his old swing. He improved slowly.

He ended the regular portion of the Nike Tour fifty-first on the money list. The top fifty get into the Nike Tour Championships. But Cook got in because Mike Brisky, thirty-fourth on the list, decided to play in the Texas Open on the big tour that week. Cook took advantage of his good fortune, playing his best golf of the year. He finished in a three-way tie for second, one shot behind winner Mike Schuchart, and jumped to thirty-fourth on the money list. That got him a free pass to the second stage (the top ten on the Nike list make the big tour; eleven to twenty-five go straight to the finals; and twenty-six to fifty go to the second stage) and gave him a big boost of confidence.

"I've struggled with my putting all year," Cook said. "Now for the first time, I feel good about my swing and my putting. If I can keep that feeling at the school, I think I've got a good chance." He cruised through the second stage and was back where he had been twelve months earlier: the finals. Once again though, he didn't make it. Once again, at least for one more year he said, it was back to Nike land.

Mike Donald was certainly hoping to keep the feeling he had during the fall. He had bounced back and forth from Nike events to big tour events all summer. Late in August, he decided he was wasting his time in Nike events. "I wasn't playing bad, I wasn't playing great," he said. "Every week, it seemed like I finished fifteenth. That wasn't getting me anywhere."

He decided he needed to focus on preparing for Q-School and called Paul Marchand, the Houston-based teacher he had worked with on occasion in recent years. They spent three days together, and Donald came away hopeful again. There had been times during his two-year slump when he had thought his game was coming back only to find that it wasn't.

Much to his surprise, he received a last-minute sponsor's exemption into Milwaukee. A 72 the first day was discouraging, but he hung in on Friday and came to 18 needing a birdie to shoot 68 and make the cut. It was late in the day, so there was no doubt what the number would be. Facing a six-foot putt, he rammed the ball into the back of the cup. Then he shot 65–70 on the weekend and finished eighteenth.

"It's amazing how delicate the game is," he said later. "If I miss the six-footer, I leave town down on myself, thinking, well, here we go again, playing just well enough to miss the cut. Instead, I show up Saturday feeling great and play great and end up leaving feeling like eighteenth was a great week. There was a time when making the cut on the number felt like a waste of time to me. Now I was really excited that I had hung in there and made it."

He finished thirty-second at the B.C. Open, again coming back from a bad start (five over par after eight holes) to make the cut and went to the Hardee's Classic feeling better than he had in three years. "There's a huge difference between hoping you'll play well and knowing you'll play well," he said. "Hardee's was the first time in a long time I started the week knowing I was going to play well."

He was right. He shot 68–66–64–67 and finished tied for third. The $58,000 check was the biggest he had cashed since the Open in 1990 and was worth more than he had made in all of 1993. He then played two more solid weeks, finishing nineteenth at the Southern and fifteenth at Disney.

In five weeks, he had made just under $100,000 after having made $70,000 in the previous twenty months. He had one tournament left — Texas — and knew he probably needed a top-ten finish to make the top 125. Maybe it was pressure, maybe it was just exhaustion after making five straight cuts, but on Friday, after an opening 69, he shot 75 to miss the cut, fading on the last nine holes.

That was a letdown. But he still finished with $119,065 for the year. That put him 141st on the money list, meaning he was straight into the Q-School finals and, perhaps just as important, as a top-150 player, he was guaranteed entry into fifteen to seventeen tournaments in 1995 even after playing poorly for a second straight year at Q-School.

"The best part is that I have hope again," he said. "For a long time, I had no game and no hope and no answers. I went to Q-School last year having missed eleven straight cuts. My attitude was awful and it showed. Now I feel good about myself and my game again. I have a chance to compete. That's all I can ask for."

The year would not have been complete without another round of bizarre behavior from John Daly.

Throughout the World Series of golf, Daly seemed intent on hitting into players in front of him. When he did it to Norman's group on Thursday, Norman's caddy, Tony Navarro, peeled back and asked Daly what the rush was.

"If you guys would get going, maybe we could play some fucking golf out here," Daly told Navarro.

"Are you in such a hurry to shoot eighty?" Navarro asked, before turning around to rejoin Norman.

On Friday, it was Andrew Magee who was upset with Daly for not waiting until his group was out of range. Saturday passed with no new troubles, but things got worse on Sunday. Daly kept hitting shots into or close to the group in front of him, one that included a club pro named Jeff Roth, who had gotten into the tournament by virtue of his victory at the National Club Pro Championships. At the 15th hole, a reachable par-four for most players and especially for Daly, he pulled out his driver with Roth's group still on the green.

"Maybe you ought to wait," Neal Lancaster, his playing partner, suggested.

"Why?" Daly answered. "It's a fucking par-four, isn't it?"

With that, he blasted away, landing the ball pin-high, next to the green. When he came up to the green, Roth's parents were waiting there to give him a piece of their minds. Daly turned to Roth's mother and, repeating what had become his favorite line, said, "You know something, you remind me of my ex-wife."

When the round was over, Roth and Daly exchanged angry words in the parking lot. Then Daly got into it again with Roth's parents. Before anyone knew what was happening, Roth's sixty-two-year-old father had jumped on Daly's back and the two men had to be separated.

A few minutes later, when Curtis Strange finished his round, he walked into the locker room and heard several players talking about Daly's antics on the golf course. He rounded a corner and found Tim Finchem talking to someone.

"You know something, Tim, I may be out of line saying this, but if you don't do something soon, I'm afraid Daly's going to end up in a fight," Strange said.

Finchem smiled wanly. "Too late," he said. "There's already been a fight."

Naturally, the incident made national headlines. Just as naturally, Finchem was circumspect about what he would do next, saying he would "investigate."

The last thing anyone heard Daly say as he left that day was, "Fuck the PGA Tour. I'm sick of it. I'm outta here."

Two weeks later, at a player meeting before the Canadian Open, the subject of Daly came up. Bruce Lietzke, the quiet Texan who has become a legend on tour by playing no more than sixteen or seventeen weeks a year and still remaining a consistent winner, stood when Daly's name came up.

"Whatever you feel you have to do, Tim, you do it," he said. "We all know this is a tough situation for you, but we're behind you."

The overwhelming sentiment in the room was anti-Daly. Most players felt he had used up more lives than a cat. And yet they understood that if Finchem simply brought the hammer down on him with a long-term suspension, sponsors would scream and many in the public would view Daly as a martyr, no matter how ludicrous that notion might be.

Finchem talked to Daly and his agent the following week. A compromise was reached: Daly and Finchem would announce that Daly had "voluntarily" decided to take the rest of the year off. "Voluntarily," in the same sense that someone with a toothache "voluntarily" goes to the dentist. "John can come back to the tour as early as the

Mercedes [Tournament of Champions] Championships in January," Finchem said.

The phrasing was important. "As early as" clearly meant that his return was conditional and would be based on whether Daly finally got himself counseling and appeared — déjà vu — to be ready to act like an adult on tour. His "everyone picks on me" act had worn thin with most of his fellow pros.

A month after Finchem announced the "voluntary" decision, Daly was quoted in the *Atlanta Journal-Constitution* as saying that the decision not to play the rest of 1994 was entirely his and had nothing to do with Finchem and everything to do with a sore back he had been nursing. If telling the truth was a criterion for Daly's return, he was going to be in trouble.

He still managed to win sympathy from people. At the Tour Championships in San Francisco, Norman, who had been virtually frothing at the mouth at the mention of Daly's name throughout the summer, was asked about Daly. Norman promptly launched into a monologue about what a fine young man Daly was, saying he was good for the game and he would do anything he could to help him in the future. No doubt he thought now that Daly had been quoted "out of content" in the British tabloids.

As it turned out, Daly had called Norman, apparently seeking forgiveness for his behavior during the summer and, after a forty-five-minute conversation, Norman had decided that Daly was his new best friend. Could their "friendship" have anything to do with both having multimillion-dollar deals with Reebok? Could it have been Reebok that "suggested" they chat? All one can do is speculate.

Daly returned at the Mercedes Championships saying he had learned his lesson — again. The saga continues.

As for the PGA Tour itself, it was a fascinating year. It began with Deane Beman as commissioner and ended with Finchem as commissioner. How different were the two men? On the Saturday of the Tour Championships, Finchem took several players to a Rolling Stones concert. Beman could not have handled all the noise.

There was a victory by a grandfather/TV announcer (Johnny Miller) and, for the first time ever, not a single victory in a major championship by an American. American stars were an endangered species. Azinger missed almost the entire year with cancer, Fred Couples missed most of four months with back troubles, and Phil Mickelson missed three months with both legs broken while skiing.

The second leading American-born money winner in 1994 was Tom Lehman, who five years ago was ready to quit to become a college golf coach. The top American was forty-three-year-old Mark McCumber, who, after going six years without a victory, won three times in less than four months, including the Tour Championship. Hale Irwin, who will be eligible for the senior tour in June, finished tenth on the money list. With half the total prize money, as many players (six) won more than $1 million on the senior tour as on the regular tour.

The Presidents Cup was invented in 1994 in about fifteen minutes. The tour decided it had to be up and running *now* in order to take advantage of Ryder Cup mania and to keep IMG from inventing a similar event. Even though Ernie Els didn't play because he had a $200,000 guarantee to play that week in Europe, and Norman had to pull out because he got sick, the first Presidents Cup was successful enough that there will be a second one in 1996.

Many of the Americans didn't want to play, but after considerable arm twisting by Finchem and his staff, all those who qualified showed up and, for the most part, enjoyed the week in northern Virginia, even though the tour put everyone up at a Hilton (corporate deal, of course) that was a forty-five-minute trip through brutal traffic from the golf course.

This time, no one raised any objections — political or otherwise — when both teams were invited to the White House for dinner. Come 1995's Ryder Cup, President Clinton and Paul Azinger (who was named an honorary co-captain of the American team when captain Hale Irwin qualified to play) will probably be the best of friends.

The Americans won the Presidents Cup 20–12, dominating most of the weekend, although there was just enough suspense on Sunday that Fred Couples's nine-iron to two feet for a clinching birdie at the 18th hole in his singles match against Price was dramatic. Or at least almost dramatic since the U.S. probably would have won with or without his clinching shot, a few minutes later.

Fifty-nine golfers made more than $300,000 on the PGA Tour in 1994, ninety-one of them made more than $200,000, and 154 made more than $100,000. That's pretty good money, even if it costs close to $75,000 a year to travel the tour, not luxuriously, but comfortably. In all, 328 players received at least one check on tour in 1994. That means less than half of them broke even for the year. And they were the ones lucky enough to play on the big tour at all.

Golf remains a life that makes a chosen few very rich, a reasonable number very comfortable, and about 150 of the several thousand who play it professionally a good living each year. The competition becomes more intense with each passing year. Succeeding on tour has never been more lucrative or difficult than it is right now. Just getting there is brutal.

It is impossible to forget the joy and the despair of the last day of Q-School. The forty-six who survived at PGA West in 1993 left that evening with a grand future in front of them. They were on *The Tour.* They would share locker rooms with Price and Norman, Nicklaus and Palmer, Azinger and Couples. All the big names, all the great tournaments. There was huge money to be made.

"It's almost impossible to explain what this means," said Brad Lardon, who had somehow made a five-foot putt on the last hole to get his card. "You grind and you grind for six days and if you make it, the whole world opens up for you."

But that opening guarantees nothing. In January, Brad Lardon began 1994 — like everyone else on tour — at zero. Ten months later, Lardon had played in twenty-one tournaments. He had earned $21,429. Like twenty-eight others who had left PGA West deliriously happy, he was going back to school.

Back to the grind. Those who made it through the grueling six days would joyously rejoin the big boys in January. *All* of them would be back to the grind.

In golf, there is no higher compliment than having someone say, "He was really grinding out there." From Price to Mark Pfeil (the last name on the 1994 money list) they all grind. They have no choice. It is the only way to keep playing the game they love so much.

INDEX

Aaron, Tommy, 241
ABC network, 154, 320, 334, 343, 353, 408
ACC. *See* Atlanta Country Club
Adams, Chuck, 82, 207
Advantage International, 204, 292
Allem, Fulton, 255, 287
Alliss, Peter, 265–266
Andrade, Billy, 128, 133, 206, 296, 340, 372, 410, 422, 450, 451–452
    personal history of, 178–190
Andrade, Cameron James, 190
Andrade, Jody (née Reedy), 128, 181–189
Anheuser-Busch Classic, 157, 366, 371, 374, 411
Armour, Tommy, 296, 448
Armour, Tommy III, 362
Ashe, Arthur, 425
Asian Tour, 342, 362–365
Atlanta Country Club (ACC), 244, 305, 309, 313
AT&T Pro-Am, 104, 107, 423
    See also Crosby Clambake; Pebble Beach
Augusta, 151, 210, 226, 230, 269–281
Augusta National Golf Club, 239–240
autograph incident, 29–30, 53
Avenel golf course, 184, 323, 328
Awtrey, Jim, 18
Azinger, Jed, 59
Azinger, Josie Lynn, 59, 64, 412
Azinger, Paul, 8, 10, 19, 24, 27, 34, 41, 63, 179, 423, 434
    and autograph incident, 31
    and British Open, 265–266
    and cancer, 57–59, 64–66, 177, 411–419
    and "major question," 140
    and New England Classic 1992, 123
    personal history of, 59–62
    quoted, 120, 228

and Ryder Cup, 36–38, 46–47, 51
and Skins Game, 56–57
and Westchester 1993, 140
mentioned, 104, 122, 136, 170, 171, 429
Azinger, Ralph, 59–60
Azinger, Sarah Jean, 59, 64, 412
Azinger, Toni, 59, 61, 412

Baker, Peter, 34, 41, 42, 43, 45–46, 47, 202
Baker-Finch, Ian, 128, 236
Ball, Elizabeth, 148
Ballesteros, Seve, 9, 11, 12, 15, 19, 27, 28, 32, 33, 41, 47, 176, 215, 226, 258, 277, 334–335
    mentioned, 45, 52, 53, 62
Baltusrol, 198–199, 200, 271
Barkley, Charles, 425
Barrow, Lance, 222
Bates, Patrick, 365
Baugh, Laura, 70
Bay Hill, 191, 195, 196, 198, 205, 225
    See also Nestle Invitational
    See also Palmer Bay Hill Classic
BBC network, 396, 397, 407
Beck, Chip, 10, 27, 39–41, 43, 44, 46–47, 125
Belfry golf course, 3–5, 10, 87, 125
    See also Ryder Cup
Belfry Hotel, 11, 27, 28, 35
Bell, Judy, 354
Beman, Deane, 55, 104–109, 152, 209–210, 212, 307, 308, 319, 421
    resignation of, 162–163, 166–167, 328–329
Bemen, Judy, 108
Bender, Pete, 291
Bendle, Jon, 236
big tour. *See* PGA Tour
Block, Henry, 426
Boldt, Rob, 101

Borg, Bjorn, 191
Boros, Julius, 287, 359
Brendencamp, John, 433
Brendle, Jon, 177
Brisky, Mike, 459
British Amateur, 171, 173, 241
British Open, 15, 25, 105, 123, 141, 142, 171,
    175, 176, 201, 220, 222, 223, 227, 228,
    240, 262, 264–266, 266–267, 271, 371–
    406
Brodie, Steve, 101
Brooks, Mark, 321, 323, 325, 328, 448
Brouse, Devon, 246
Brown, Billy Ray, 450
Brown, Cindy, 450
Brown, Pete, 424
Brundred, Ben, 368
Bryant, Brad, 185, 190, 299, 300
Buccholz, Butch, 210
Buick Classic, 104, 106, 336, 450, 460
Buick Invitational, 104
Buick Open, 104, 188, 415, 423, 450
Buick Southern Open, 104, 189, 366, 450
Burke, Patrick, 83, 94, 194
Burns, George, 71, 97
Bush, George, 24, 25
Byrum, Curt, 449

Caffey, Marty, 166, 374
Calcavecchia, Mark, 220–221
Calfee, Bill, 374
Canadian Open, 124, 176, 228, 462
Canon Hartford Open, 371
Carrick, Mike, 215, 420
Carter, Jim, 362
Carter, Jimmy, 329
Casper, Billy, 193
Cave Valley golf course, 217
CBS Golf Classic, 55
CBS network, 109, 111, 183, 222, 239, 242,
    254, 279, 299, 313–315, 318–323, 343,
    367–368, 441
Chirkinian, Frank, 55, 222, 243, 279, 314,
    318–327, 329, 343, 441
Cimarillo, Craig, 355–357
Claar, Brian, 178
Clampett, Bobby, 93
Cleveland Classics clubs, 274, 296
Clinton, Bill, 23, 24, 26, 124, 137, 329, 464
Clinton, Chelsea, 26
Clinton, Hillary, 26
Cobra clubs, 274, 286
Cochran, Russ, 134
Cole, Bobby, 70, 93
Congressional golf course, 184
Connolly, Wayne, 260–261
Coody, Charles, 241, 260

Cook, Jan, 120, 121, 292–293
Cook, Jason, 349
Cook, Jeff, 84, 86–88, 92, 96, 98–101, 103,
    302, 315–316, 362–365, 458, 459
Cook, Jim, 121, 292–293
Cook, John, 10, 24, 27, 39–41, 44, 47, 120,
    146, 267, 296, 441–442, 453–454
  at Greater Greensboro Open, 291, 294
  personal history of, 120–130, 292–293
  and U.S. Open, 348–349, 351, 357
  mentioned, 43, 48, 431
Cook, Kristin, 349
Couples, Deborah, 142
Couples, Fred, 10, 27, 34, 372, 408, 417–419
  and back trouble, 177, 417
  and Brian Henninger, 85
  and Canadian Open, 124
  and Doral Ryder Open, 166
  and Los Angeles Open, 139–142
  and Mike Donald, 74
  and off-season play, 54–55
  and pep talks, 41–43
  and Riviera Country Club, 119, 139–142
  and Ryder Cup, 36–37, 46, 202
  mentioned, 280, 289, 309, 429, 448, 464
Cowlings, Al, 348
Crenshaw, Ben, 214, 286, 287, 335, 342, 382,
    415–416, 439
Crosby, Bing, 107
Crosby, Kathryn, 107
Crosby Clambake, 104, 106–107
  See also AT&T Pro-Am
Cupit, Jacky, 359
Cypress Point, 107, 423

Dallas Open, 214, 282, 330
Dalpos, Rick, 86, 94
Daly, Bettye (née Fulford), 306, 307
Daly, John, 10, 19–20, 55, 90, 128, 212, 226,
    237, 253, 256–257, 321, 342, 362, 423,
    430–431, 461–463
  and alcohol, 318, 373–377
  and British Open, 373–377, 380–381, 397–
    398
  at Greater Greensboro Open, 289–290, 306–
    317
  and tobacco, 287
  mentioned, 285, 333
Daly, Shynah, 306, 307
Davis, Ann, 277
Day, Glen, 449
Deane, Paulette, 312–313, 317
DeLong, David, 128
Dennis, Clark, 357
Dent, Jim, 424
Deposit Guaranty Classic, 264, 409–410, 436,
    449

Dey, Joseph, 163
Diaz, Jaime, 312
DiMaggio, Joe, 191
DiMarco, Chris, 305
Disney World Classic, 452, 453
Dodd, Tawnya, 43, 74, 142
Dolby, Tom, 91–92
Donald, Mike, 71–75, 89, 91–92, 94, 128,
    365–370, 458, 459–461
Donald, Pearl, 72
Doral Ryder Open, 165, 189–190, 194, 205,
    228, 304, 451
Dorman, Larry, 312, 367
Drum, Bob, 279
Dunes Course, 68, 69, 83, 86, 89, 91, 94
DuVal, David, 93
Dye, Pete, 209–210

Edwards, Bruce, 4, 6, 115–116, 391, 398, 399,
    400
Edwards, David, 288, 349
Edwards. Joel, 298–299
Elder, Lee, 424
Elkington, Steve, 180, 227
Els, Ernie, 257, 258, 273, 279, 429, 464
    and British Open, 386, 394
    and U.S. Open, 336–337, 342, 349, 350–
        353, 355–360
Emery, Mike, 99–100
Emery, Mike Sr., 101, 102
Enberg, Dick, 320
ESPN network, 106, 323, 331, 374
Estes, Bob, 146, 311
European PGA, 13, 28
European tour, 171, 224, 257, 258, 261

Faldo, George, 260–261
Faldo, Georgia, 270
Faldo, Gill (née Bennett), 263, 270
Faldo, Joyce, 260–261
Faldo, Matthew, 270, 386
Faldo, Natalie, 265, 270
Faldo, Nick, 8, 9, 18, 19, 27, 34, 156, 166,
    177, 214, 227, 229, 256, 423, 455
    and British Open, 228, 386–390, 393, 398–
        399
    and Muirfield, 122–123
    personal history of, 258–271
    quoted, 127, 211
    and Ryder Cup, 36–38, 41, 47, 51, 53, 125
    and U.S. Open, 349–350
    mentioned, 60, 62, 113, 192
Fall Classic, 75, 184
Farr, Heather, 58, 65
Faxon, Bonnie, 408
Faxon, Brad, 166, 189, 382, 392, 396, 404,
    408

Fehr, Rick, 166, 211, 254
Feldman, Loren, 414
Ferris, Dick, 162, 166–168, 196–197, 211
Ferris, Richard, 329
Finchem, Tim, 166, 209, 211–212, 328–331,
    373–374, 380–381, 424, 458, 462–464
Finsterwald, Dow, 17
Fleck, Jack, 71, 333
Fleisher, Bruce, 233–238, 435–437, 458–459
Fleisher, Herbert, 233
Fleisher, Jessica, 234–235
Fleisher, Wendy, 234–235
Floyd, Maria, 52
Floyd, Raymond, 10, 18, 19, 27, 34, 39, 41,
    43, 45, 47, 50, 255, 271
Ford, Gerald, 145
Ford, Joe, 242
Forsman, Dan, 146, 257, 273
Fox Network, 323, 456–457
Frazee, Jack, 330
Frost, David, 225

Gallacher, Bernard, 4, 6, 13, 27, 31, 41, 44, 46
Gallagher, Jim Jr., 10, 27, 34, 40, 43, 47, 202,
    146, 157–158, 171, 334–335
Gamez, Robert, 225, 451
Garrison, Zina, 425
Gatlin, Rudy, 112–113
Gaudino, Jean, 59–60
Gaudino, Jeff, 59
Gaudino, Joe, 59
Gaudino, John, 59
Gilder, Bob, 212
Giles, Vinny, 234, 251
Golden Bear Inc., 204, 320
golf
    compared to other sports, 120
    and drugs, 373–376, 380–381
    and exactness, 210
    and gender issue, 241, 423
    graying of, 286–287
    and racism, 241–242, 422–427
    and rules, 241–242
    and tradition, 239–241, 253
Golf Course Board, 249
Goydos, Chelsea, 80, 233, 285
Goydos, Courtney, 233, 285
Goydos, Paul, 92–93, 96, 98, 127, 206, 232–
    233, 362, 449–450
    and Brian Henninger, 303, 310, 311
    and Greater Greensboro Open, 294–295,
        312
    and Hilton Head, 285–286
    nicknamed Aquaman, 207
    and Pebble Beach, 143–144
    personal history of, 76–84
    and Pro-Ams, 143

Goydos, Paul (*continued*)
   and Qualifying School, 69–70
   and U.S. Open, 340, 354
Goydos, Wendy (née Madak), 69–70, 77, 80,
   83, 93, 98, 233, 285, 450
Grady, Wayne, 128, 220
Graham, David, 71, 358
Grand Slam, 58, 204, 267
Greater Greensboro Open, 178, 282, 285–286,
   288–289, 291, 297–300
Green, Hubert, 418
Green, Iva, 167
Griggs, Jim, 249
Gumbel, Bryant, 111–112, 116, 320

Haas, Jay, 151, 166, 185, 211, 286, 441
Haas, Jerry, 362
Haddock, Jesse, 180
Haeggman, Joakim, 41, 43, 47, 125, 335
Hagen, Walter, 13, 192
Hannigan, Frank, 334–335, 353
Hardee's Classic, 366, 460
Harmon, Butch, 227, 228, 230, 395
Harmon, Craig, 437
Hart, Dudley, 79, 110–111, 113–114, 132,
   133
Hartford Open, 178, 371
Hattiesburg, 264, 284, 366, 409
Hawaii, 107, 120, 125–126, 130, 247–248,
   251, 302
   See also Kapalua; Maui
Heinen, Mike, 99–101, 449
Henderson, Hollywood, 307
Henke, Nolan, 311, 313, 316
Henninger, Brian, 68, 84–86, 92–93, 94–98,
   289, 361, 362, 410, 449–450
   and Deposit Guaranty Classic, 410
   at Greater Greensboro Open, 301–306, 308–
      317
   and Nike Tour, 362
   and Q-School, 68
Henninger, Carlin, 85, 96, 304–305, 317
Henninger, Cathy, 85, 96, 301, 304–305, 310,
   317, 410
Heritage Classic, 247, 261, 282
Heritage Open, 178
Hilcoff, Eric, 126, 294
Hobe Sound, 195, 320
Hoch, Scott, 165, 372
Hogan, Ben, 18, 146, 192, 259, 267–268, 333,
   334
   See also Hogan Tour; Nike Tour
Hogan Company, 204, 296, 337
Hogan Tour, 79–80, 84, 164, 236, 361
   See also Nike Tour
Holland, Trey, 353, 358
Holloway, Tad, 364

Honda Classic, 191, 205, 251, 290, 308, 367–
   368, 436
Hope, Bob, 120, 145
   See also Hope Chrysler Classic; Hope De-
      sert Classic
Hope Chrysler Classic, 104, 143, 313
Hope Desert Classic, 72
Hope Shootout, 162
Huber, Dan, 204
Hulbert, Mike, 126, 129, 132, 369
Humenik, Ed, 298
Hurlburt, Cathie, 373
Huston, John, 146, 177–178, 190, 299
Hutton, Randy, 415

IMG, 135, 176, 186, 195, 263, 269, 272, 432–
   433, 453, 464
Infiniti Tournament of Champions, 105
Inman, John, 128, 189, 212
International, 250, 446, 448
Irwin, Hale, 71, 178, 232, 257, 286, 288, 298–
   300, 329, 342, 351, 354, 372, 408, 464
Isenhour, Tripp, 305
Ives, Doug, 77

Jack, Charles, 405
Jacklin, Tony, 13, 18, 28, 261
Jacobsen, Peter, 146, 162, 195, 212, 215, 292,
   307, 372, 380, 421–422
James, Mark, 27, 32, 40, 47
Janzen, Bev, 199, 201, 203, 205
Janzen, Connor, 203
Janzen, Lee, 10, 23, 27, 34, 44, 135, 206, 231,
   272, 282, 296, 454–455
   personal history of, 198–205
   and Ryder Cup, 47, 53
   and U.S. Open, 336–338, 349–350
Jastrow, Terry, 320
Jenkins, Dan, 106
Jiminez, Mark, 37, 423
Jobe, Dr. Frank, 57–58, 64, 413–414
Jones, Bobby, 192, 240, 274
Jones, Charlie, 320
Jordan, Michael, 156, 192, 246, 424–425

Kapalua Invitational, 67, 247–248, 290, 307,
   450
Kelly, Jim, 374–375
Kemper Open, 142, 184, 219, 318, 319, 321–
   328, 336, 368–369
Kempner, Arnie, 325, 327
Kendall, Skip, 303, 362, 365
Kennerly, Ken, 135, 204
Kite, Christy, 33, 216, 218–219
Kite, Stephanie, 217
Kite, Tom, 4, 6, 8–9, 10, 12, 27, 32, 33, 144,

145, 164, 232, 251–252, 255, 297, 321, 455
at Bay Hill 1994, 205
and Davis Love III, 297–298, 395
and Greater Greensboro Open, 297
and "major question," 140–141
at Oak Hill, 156
and Pebble Beach, 110–114
personal history of, 213–220
quoted, 120, 211, 213, 250, 372
and Ryder Cup, 47
and U.S. Open, 62
mentioned, 257, 279, 286, 294, 304, 364, 431
Kite, Tom Sr., 214
Klauk, Fred, 212
Kmart, 106, 288, 299
Knox, Kenny, 128, 138
Koch, Gary, 374–375
Kodak, 131

LaCava, Joe, 42
La Costa Resort, 104, 107, 142
LaMontagne, Steve, 100
Lampley, Jim, 320
Lancaster, Neal, 461
Lane, Barry, 46
Langer, Bernhard, 9, 27, 40, 47, 155, 219, 229, 281
Lardon, Brad, 102, 465
Lardon, Mike, 102
Las Vegas Invitational, 58, 82, 284, 447
Leadbetter, David, 175, 227, 262, 263, 269, 363, 387–388, 459
Lehman, Tom, 257, 273–281, 283, 288, 348, 362, 464
Lema, Tony, 64
Lemmon, Jack, 108
Letterman, Dave, 324
Levet, Thomas, 88
Lietzke, Bruce, 451, 462
Limbaugh, Rush, 23, 124
Littler, Gene, 65
Long Beach Open, 79, 207
Los Angeles Open, 119, 194, 367
Love, Davis III, 27, 32, 33, 45–46, 178, 189, 228, 447–448, 450
  and British Open, 382–386, 393–395, 398
  and Greater Greensboro Open, 294–298, 311
  and Greg Norman, 230–231
  and Hilton Head, 282–285
  nicknamed Slick, 133, 332
  personal history of, 243–253
  quoted, 194, 199, 371
  and Ryder Cup, 3–13, 47–51, 215
  and Tom Kite, 297–298, 395

and Tom Watkins, 25–26
and Tylenol incident, 35–36, 41–43
Love, Davis IV, 251
Love, Davis Jr., 244–245, 247–249, 284
Love, Lexie, 247, 283
Love, Mark, 50, 244–245, 247–249
Love, Mary Elizabeth, 283
Love, Penta, 245, 247, 284
Love, Robin (née Bankston), 35–36, 41–43, 246–249, 283, 384, 408, 450
Lowery, Steve, 133, 287, 356
Lumpkin, Jack, 385
Lyle, Sandy, 132, 204, 262, 337
Lytham and St. Anne's, 31, 176

MacGregor clubs, 296
Madak, George, 77
Magee, Andrew, 205, 207, 383, 385, 461
Maggert, Jeff, 116, 232, 257, 362
Maginnes, John, 90–92, 94
Maginnes, Philip, 90
Mahaffey, John, 210, 344–346
majors, 69, 140–141, 200, 209, 219, 277, 421
  See also British Open; Masters; PGA Tour; U.S. Open
Maltbie, Roger, 271
Mantle, Mickey, 191
Marchand, Paul, 460
Marr, Dave, 154, 267, 287, 397
Martzke, Rudy, 318, 324
Maruman clubs, 296
Mascari, Tommy, 237
Mast, Dick, 138
Masters, 14, 16, 105, 165, 206, 225, 239–240, 258, 259, 271, 301, 409, 422
Masters 1935, 253, 378, 429
Masters 1985, 151, 155
Masters 1986, 175
Masters 1987, 200
Masters 1989, 165, 259
Masters 1992, 10, 130, 217, 244
Masters 1993, 228, 230, 272
Masters 1994, 243, 251, 322–323
Maui, 248, 450
Mazziotti, Chris, 94–95, 305, 310, 311
McClusky, Ken, 144
McCord, Gary, 161, 239, 242–243, 308, 313, 321–324, 343
McCumber, Mark, 464
McDonough, Sean, 186
McGovern, George, 25
McGovern, Jim, 386, 388
McNeil, Lori, 425
Mediate, Rocco, 199, 338, 344–346
Medinah Open, 156–157
Medlen, Jeff (Squeeky), 168–169, 288, 306, 402, 404–405, 408, 420, 443–444

Melnyk, Steve, 154
Memorial Tournament, 194, 209, 348, 413
Mercedes Championships, 104–107, 273, 427,
    463
Merrill Lynch, 146, 292
Micheel, Shaun, 101–102
Mickelson, Phil, 142, 166, 177, 321, 383, 429,
    441, 443
Miller, Johnny, 65, 110–118, 154, 286, 319,
    320, 334, 463
Mingolla, Ted, 411, 414
Mize, Larry, 20, 200, 225–226, 252, 255, 257,
    272, 273, 274, 280
Montgomerie, Colin, 27, 34, 214, 218, 389,
    393, 434
  and Ryder Cup, 36–37, 41, 47, 125, 202
  and U.S. Open, 348, 351–352, 355–360
Montgomery, Bob, 186
Moody, Larry, 414
Moody, Orville, 71, 137, 333
Morgan, Gil, 217, 299
Morris, John, 166, 373
Morris, Old Tom, 239, 378
Morris, Young Tom, 239
Morse, John, 299–300
Moss, Perry, 94
Muirfield, 122–123, 264–266, 379, 426
Murchison, Bill, 97
Murdoch, Rupert, 456
Murray, Bill, 108–109, 162
Musberger, Brent, 321
Musgrove, David, 204, 337

Nantz, Jim, 63, 115, 279, 315, 320, 321, 325–
    327
Navarro, Tony, 134, 276, 443, 461
NBC network, 110, 154, 242, 319, 320
Nelson, Byron, 16, 178, 192, 253–255
Nelson, Larry, 194, 228, 334
Nelson Classic, 330
Nelson Open, 176, 184
Nestle Invitational, 104, 191
New England Classic, 57, 85, 123, 158, 236,
    411
Nicklaus, Barbara, 225, 408, 428
Nicklaus, Jack, 14–15, 16, 110, 209, 218, 220–
    221, 225, 241, 254, 255, 259–260, 271,
    408–409, 427–429
  and ABC, 320
  and British Open, 381–382
  and Deane Beman, 165, 197
  flying elbow of, 179
  instructional books of, 224
  and John Daly, 308
  and racism, 424, 425–427
  respect for, 192, 376
  and Skins Game, 56

  and tobacco, 287
  TV production company of, 56
  and U.S. Open, 333, 334, 341–342, 349
  mentioned, 137
Nicklaus Resort Course, 76, 89, 92–94, 97
Nike Tour, 90, 94, 101, 102, 164, 247, 288,
    302–303, 310, 361–370, 449, 459
  versus big tour, 67, 361
Nissan Open, 119, 204
Nobilo, Frank, 342, 351, 352
Norman, Greg, 37, 38, 116, 128, 143, 194–
    195, 200, 217, 220–221, 255, 259, 385,
    387, 423, 431–432, 441–443, 447, 455–
    457, 463
  airplane of, 176, 407
  appearance of, 214
  at Augusta, 273–277, 278–279
  at Bay Hill, 205
  and British Open, 141, 376–378, 381–382,
    395–397
  and Doral Ryder Open, 166, 177
  and "major question," 140
  and off-season play, 54–55
  personal history of, 220–232
  at PGA Tour, 62–63
  quoted, 194
  and U.S. Open, 272, 338, 357
  mentioned, 134, 170, 171, 192, 286, 287
Norman, Gregory, 377
Norman, Laura, 223–224, 225
Norman, Merv, 224
Norman, Toini, 224
North, Andy, 194, 240, 333

Oak Hill, 156, 216, 333
Oakmont Country Club, 332–360
O'Brien, Andy, 427
O'Brien, Larry, 427
Ogle, Brett, 70, 109, 251
O'Grady, Mac, 338
Ogrin, David, 264
Ohlmeyer, Don, 56
Olazabal, José María, 11, 12, 13, 27, 32, 33,
    41, 43, 47, 50, 51, 52, 215, 252, 257–258,
    273, 274, 277–281, 429, 447
Olsen, Jack, 144
O'Meara, Mark, 126, 129, 292–293
Open Championship. *See* British Open
Order of Merit, 174, 258, 261, 263
Ozaki, Jumbo, 342

Paige, Satchel, 305
Palmer, Arnold, 14–15, 56, 148, 151, 154, 179,
    191, 241, 308
  and Augusta, 272–273
  and Deane Beman, 165, 197
  and his role in golf, 192–198

quoted, 153, 298
and tobacco, 287
and U.S. Open, 333, 334
and U.S. Open 1994, 340–341, 344–347
mentioned, 359
See also Palmer Bay Hill Classic
Palmer, Deke, 193
Palmer, Gary, 194
Palmer, Jack Jr., 194
Palmer, Steve, 194
Palmer, Winnie, 197
Palmer Bay Hill Classic, 104–105
See also Bay Hill; Nestle Invitational
Palm Springs, 68, 108, 143, 308
Parks, Sam Jr., 333
Parvenik, Jesper, 392, 397, 399–405
Pate, Jerry, 212, 352, 360
Pate, Steve, 44, 133
Pavin, Corey, 10, 12, 27, 32, 34, 40, 116, 140,
    146, 177, 220, 296, 382, 415–416, 443
    and Los Angeles Open, 139–142
    and Ryder Cup, 47
    mentioned, 43
Pebble Beach, 107–108, 126, 194, 217, 251,
    302, 333, 367
See also AT&T Pro-Am; Crosby Clambake
Peete, Calvin, 424
Penick, Harvey, 215, 219
Peoples, David, 311, 312
Perry, Chris, 362
Pesci, Joe, 108
Pfeil, Mark, 465
PGA, 10, 18, 20, 57, 240, 268, 306
PGA of America, 13, 209, 420–421
PGA Tour, 23, 54, 67, 79, 102, 104, 105, 200,
    215, 236, 409, 465
    compared to the Masters, 240
    description of, 301
    Greater Greensboro Open of, 288
    policy board of, 166
PGA Tour headquarters, 163
    description of, 209
    See also Ponte Vedra
PGA Tournament, 91, 421, 446
PGA West, 76, 465
Phoenix Open, 107, 125–126, 160, 203
Ping clubs, 165, 212
Player, Gary, 56, 258, 277
Players Championships, 13, 132, 143, 191,
    209, 229–232, 237, 244, 251, 269, 288,
    432, 435
Players Clubs, 163, 211
Pleasant Valley, 236, 411
Ponte Vedra, 118, 163, 191, 209–210, 231, 331
    See also PGA Tour headquarters
Poppy Hills, 107, 111
Presidents Club, 464

Presidents Cup, 448
Prestonwood Country Club, 361, 364–365
Price, Nick, 14, 164, 168–169, 200, 218, 222,
    232, 256, 258–259, 408–409, 420, 429,
    431–435, 441, 443–445, 447, 456
    at Bay Hill, 205
    and British Open, 381–382, 392–393, 397,
        402–406, 407
    and Doral Ryder Open, 166
    and Greg Norman advice, 298
    personal history of, 168–177, 306
    as player of year 1993, 54
    quoted, 194, 223
    and tobacco, 287–288
    and U.S. Open, 342–343
    mentioned, 123, 251
Price, Raymond, 172
Price, Sue, 405, 444
Price, Tim, 172
Price, Wendy, 172
Pride, Dicky, 449
Pro-Am, 143, 283, 414, 425
Purtzer, Tom, 126, 180

Q-School. *See* Qualifying School
Qualifying School, 57, 61, 68, 75–88, 80–83,
    94, 175, 184, 234, 246–247, 288, 436,
    459, 465
    and Nike Tour, 362
    three stages of, 70
Quayle, Dan, 329
Queen Mary Open, 79

Rafferty, Ronan, 397
Reagan, Ronald, 25
Redman, John, 60
Reebok, 463
Reilly, Rick, 141
Rhodesia, 173
Riggins, John, 192
Rinker, Larry, 212
Riviera Country Club, 119, 126–130, 139,
    141
    See also Los Angeles Open; Nissan Open
Robbins, Tony, 200
Roberts, Loren, 207–208, 286, 351, 352–353,
    355–360
Robinson Open, 163
Rocca, Costantino, 3–8, 40–41, 47–51, 250
Rodriguez, Chi-Chi, 426
Rolfing, Mark, 346
Roosevelt, Theodore, 51–52
Rosaforte, Tim, 276
Rosburg, Bob, 343, 353
Rose, Pete, 192
Rotella, Bob, 50, 189, 248, 395
Roth, Jeff, 461–462

Royal Lytham, 17
  See also Lytham and St. Anne's
Royal St. Georges, 229
Royal Troon golf course, 220–221, 379
Russell, Mark, 312, 316–317
Ryder, Samuel, 266
Ryder Cup, 17, 158, 281, 421, 464
  and Belfry hotel, 28
  captains of, 13–14, 17
  format of, 32
  and nerves, 8, 11
  and pressure, 9
Ryder Cup 1993, 4–13, 51–52, 124, 201–202,
    202, 215, 250

San Francisco, 77, 284, 447, 463
Sarazan, Gene, 253–255
Satyshur, Dennis, 217
Scherrer, Tom, 364
Schuchart, Mike, 459
Scottish Open, 373, 380
Scully, Vin, 320
Sea Island, 245, 247
Seeley, Wes, 166, 374
Senior, Peter, 124
senior tour, 164, 237, 334, 429
Shapiro, Leonard, 318
Sheehan, Jack, 430
Shell's Wonderful World of Golf, 55, 106, 259,
    387
Sherrod, Blackie, 241
Shipnuck, Alan, 325
Shoal Creek, 107, 241, 422–423
shootouts, 67, 145–146, 161, 283
Sifford, Charlie, 424, 426–427
Silvera, Larry, 305
Simpson, Jim, 320
Simpson, John, 263, 267
Simpson, O. J., 144, 192, 348, 360
Simpson, Scott, 146, 162
Simpson, Tim, 414
Singh, Vijay, 205, 207, 424
Skins Game, 56, 67, 219
Sluman, Jeff, 166, 184–185, 189, 200, 212,
    218, 240, 271, 332, 372, 437–440, 450–
    451
  personal history of, 130–139
  quoted, 191, 427–428
  mentioned, 62, 282
Sluman, Linda, 133–134, 137
Smith, Lee, 336
Smith, Rick, 189, 202, 451
Snead, Sam, 192, 253–255, 287, 334
Solheim, Karsten, 165, 212
Sony Rankings, 431–432
South Africa, 55
Southern Hills, 271, 412, 420, 428, 434, 436

Southern Open, 128, 452
Spalding clubs, 296
Spanish Open, 264
Springer, Mike, 287, 298–300, 362
Sprint Western, 105
Spurrier, Steve, 132
St. Andrews, 15, 16, 239, 266, 379, 453
St. Anne's, 17
St. Georges. See Royal St. Georges
Stadler, Craig, 146, 165, 286, 287, 448
Stallings, Rick, 60–61
Standly, Mike, 79
Stephens, Jackson, 241, 253–254, 281, 322
Stewart, Payne, 10, 24, 27, 34, 39, 41, 198,
    296, 414–415
  and Paul Goydos, 81
  and Ryder Cup, 47, 53
  and Skins Game, 57
  mentioned, 43, 65
Stewart, Tracy, 41
Stockton, Dave, 13, 413
Strange, Allan, 148–149, 151, 153, 154
Strange, Curtis, 20, 65, 128, 197, 206, 216,
    372, 408, 430–432, 452–454, 462
  and Anheuser-Busch Classic, 374–375
  as grinder, 164
  and Kemper Open, 321
  personal history of, 146–161
  and Qualifying School, 68
  quoted, 333, 366
  and U.S. Open, 219, 339–343, 349–352,
    354–357, 359
  mentioned, 287
Strange, Sarah, 68, 147–148, 153–161, 197,
    339, 343, 351, 359, 453
Strange, Tom, 148–150, 154
Sullivan, Mike, 410, 450
Summerall, Pat, 243, 320, 321
Sunneson, Fanny, 259
Sutton, Hal, 304, 352–353

Tatum, Sandy, 112
Taylor-Made, 326
TBS network, 106
television and golf, 54–56, 67, 104–106, 164,
    242, 267, 322–323, 446, 456
  See also individual networks
Ten Broeck, Lance, 75, 94
Tennyson, Brian, 128, 138
Texas Open, 189
Thompson, Bobby, 253
Thompson, Hall, 422
Thore, David, 148
Thorpe, Jim, 424, 425
Titleist dog, 101
tobacco, 90, 92, 172, 287–288
Tommy Armour clubs, 295–296

Toms, David, 138, 353
Toms, Sonya, 353
Torrance, Sam, 27, 29, 31, 32, 38, 44–46, 202
Tour Championships, 54, 250, 288, 301, 446, 447, 452, 463
Tournament of Champions, 104, 409, 446
    See also Infiniti Tournament of Champions; Mercedes Championships
Tournament Players Championship, 234
Tournament Players Clubs, 163, 184, 191, 209, 323, 328
Travelers Insurance, 242
Trevino, Claudia, 384
Trevino, Lee, 28, 264, 287, 333, 383–384
Triplett, Kirk, 116
Troon. *See* Royal Troon golf course
Trump, Donald, 144, 329
Turnberry, 16, 222, 376–406, 434
Turner, Greg, 385
Tway, Bob, 225–226

U.S. Amateur, 234, 241
U.S. Golf Association (USGA), 186, 332–335, 347, 353–354, 360, 421, 423
U.S. Open, 10, 14, 16, 105, 137, 151, 193, 216, 228, 244, 297, 301, 369, 422
    compared to the Masters, 240, 282
U.S. Open 1984, 206, 225
U.S. Open 1990, 178, 366
U.S. Open 1992, 62, 130, 217
U.S. Open 1993, 135, 198–199, 272
U.S. Open 1994, 332–360
U.S. Public Links Championship, 77
USA Network, 222, 323
USGA. *See* U.S. Golf Association

Van Halen, Eddie, 145
Vardon Trophy, 54, 214, 447, 455
VAS clubs. *See* Cleveland Classics clubs
Venturi, Ken, 117, 121, 243, 254, 315–316, 320, 325–328

Wadkins, Bobby, 321, 323
Wadkins, Lanny, 4, 6, 10, 12, 19–20, 27, 32, 34, 45, 50, 202
Wagner, Jeff, 323–328
Waite, Grant, 70, 219
Wake Forest, 147–148, 154, 179, 180–181
Walker, Jim, 138
Walker Cup, 241
Walrus. *See* Stadler, Craig
Wannamaker Trophy, 444
Watson, Denis, 174
Watson, Linda, 35–36, 53, 117, 384, 408–409
Watson, Meg, 15

Watson, Michael, 15
Watson, Tom, 4, 6–7, 14, 27, 31, 45–46, 179, 218, 255, 322, 408–409, 440, 454
    and autograph incident, 29–31, 53
    at Bay Hill 1994, 205
    and British Open, 175, 378, 381–384, 390–393, 397–402, 399–402
    and Couples pep talk, 41–42
    and Davis Love and putting, 25–26
    and Greg Norman, 228, 230–231
    and infected toe incident, 44–45
    and John Daly, 307–308
    and Pebble Beach 1994, 110–118, 141
    and politics, 24–25
    quoted, 210, 372, 376, 429
    and racism, 426
    and Ryder Cup, 9–10, 14–22, 37, 46–47, 51–52, 53, 158
    and Skins Game, 56
    and tobacco, 287
    and U.S. Open, 333, 334, 342, 349, 351, 354, 355, 357
    mentioned, 39, 41, 136, 192, 257, 261, 271, 274, 279, 286, 364, 431, 434
Weiskopf, Tom, 214
Westchester Open, 178, 185
Western Open, 85, 105, 144, 178, 309, 383, 392, 414, 423, 434
Whitaker, Jack, 239, 242, 314
Wiebe, Cathy, 188
Wiebe, Mark, 188
Will, Chuck, 183, 327
Williams, Frank, 4, 6, 12, 49–50, 284, 385, 395, 396
Williams, Roy, 21–22
Williamsburg, 72, 371
Wilson, Sid, 374
Winged Foot, 16, 228
Woods, Tiger, 424, 425
Woosnam, Ian, 27, 41, 42, 43, 46, 202, 256, 257
World Cup, 448
World Gymnastics Championships, 217
World Series of Golf, 121, 124, 136, 175, 200, 258, 301, 409, 446
World Tour, 456–458
Wrenn, Robert, 348
Wynn, Rick, 237–238

Yates, Charlie, 241, 256
Yates, Dan, 241, 256
Yates, Dan Jr., 241

Zebra clubs, 303
Zoeller, Fuzzy, 20, 205–206, 225, 232, 286, 287, 308, 396